GRANITE CITIES, YANKEE HEROES, AMERICAN DREAMS

A NATIONAL HISTORY OF BOSTON'S
BUNKER HILL MONUMENT

MICHAEL E. CHAPMAN

Trebarwyth Press

Reading, Massachusetts

Publishing and Printing

Published 2012 by Trebarwyth Press, Reading, Massachusetts

mail@trebarwyth.com

Typeset in Adobe Garamond Pro, 12.2pt and 8.5pt

Printed in the People's Republic of China

Paperback: 80gsm Galaxy acid-free paper, perfect binding

Hardcover: 100gsm Caijiaobante zhongzhiye acid-free paper, case binding, saddle stitched

16 15 14 13 12   1 2 3 4 5

Paperback edition: ISBN-13: 978-0-9786597-4-5

Hardcover edition: ISBN-13: 978-0-9786597-6-9

Library of Congress Control Number: 2012942338

Parts of this manuscript previously appeared in different forms in the following articles and are re-published with permission: "Taking Business to the Tiger's Gate: Thomas Handasyd Perkins and the Boston–Smyrna–Canton Opium Trade of the Early Republic," *Journal of the Royal Asiatic Society Hong King Branch*, 52 (2012); "Pragmatic, Ad Hoc Foreign Policymaking of the Early Republic: Thomas H. Perkins's Boston–Smyrna–Canton Opium Model and Congressional Rejection of Aid for Greek Independence," *International History Review* (2013, forthcoming).

Liability Disclaimer

Author and publisher disclaim liability for loss or damage resulting from the application or publication of information or opinion contained herein. Opinions and practices, including statements of a political, philosophical, moral, or legal nature outlined herein are those of the author alone; they are not reflective of the views, policies, or procedures of any organization or institution where this book may be sold or otherwise distributed. Where the author makes statements of a contentious nature, particularly in reference to personal or ongoing legal issues, he does so based on the available documentary evidence, for the sake of academic inquiry, and to raise constructive debate, not to defame, slander, or offend the persons or parties under discussion. In the event that persons or parties mentioned herein disagree with the evidence presented, or any of the statements, interpretations, or arguments that the author has advanced, and especially if they feel offended or wronged, the author solicits their feedback, will undertake revision as necessary in subsequent printings, and apologizes in advance because he intends neither harm nor insult.

Quotation Marks

This book reserves quotation marks to enclose quotations, never using them as a rhetorical device or to denote irony; for added precision, it encloses quotations that were themselves quotations in the source in a double set of quotation marks.

Cover Illustrations

Front: *Col. Prescott and the Bunker Hill Monument*, by Michael E. Chapman, © 2008.

Back: *The Death of General Warren at the Battle of Bunker Hill*, by John Trumbull, 1786 (original, Museum of Fine Arts, Boston; 1834 copy, Wadsworth Atheneum, Hartford).

CONTENTS

fig. 1

INTRODUCTION

Some three million tourists each year tackle Boston's 2.5-mile Freedom Trail, which starts from a visitors' center on Boston Common, follows a red line on the sidewalk from one historic site to the next, and finishes at the Bunker Hill Monument in Charlestown, a 220-foot granite obelisk that commemorates the first pitched battle between rebels and redcoats, on 17 June 1775, at the outset of the American War of Independence. Those with the stamina to climb 294 steps to the Monument's pinnacle catch their breath by marveling at the panoramic outgrowth of what began—a dozen generations ago—as a tiny colony of English Puritans. While crossing the Atlantic in 1630 prior to founding this colony, John Winthrop impressed on his fellow "professors for God's sake" that because "The eies of all people are uppon us" they must "be as a citty upon a hill." Their survival and prosperity in New England, he cautioned them, depended solely on "obeyeing His voice and cleaveing to Him." Vivid imagery was as vital for colonists then, as it was for the Monument's nineteenth-century founders and chroniclers. In his seminal 1877 history, George Washington Warren concluded that the Monument symbolized "a fit type of the national unity." By its "use of many separate blocks" of granite, through "the beautiful adaptation and harmony of its several parts," and in its "grandeur as a single object," the Monument aptly illustrated the "national motto, 'E pluribus unum.'" For Warren, a state legislator, the first mayor of Charlestown, and relative of a famous rebel killed in the battle, the Monument signified that "out of many States there has sprung up, by a sort of natural growth, our glorious Union." There was a strange yet compelling synergy here, between an obdurate, volcanic extrusion, the mystery of an ancient language, the encouraging benevolence of a supreme being, and the empowering social identity of republicanism.[1]

Orators like Edward Everett and Daniel Webster, who similarly extolled the Monument's republican spirit, believed that the Monument had special powers. When they planted their feet on the battleground, the moral character of their Puritan ancestors flowed into them. When they delivered addresses on the spot where their heroes fell, it was as if the Monument spoke through them. Visitors still marvel at this cold, silent, granite obelisk, always recognizing its shape but often passing over its most singular characteristic. Unlike the Pharaonic obelisk of Paris's Place de la Concorde or Trajan's Column in Rome, it is not a billboard for hieroglyphic inscriptions or bas-reliefs acclaiming a conqueror's rule. Unlike Nelson's Column in London's Trafalgar Square, it is not a plinth for an eighteen-foot statue of an imperial hero. Other than four small viewing windows set nine courses down from its conical capstone, it is utterly plain (fig. 1). It is natural to look at the Bunker Hill Monument, as well as its later twin, the 555-foot white marble Washington Monument in the nation's capital,

---

1. *Out of Many, One* was the national motto until 1956, when Congress replaced it with the religiously explicit *In God We Trust*. John Winthrop, "A Modell of Christian Charity," sermon aboard the *Arbella*, 1630, in *Collections of the Massachusetts Historical Society* (Boston: Charles C. Little and James Brown, 1838), 3rd series, vol. 7, pp. 31–48; George Washington Warren, *The History of the Bunker Hill Monument Association During the First Century of the United States of America* (Boston: James R. Osgood and Company, 1877), p. 376.

and presume that American monuments commemorating the Revolutionary War are supposed to be plain obelisks, yet nothing could be further from the case. When a group of elite Bostonians formed the Bunker Hill Monument Association in 1823 and began raising funds, they planned to erect a triumphal column, just like Trajan's. Why did they change their minds? What was it about a plain obelisk that the descendants of Puritan colonists could find so inspirational? Might there be a link between the physical form of the Monument and American exceptionalism, the notion that a Providential hand has always guided Yankee prosperity, progress, and territorial expansion?

Successive chapters that present a revision of the battle, a history of the Monument, and a discussion of Boston's granite building boom inspired by construction manager Solomon Willard suggest that the Monument's unblemished surfaces and its frugal, minimalist lines stood as an uplifting testament to Puritan virtue, as well as an unpretentious yet virile statement of Yankee power and mercantile profit. Willard's Monument came to symbolize the granite-like moral qualities of the shining city upon a hill, and the hopes as well as fears of immigrants who search for—and may fail to find—the American Dream. Some of those failed dreams, along with a vibrant youth counterculture centered on Quincy's abandoned granite quarries during the 1970s–90s, produced a range of stories that have challenged and attempted to modify the dominant national narrative. In seeking to establish relationships between founding myths, national core values, and a nineteenth-century granite obelisk, this book ponders the extent to which a single pillar of republicanism still defines American society.

Granite Cities' overarching premise is that historicized myths, the monuments celebrating them, and the official discourse they engender play a crucial role in the construction, affirmation, and subsequent modification of national identity, a process that is no less important for Americans today than it was for the Warrens, Websters, and Everetts of the Early Republic. Despite historians' best efforts to study global phenomena, or ethnic groups, or non-state actors, citizens' understanding of their history is ultimately national. Given the seductive power and fixedness of the prevailing nation-state system, this is inevitable, even necessary, because it is only through history that we know who we are and, hence, can feel comfortable within ourselves and play a productive role in society. We like to feel good about our country and take pride in its accomplishments. And yet, if our history is not so much fact as fancy, an interleaved web of exaggerations, half-truths, and omissions, then we are in danger of making flawed judgments with negative consequences. Were Americans' actions to belie their national ideology, particularly when that ideology is so moralistic, then, not being true to themselves, others would judge them to be hypocrites. Each chapter of *Granite Cities* challenges a central premise of Americans' received wisdom, not from any unpatriotic intent but rather in the belief that introspection is the bedrock of civil society, and in the hope that from civil society a more compassionate, enriching, and sincere global village will grow.

1. JOSEPH WARREN: FOUNDING MYTH

A confluence of four factors led to the founding in June 1823 of the Bunker Hill Monument Association (BHMA), an organization of elite Bostonians who purchased the land on which the Monument would stand, decided its form, raised funds for its construction, chose a superintendent, and even in some cases profited from their apparently altruistic endeavor. First, as so often happens two generations after a war—when the number of veterans has dwindled and those remaining fear their imminent death—there was a crescendo of interest in the Charlestown battle, an urge to capture for posterity the memory of the surviving heroes. Second, and fueling the interest, was a controversy over charges of delinquency against Gen. Israel Putnam, one of the rebel leaders, made in a recently published memoir of the battle by Henry Dearborn, a doctor turned soldier-statesman.[1] Third, and perhaps sensing a windfall from the interest, a farmer offered for sale a few acres of the battle site. Fourth, Boston's leading merchants, academics, lawyers, and legislators were feeling sufficiently confident about their achievements in the fledgling republic to collectively celebrate and display their wealth, authority, and prestige.

From their inaugural meeting onward, BHMA directors sought to establish and promote a particular version of the battle, central to which was the death, or martyrdom as some called it, of rebel leader Joseph Warren. Despite its inherent falsehoods, they convinced themselves that this was the true account; they ignored contrary evidence, and they ridiculed anyone who disputed its facts. Their behavior was understandable, especially in this case when the stakes were so high. Nations, ethnic groups, even small organizations often construct and then legitimate their collective identity around a romanticized or fictitious account of their creation, which then becomes their *founding myth*. A battle story that deviated from one of heroic sacrifice leading to the founding of the American republic would not only reveal the monument building endeavor to be a hollow sham but also challenge the directors' sense of self as Americans.

Fighting the Battle

Tactical and logistical blunders, divided command, personal initiative, infectious cowardice, and astonishing bravery characterized the "decisive day," as one historian dubs the Battle of Bunker Hill.[2] During a police action in April 1775 to seize illegal weapons' caches from uppity farmers at Concord, redcoats took an unexpected mauling on their way back to Boston through the lanes of Merriam's Corner, Lexington, and Menotomy (Arlington). Since then, Sons of Liberty, whom British authorities regarded as rebellious Sons of Violence, had escalated the conflict by encircling Boston

---

1. Henry Dearborn, *An Account of the Battle of Bunker's-Hill*, printed with Daniel Putnam, *A Letter to Maj. Gen. Dearborn, Repelling His Unprovoked Attack on the Character of the Late Maj. Gen. Israel Putnam* (Boston: Munroe & Francis, 1818).

2. Richard M. Ketchum, *Decisive Day: The Battle for Bunker Hill* (1962, repr.; New York: Henry Holt and Co., 1999).

with a hodgepodge of militia companies 20,000 strong, drawn from Connecticut to Maine. Even besieged, Boston made a secure base for the redcoats, provided they could resupply by sea, for it was a peninsula connected to Roxbury and Dorchester by a narrow neck (fig. 2). After reinforcements arrived from Britain, along with three generals and orders to impose martial law, Gen. Thomas Gage, the royal governor of Massachusetts and commander-in-chief of British forces in North America, decided to gain control of the Dorchester Heights, which overlooked Boston from the south, and then fortify them, because were the rebels to mount cannon on the Heights they could interdict ships as they tacked, across the offshore wind, into Boston Harbor.[3]

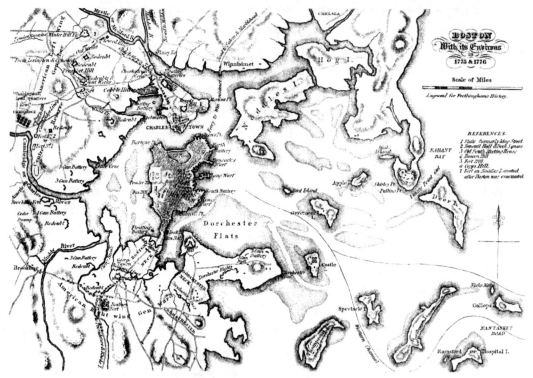

fig. 2: Boston in 1775, at center, with Charlestown above it and Cambridge to the left

In nearby Cambridge to the northwest, the rebels' Committee of Safety soon learned of Gage's plan. On 16 June, a hurriedly convened war council under Gen. Artemas Ward debated preemptive action. A Harvard-educated shopkeeper turned public official, Ward had been a militia colonel during the French and Indian War (1754–63), though a kidney stone had kept him from his only battle at Fort Ticonderoga. Young officers, confident after Lexington and spoiling for a fight, wanted to taunt the redcoats with a diversionary move into Charlestown, and Ward, though he surely understood the strategic importance of retaining control of Dorchester, went along. Perhaps he worried about mounting an adequate defense of Dorchester at

---

3. Distilled primarily from: Richard Frothingham, *The Battle-Field of Bunker Hill: With a Relation of the Action by William Prescott and Illustrative Documents* (Boston: By Author, 1876); id., *History of the Siege of Boston and of the Battles of Lexington, Concord, and Bunker Hill* (Boston: Little, Brown, and Company, 1903); W.J. Wood, *Battles of the Revolutionary War, 1775–1781* (Chapel Hill, NC: Algonquin Books of Chapel Hill, 1990), pp. 3–34; Brendan Morrissey, *Boston 1775: The Shot Heard Around the World* (London: Osprey Military, 1993), pp. 51–67; Ketchum, *Decisive Day.*

short notice; also—as seemed to happen whenever a battle was imminent—a painful stone was bothering him, so he may have agreed on Charlestown for its proximity to his command post. Charlestown, a square mile of undulating farmland with a now-deserted settlement on its southwesterly corner, lay a cannon-shot across the harbor from Boston's Copp's Hill.[4] It was a smaller version of Boston's peninsula, connected to Cambridge in the northwest by the narrow Charlestown Neck, while the estuaries of the Mystic and Charles Rivers washed its northeast and southwest flanks. Asking disparate militias to defend such a tiny promontory against a professional army backed by three heavy frigates and assorted gunboats was expedient at best, suicidal at worst, but as a venue for a pitched battle in fine view of Boston's citizenry, it was perfect.

Contingents of militia 1,200 strong crossed into Charlestown about 10 PM, under the nominal command of Col. William Prescott, a farmer from Pepperell, Massachusetts, and a veteran of King George's War of the 1740s. Prescott's orders were to occupy Bunker's Hill, but he was soon arguing with other officers over what that meant. There were three hills: Moulton's, more of a rise than a hill at thirty feet above sea level, was adjacent to brick pits and marshy sandbanks at the peninsula's southeastern tip; Breed's, at sixty feet, sat in the center; while overlooking the Neck rose the more commanding and flat-topped Bunker's at 110 feet. Breed's Hill, which only acquired that name after the battle, was actually Breed's Pasture, and Prescott, it seems—visiting Charlestown for the first time, and then in the dark—presumed Bunker's Hill referred to both hills, connected as they were by a stretch of higher ground. Col. Richard Gridley, an elderly veteran of the French and Indian War, chief army engineer, and commander of an artillery battalion of two 4-pounders, pressed to fortify Breed's, where his guns could range over British landing parties on the flanking beaches. But Gen. Putnam, a Connecticut farmer, tavern keeper, and Indian fighter with a reputation for reckless adventures, who had arrived in an ad hoc capacity with wagons of entrenching tools, pleaded with Prescott to fortify Bunker's.[5] After an hour of bickering, Gridley began laying out a 130-foot-sided redoubt at Breed's, and the militia, more comfortable with yeomanry than soldiery, spent the next five hours in frantic digging with spade and pickaxe. While they must have been grateful for an activity to alleviate their fear, their labors left them exhausted. Few of them, moreover, despite an order to do so, had brought any food or water, although several had flasks of rum or peach brandy.

Booms echoing around the waterfront awakened Gage at first light on 17 June 1775, for at 4 AM the frigate HMS *Lively* had spotted the half-built redoubt and begun a noisy, if largely ineffective, bombardment. Sleepy but excited Bostonians gathered on Copp's Hill to watch the action, and Gage called his officers to council. Henry Clinton, one of the three new generals in Boston, always maintained that he had advocated an immediate two-prong amphibious assault: a feint from the southeast, while

---

4. Here, the term *Charlestown* is geographic, referring only to the peninsula, because the boundary of the township in 1775 included all of present day Somerville.

5. Contemporary accounts of Putnam's actions are inconsistent, so "probably pleaded" may be better.

the main force, bracketed by naval gunnery, would land near the Neck, cut the rebels off from resupply, and then take their fort in the rear. A swift implementation of this plan might have succeeded, but Gage preferred Gen. William Howe's idea: a similar holding attack from the front, while a flanking force came around the fort from the east. Had Gage executed this plan as soon as the first troops to muster could board transports, say by 8 AM, hindsight suggests that it too may have worked. Instead— and perhaps wisely, for he surely presumed that rebel militia would flee in the face of an overwhelming show of strength—Gage decided to roust up all the troops from their billets scattered around Boston, requisition sufficient boats and crews to convey them as well as their artillery, and coordinate the landing for high tide, at about 1 PM, when the marshy ground at Moulton's Point would be safely submerged.[6] This delay, though, did give the rebels an additional five hours to devise further fortifications and bring up more detachments.

Even though Putnam, one of the few rebels with both a sense of Prescott's pending predicament and a horse, had twice ridden to Cambridge to plead for fresh troops, Ward refused to release any, for he was preoccupied with defending his base at Cambridge, and perhaps with his kidney stone. It was only after an angry Putnam forced a vote from the Committee of Safety that Ward agreed to detach Col. John Stark—another seasoned Indian fighter—with two hundred New Hampshire militia from their position at Medford. Stark's farmers had a reputation for marksmanship, although few if any had rifles and they were all chronically short of ammunition. Hours therefore passed while they begged powder and vengefully stripped the lead from organ pipes in a Cambridge Anglican church, which they then mangled into musket-sized lumps because none of them owned a bullet mold.[7] Meanwhile, Putnam was determined to fortify Bunker's Hill, for he appreciated the inevitability of a retreat by Prescott's force from the redoubt. Unable to persuade any of the Massachusetts militia to work for a Connecticut outsider, Putnam eventually convinced Prescott to release half of his weary force on the promise that they would return later. But glad to be out of the redoubt, and as thirsty and hungry as they were sleepy, most of these men simply went home. When the British warships ceased their frightening preparatory barrage around 1 PM, there were about two hundred men in the redoubt, supported in a defensive line by twelve hundred or so combat-ready militia: snipers in orchards, a barn, and the town to their right, and, to their left, contingents manning an earthen breastwork, three *flèches* (angled shelters of bundled sticks) in a dogleg, and, set back from the flèches, a rail fence (fig. 4). Because uncommitted groups wandered aimlessly around the peninsula and new arrivals swapped places with deserters, it is difficult to estimate the numbers of actively engaged rebels at any time, although once the battle began in earnest, losses exceeded gains.[8]

6. I am grateful to Joseph McCarthy for this interpretation of Gage's reasoning; and see Michael Stephenson, *Patriot Battles: How the War of Independence Was Fought* (New York: HarperCollins Publishers, 2007), pp. 213–15. A plaque on the wall of a disused Navy Yard factory, on 1st Ave. just past 9th St., marks the landing site.

7. I am presuming that no one owned a mold; at least, no one had remembered to bring one. Samuel Swett, in *History of Bunker Hill Battle, with a Plan* (Boston: Munroe and Francis, 1827), fn., p. 18, commented that the rebels "had quite as little respect for Episcopal churches as the enemy had for puritanical meeting houses."

8. When the first redcoats advanced around 3:30 PM, Prescott—in his report to John Adams of 25 August 1775—

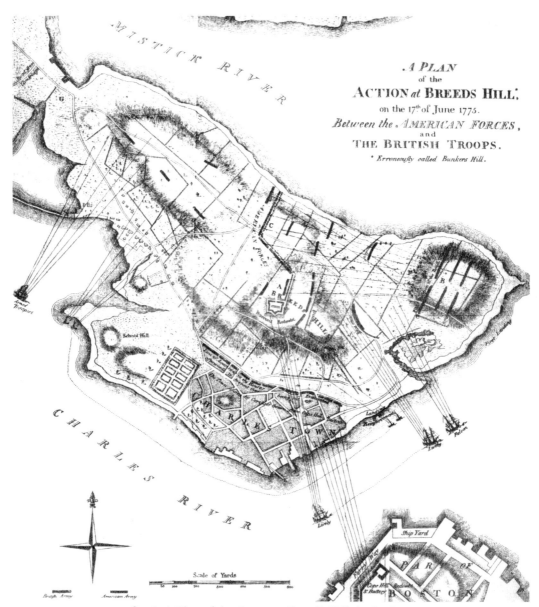

fig. 3: A Plan of the Action at Breed's Hill, by Lt. Page

After the lull in the bombardment, the rebels saw thirty or forty barges and row-boats crossing the harbor, in what was the first wave of eleven hundred redcoats. Prescott ordered the artillery forward to interdict them, but once away from the re-doubt, Capts. John Callender and Samuel Gridley (son of Col. Richard) and their crews turned the horses for Bunker's Hill, where they left the fieldpieces, and the offi-cers went home to Cambridge. By the time Putnam had found men to bring the guns back to the breastwork, the redcoats had established a safe beachhead at Moulton's Point.[9]

estimated there were as few as 150 men in the redoubt, in William W. Wheildon, *New History of the Battle of Bunker Hill, June 17, 1775: Its Purpose, Conduct, and Result* (Boston: Lee and Shepard, 1875), p. 40; one rebel soldier told a friend that there were 150 men in the redoubt, 200 manning the breastwork, and 400 or 500 at the rail fence, in Frothingham, *Siege of Boston*, p. 398.

9. Letter of Peter Brown (enlisted under Prescott) to his mother, 25 June 1775, from Frothingham, *Siege*, p. 392;

When shortly after 2 PM Stark's contingent arrived at Charlestown Neck, with its causeway narrowed to a few yards in places by high tide, the scene was chaotic. So many men were milling around that the New Hampshire militia had to elbow their way through. Stark found similar conditions at Bunker's Hill, where retreating deserters had so commingled with volunteer engineer companies that inexperienced officers had lost control, and there was little progress with entrenchment. At a steady pace so as not to tire them, Stark marched his men forward, coming upon Capt. Thomas Knowlton, whose company was reinforcing their rail-fence barricade by scavenging extra rails and stuffing hay into the gaps. After taking command of Knowlton's position, Stark strode to the end of the fence, where, beneath the riverbank by the Mystic, lay a stretch of unprotected beach; Stark soon had his men gathering stones to improvise a wall down to the waves. Historians seem to think this wall was waist high or chest high, and perhaps it was, but that would be a lot of stone to collect and stack in under an hour; Henry Dearborn, who fought with Stark, mentioned that they built a "slight" wall, behind which men laid down to fire, so it may not have been much above a foot high.[10]

Since coming ashore, reconnoitering the redoubt, which by now looked impressive, and consequently sending for his reserve, field-commander Howe never attempted to impede Knowlton's and Stark's preparatory endeavors. Redcoat scouts on Moulton's Hill would have had a good view of the defenses, and Howe carried a telescope. While he may well have judged a quick charge by redcoats already ashore too risky, it seems negligent of him—at least to a modern commentator—not to order one of the frigates to tack up the Mystic, drop anchor, and enfilade the rebel line.[11] Yet such tactical blunders were a commonplace by-product of the formal, set-piece approach to linear warfare. Howe, an intelligent and enterprising general of forty-six, was also as popular with his troops as he was sympathetic to the colonists, and he may have hoped to avert bloodshed through a last minute parlay. By 3 PM, Howe had prepared his attack. Sniper fire from houses and barns to his left had forced him to order the frigates in the Charles River to lob incendiaries, and now black smoke was wafting over the battlefield from the burning town. His reserve had disembarked, and he could count on around 3,500 men, half of whom were crack troops led by experienced officers, with twelve field guns including four 12-pounders. Gen. Robert Pigot would mount the frontal assault on the redoubt, while Howe directed the encircling force of light infantry up the beach, and personally led the grenadiers—physically large men made larger by wearing a mitered cap—against the rail fence. But Howe seems to have been oblivious to the stone wall, just as he underestimated the ability of officers like Prescott and Stark to regulate the rebels' firepower.

Brown thought 4,000 redcoats were landing, but Howe stated in a letter to his brother Lord Howe that with all the boats full, each wave of landings could not bring more than 1,000, in Harold Murdock, *Bunker Hill: Notes and Queries on a Famous Battle* (Boston: Houghton Mifflin Company, 1927), p. 148. Because only the wealthiest owned pocket watches, there are necessarily discrepancies in timing across the various accounts (Brown gave 3 PM, although he might have been thinking about the second wave of landings, which occurred around 2:30).

10. Dearborn, *Account of the Battle*, p. 4.

11. Adverse currents had precluded an earlier attempt to tow an artillery barge up the Mystic River.

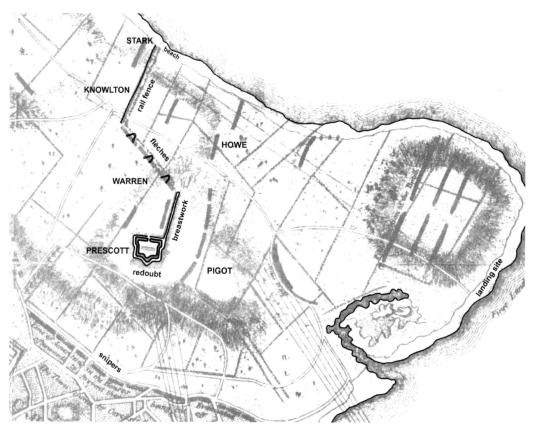

fig. 4: rebel defenses and disposition of forces

From his experiences in the French and Indian War, Stark knew that once the first line of redcoats had volleyed, a second disciplined line would advance and fire, followed, if necessary, by a third, before the final bayonet charge; his militia, moreover, had only enough ammunition for a half-dozen shots apiece. Because it was therefore crucial that every shot counted, he too divided his men into three lines, and placed a stake fifty yards ahead as a firing marker. Still, Stark was unprepared for the speed at which the first wave of light infantry advanced to the stake, and the almost suicidal bravery with which the second wave followed them, after his militia had leveled their comrades. By the time the remnants of the puzzled third wave retreated, ninety-six redcoats, including most of the officers, lay dead in the sand; many more died later from the ragged and easily infected wounds caused by the assorted metal objects that rebels had fired in lieu of cast lead bullets.[12] Over by the rail fence, Howe's grenadiers were faring no better. After Knowlton repulsed their first attack, Howe sent in a second wave of light infantry, while he led a flanking assault on the flèches with 6-pounder guns in support. For thirty minutes, the rebels raked the redcoats, whose artillery was little help for it had the wrong caliber ammunition. When Howe abandoned the

---

12. "Their muskets," reported a British surgeon named Grant, "were charged with old nails and angular pieces of iron," in consequence of which many redcoats had died of their wounds or required the amputation of one or both legs, cited in Margaret Wheeler Willard, ed., *Letters on the American Revolution, 1774–1776* (Boston: Houghton Mifflin Company, 1925), p. 141.

attack, he had lost his entire staff of twelve and he was lucky to be alive. Of some 1,350 light infantry and grenadiers committed by Howe on the right wing during the afternoon, those killed and wounded totaled 790, a staggering 60 percent.[13] Though the slaughter must have horrified him, Howe never relented—British honor was now in jeopardy—and he ordered Gen. Clinton to make haste from Boston with his marines and whatever reinforcements he could muster. At the redoubt, Pigot had also taken many casualties and given few, although, unbeknownst to him, the rebels were down to their last rounds.

Too late in the day, as it turned out, Ward over in Cambridge had decided to throw more contingents into the fray, but those that made it over the crowded Neck then acted autonomously, their officers and men thinking better of venturing anywhere near the hellish redoubt. They would have been at that pre-combat level of emotion, where flighty terror overrides the productive adrenaline of bravado, and their inexperienced officers lacked the authority to discipline them into action. Nonetheless, they could still have made a vital contribution to Prescott's spent force by donating their ammunition and whatever water they had brought, were they not so fearful for their own survival.

Once Clinton's marines had landed at 4:30 PM, Howe regrouped. Pigot's men stripped off their packs, mounted bayonets, and ran at the redoubt, while 6-pounders from their right flank enfiladed first the breastwork and then the redoubt with grapeshot. Firing their last cartridges, and without bayonets with which to defend themselves, Prescott's doomed rebels dashed to the rear of the fort that had served them so well, where they now fumbled in the smoke for the narrow sally-port, while redcoats who had jumped from the parapet gored them down. Prescott, whose swordplay helped him survive, later counted a half-dozen bayonet cuts in his tunic, although Gen. Joseph Warren, a doctor turned politician and rather naive warrior, was not so lucky, killed instantly by a bullet through his skull. Had Ward managed to resupply Prescott at any point during the afternoon then the rebels may well have beaten back even this determined attack, and prevailed. As it was, every man was now fending for himself. Indeed, the rout would have been total were it not for a valiant fighting retreat by the men under Stark's command, who even managed to drag with them one of their 4-pounders. Massachusetts militia on the still unfortified Bunker's Hill panicked, leaving it to three Connecticut companies to cover Prescott's desperate retreat across Charlestown Neck. Although the rebels abandoned Charlestown, it was really their victory, for they had not only bested the most professional fighting force of the time but also undermined the redcoats' confidence. Howe, especially, would in future be hesitant, even timid, before committing to battle.

In addition to the rebels' problems of logistical deficiencies, anarchic command, and parochial loyalties, this synthesis of the battle suggests three further observations:

---

13. Calculated from unit rolls in Morrissey, *Boston 1775*, pp. 60, 62–63, and Victor Brooks, *The Boston Campaign, April 1775–March 1776* (Conshohocken, PA: Combined Publishing, 1999), pp. 239–43.

First, despite Dearborn's later criticism of Putnam (who was indeed away from the fighting for much of the afternoon), Putnam's tactical contribution was crucial to the whole course of the battle. In the war council of 16 June, he had stressed that while green militia would turn and run from disciplined redcoats in linear combat, they would stand their ground if protected by a barricade. "'Americans,'" he had explained to Ward, "'are not at all afraid of their heads, though very much afraid of their legs; if you cover these they will fight forever.'"[14] He had then organized and delivered the wagonload of tools that had made entrenchment feasible, as well as fascines (bundles of sticks), and empty barrels that when filled with earth made effective firing positions. Second, correct artillery placement on one hand, and well-executed earthworks on the other, were critical adjuncts to the final assault; once Howe's 6-pounders were far enough forward to rake the breastwork with close range fires of grapeshot, they decimated the defenders, and yet had Prescott given orders to terminate the breastwork with a right-angled defilade, this would have been impossible. Third, and most importantly, Howe had to learn that it was futile to send lines of fully-kitted men—at walking pace over rough ground littered with obstacles—against prepared defenses; after switching to less formulaic tactics, he carried the redoubt by storming it with a running column of stripped-down troops with bayonets, who did not fire a shot until they were inside the fort.

With the benefit of hindsight, it is tempting to smirk at the stupidity of Howe's first orders and his men's suicidal adherence to them, just as it is easy not to notice that rebels and redcoats were attempting to fight a pitched battle according to the rules of two different games. Howe's professionalism becomes apparent upon appreciating the radical adjustment he had to make to adapt the redcoats' game of mobile linear warfare to the rebels' game of static defensive entrenchment. Had he been able to make that adjustment at the outset, then, following a feint from the right, say, to draw the rebels' fire, a shock column running from the left might have reached the redoubt before the defenders could reload, thereby reversing the carnage. A complementary factor requiring lateral thinking by the redcoats was that while they had a bayonet apiece, the rebels had but a few dozen between their entire force, which gave the redcoats an overwhelming advantage at close quarters.[15]

Warren's Founding Myth

Twenty-five of Boston's most prominent citizens, all "gentlemen of culture and high character," according to their historian George Washington Warren, met for lunch on 13 May 1823 in a private room at the Exchange Coffee House, a five-floor tavern-restaurant on the corner of Boston's State and Devonshire Streets recently rebuilt after a fire, to discuss the formation of the BHMA. Each of them had no doubt read one or more of the reasonably objective accounts of the battle, including that by

---

14. Swett, *History of Bunker Hill Battle*, p. 14; and see recollection of Maj. John Brooks, in Frothingham, *Siege of Boston*, p. 116.

15. Dearborn, *Account of the Battle*, p. 5, estimated less than fifty bayonets, there being only one in his company.

Col. Samuel Swett, a veteran of the War of 1812, who lunched with them. William Tudor, another of their company, was the son of a judge-advocate at the courts martial of officers accused of cowardice on the field. Two of them had a father or uncle who participated. And yet, perhaps without realizing it, they had constructed such a definitive conception of the event they were about to commemorate that it became mythical. So convincing was their shared vision, which they further embellished during the lengthy process of shepherding the project to completion, that the battle's myths have become received wisdom today.[16]

An anecdote favored by grade school history books is that Prescott told his men not to fire until they saw the whites of the redcoats' eyes, an order one military historian calls "absurd."[17] Like Stark who placed a fifty-yard marker in the sand, and Knowlton (or Putnam, according to some accounts) at the breastwork who waited to shout *Fire* until the grenadiers were clambering over a fence forty yards away, Prescott knew his men had to make every round count, so he did discipline them to hold back until a nerve-wracking thirty or forty yards. Smoothbore muskets—of which the militia had a varied assortment—were wildly inaccurate. Lead balls had a rough, irregular shape and fitted the barrel loosely; already wobbling as they left the gun, they caught the air with a random trajectory. At trigger pull, there was a significant lag between the flint flashing the pan and the charge igniting. Sparks from the pan singed hand and face, while the flash was disorienting, so at the instant of discharge the barrel would tip upwards if the shooter involuntarily winced backwards. When firing at ranges over fifty yards, balls therefore tended to pass harmlessly over the heads of the enemy, as happened with most of the redcoats' volleys. It was for this reason that rebel officers reminded their men throughout the afternoon to aim at the redcoats' legs. But whites of their eyes? There would have been so much dust and smoke in the air that even faces would have been hard to discern at twenty yards. An advantage worth noting is that many of the rebels rested their muskets on a barricade or fence rail before firing, and some even fired prone, whereas the redcoats fired standing.[18]

Nineteenth- and twentieth-century histories emphasize how hot it was. Samuel Swett began his account of the battle by noting that, "the sun fell with its full force on the American camp," leaving the earth "parched up," and stressed later how "the heat was excessive." Another historian talks about "sweltering heat" three times in as many pages, in addition to high humidity. Col. Prescott's son stated that, "the day was clear

---

16. For the Exchange Coffee House, see Samuel Adams Drake, *Old Boston Taverns and Tavern Clubs* (Boston: W.A. Butterfield, 1917), p. 108, ill. fp. 110. A popular textbook that they may have read at school was William Gordon, *The History of the Rise, Progress, and Establishment of the Independence of the United States of America: Including an Account of the Late War . . .* (New York: Samuel Campbell, 1794). George Washington Warren, *The History of the Bunker Hill Monument Association During the First Century of the United States of America* (Boston: James R. Osgood and Company, 1877), p. 46.

17. Morrissey, *Shot Heard*, p. 61.

18. For "laying down behind" the wall on the beach, and "rested their muskets over the fence," see Dearborn, *Account of the Battle*, pp. 4, 6; Dearborn estimated that of fifty balls fired at them, forty-nine flew six feet over their heads, noting the marks on an apple tree as proof. Under controlled conditions, the odds of hitting a man-sized target at fifty yards were about 30 percent, falling to 3 percent at a hundred yards. See Alexander Rose, "Marksmanship in 1775: Myth or Reality?" *American Rifleman*, 158:7 (July 2010), pp. 45–47, 70.

and very hot." Yet Prescott's reminiscence was sixty-three years after the fact by someone who, at age thirteen, was home in Pepperell, forty-two miles away. What might the weather really have been? From a sample of thirty-five accounts written at the time by combatants on both sides, none of the rebels mentioned anything about it being particularly hot. Conversely, redcoat writers typically referenced the "heat of the action," and three complained about "the heat of the weather" or "the heat of the day." These writers, who belonged to regiments newly arrived from Britain after a cool sea crossing, were perhaps looking for excuses to justify their heavy casualties. One pointer is the logbook of HMS *Preston*, which for 12 PM recorded, "light airs and calm [water]." A better indication might be the account of rebel Capt. Joseph Chester, from Connecticut, who "ran" from his lodgings where he was finishing lunch because Putnam had galloped in to say the redcoats had landed. Chester "hasted" to his company, and marched them to Charlestown, "with our frocks and trowsers on over our other clothes (for our company is in uniform wholly blue, turned up with red,) for we were loathe to expose ourselves by our dress." If it was hot then it seems odd that after dashing around Cambridge at 2 PM, Chester would have pulled on extra clothes for a two-mile march. Most likely it was a typical June day by the ocean during the Little Ice Age, when average temperatures were lower than today: cool and breezy in the morning, with low humidity, warming in the afternoon to the mid-seventies. Certainly it would have felt hot, from the sight of Charlestown burning, the flash of weapons, and of course the adrenaline of battle. Even though they lacked water, the stationary rebels nevertheless had a clear advantage, for they wore loose shirts and wide-brimmed hats, while the redcoats were struggling uphill across rough pastures of unmown hay, wearing wool jackets, tight-fitting headgear, and heavy knapsacks.[19]

BHMA members and contemporary accounts made much of British barbarity, especially the burning of Charlestown. In a letter to a friend shortly after the battle, Samuel Gray, a native of Roxbury, wrote that, "The savages set fire to the town, beginning with the meeting-house." British officers had a different view. When Pigot attempted to advance the companies of his left flank into position, they had come under heavy skirmishing fire from buildings on the outskirts of the town, which were only two hundred yards from the redoubt. "Being much exposed to the enemy's fire from the houses of Charlestown," wrote one Royal Marine, they "sustained considerable loss." Before launching the assault, Howe consequently sent orders to the Copp's Hill battery and marines on HMS *Somerset* to burn Charlestown; the conflagration that soon consumed the wooden buildings flushed out Capt. Walker's militia company stationed there, although later in the day sniper fire from houses near the waterfront killed two of Clinton's officers as they came ashore. With the exception of Gen. William Tryon's attacks on Fairfield and Norwalk, Connecticut, in July 1779 in the

---

19. Swett, *Bunker Hill Battle*, p. 18; "sweltering heat," Brooks, *Boston Campaign*, pp. 151, 153; Prescott, in Frothingham, *The Battle-Field*, p. 20; redcoat accounts, in Samuel Adams Drake, *Bunker Hill: The Story Told in Letters from the Battle Field by British Officers Engaged* (Boston: Nichols and Hall, 1875), pp. 25, 50; logbook, in Frothingham, *The Battle-Field*, p. 9; Chester, in Frothingham, *Siege*, p. 391.

hope of luring Gen. George Washington's army out of West Point, British forces during the war did not burn towns, which, after all, were British property. Frustrated though he was, Howe did not relish Charlestown's destruction; rather he reacted to a tactic he viewed as underhanded, if not contrary to the established rules of honorable warfare. After Concord and Lexington, moreover, Gage had warned Charlestown's selectmen that were the rebels to occupy the town, the townsfolk would suffer the consequences. Prescott nevertheless made the decision to set up a defensive line of which the town formed a part, instead of defending Bunker's Hill.[20]

As paintings, prints, plays, and public orations over the following decades made plain, the central myth that members celebrated was the heroic death and republican spirit of Dr. Joseph Warren. Some members might have questioned Warren's sensibilities: why was such an important politician—as head of the Massachusetts Provincial Congress he was the putative state's chief executive—a valuable surgeon, and a single parent of five children, so determined to place himself in harm's way? Indeed, Putnam and Prescott had both entreated him to return to Cambridge on that fateful day. Most members surely appreciated that Warren's appointment to major general three days before the battle was titular; other than a similarly impetuous brush with redcoats at Lexington in April, which almost proved fatal when a ball whistled out one of the pins that held up his long powdered hair, he had no military experience and may not even have known how to properly load a musket. But all of them must have understood that the lead ball that crashed into the back of his skull as he fled the battlefield knocked him dead to the ground.

Yet the story that members wanted to believe, and did their best to promote, was far more romantic, even biblical. "Those who saw General Warren fall, as he slowly retreated in the rear," the BHMA's historian wrote in 1877, heard him exclaim, "'I'm a dead man; fight on, my brave fellows, for the salvation of your country!'" "'Country,'" the historian reiterated, "was the last word on the heroic martyr's lips." To the members of the BHMA and their acolytes, Warren was even more than their founding father: he was a deity. "But, ah! Him! The first great martyr in this great cause! Him!" BHMA president Daniel Webster eulogized in one of his most famous orations, as if to conflate Warren with Christ, "the premature victim of his own self-devoting heart! Him! Cut off by Providence in the hour of overwhelming anxiety and thick gloom; falling ere he saw the star of his country rise." In the hands of a master rhetorician like Webster, Warren became as central to the creation story of the United States as George Washington.[21]

---

20. Gray, in Frothingham, *Siege*, p. 393; "Historical Record of Royal Marine Forces," in Drake, *Letters from the Battle Field*, p. 33; Clinton, in Allen French, *The First Year of the American Revolution* (Boston: Houghton Mifflin Company, 1934), p. 243; Charles Hervey Townshend, *The British Invasion of New haven, Connecticut, Together with Some Account of Their Landing and Burning the Towns of Fairfield and Norwalk, July 1779* (New Haven, CT: Tuttle, Morehouse and Taylor, 1879).

21. Warren, *Monument Association*, p. 28; Daniel Webster, at the laying of the Monument's cornerstone, 17 June 1825, *Two Orations by Daniel Webster: The Bunker Hill Monument; Adams and Jefferson* (Boston: Houghton Mifflin Company, 1893), pp. 18–19, discussed further, below.

THE DEATH OF WARREN

fig. 5: frontispiece of H.H. Brackenridge's play, *The Death of Warren*

Illustrations of Warren's death, such as the frontispiece to a 1776 playbook by H.H. Brackenridge (fig. 5), consistently showed him mortally wounded, hand on heart, staring toward heaven, surrounded by grieving patriots. John Trumbull's *The Death of General Warren at the Battle of Bunker Hill* (1786, and reproduced widely as an engraving), a classic Republican-genre battle scene, depicted redcoat Maj. John Small staying a grenadier's bayonet thrust at the dying Warren, supported in the arms of another rebel. Trumbull dressed Warren in white shirt and breeches, which, together with his fair complexion and baby face, created a sense of the spiritual, the otherworldly (back cover ill.). Warren's two aides, also in white shirts but with khaki breeches, might have been angels waiting to transport their master to heaven. BHMA members stressed Warren's republicanism, making much of his impromptu arrival at the redoubt. According to contemporary accounts, when Col. Prescott offered his command to the general, Warren answered that he "'came as a volunteer, with my musket, to serve under you, and shall be happy to learn from a soldier of your experience.'" He was a regular soldier who "stood among equals, without selfish rivalry, in devotion and patriotism"; his purpose was pure, historian George E. Ellis wrote in 1875, "mingling with his countrymen on that hill." "Declining all command, insistent on serving as the pupil of more experienced men," wrote another historian in 1927, Warren made "but a dim and modest figure on the battle canvas, hardly distinguishable in the throng." Webster's eulogy had Warren "pouring out his generous blood like water, before he knew whether it would fertilize a land of freedom or of bondage." Warren's self-sacrifice was as pure as it was egalitarian.[22]

And yet the reality of Warren's presence on the field was a different story. Leaving aside that some battle memoirs place a fancy sword in his hand rather than a simple musket, he sported a finely tailored light-blue jacket adorned with rows of silver buttons, a white satin waistcoat, and silk breeches tied with silver loops. So valuable were his clothes that soon after the redcoats gained the field, someone stole them.[23] Other than his French Enlightenment idealism, Warren in 1775 was in fact just like the BHMA's elite members of 1823, with his Harvard education, cultured tastes, and a Freemason's business connections. He was a privileged, slave-owning aristocrat of high taste and expensive habits.[24] Freshly resplendent in bright silver and perfumed silk, Warren had no intention of standing as an equal among rough laborers and rustic yeomen, with their soiled homespun garments dyed in vegetable extracts. Rather, he set himself apart as a spiffy, swashbuckling firebrand. Even the proud Prescott knew enough about militia leadership to exchange his uniform and wig early in the day for a farmer's linen shirt and wide hat.

Accounts of the battle, then and since, are unanimous in placing Warren in the redoubt, explaining how he fought under Prescott as a common soldier. Richard Frothingham's respected 1903 history provides an especially detailed picture of Warren's arrival on the field at around noon. Going first to Putnam at the rail fence, Warren asked where he would be most useful. Putnam directed him to the redoubt, for it offered good protection. "'Don't think I come to seek a place of safety,'" Warren replied, "'but tell me where the onset will be most furious.'" Putnam was still pointing, so Warren "passed to the redoubt, where the men received him with enthusiastic cheers." Once the battle started, Warren "mingled in the fight, behaved with great bravery, and was among the last to leave the redoubt." Subsequent historiography has followed Frothingham's version of events. In a typical recent history, Richard M. Ketchum writes, "After asking where he would be of most use, Warren went out to the redoubt," where he "[took] his place in the line," adding a "graceful word about how he would consider it a privilege to fight under Prescott."[25] At the Monument's reception center, the National Park Service's official history informs visitors that "Warren

22. Hugh Henry Brackenridge, *The Battle of Bunkers-Hill: A Dramatic Piece, of Five Acts in Heroic Measure, by a Gentleman of Maryland* (Philadelphia: Robert Bell, Printers, 1776), frontispiece. John Burk's *Bunker Hill, or the Death of General Warren*, which opened at Boston's Haymarket Theatre on 20 February 1797, became a perennial favorite into the 1820s. "'Volunteer,'" account by Prescott's son, Judge William Prescott, cited in Wheildon, *New History*, p. 45; George E. Ellis, *History of the Battle of Bunker's (Breed's) Hill, on June 17, 1775* (Boston: Lockwood, Brooks, & Company, 1875), p. 88; Harold Murdock, *Bunker Hill: Notes and Queries on a Famous Battle* (Boston: Houghton Mifflin Company, 1927), p. 53; *Two Orations by Daniel Webster*, p. 19.

23. One rebel wrote that Warren "had dressed himself like Lord Falkland [Lucius Cary, 2nd Viscount, who died at the First Battle of Newbury in 1643], in his wedding suit," cited in Willard, ed., *Letters on the American Revolution*, p. 151; Lt. John Clarke, "I saw the soldier soon after strip off his body," in Drake, *Letters from the Battle Field*, p. 50.

24. For Warren as slave owner, see "The Armies Face Off: The Patriot Militia," Bunker Hill Monument Museum exhibit panel, National Park Service, exhibition panel, National Park Service, from research by Martin Blatt and Alfred F. Young.

25. Frothingham, *Siege of Boston*, p. 170; Ketchum, *Decisive Day*, pp. 150–51.

took up a musket to fight alongside the other men in the redoubt. As the British troops stormed the redoubt, Warren was one of the last to leave."[26] Placing Warren in the redoubt was as obvious as it was natural to these historians: where else would the principal hero be but fighting to the last man in the battle's metaphorical heart? Yet again, though, as a previously overlooked account of Warren's presence on the battlefield indicates, the need to create a founding national myth has driven historical reality.

Born in Framingham, Massachusetts, in 1755, Nedham Maynard was an eighty-five-year-old retired judge who still served as a magistrate in Seneca Falls, New York, when he related his story of the battle to an *Albany Evening Journal* reporter. Rheumatism had stiffened Maynard's gait, but he impressed the reporter as having a sharp mind. A matter-of-fact quality pervades the article—it gives no sense that Maynard was trying to set straight any records, rather it reads as an eyewitness account of immediate events—indeed, Maynard's story was peripheral to the article's purpose, which was to support the presidential election campaign of Gen. William Henry Harrison, an elderly Whig, by showing how someone seventeen years older than Harrison was still an active public servant (ironically, Harrison died after only a month in office). As Maynard explained, although Warren was the senior officer on the field at the rank of major general, he had no staff, and consequently "required the services of some one to transmit his orders." Col. Jonathan Brewer, Maynard's commanding officer, volunteered Maynard to be Warren's aide-de-camp. Maynard "repaired with him [Warren] to the centre" of the field, where Warren "immediately" ordered improvements to the defenses, by "doubling a post and rail fence," and having the men stuff hay, mown only the day before, into the remaining gaps. (*Doubling* meant adding extra rails scavenged from other fences.) Once the redcoat advance was underway, Warren soon had Maynard busy delivering more orders, the first to Col. John Nixon on the left flank by the Mystic River, to "'reserve his fire until the firing commenced in the centre,'" and then "the same order to Col. Prescott and the other officers along the line." When the redcoats were within ten or twelve rods (sixty yards), Warren gave the order to "'fire,'" and then when the redcoats retreated, an order to cease fire. Towards the end of the battle, Warren ordered sixty men to the redoubt, and he dispatched Maynard to Prescott with a message that he would send more men if Prescott required them. It was while Maynard was in the redoubt awaiting Prescott's reply that a redcoat shot the fleeing Warren.[27]

There is no reason to doubt the central facts behind Maynard's recollection, which make evident that Warren spent the battle not as a humble soldier in Prescott's service at the redoubt but rather as a presumptuous commander barking orders and expecting

---

26. "Doctor Joseph Warren," exhibit placard next to the Henry Dexter statue of Warren, Bunker Hill Monument visitors' reception hall, photographed 25 July 2011.

27. "The Battle of Bunker Hill," reproduced in the *Bunker-Hill Aurora*, 11 July 1840, p. 1. Solomon Willard's biographer William H. Wheildon was the editor of the *Aurora*, a weekly Charlestown newspaper, which also appeared downtown as the *Boston Mirror*.

deference—as befit a man of aristocratic station—while strutting left and right, perhaps at the rail fence, or more likely, by the flèches or behind the hundred-yard-long breastwork, where he played the role of the absent Putnam. This interpretation is consistent with Warren's behavior at Lexington, and meshes with other reports that he ordered militia about, jeered at redcoats, and was anything but self-effacing.[28]

Of all the myths, the most enduring has been that of numbers. According to "Looking Back at the Battle that Changed the World," the *Charlestown Patriot-Bridge*'s lead editorial for Bunker Hill Day 2008, a small band of "1,000 Patriots" repeatedly repelled a far larger force of redcoats (the editorialist was careful to say "more than 1,000 Patriots," but it is the number that sticks in readers' minds). "History tells us that 5,000 crack British soldiers marched up the hill and were met with a deadly fusillade from the American 'rebels.'" But that is not what history—a less subjective history—has to say. Approximately 3,500 redcoats (officers and men) landed on the peninsula during the afternoon, of which several hundred took no active part (porters, medics, messengers), and eight hundred arrived later with Clinton's third wave to replace redcoats already dead or evacuated. In each attack, when "soldiers marched up the hill," there would have been 1,200–1,800 redcoats engaged, spread out from the beach to the town, with a thousand at most on Breed's Hill. By contrast, the rebels had a total force in Cambridge of about 10,200, of which four or five thousand were on the Charlestown peninsula as the redcoats marched up the hill. Of those, Prescott, Knowles, and Stark expected that at least three thousand would be fighting next to them, but half were too afraid, which made the numbers actively engaged at any one time evenly matched. Musket-to-musket numbers were of course important, yet the defensively entrenched rebels enjoyed a five- if not ten-to-one superiority in effective firepower over the attacking redcoats, hence the disproportionate casualty ratio. Even here the *Patriot-Bridge*'s "history tells us" figure of "1,000 British laid dead" on the battlefield adds to the glorious myth of Bunker Hill; in fact, 226 lay dead or subsequently died of their wounds, with 828 evacuated wounded, tragically high numbers nevertheless.[29]

An intriguing story to emerge from the historical record of 1775 with a ring of plausibility is the origin of *Yankee*. Redcoats derided rebel skirmishers at Lexington and Bunker's Hill who fired at them from the cover of hedgerows and buildings as Yankees or Yankee Doodles. "[Our] troops then laughed," wrote a redcoat, "and damned the Yankees" as cowards who "could not bear the smell of gunpowder." But the rebels adopted the term as a badge of honor for a successful "*Yankee* way of bushfighting," as one letter writer put it, going on to explain that it was "an Indian word,

---

28. For colonial-era deference, see for instance Alfred F. Young, *The Shoemaker and the Tea Party: Memory and the American Revolution* (Boston: Beacon Press, 1999), p. 4. There was also a rail fence in front of the flèches (running northeast–southwest, in line with the redcoat line of advance and at 110 degrees to the breastwork). At Lexington, Warren "was, perhaps, the most active man in the field," according to historian Samuel Atkins Eliot, cited in Frothingham, *Siege of Boston*, fn. 4, p. 77.

29. *Charlestown Patriot-Bridge*, 12 June 2008, p. 6. Figures from Morrissey, *Shot Heard*, pp. 60–61, and Frothingham, *Siege*, p. 194.

and was given our forefathers, signifying Conquerors." There is corroboration for this etymology in Frank Moore's *The Diary of the American Revolution*, which cites a diarist called Clift who appeared—according to Moore—in the *Virginia Gazette* of 10 June 1775. Early New England colonists, Clift wrote, had particular difficulty subduing a tribe called Yankoos, which in the native language meant *invincible*. When the colonists eventually beat them into submission, the Yankoo survivors "transferred their name to their conquerors." Clift hoped that the derivation *Yankee* would "soon be equal to that of a Roman, or an ancient Englishman." First published in 1860, Moore's edited collection contains as much fact as fancy yet, in this case, it is an appealing story to believe.[30]

Forming the BHMA

Settled no doubt with brandies and smokes around a table in an upper room at the Coffee House as they adopted their new association's mission statement, the twenty-five gentlemen of culture and high character were of a piece. They were scions of elite families of long standing, who owned substantial homes in Boston or its environs, and depended on servants for their wellbeing and transportation. Groomed from early childhood for achievement and leadership, most had personal tutors, went to exclusive schools, and read Greek, Latin, and French by the time they were teenagers. Half were Harvard educated; fifteen were lawyers, doctors, or academics; seven were mercantilists or manufacturers; and by their close average age of forty-two, fourteen of them were sufficiently wealthy to be in public service. Six, moreover, were, or had been, top-ranking officers of the state's military apparatus. Except for a few Unitarians, they were all Protestants of one denomination or another, and most were members of gentlemen's clubs or Masonic lodges. Yet these men were not the types to rest on the laurels of old money.

Nathaniel Pope Russell had made his fortune in shipping insurance, before two terms in the state house. BHMA secretary William Tudor, whose more entrepreneurial brother Frederic was Boston's famous Ice King, was the founder-editor of the *North American Review*. Dr. John Collins Warren, Joseph Warren's nephew, was a cofounder of the Harvard Medical School and in the 1840s would pioneer anesthesiology. Isaac P. Davis had supplied the cordage for USS *Constitution*. Henry A.S. Dearborn, a lawyer whose father fought with Stark, was Boston's Collector of Customs (as his father had been), and rode in a curtained four-wheel carriage of his own design, to which he gave his name. Harvard law professor Joseph Story served on the U.S. Supreme Court, and wrote the opinion in *Martin v. Hunter's Lessee*, a case about the right of Virginia to confiscate Loyalists' property, which set the precedent for the Court's authority over state courts in matters of federal law. By five years the oldest at fifty-nine and by far

---

30. Redcoat, cited in Frank Moore, ed., *Diary of the American Revolution, from Newspapers and Original Documents* (New York: Charles Scribner, 1860), vol. 1, p. 64; "bush-fighting," cited in Willard, ed., *Letters on the American Revolution*, pp. 84–85, emphasis original; Moore, ed., *Diary of the American Revolution*, vol. 1, p. 86. For a critique of Moore and whether Clift's name might have been Solomon E. or Joseph W., see Glenn B. Skillin's review of the republished book in *New England Quarterly*, 40:4 (December 1967), pp. 622–24.

the wealthiest, Thomas Handasyd[31] Perkins would be the BHMA's co-vice president with Story. As a commission merchant at Saint-Domingue (Haiti) in the 1780s, Perkins had built his business trading salt cod, flour, horses, and slaves. Now he operated a fleet of packet ships and a factory in Canton to trade furs, metals, and Turkish opium for Chinese silks, dyestuffs, and tea. Restless and competitive, Perkins was already experimenting with investments in the textile factories and infrastructure of the industrial age.[32]

Pledging their initial subscription of $5 ($400[33]), they agreed to incorporate, raise funds, and erect a suitable monument. In essence, the statement they prepared that day, and their submission for incorporation to Massachusetts General Court two weeks later, observed that almost fifty years after the opening salvos of the Revolutionary War, no state had built a monument of any substance. (They either conveniently ignored or were unaware of a 178-foot column to honor George Washington rising in Baltimore, Maryland.) It was only fitting, they reasoned, that the first colony stained with the blood of patriots should be the first state to erect a column in their honor. These documents, though, reveal far more about how they saw their world, and their place in it, than simple patriotism. Since emerging from the War of Independence, "every American"—or at least, those in their circle—daily felt the advantages accrued, whether in agriculture, manufactures, commerce, literature, science, or the arts. Americans had "advanced in the route of national glory with a rapidity unprecedented in the annals of empire." It was now time that they, who were the "generous spirit of an intelligent and prosperous community," fulfilled their obligation to the patriots who had "braved the hardships, privations, and dangers of the conflict, for the boasted privileges we enjoy." An interpretation at the parochial level, in other words, is that they wanted to celebrate their achievements and status.[34]

But the men gathered at the Exchange Coffee House that May day in 1823 had a grander design, one that encompassed the globe, in parts of which, principally the European Enlightenment centers of London, Paris, and Göttingen, half of them had studied or traveled. At Bunker's Hill, their heroes had fought the battle that commenced an era "more wonderful in its progress" than any before. It was at Bunker's Hill that Warren, Prescott, Putnam, Stark, and the rest had "laid the everlasting foundations of *liberty*," from whence the spirit of representative government had gone forth, "advancing, with the general and irresistible march of intelligence, round the globe." If only the BHMA could erect a sufficiently impressive monument then "the whole human race" would venerate those gallant New Englanders, who "breasted the

---

31. Pronounced Handy-side.

32. Carl Seaburg and Stanley Patterson, *Merchant Prince of Boston: Colonel T.H. Perkins, 1764–1854* (Cambridge, MA: Harvard University Press, 1971), pp. 40–41, 266–69, 312–14.

33. Based on "Inflation Data, 1823," spreadsheet, compiled by author (available on request), of a basket of goods, services, rents, and wages, this study uses a factor of 80 to adjust for inflation from 1823–40 to 2011 (for consistency, 80 is used throughout, even though the 1820s were deflationary and the 1840s were inflationary).

34. Formative agreement, and petition to the Commonwealth, in Warren, *Monument Association*, pp. 40–41, 42–43.

tempest of war for the '*unalienable rights of man*.'" Their monument—their "*first pillar* of the Republic"—on Bunker's Hill would stand as an example to the rest of the world of the civilizing progress of republican governance.[35]

With such an august body behind it, their application for incorporation sailed through the Massachusetts legislature (until the 1860s, public corporations, of which there were few, required a state-approved charter). There was so much enthusiasm for their project that they acquired the good offices of Massachusetts Governor John Brooks as their first president. After training to be a doctor in Medford, Brooks practiced in Reading, thirteen miles north of Boston. A twenty-three-year-old Minutemen company commander in April 1775, he had marched his men from Reading to Lexington, where they killed redcoats who were fleeing back to Boston down the wooded lanes. Brooks liked to say that he fought at Bunker's Hill too, but although Col. Ebenezer Bridge, whose regiment included two companies commanded by Maj. Brooks, paraded in Cambridge on 16 June, Brooks's companies had still not reached the hill by the time Prescott was retreating on the afternoon of 17 June; Bridge was subsequently acquitted at a courts martial for excessive caution. In the event, Brooks contributed little to the BHMA—he did not stand for a seventh term as governor and died in early 1825—and it is beside the point whether he and his men were too afraid to fight with Prescott. What matters here, is the process that links the battle, through memory, to the official sanctioning of the mythicized event, and how that legitimated history created a foundation for national identity.[36]

In 1818, Henry Dearborn had published a short memoir of the battle, which was critical of Putnam's conduct. When an angry Daniel Putnam, son of the now-deceased general, published a refutation, also in pamphlet form, the old wounds he opened focused attention on the sanctity of the founding myth. "It grieves me," Secretary of State John Quincy Adams wrote to his mother Abigail, to watch "cotemporaries and eye-witnesses disputing with each other whether Putnam was a hero or a coward." Adams was typical of Yankee elites who understood the necessity of protecting the "reputation" of the "patriots and warriors of our Revolution." Writing against Dearborn in the *North American Review*, Daniel Webster made explicit the centrality of the hero to the national story: "Let us remember that we have nothing more precious than the reputation of our distinguished men," he cautioned; his readers must "deprecate the spirit that deprecates merit," and earnestly embrace "in all its extent and spirit" the maxim that "*character is power*." Brooks then threw his gubernatorial hat into the ring, visiting the battle site accompanied by two aides—one of whom was Gen. William H. Sumner, commander of the state militia and eponym of Boston's Sumner Tunnel—with a view to undermining Dearborn's version of events. Even though Brooks never reached Breed's Hill on 17 June 1775, by his own admission did not go there subsequently, and therefore had no first-hand knowledge of the

---

35. Ibid., emphasis original.

36. Frothingham, *Siege*, pp. 72–73, 176–77. Massachusetts governors served a one-year term until 1918, when the term became two years, and then four years in 1966. See also Sarah J. Purcell, "Sealed With Blood: National Identity and Public Memory of the Revolutionary War, 1775–1825" (PhD diss., Brown University, 1997).

fortifications, he located a plowed-over ridge in the tall grass that he declared was the remains of the breastwork. Because its location was at odds with a map included in Dearborn's account, he concluded that Dearborn's version of the battle was faulty, leaving Putnam, and of course Warren, as the true heroes of the day.[37]

Indeed, the facts—or rather the myth—of Warren's death lay at the heart of the debate. In his pamphlet, Dearborn mentioned, quite unemotionally, that with his ammunition expended and redcoats storming the redoubt, he had walked toward the melee in the hope of collecting ammunition from a fallen soldier; he had not gone far when he noticed a finely dressed body by a locust tree, which a fleeing rebel said was Warren. Daniel Putnam's pamphlet pounced on Dearborn's version of the "death of the immortal Warren," citing a letter from the patriot-artist John Trumbull, who had befriended the redcoat Maj. John Small while in London in 1786. Trumbull stated that Small had been assisting Howe, who had a bruised ankle, when Howe spotted an "'elegant young man who has just fallen.'" Recognizing Warren, whom he knew, Small rushed over, and said, "'My dear friend, I hope you are not badly hurt.'" Warren then "looked up, seemed to recollect me, smiled and died!" As Daniel Putnam pointed out, "both statements *cannot* be true," for Dearborn saw Warren dead before the redcoats had claimed the field, whereas Small held the dying Warren some time after the rebels, including Dearborn, had fled. "You," Putnam leveled at Dearborn, a man who would stoop so low as to "rifle the dying and the dead," and use "unworthy means" to defame the character of brave patriots, "*know* to which the truth belongs." Those who read the pamphlets and debated their contents in literary magazines or around dinner tables had to decide between two stories, one cold-blooded and sometimes sordid, the other glorious and honorable. For those who understood that character was power, choosing the romantic myth was an easy decision.[38]

Brook's visit after forty-three years not only established his presence on the battlefield in 1775, and presumably his contribution to the glorious outcome, but it also stamped his imprimatur on the received wisdom of the day, thereby authenticating the founding myth. As a corollary to the process, when elites like Brooks, Russell, Tudor, Davis, Story, and Perkins formed their association to build a monument, they appropriated that myth, becoming one with the nation's founders, and securing their—and their families'—legitimacy as the new Republic's rightful rulers and power brokers. It is a telling irony that Brooks rose through the ranks of the state legislature after leading his Middlesex Militia in 1786 to suppress the disgruntled yeomen farmers of Shays's Rebellion, many of whom had fought in the ranks at Breed's Hill for liberty of a different kind. Backwoods sharecroppers, itinerant laborers, and underemployed

37. John Quincy Adams to Abigail Adams, 25 May 1818, in *The Writings of John Quincy Adams*, ed. Worthington Chauncey Ford (New York: Macmillan Company, 1916), vol. 6, p. 338; Daniel Webster, book review of *An Account of the Battle of Bunker Hill*, by Henry Dearborn, and *A Letter to Major General Dearborn*, by Daniel Putnam, *North American Review and Miscellaneous Journal*, 7:2 (July 1818), p. 258, emphasis original; Brooks's visit, in Warren, *Monument Association*, pp. 33–35. See Patricia Roeser's PhD diss., "Bunker Hill Monument in Memory and Rhetoric" (Arizona State University, 2010), pp. 55–75, 366–67, for an interpretation of the debate as a partisan, political attack by the Republican Dearborn on beleaguered New England Federalists, as represented by their icon Israel Putnam.

38. Dearborn, *Account of the Battle*, p. 6, and Daniel Putnam, *Letter to Maj. Gen. Dearborn*, pp. 8–10, emphasis original. In 1786, Small was a colonel.

artisans, all those who in the tumultuous years of 1765–74 tarred and feathered tax collectors, rioted outside Governor Thomas Hutchinson's mansion, and roughed up redcoats with whom they competed for Boston's scarce jobs, thought they were fighting for a social revolution. Elites, whose primary aim was to govern in place of the crown thereby reinstituting lost perquisites, had only listened to the would-be revolutionaries for as long as it took to foment a popular insurrection and defeat the British, after which it was business as usual, albeit in new republican clothes. Since the American Revolution—so-called—taxation had increased dramatically, courts confiscated property for the slightest default, and the federal government sent in the army at the first sign of dissent. Disagreements during the Republic's early years, such as the Whiskey Rebellion in Pennsylvania (1791), hinged on the extent to which political power should be centralized or localized, corporate or communal. To resolve the quarrel and restore consensus, Americans had to reformulate their national identity.[39]

Historians propose a range of theories to explain the rise of nationalism in the nineteenth century: most begin with the Marxist presumption that the Industrial Revolution was a necessary precursor; one school argues that print capitalism and mass media made nationalism possible; another believes that wars create feelings of otherness, which one's enemy then reciprocates, leading to a spiral of nationalistic fervor; several postmodernist scholars suggest that nationalism is not so much an ideology as a location for discourse, a sort of civic arena in which different groups contend to build a suitable identity. These theories are all informative, yet in the case of the Monument and the seductively powerful American nationalism or *Americanism* it engendered, none is particularly satisfying. Boston, by 1823, was developing a substantial manufacturing sector on top of its mercantile base, but its economy was pre-industrial, in the sense that its workforce still felt proudly artisanal rather than abjectly proletarian; it had plenty of newspapers and journals, but the BHMA's members promoted their ideology through meetings in smoke-filled rooms, handwritten letters, oratory, and the physical presence of the Monument; Bostonians had certainly fought a war, which they did perpetuate through civic memory, yet they soon patched up their quarrel with the mother country, to the extent of creating a tacit alliance or special relationship with England; many Bostonians sought to contest the meaning of liberty or republicanism, but once elites had expropriated the founding myth and made it their own—once they had built a granite obelisk towering to the heavens that seemed to authenticate their commercial and intellectual power on earth—it became easier for dissenting voices to fight within the accepted framework of Americanism's received wisdom than to challenge its ideology head on.[40]

39. For social conditions in Boston, see Young, *Shoemaker and the Tea Party*, pp. 26–57. My interpretation of the events of 1770–89 as counter-revolutionary follows in part Francis Jennings's in *The Creation of America: Through Revolution to Empire* (Cambridge: Cambridge University Press, 2000), esp. pp. 297–303, 315–18.

40. For industrialization, Ernest Gellner, *Nations and Nationalism* (Ithaca, NY: Cornell University Press, 1983), with BHMA members resembling Gellner's pre-industrial "clerisy"; for print capitalism, Benedict Anderson, *Imagined Communities: Reflections on the Origin and Spread of Nationalism* (London: Verso, 1983); for warfare, C.A. Bayly, *The Birth of the Modern World, 1780–1914* (Oxford: Blackwell Publishing, 2004), esp. pp. 203–10; for sites of contestation, Prasenjit Duara, "Historicizing National Identity, or Who Imagines What and When," in *Becoming National*, eds. Geoff

Rather than using a neo-Marxist or Enlightenment interpretation, it may be that in the case of the BHMA's elites Classicism fits the evidence better. Whereas it was the liberalism of John Locke and the republicanism of Jean-Jacques Rousseau that inspired Constitution writers like Thomas Jefferson and James Madison, or rebel activists like Samuel Adams and Daniel Shays, BHMA members distanced themselves from the barbarous excesses of the French Revolution while they quietly recreated Plato's Republic. Edward Everett, one of the BHMA's five founding members and its executive secretary, was professor of Greek literature at Harvard, where his influence on young minds, according to former pupil Ralph Waldo Emerson, "was almost comparable to that of Pericles in Athens." William Tudor, another founding member and the BHMA's secretary of correspondence, was also the founder of the Boston Athenaeum; Tudor even christened Boston the "Athens of America." George Ticknor, who at age ten could read the works of Cicero in Greek, had studied the Greek classics at Göttingen with his friend Everett. It is not surprising, therefore, that these highbrow aristocrats, most of whom were Freemasons, presumed that their monument would resemble Trajan's Column.[41]

Fundraising

Charter in hand, the BHMA's thirty new directors fixed the appropriate date of 17 June for their annual meetings, elected twenty-five regular members who also paid $5, made appointments to various committees—Standing, Correspondence, Finance, Design—and began raising funds, initially to buy the battle site and then for construction. In 1794, Charlestown's King Solomon's Lodge of Freemasons had erected an eighteen-foot Tuscan pillar in honor of Warren—a modest affair of wood, topped with a gilt urn—on a plot in the vicinity of the flattened redoubt, donated by local farmer-magistrate James Russell. When the entire Russell Pasture of 2.75 acres went on sale in early 1823, John C. Warren eagerly paid $1,250 for it. After BHMA directors failed to persuade the General Court to let them take sufficient land by eminent domain, they negotiated with nine farmers to buy a further 12.25 acres for $21,982 ($144,000 per acre), four times the cost-per-acre that Warren paid the Russell heirs. For some Americans, monument fever was a windfall, and it would not be long before detractors were charging the directors with extravagance. To finance this substantial sum, twenty directors and members signed sureties for a thousand dollars apiece, supplementing the first donation they received, and one of few from out of state, from the Washington Benevolent Society of $1,900, which its members had collected on the assumption that it was a patriotic endeavor of national importance. There were other handsome donations in the early months, principally $1,000 from former Lieutenant Governor William Phillips, $500 each from Peter C. Brooks and merchant David Sears, $100 each from Rev. John Codman and Cdr. William Bainbridge, and a group

Eley and Ronald Grigor Suny (New York: Oxford University Press, 1996).

41. Edward Waldo Emerson and Waldo Emerson Forbes, eds., *Journals of Ralph Waldo Emerson, with Annotations* (Boston: Houghton Mifflin Company, 1911), September 1842, vol. 6, p. 255.

of New Englanders living in New York who collected $86. Thereafter, raising funds became hard work, and Secretary Edward Everett started to notice the cost of mailing circulars—at the rate of 6¼¢ for thirty miles, 10¢ for eighty, and 25¢ for five hundred—that he had initially paid for out of his own pocket.[42]

After graduating from Harvard and a stint as a Unitarian pastor, Everett earned a PhD—the first American to do so—in Germany and returned to join Harvard's faculty in 1819; he later served as governor of Massachusetts, president of Harvard, and Secretary of State. Webster and Everett were the finest orators in America, and the BHMA was lucky to have both as directors. Everett's masterful fundraising circular of 20 September 1824 shows that the BHMA had reached a consensus on a design for the monument, and suggests what the members thought their design would accomplish. For about $37,000 ($3 million), the BHMA would erect a monumental column, "of classical model, with an elevation to make it the most lofty in the world." Of fine Chelmsford granite, it would be of "substantial strength and severe taste," to reflect the "grave and serious character" of the men who fought there, the events it would commemorate, and—no doubt—the distinguished gentlemen who would pay for it. It was the order of nature, Everett observed, that after one generation had achieved nobly, the subsequent generation would worthily record and commemorate. "We are not called to the fire and the sword," he was thankful, "to meet the appalling array of armies, to taste the bitter cup of imperial wrath and vengeance proffered to an ill-provided land." Instead, Providence had chosen his generation for an easier but no less solemn duty, of "honoring the labors, sacrifices and sufferings of the great men of those dark times." And dark those times had been. Prior to the war, a scanty population lived in poverty, while a "general languor" stalked the land. Now, homes, factories, and warehouses were rising in "unexampled numbers," and there was great prosperity. Daily since the war, he had observed in his fellow citizens an "improved, liberal, and more productive character." For Everett, who was convinced that Providence intended republican America to be the world's producing, civilizing, and moralizing exemplar, the Monument would do much more than commemorate: it would celebrate progress just as it would foster a moral, national character.[43]

Everett was confident that the members' monument would have the "happiest influence in exciting and nourishing the national and patriotic sentiment." Their monumental column of severe taste would build a special kind of national identity, for theirs was "a government of *opinion*," yet "one of *sentiment* still more." America's progressive new identity had not arisen merely from the judgment of its people, who had dictated a preference for its special institutions, but in particular from a "strong, deepseated inborn sentiment; a feeling, a passion for liberty." Readers of history throughout the world—he had explained at the circular's outset—by now well understood the

---

42. There were thirty directors by spring 1825 although there may have been somewhat fewer at the outset. Warren, *Monument Association*, pp. 9, 101–2, and passim. An acre of industrial land in Charlestown is worth about $1.5 million today, with prime residential building plots fetching considerably more. Charles R. Codman, one of the BHMA's founding members, handled the sale to John C. Warren.

43. From Everett's circular of 20 September 1824, as reproduced in ibid., pp. 109–16.

import of 17 April 1775. Gen. John Burgoyne, watching from Copp's Hill, had deemed it "'one of the greatest scenes of war that can be conceived.'" Yet despite burning Charlestown and enjoying overwhelming superiority in artillery, Burgoyne's redcoats had taken terrible casualties. America's "raw militia, badly armed, scantily provided with ammunition," had killed and wounded the "flower of the best troops in the world." After demonstrating their "coolness and intrepidity" under fire, Americans had returned that fire with "fatal precision." No event in history, Everett mused, could be more entitled to "celebration by the character of the exploits, its great national effects, its astonishing grandeur, and its affecting incidents" than the battle at Bunker's Hill.[44]

It is important to realize that the Monument was not a public project, conceived, designed, and funded by the city or state. Neither did BHMA members—at least in the early years—solicit mass collections or launch subscription drives in newspapers. Instead, Everett had his circular "handsomely printed," as historian G.W. Warren put it, and mailed to "every respectable house in Boston." This would be a personal endeavor by the members and their respectable local contributors; it would be their monument. As passages in the circular suggest, the members' primary intention was that the Monument would make a statement; it would send a message about the virtues of republican society from the "gentlemen of culture and high character" to those of inferior status at home, as well as to corrupt, immoral Europeans abroad. Built on high ground in Charlestown, which was adjacent to Boston and a convenient distance from the rival port of Salem, it would be continually visible to "the greatest masses of the community." It would remind the masses, "daily and hourly," of the boundless prosperity, harmony, and happiness that the War of Independence had brought them. Elevated on the heights of Charlestown, the members' monument would be the "first landmark of the mariner in his approach to our harbor." A visitor to its lofty summit would no doubt gaze in wonder at the "rich fields, villages, and spires, the buildings of [Harvard] University, the bridges, the numerous ornamental country seats and improved plantations," beyond which lay "a distant line of hills," forming a landscape unsurpassed in "variety and beauty," beckoning—Everett seemed to suggest—to the vast unsettled lands in the west. Their monument would be the "best proof we can exhibit to strangers that our sensibility is strong, and animated toward those great achievements and greater characters to which we owe all our national blessings." There could not be one among them, Everett prompted his potential contributors, who would not "experience a strong satisfaction in conducting a stranger to the foot of a monumental structure rising in decent majesty" on such a memorable spot. No other endeavor, Everett implied, could so inspire "America herself with the consciousness of her own power." Power—whether economic, cultural, intellectual, or military, all of which members and their immediate circle effectively monopolized—was not power unless others were conscious of it.[45]

---

44. Everett's circular, ibid., emphasis original.
45. Warren, *Monument Association*, p. 109, and Everett's circular, ibid., passim.

In 1823 when Everett, Warren, Tudor, Webster, and Perkins first discussed a monument, Everett was in residence at Harvard, where he felt constrained. Everett used the BHMA as a springboard for his political ambitions, which he fulfilled in 1824 with a move back to Boston and a successful election campaign for U.S. Congress. Disappointed over Harvard's loss, Ralph Waldo Emerson remarked bitterly that the "vulgar prizes of politics" had wooed him, and then wondered retrospectively if Everett had "neither intellectual nor moral principles to teach"; perhaps his scholarship all along had been merely "the pure triumph of Rhetoric." Many of the ideas behind themes Everett developed in later writings and orations—such as the development of technology, especially railroads—are apparent in his work for the BHMA and associated speechmaking in Charlestown, a place, he stressed on one occasion, that was "holy ground," because all its "hill-tops are the altars of precious sacrifice," scattered with the "sacred dust of the first victims in the cause of liberty."[46]

Underlying Everett's thinking was the premise that it was the "will of Providence, and for the interest of humanity, that America should be settled by a civilized race of men," to which he added an assumption that the "genius" of America's institutions—its unique government—was the "final design of Providence." Enamored as he was with ancient Greece and Rome, their republics had been short lived, prone to corruption and outside attack; at no time had the ancients been able to capitalize on a "populous and extensive region, blessed with institutions securing enjoyment and transmission of regulated liberty," as Americans now could. An expanding population with access to limitless land was central to Everett's calculus, yet had North America's colonists been continental Europeans, Providence's final design would have been unfulfilled. "One of the happiest features of the American character" was its "peculiarity" of population, for it was onto the "stock of English civilization" that time had "engrafted the languages, the arts, and the tastes of the other civilized nations." Had Americans been the "unmixed descendants of any one nation of Europe," then—even with perfect governance—they would have retained a "moral and intellectual dependency on that nation," and their experiment would have failed. One of the most "attractive and beautiful peculiarities" of Americans was that they had inherited from the English settlers all the "prominent qualities of the Anglo-Saxon," an "admixture of almost everything that is valuable" in the European states. This was why republicanism had failed in France, where the "former evil" of monarchical tyranny had existed in its most "inveterate form." So despite the "power of example" provided by the United States, the reaction was necessarily violent, with such "dreadful excesses" that the very name of liberty almost became odious. It remained for Americans alone to be "exemplars": they must never forget that because "the eyes of the world" were turned upon them, if they were to fail then they would "blast the hopes of the friends of liberty" throughout the world "to the end of time."[47]

---

46. Emerson and Forbes, eds., *Journals of Ralph Waldo Emerson*, pp. 256–57; address at the Charlestown Lyceum, 28 June 1830, in *Orations and Speeches on Various Occasions by Edward Everett* (Boston: American Stationers' Company, 1836), p. 229.

47. Address at the Charlestown Lyceum, 28 June 1830, Fourth of July Oration in Charlestown, 1828, in *Orations*

When Everett orated on the holy ground of Charlestown to mark public anniversaries, he tailored his message to have a broad—if never quite populist—appeal, but on other occasions he was less egalitarian. "It is of the utmost importance," he explained to elite audiences, "that the active walks of life be filled by an enlightened class of men," of the type, presumably, that comprised the BHMA. In Europe, where the "mechanic and manufacturing" populations were "grossly depraved," and the agricultural population was "incredibly stupid," it took gendarmes and mounted soldiers to enforce any semblance of order. Thankfully, a "general intelligence and morality" characterized both the mechanic and agricultural populations of New England. Nevertheless, to maintain the "security and order of the community"—for America's republican experiment to prevail—it was vital that an enlightened class of men "protect it" from the "evils" possessing the "laboring population" of Europe. Everett was clear, though, that the enlightened class should not maintain order by force, but rather through an "enlightened moral public sentiment," a sentiment of the kind that would "spread its wings over our dwellings, and plant a watchman at our doors," a sentiment that Everett no doubt hoped the Monument would foster.[48]

Most recipients of Everett's fundraising circular of September 1824, which he sent at the height of his election campaign, apparently favored his ideas for the enlightenment of public morals, for in addition to sending him to Congress they donated five, ten, occasionally twenty or more dollars to the Monument fund. Some, though, were lukewarm, and a few were downright disparaging. Maj. Caleb Stark, who at sixteen had fought with his father on the beach at Breed's Hill, was incensed that the federal government had honored all its international obligations and yet it had failed to pay promised compensation to its soldiers, who had made the revolution possible. And now, to compound the travesty, instead of giving the remaining 14,000 pauper-veterans bread, the BHMA was lavishing a fortune on "a stone." Stark was livid. It would "redound more to the honor of this rising, powerful nation to obliterate every vestige of the Revolution," he fumed, than to couple the "heroic deeds, privations, and sufferings" of the Revolution's true authors with such a "foul stain of ingratitude" as the proposed monument. If anything, Stark's figure of 14,000 was conservative. In 1818, the federal government had passed—belatedly, by thirty-five years—the Revolutionary War Pensions Act (the forerunner of all subsequent veterans' benefits provisions), which agreed to pay $240 ($19,200) a year to officers and $96 ($7,700) to enlisted men. Six months later, when 20,000 applications had arrived at the War Department, there was congressional backtracking, because claims of $175 million would overwhelm the original estimate of $155,000. By 1820, amid much political squabbling, Congress suspended all payments, pending a means test; when this revealed that some 20,000 veterans were destitute, payouts resumed, so that by 1823 about 12,000

and Speeches . . . by Edward Everett, pp. 203–4, 143, 151, 157–58, 161, 157.

48. "A Discourse on the Importance to Practical Men of Scientific Knowledge, and on the Encouragements to Its Pursuit," ibid., p. 250; this discourse was a compilation prepared in 1836 either by Everett or his editor, from speeches given at Boston's Mechanic Institute (November 1827), Middlesex County Lyceum, Concord (November 1829), and the Columbian Institute, Washington (January 1830).

veterans were receiving a stipend, low though it was. G.W. Warren, to his credit, did include Caleb Stark's letter in his history of the Monument, though it seems that Everett never sent Stark a reply.[49]

Design Competition

A year had passed since the BHMA's directors held their inaugural meeting, and there was only nine months to go before the battle's fiftieth anniversary, when they intended to lay a cornerstone. Everett's circular letter promised a classical column—the tallest in the world—of substantial strength, severe taste, and serious character, made of hewn Chelmsford granite. Beyond some sort of a consensus for the Monument's style and material, they still had nothing on paper, which suggests both a preoccupation with the empowering yet often futile business of holding meetings and a complacency toward the enormity of the task they were proposing. Before examining how the column became an obelisk, it is necessary to ask why a column, as well as why granite.

Only a few of the directors had visited Athens or Rome, but from early childhood, parents and educators had immersed them in the art and architecture of the ancient world. Heroic statuary, triumphal arches, and victory columns were more vivid in their imaginations than New England's mundane town centers. Of these three basic categories of monumental architecture, statuary would have been the least appealing. Breed's Hill as a location was a given; that was where Gen. Warren died, and founding member John C. Warren had already purchased part of the battle site. Yet most directors lived in Boston, and Bostonians were the primary subjects of their endeavor. Viewed from Beacon Hill—let alone down by Mill Dam, recently built by BHMA director Isaac P. Davis to power gristmills but which served as a turnpike and fashionable strolling ground—heroic statues, even at monumental scale, would have appeared like stick creatures, soon to be hidden behind Charlestown's rising three-floor houses. Triumphal arches, under which Roman centurions led their enslaved captives, hardly suggested republican ideals, and, as in the case of Napoleon's unfinished Arc de Triomphe, arches best suited flat ground and city boulevards. Whereas an arch, such as that of Constantine I in Rome, symbolized the tyranny of triumph, a column stood for the heroism of victory. At the same time, the bas-reliefs of a column like Trajan's, with which members were most familiar, told stories of good governance, inspirational priests, and industrious citizens. A column of some sort, therefore, was an obvious choice requiring little discussion.[50]

In addition to being visible from miles around, a column perched atop Breed's Hill would offer an inspiring view. Everett's circular pointed to an important feature that members wanted for their column: an internal staircase would allow a visitor to

---

49. Ibid., pp. 65–66; see John P. Resch, "Politics and Public Culture: The Revolutionary War Pension Act of 1818," *Journal of the Early Republic*, 8 (Summer 1988), pp. 139–58.

50. Construction of the Arc proceeded so slowly that in 1810 Napoleon ordered a wooden replica erected on the foundations. Davis completed his Mill Dam in 1821, seven years after receiving a charter; once filled, it became Boston's Back Bay district.

climb to the top and gaze out over the universities, churches, and improved plantations, on, to the beckoning hills stretching west. Taking a carriage all the way over to
Charlestown, though, and then puffing up the hundreds of stairs of a dark, smelly
shaft, would have held little appeal. It would be sufficient for members to imagine
what a visitor could see from the top, hence, their monument would not need a spa-
cious—and esthetically problematic—viewing gallery, when a few discrete peepholes
would suffice.

As for a building material, freestones (sandstones) were easy to shape but prone to
fractures from New England frosts, and the nearest freestone quarries were in Connecticut. Marbles, also easy to work, were ostentatious, and, other than a low-grade white
marble from a small quarry at West Stockbridge in the Berkshires, they required importation, either from states such as Maryland or as far as Italy, which made them expensive. Directors saw their monument as a Massachusetts affair, and, despite their
personal wealth, they could be remarkably tightfisted. Granites perfectly fitted their
"substantial strength and severe taste" requirement, and were available locally. Several
new civic buildings in Boston had granite façades, and directors appreciated the link
between the stone's rising popularity and its affordability, because they knew that convicts at the Massachusetts State Prison in Charlestown spent their days hewing (or facing) granite. Everett was interested in the work of a new BHMA member, Solomon
Willard, a sculptor who was carving Ionic capitals in freestone for the portico of St.
Paul's Church in downtown Boston, which had walls faced in granite. Willard had
earlier made plaster models of the Athenian Parthenon and Roman Pantheon for
Everett to use in his lectures.

In November 1824, the directors commissioned Willard to supply a design for a
column. Willard drew up the plans, and the directors judged them admirable. Then,
in the *Boston Commercial Gazette* of 27 January, they advertised a design competition
with a $100 prize, giving a preference for a 220-foot column of hewn granite but so-
liciting all suggestions offered by the "architectural skill and genius of the country."
Everett kept Willard's plans, postponed his compensation, and explained how the
BHMA had a duty to discharge its public trust through a general advertisement. Willard
was miffed. But whatever the directors liked to say about their own moral character,
they had met their match. In a brusque note to Warren, Willard mentioned that at
220 feet, the BHMA's column would not be the tallest in the world. He had just read
in a journal about La colonne Vendôme, a brash celebration of Napoleon's victory at
Austerlitz, modeled on Trajan's Column, which was 235 feet high, plus an 11-foot
statue of the emperor. Perhaps the journal published incorrect figures or Willard
could not yet cope with France's new metric system, for Vendôme's column was just
144 feet, or maybe it was Willard's idea of fun. Willard regretted he would not be in
a position to furnish any more assistance, offered the plans as a gift in lieu of a donation, and wished a "'God-speed'" to the BHMA.[51]

---

51. *Boston Commercial Gazette*, 27 January 1825, p. 1; Warren, *Monument Association*, p. 157, in Warren's words.

fig. 6: Robert Mills's original design for Baltimore's column

This was not the first time that the directors had learned of a rival column. As early as 1811, Maryland's General Assembly had authorized lotteries to raise funds for the erection of a monument in Baltimore, settling in 1815 on a simplified version of a design by Robert Mills, for a hollow 178-foot Doric column in white marble topped by a statue of Gen. Washington (fig. 6). It was essentially a replica of Trajan's Column, except it had an oversized rectangular plinth containing a museum, a clunky-looking viewing platform, and no bas-reliefs. Even though the Baltimore column was still rising in 1823—it would take until 1829 to complete—BHMA directors did not acknowledge this ambitious endeavor in their inaugural communiqués. In his circular of September 1824, though, Everett did mention that the BHMA must "improve upon the example" of Baltimore's citizens, presumably by building a significantly taller column, hence the height specified in the competition of 220 feet. Early nineteenth-century America was a provincial place, and news traveled slowly. Yet it seems odd that someone with Everett's connections had not heard about such a massive civic project as Baltimore's until nine years after construction commenced. A more likely explanation is that BHMA directors knew about the column but were intent nonetheless to claim the history of the revolutionary war exclusively for Massachusetts, and for themselves.[52]

To judge the fifty or so entries, the directors formed a talented Board of Artists, comprising Daniel Webster; George Ticknor; Gilbert Stuart, a painter most noted for his unfinished and slightly sad-eyed portrait of President Washington, which graces the dollar bill; Washington Allston, a poet and Romanticist landscape painter, the so-called American Titian; and Loammi Baldwin Jr., a Harvard-educated civil engineer who had used Chelmsford granite to construct the Middlesex Canal (1803) as well as for ongoing projects in the Charlestown Navy Yard and had just returned from an architectural tour of Europe. All the entrants submitted designs for columns of varying degrees of fanciness and classical detailing, with the exception of a couple of mausoleums, and three designs proposing an obelisk. On 20 March, Mills, the South Carolina architect who had designed Baltimore's rival column, submitted some drawings and two oil paintings, one of a column and the other of an obelisk. As his painting of the obelisk is not extant, the character of its "simple decorations," as he put it, is a matter for imagination. His covering letter described an entrance through a "rich bronze palisade," "oversailing platforms, enclosed by balustrades," "winged globes," a "great body of inscriptions," a "series of shields," a "great star" near the apex, the whole "surmounted by spears and wreathes" and topped with a gas-lit tripod that would serve as a beacon for shipping. An 1832 letter complaining about why he had never received the $100 prize enthused about a "grand gallery" one-third up the shaft. Like all Mills's proposed monuments, it seems his obelisk would have been both elaborate and extravagant. Mills, though a Freemason, was not a New Englander, which surely weighed against him. On 19 May, the final day of the competition, Boston architect G.W. Brimmer presented plans for a solid obelisk, necessitating external stairs to reach its viewing gallery, which sported all manner of statuary. Even if these fussy designs had passed the Board of Artists, the directors would no doubt have dismissed them as being insufficiently severe.[53]

Sufficiently severe to impress the judges, and ultimately the directors, was a scale model of an obelisk presented on 25 April by Horatio Greenough, a twenty-year-old Boston-born sculptor and graduating senior at Harvard (fig. 7). To the same proportions as the red granite obelisks at the Pharaonic temple of Karnak, Thebes (Luxor), it would be only a hundred feet tall, but would stand on a plinth twenty feet high, with provision for four statues, cannon, or other memorabilia on blocks at each corner. Despite its diminutive height, Greenough's idea for a plain granite obelisk—with the narrowest of slit windows and no embellishments of any kind—immediately struck a chord. Perhaps, too, a physical model helped the directors envisage the finished

---

52. Warren, *Monument Association*, p. 116.

53. Baldwin's father, a Revolutionary War hero who gave his name to New England's popular apple, was the principal engineer and primary contractor of the ten-year canal construction project. William W. Wheildon, *Memoir of Solomon Willard: Architect and Superintendent of the Bunker Hill Monument* (Boston: Bunker Hill Monument Association, 1865), p. 88; "globes," in H.M. Pierce Gallagher, *Robert Mills: Architect of the Washington Monument, 1781–1855* (New York: Columbia University Press, 1935), pp. 204–7; Brimmer, in Warren, *Monument Association*, p. 163.

product. Remarking that an artist never carried a pencil, Gilbert Stuart borrowed one from director Warren Dutton and wrote on the model, "Approved."[54]

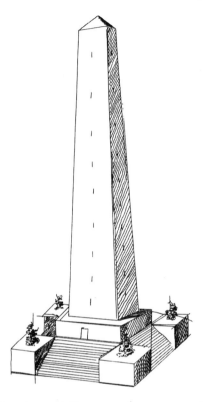

fig. 7: Horatio Greenough's
sketch of his model

It was not to be that simple, and Greenough never received the $100 prize money. A majority of the directors still favored a column, not least Warren, who hoped to see a statue of his uncle grace the entablature. There would be months of bickering, requiring two more Boards of Artists, before the directors settled on an obelisk to their original height of 220 feet, lofty enough to trump all other columns then in existence. Intent as they were to claim the Monument for themselves, the directors made sure to imprint it with their own character, not that of a novice sculptor, even if he was at Harvard. They "'substantially adopted'" Greenough's design, as the Building Committee's Amos Lawrence put it, but they left it to the "'talents, taste and influence'" of Loammi Baldwin, the BHMA's pedigreed civil engineer, to make it their own. As for the prize money, that was a hundred dollars that "the Association could ill afford to pay," according to G.W. Warren, even though they had members like Lawrence, whose father founded Groton Academy while he ran a dry goods empire and would soon bankroll a cotton mill in Lowell. Greenough, who left for Europe after graduating, did not resent the BHMA's mean-spirited dissembling, perhaps because it was satisfaction enough to know that his model had helped to steer the Board of Artists away from a gaudy triumphal column.[55]

54. Warren, *Monument Association*, p. 162, and Greenough's covering letter to the BHMA, pp. 159–60. In 1825, there were two obelisks at the entrance to Karnak, one of 82 feet, the other of 75 feet, gifted by Mehemet Ali to France in 1831, and erected at the Place de la Concorde.

55. Samuel Swett, *Original Planning and Construction of Bunker Hill Monument* (pamphlet, Albany, NY: J. Munsell,

Contemporary historians struggled to decide who deserved credit for the design, while acrimony among contestants over the un-awarded prize money fueled the debate. Leading the pack was Mills, who in 1836 would win the design competition for the Washington Monument, a 555-foot replica of the BHMA's obelisk. Washington's city planners wisely omitted the flamboyant 120-foot-tall colonnade with thirty heroic statues that Mills specified, did not begin construction until 1848, and could not complete it until 1885, thirty years after Mills's death. BHMA directors tried to argue at the time, and Willard's sympathetic biographer and friend William W. Wheildon reiterated in 1865, that there was nothing original in the design of an Egyptian obelisk. Wheildon even suggested that if anyone could claim the design then it ought to be Willard, because he drew the plans. Credit for the concept, which should surely be the criterion to adjudicate origination of design, nevertheless belongs to Horatio Greenough. Still, it is remarkable that the directors abandoned the column, for they had no availing precedent to link the commemoration of a battle, let alone the celebration of republican values, to an obelisk. Mills himself had proposed in an 1820 *Analectic Magazine* article that obelisks were symbolic of death. And from their classical studies—in several cases from their visits to Rome—BHMA members would have been familiar with the obelisk in St. Peter's Square. Raised in 1586 during the papacy of Sixtus V, this was the second tallest surviving Pharaonic obelisk at 84 feet, topped with a cross, and it mourned the martyrdom of St. Peter.[56]

Since the publication in 1809 of the first volumes of *Description de l'Égypte* by the French savants who accompanied Napoleon on his ill-fated expedition to the Nile, there had been renewed interest in Egyptology. By 1824–25, though, so-called Egyptomania was still primarily a phenomenon among European aristocrats, as when in 1821 Sir John Banks graced his country estate at Wimborne, Dorset, with the 10-foot Philae Obelisk of Ptolemy IX. Members like Everett who taught classics at Harvard, as well as Baldwin who had just returned from France when he joined the Board of Artists, would no doubt have seen *Description*. Yet rather than Egyptomania driving the BHMA's decision to erect an obelisk, it seems that the reverse prevailed, with the BHMA's Monument and promotional activities inspiring the American Egyptomania that followed. When a dying Thomas Jefferson sketched an obelisk for his own grave marker in March 1826, he had just received a letter from Mills who, after taking credit for designing the Bunker Hill Monument, recommended that Jefferson choose an obelisk for his grave. "Your idea is a very fine one," Jefferson replied to Mills. In the following years, obelisks became popular tombstones throughout America.[57]

1863), p. 6.

56. Wheildon, *Solomon Willard*, pp. 90–92, 84; Robert Mills, "Essay on Architectural Monuments," *Analectic Magazine*, 1 (1820), p. 288.

57. From Andrew Burstein, *Jefferson's Secrets: Death and Desire at Monticello* (New York: Basic Books, 2005), p. 11. Robert Mills was one of the first architects in America to use the obelisk form for monuments; he followed his grave-marker-sized North Point Monument in Baltimore (1817), with the slightly bigger DeKalb and Maxcy Monuments, in Columbia and Camden, SC, respectively (both 1827).

A further repudiation of Mills's theory that obelisks symbolized death—and a clue to the members' embrace of the obelisk—lay in a letter Greenough included with his submission. He apologized for disregarding the BHMA's preference, but columns, he felt, lacked coherence; they were awkward assemblies of "*useless* appendages and *unmeaning* parts," whereas an obelisk was "purely *monumental.*" Once the members had started to think of an obelisk as purely monumental, and with Greenough's unembellished model on the table before them, they could begin to appreciate that a plain obelisk would be symbolic of whatever meaning they attached to it, whether through its location on the battlefield or by rhetorical association with the myths they were creating.[58]

fig. 8: *Description de l'Égypte*, frontispiece, 1809 edition

Egyptian obelisks were inherently mysterious, covered as they were with unintelligible hieroglyphs. Neither did they necessarily embody any fixity of purpose or message. Sixtus's obelisk, like theirs, was oddly devoid of hieroglyphics, while supporting its cross were the arms of the Chigi-Albani family, fabulously rich Renaissance bankers, statesmen, and patrons of the arts. Amid the sidewalk cafes, food stalls, and

---

58. Warren, *Monument Association*, pp. 159–60, emphasis original.

chapmen of Rome's Piazza della Rotunda, a fountain played on a 21-foot obelisk from the Temple of Ra in Heliopolis, albeit with a star and cross on the top. For the centerpiece of their sumptuous Boboli Gardens, in 1790 the Medici family had erected a 16-foot obelisk as an ornament. Egyptian obelisks conveyed a romantic idealism. Those who had seen the second (1821) edition of *Description de l'Égypte* no doubt marveled at its hand-colored frontispiece, featuring exotic artifacts, a nubile goddess, and painted pylons set against fanciful scenery, while a magnificent obelisk thrust skyward in the upper center of the engraving. No image of death, this was rather a vision of fecundity.[59]

fig. 9: Piazza San Giovanni, Rome, by Giuseppe Vasi, 1752

Egyptian obelisks were certainly urban; might they be republican too? During their course work, it is possible the four members who were in Harvard's classes of 1809–12 looked through *Description*'s first edition, which had a similar—though uncolored—frontispiece to the 1821 edition (fig. 8), but it is far more likely that they derived their sense of what an obelisk symbolized from one or more of the many eighteenth-century engravings of obelisks in classical textbooks, such as Giuseppe Vasi's view of the Piazza San Giovanni (fig. 9). These engravings showed obelisks in urban settings, with imposing civic buildings as a backdrop. In Vasi's engraving, peasants (with a cart at the far right), priests, and regular townsfolk were tiny, almost insignificant figures. Bathed in sunlight as it pointed heavenward through a break in the

59. Frontispiece from *Description de L'Égypte, ou recueil des observations et des recherché qui ont été faites en Égypte pendant l'expedition de l'armée Française* (Paris: De L'Imprimerie Impériale, 1809). There were two separate editions of the multivolume series of *Description*—twenty-three and thirty-seven books respectively—published from 1809 to 1830.

glooming cloud, the obelisk commanded the public space. Local gentry in their opulent carriages took center stage, while a second obelisk awaiting erection lay in the immediate foreground. Vasi depicted the tiny figures looking at or walking towards the obelisk, as if it was bringing them together as a common polity, while the gentry, a safe distance away with their carriages, could almost have been orchestrating the scene. Following this interpretation, the second obelisk acted as the gentry's reserve, a sort of threat card, which they could erect if the symbolic power of the first obelisk proved insufficient to both unite and control the masses.[60]

An obelisk, BHMA members were beginning to realize, particularly if it was of a grave and serious character, would be the perfect vehicle for their own designs. Of all the classical forms of monumental architecture—cenotaph, mausoleum, tower, arch, column, statuary—a plain obelisk was the only one devoid of representation; it was a clean slate primed for the BHMA's founding myths.

With just ten days to go before the cornerstone laying ceremony, sixteen directors gathered at one of their favorite downtown restaurants, probably the Park House or Exchange Coffee House, to vote on the final design. They made a point at their regular meetings of wining and dining at their own expense, and, according to G.W. Warren, they were relatively frugal. "The highest one paid was $1.84. Happy days those of olden time!" Still, $1.84 was more than a mechanic's daily wage and four times that of an apprentice's. Planning committee chairman Henry A.S. Dearborn presented a report detailing both an obelisk and a column. Having examined engravings of Egyptian obelisks, his committee had concluded suggestively that they were "naked, and rude," only becoming "interesting and imposing from an association of their great antiquity, and the imagined legends of their unintelligible hieroglyphics." Ancient columns, by contrast, were "monumental, honorary, historical, and triumphal." "Learned travelers, of every age and country," had been lavish in their praise of Trajan's, "the most perfect in form and magnificent in execution" of any column. After braving the ravages of time and barbarian incursions for nearly seventeen centuries, it "still proudly stands, the admiration of the world." Because the committee was "unwilling to run the risk of compromising the character of the Association" on such a "solecism in architectural taste" as an obelisk, it recommended a vote for a 220-foot version of Trajan's Column. Dearborn held a strong personal bias for an elaborate victory column, perhaps because such a memorial would better requite the honor his father had lost by impugning Gen. Israel Putnam's courage in 1818. Yet much as he wanted to, Dearborn found he could not coerce his fellow directors. A change of heart by Warren, who had long dreamed of a statue of his heroic uncle astride the pediment of a Roman column, must have influenced those still undecided; G.W. Warren thought Warren's vote for an obelisk was a "noble relinquishment" of family honor that demonstrated an "unselfish desire" for a "purely national" monument. Another factor was the absence of Everett and Perkins, both advocates of a column. Over Dearborn's

---

60. There are twelve Pharaonic obelisks in Rome, ranging in height from 32.18 meters to 2.68 meters.

insistent pleas for a triumphal column, a clear majority of eleven to five directors voted for an obelisk, naked and rude, but nonetheless interesting through association with antiquity, and capable, moreover, of bearing their imagined legends.[61]

Laying the Cornerstone

Even as successive Boards of Artists were arguing over the Monument's final form, many more members, spread across several committees—Welcome, Escort, Meeting-House, Cornerstone, Dinner, Executive—were organizing the grandest of ceremonies to lay its cornerstone. They booked America's newly inaugurated president John Quincy Adams, Webster as orator, and the Marquis de Lafayette, hero of both the American and French Revolutions, as guest of honor. They orchestrated every detail of the daylong extravaganza to mark the fiftieth anniversary of what everyone by then called the Battle of Bunker Hill, right down to commissioning hymns, odes, and songs to accompany the various services and dinners. As many as a hundred thousand people—some newspapers estimated 150,000 and Lafayette thought 200,000—half of whom had traveled from other towns and states, flooded the BHMA's Bunker Hill celebration on Friday, 17 June 1825, making it the largest gathering to date in North America.[62]

Freemasons from all over New England began the festivities by gathering before 7:30 AM at different locations—Concert Hall, Faneuil Hall—for there were more of them than would fit inside one building. Facing mounting hostility from religious leaders and anti-Masonic politicians, Masons were trying to claim the day, and hence their rights to the battle, its founding myths, and their own legitimacy. Their claim was strong: martyred hero Joseph Warren was the first Provincial Grand Master of America's first accredited Scottish-rite Grand Lodge; Charlestown's Masons had erected the Tuscan pillar to honor Warren in 1794; Lafayette was one of Europe's most famous Masons; and many of the BHMA's members were themselves Masons. But along with veterans, another group vying for battle rights, they were only bit players in the BHMA's dramatic production.[63]

Long before 10:00 AM, the BHMA's parade organizer, thirty-three-year-old Theodore Lyman Jr.—of Exeter Academy, Harvard College, and his father's mercantile business, a state representative (later governor) and brigadier general of the state militia—began forming up the procession with military precision outside the State House. Lyman could not have wished for a better day. "Not a cloud obscured the smallest portion of the firmament," reported the *Boston Courier*. Showers the previous day had "brightened the emerald hue of the earth," and now it was as if the "whole face of

61. Warren, *Monument Association*, pp. 57, 164–68.

62. For instance, the *Farmers' Cabinet* (Amherst, NH), 18 June 1825, p 3, estimated 100,000, and the *Boston Commercial Gazette*, 20 June 1825, p. 2, thought it "no exaggeration" to estimate 150,000. Note: newspapers of the day traded stories and copied from each other profusely, frequently without acknowledgement or bylines, so provenance is often inexact. *Mémoires, correspondance et manuscrits de Général Lafayette, publiés par sa famille* (Brussels: Société Belge de Librairie, 1839), p. 389.

63. This was just a year before the disappearance of William Morgan, a disgruntled Mason who had begun publishing the secret activities of his local lodge in Batavia, NY; New Yorkers formed the Anti-Masonic Party in 1827.

nature wore its loveliest aspect; the flooring was spread with her richest variegated carpet; the canopy was all azure and sunshine." At the head, Lyman stationed twenty companies of militia, followed by forty aged veterans of the battle riding in eight open carriages, and over a hundred veterans of the war on foot behind. Then came BHMA members, also in carriages, followed by five thousand bejeweled Masons resplendent in their regalia of white aprons and blue scarves; there were bright Masonic banners, a Masonic band, and an urn containing a relic of George Washington who was another famous Mason. Lafayette in a coach-and-four (one account mentioned six white horses) was next, and then, on foot, the civic and military dignitaries—the governor, senators, and congressman of Massachusetts, Secretary of War James Barbour (but not President Adams who was stuck in Washington), politicians from other states, U.S. Army and Navy officers—with everyone else tailing along behind. As the vast column moved off, a little late around 10:30, distant guns boomed, the bells of Boston's churches peeled out, and the women and children lining the streets or jostling for a view from windows and balconies—for this was a masculine parade—waved their handkerchiefs. Every face, said the *Courier*, whether of the "feeble veteran of the silver lock, the manly soldier decorated with plume and sword, the inquisitive and admiring child, or the woman, the still more interesting product of heavenly skill and goodness," every face inspired the others, every face "beamed with gratulation, and reflected back the smile of the Creator." So vast was the procession that by the time the honor guard passed over the Charles River Bridge, at which toll collectors had waived their fee, the rear had not left the Common, a mile-and-a-half behind.[64]

Special contingents of police, recruited by the BHMA, lined the route to keep order. As the band approached Breed's Hill, it struck up "Yankee Doodle," a tad discordantly, perhaps, as all the bells in the town were ringing. Other parties, too, were converging on the battle site, such as those at a service at the Congregational meetinghouse in Charlestown of Jedidiah Morse, father of Samuel F.B. Morse. Those that could find a vantage point clustered round the site laid out for the Monument to watch John Abbott, Most Worshipful Grand Master of the Grand Lodge of Massachusetts, place and adjust the cornerstone. Unsure whether the stone they had purchased would ever form part of the obelisk, the directors had provided a silver informational plaque complete with a Masonic inscription, and a box containing a printed book of subscribers, various public addresses, and a history of the battle, both plaque and box to be set under the stone. Abbott then handed his ceremonial silver trowel to Lafayette, who did not make a speech but earlier that morning had declared, perhaps apocryphally, "In all my travels through the country, I have made Bunker Hill my pole star." After Lafayette had spread mortar on the stone, and Abbott had sprinkled corn, wine, and oil over it, the throng moved off to a still undeveloped part of the hill. There they found a stage with a canopy topped by a golden eagle, seating with awnings for a thousand ladies, and then, rising up the hill, rows of benches for veterans, dignitaries, and the other

---

64. *Boston Courier*, reproduced in the *Eastern Argus* (Portland, ME), 28 June 1825, p. 1; *Boston Centinel*, reproduced in the *Boston Commercial Gazette*, 20 June 1825, p. 2.

parade marchers. Accounts estimated the seated audience at 15–20,000, with another thirty thousand or so clambering for a place on the hillside behind them.[65]

fig. 10: Daniel Webster

Eighty-three-year-old Rev. Joseph Thaxter, the Unitarian chaplain of Prescott's regiment who had tucked a brace of pistols in his belt and called for God's aid in the battle fifty years earlier, gave a barely audible though moving benediction. To that most ponderous yet well known of Christian melodies, "Old Hundredth,"[66] the band played while the crowd sang one of the specially commissioned hymns: "O is not this a holy spot! / 'Tis the high place of Freedom's Birth; / God of our Fathers! Is it not / The holiest spot of all the earth?" Daniel Webster—with the presence of a preacher at what might have been a southern Baptist camp meeting—rose to speak. Presuming that they would not be able to hear, thousands of people pushed forward, and a tier of seating collapsed. There was pandemonium as the marshals barked instructions, and the apologetic BHMA organizers turned to Webster to say, "'It is impossible to restore order.'" "Nothing is impossible," Webster snapped back. "*Be silent yourselves*," he bellowed to the marshals, "*and the people WILL obey!*" To whatever extent this story was accurate, it became integral to the Bunker Hill Oration myth, and essential to even recent scholarly accounts. Another part of the myth described Webster's preparations

65. *Courier* and *Centinel* as above, and Warren, *Monument Association*, pp. 142, 135, 146–49.
66. Usual accompaniment to Psalm 100, "All people that on earth do dwell."

for the speech. According to his twelve-year-old son, Fletcher, who first told the story (repeated over the years at Webster's encouragement) they had gone trout fishing to Cape Cod. Fletcher watched his father wading around the stream, gesturing to a tree here, a rock there, and roaring out his lines, using the reflections from the water and riverbank to gauge the timbre, the tone, the rhythm. Now, in amazement that a human voice could possibly be so loud, the crowd fell silent.[67]

"This uncounted multitude before me," he began, "proves the feeling which this occasion has excited." They were among the sepulchers of their fathers, he assured them, on ground hallowed by the blood, the valor, the constancy of those who fell. There could be no greater event, no greater prodigy of modern times, than the American Revolution. To the wonder and blessing of the world, 17 June 1775 had poured its light on all subsequent history. Because of that day of guiding destiny, they were Americans; they could look forward to a probable train of great events, to fortunes happily cast.[68]

Reprinted into dozens of editions by fifteen major publishing houses, Webster's *First Bunker Hill Oration* became required reading for the College Entrance Examination, alongside Washington's "Farewell Address," for generations of American schoolchildren, at least until 1911. According to instructor of rhetoric A.J. George in his preface to one edition, the oration demonstrated "the quality of imagination, the depth of passion, the breadth of sympathy, the steady and strong undercurrent of the religious feeling" that were the essential elements of Webster's art. His genius, George wrote, was to combine the national spirit with the classical form, to merge prophecy with history, to reveal what has been and to give glimpses of heights yet to come. George was certain that God's plan reached Americans through great orators like Webster.[69]

Perhaps Webster's true genius was to tell those newly patriotic, increasingly confident, and yet nationally anxious Americans what they needed to hear, in a setting and with a voice that was as memorable as it was authoritative. His genius was to take the myths of heroic battle, of boundless progress, of republican liberty, of an exceptional civilization, and of a Providential destiny and stitch them into a respectable, dignified—and hence believable—suit of national cloth. Veterans, Masons, Lafayette, the dignitaries, all those people gathered so expectantly, and of course the Monument itself (or at least its cornerstone) served to give substance, served to add meaning to Webster's otherwise empty rhetoric; those physical elements, set against the proof of so many tall ships crowding Boston's waterfront, made his genius possible.

67. Brand Whitlock, *La Fayette* (New York: D. Appleton and Company, 1929), pp. 273–74; Claude Moore Fuess, *Daniel Webster* (Boston: Little, Brown, and Company, 1930), vol. 1, pp. 298–99; "*Be silent,*" from Josiah Quincy, *Figures of the Past: From the Leaves of Old Journals* (Boston: Roberts Brothers, 1883), p. 137, emphasis original. And see, for instance, Irving H. Bartlett, "Daniel Webster as a Symbolic Hero," *New England Quarterly*, 45:4 (December 1972), pp. 498–99.

68. *Two Orations by Daniel Webster*, pp. 10–11; Webster's infatuation with the passive voice, through which he rendered doers transparent, necessitates heavy paraphrasing, as here.

69. A.J. George, ed., *Webster's First Bunker Hill Oration* (Boston: D.C. Heath & Co., 1894), pp. x–xii.

First, he addressed the veterans, the veterans whose day it really was but to whom the BHMA had allowed no voice. "*Venerable men!* You who have come down to us from a former generation." How different it was now, how changed. "You hear now no roar of hostile cannon, you see no mixed volumes of smoke and flame rising from burning Charlestown." No dead and dying strewed the ground. All was now peace. "Yonder proud ships" were now America's means of distinction and of defense. "God has granted you this sight of your country's happiness," he told them, just as God had allowed the present generation, "in the name of your country, in the name of liberty, to thank you!" "But, alas! You are not all here!" Where were "Prescott, Putnam, Stark, Brooks"? (*Brooks* some of the veterans must have wondered?—where was he on 17 June 1775?) "Our eyes seek for you in vain amid this broken band." And what of Warren, "immortal Warren"? He lived on, through the Monument, and on through memory, as perhaps they all might. "Our poor work may perish; but thine shall endure! This monument may molder away; the solid ground it rests upon may sink down to a level with the sea; but thy memory shall not fail!" He gestured at a similarly voiceless Lafayette, their hero who connected both hemispheres, both generations, and both revolutions. "Heaven saw fit to ordain that the electric spark of liberty should be conducted through you, from the New World to the Old." To hear Webster weave the founding myth, Lafayette—and the French, who supplied virtually all the gunpowder, half the cash, and the fleet that finally forced Gen. Charles Cornwallis's surrender at Yorktown—did not so much contribute to the American War of Independence as take from it. "You see the lines of the little redoubt thrown up by the incredible diligence of Prescott; defended, to the last extremity, by his lion-hearted valor. . . . You see where Warren fell." Here now were those who survived that day. "Behold! They now stretch forth their feeble arms to embrace you." Many of the veterans, of whom several were not yet seventy, were still no doubt lion-hearted, yet Webster was turning them into pathetic rag dolls, sad extras in his patriotic play (later accounts would reduce them to "living relics" or mention white hair).[70]

Next, he noted the boundless progress in the fifty years since the battle, especially in knowledge, in intelligence. Nations were making separate advances, as they always had, yet this new age was distinctive, for there was a community of opinion in the "civilized and Christian world," a realization that national difference no longer meant war. "Every breeze wafts intelligence from country to country," creating a vast commerce of ideas. "A superior tone of education, manners, and habits prevails." Of course, this superior moral tone was most true in America, and "only partly true when applied elsewhere." Americans had witnessed a vast and concomitant increase in consumption, manufacture, and commerce; incredible new machines seemed to threaten labor, and yet "Providence adjusted men's wants and desires to their condition and

---

70. Quotations here, and for following paragraphs, from *Two Orations by Daniel Webster*, passim. Col. Clark, of Lebanon, CT, was ninety-five, but accompanying him was his son of about sixty-five, who as "quite a boy" in his early teens had been the company's fifer, *Middlesex Gazette*, 8 June 1825, p. 3. "Relics," in Bartlett, "Daniel Webster," p. 499.

their capacity." In America, Webster implied, Providence would ensure that industrialization would be a republican good, not a social evil.[71]

Above all, the question of politics and government had been "the master topic of the age." Now that the smoke of battle had cleared, it was evident that a permanent change had occurred in the state of society, a change that was highly favorable "to human liberty and human happiness." In America, that great wheel of political revolution had first begun to move. "Here its rotation was guarded, regular, and safe." Sadly, when transplanted to the Old World, "it received an irregular and violent impulse; it whirled along with a fearful celerity;" at length, like the wheels of Roman chariot races, "it took fire from the rapidity of its own motion, and blazed onward, spreading conflagration and terror around." From the failure of the republican experiment in Lafayette's France, Americans could learn "how admirably the character of our people was calculated [God was the calculator] for setting the great example of popular governments." Long accustomed to representative bodies, Americans understood the doctrine of dividing power among different branches, with checks on each. Above all, Americans enjoyed a special character, for they were "sober, moral, and religious." No American revolutionary had ever wished for plunder or spoil. Indeed, if Americans had possessed any "tendency adverse to the Christian religion" then their republican revolution would have been impossible. It should be no wonder to them that republican revolutions had failed elsewhere. It was "the masterwork of the world," Webster explained, "to establish governments entirely popular on lasting foundations," just as they had done, and they should thank God that their influence might yet prevail in the struggle for independence by civilized Greeks, who currently lay "at the foot of the barbarian Turk." To ensure everyone grasped his central point, which was, by implication, that the BHMA's new monument symbolized the perfect republican city on a hill, Webster presented another example.

Before Americans fought the Battle of Bunker Hill, the civilized world barely noticed South America. "Borne down by colonial subjugation, monopoly, and bigotry, these vast regions of the South were hardly visible above the horizon." Since the battle—since the American example of republican governance—the southern hemisphere was emerging from the sea. "Its lofty mountains begin to lift themselves into the light of heaven; its broad and fertile plains stretch out, in beauty." To the eye of civilized Americans, it was clear that "at the mighty bidding of the voice of political liberty the waters of darkness retire." Webster prompted the assembled company to indulge in an "honest exultation" of the benefits that their republican example was bestowing, and must continue to bestow, on human freedom and happiness. He adjured them to comprehend the importance of the part assigned to them—God being the assignor—in the great drama of human affairs, a drama, no doubt, that they felt so palpably at

71. I am thinking here of John F. Kasson's argument in *Civilizing the Machine: Technology and Republican Values in America, 1776–1900* (New York: Hill and Wang, 1999) that Americans like Everett, Ralph Waldo Emerson, or Francis Cabot Lowell embraced technology because they thought it would perpetuate Jeffersonian producerist republicanism, and combat rather than cause the social decay of industrialization.

that very moment. "We are placed [God had placed them] at the head of the system of representative and popular governments." Their own example taught them that such a government was compatible "not only with respectability and power, but with repose, with peace, with security of personal rights, with good laws, and a just administration." Webster had turned a simple cornerstone laying into an unforgettable civics lesson.

Despite all his example-setting talk, part of the myth he was spinning was that Americans "were not propagandists." He entrusted them, nevertheless, with a sublime responsibility, for should representative government fail in America, it must be doomed everywhere, forever. There could never again be a set of circumstances more favorable to republicanism than in America; the failure of their experiment would sound the death knell of popular liberty throughout the earth. "The last hopes of mankind, therefore, rest with us." Neither could they sit on their laurels, for their proper business was progress. "Let our age be the age of improvement." They must advance both the arts and the works of peace. "Let us develop the resources of our land, call forth its powers, build up its institutions, promote all its great interests." Like the heroes of Bunker Hill, they too must achieve something worthy of remembrance. As Webster built to a close, it must by now have been obvious to the thousands gathered round the Monument's cornerstone that as they set about achieving everything Webster had mapped out for them, they would also be propagandizing their seductively empowering republican ideology. "Let us extend our ideas," he urged them, "over the whole of the vast field in which we are called to act." And yet, if they had stopped to piece together all he had said then they would have realized that the propaganda could only be self-serving. Not only did the peoples of other nations lack Americans' special moral character but outsiders did not also have the benefit of God's providential hand. Non-Americans' perpetual doom, therefore, was to be a sorry second best. Americans' unique disposition had made the experiment possible; because other nations would always fail to match America's example, those failures would prove to Americans that they were indeed exceptional. Like the immortal Warren, whose martyrdom gave America life, the immortal core of the founding myth, spun so brilliantly by Webster and perpetuated by the BHMA's directors through the Bunker Hill Monument, would be the circularity of its self-fulfilling prophecy.

For ninety or so minutes, the crowd was spellbound, following every sonorous word, every gesture, the rapture punctuated only by occasional clapping. Webster had been unusually emotional, with a crack in his delivery—a tear in his eye, some accounts said—when he addressed the veterans. Now, in the closing moments as he paraphrased medieval English jurisprudence, he was almost deafening: "Let our object be, *our country, our whole country, and nothing but our country.*" By the "blessing of God," he promised them, America would become "a vast and splendid monument, not of oppression and terror, but of Wisdom, of Peace and of Liberty, upon which the world may gaze with admiration for ever." Unsure if he had finished, and perhaps hoping for more, the crowd was silent, absorbing the last ringing phrases. Then wave after wave of applause began rolling around the hill. As it subsided minutes later, the band struck up another hymn, there was a concluding prayer, an ode, and a final benediction to end the sacred event.

Chatting, no doubt, about the oration, four thousand guests who paid $1.50 a ticket made their way to a marquee at the summit of Bunker Hill (the real Bunker Hill, above Breed's Hill), and found their places at twelve tables, each four hundred feet long. Behind the 38,400-square-foot tent were three kitchens, a crockery store, and a glass store. After the meal, there were thirteen rounds of toasts (to signify the thirteen original colonies), and thirteen musical performances, each scripted by the BHMA. Celebrations continued into the night, with two concurrent grand receptions, the first in Charlestown, at a mansion on a two-acre estate purchased in 1814 by Col. Samuel Jacques, who had made his fortune from Caribbean trade, and was now a stock breeder, hop exporter, and fox hunter. Webster hosted the second reception, at his home on Summer Street in Boston, where carpenters had doubled the accommodations by knocking through the wall to the house of his neighbor, Col. Israel Thorndike. Webster would later give his Bunker Hill Oration to the BHMA, which sold the copyright for $600 ($48,000). And once the last onlookers had drifted away from Breed's Hill, the BHMA's workmen lifted and preserved the cornerstone, the silver plaque, and the box of documents. It would be two years before the Monument began to rise. "Let it rise!" Webster had told the crowd that afternoon, his unusually large bald forehead glinting like a miniature version of the obelisk to come. "Let it rise till it meet the sun in his coming; let the earliest light of the morning gild it, and parting day linger and play on its summit." Perhaps only Solomon Willard understood then the enormity of the task ahead. It would take eighteen years of Yankee ingenuity and industriousness, backed by several rounds of orations and fundraising, before the sun glinted off the Monument's polished granite capstone, completing the link between the founding myth and the shining city.[72]

---

72. *Farmers' Cabinet* (Amherst, NH), 23:40 (18 June 1825), p. 3; Warren, *Monument Association*, p. 151; Thorndike, in Quincy, *Figures*, p. 138.

2. SOLOMON WILLARD: YANKEE MYSTIQUE

A coterie of the most influential and powerful Bostonians—educators, orators, merchants, investors, lawyers, legislators, militia commanders—had formed an association, raised funds, settled on a design, and held a remarkable cornerstone-laying ceremony for a monument to commemorate the opening battle in America's War of Independence from Britain. Yeoman farmers, craft workers, apprentices, sailors, and itinerant laborers had done the bulk of the fighting and dying in that battle. Over three dozen Blacks fought at Breed's Hill, including Salem Poor, who received a citation for valor from his commanding officers and may have killed redcoat Col. James Abercrombie; only six years earlier in 1769, Poor had bought himself out of slavery in Andover, Massachusetts.[1] Thousands of women, the leading players in the boycott of British goods during the 1760s–70s, had stitched the uniforms, dressed the wounds, and grieved over the bodies of dead rebel soldiers. Half of those in the battle line had marched from outlying colonies; many were born abroad, in the Caribbean, Ireland, or continental Europe, such as Bernard Romans, a Dutch surveyor and botanist, who produced a fanciful engraving, *An Exact View of the Late Battle at Charlestown, June 17th, 1775*. And yet, the Bunker Hill Monument Association (BHMA)'s paternalistic directors, who originated the Monument and orchestrated every detail of its inaugural jubilee, rendered all these actors voiceless, if not necessarily invisible. Several hundred women occupied reserved seating at the inauguration, but they were mostly elites who arrived separately by carriage. Forty veterans sat in the front rows, by invitation of the directors who had paid them a bonus plus traveling expenses. Thousands journeyed from other states, although few attended the grand dinner because tickets were only available in advance at downtown Boston bookstores. But once the party hangovers had faded, BHMA directors awoke to the reality of erecting a 220-foot granite obelisk, which forced them to relinquish some of their exclusive power over the Monument.

Because of the restless intellects, principled values, and disciplined work habits of those who quarried its stone and stacked its blocks, the ideology that the Monument embodied—and hence the kind of national identity it had the power to create through symbolism and myth—began to change. Here, too, the historical record of Solomon Willard, the farmhand turned architect who for eighteen years patiently supervised the Monument's construction, is the stuff of legend, primarily because Willard both felt comfortable with and cultivated a stereotypical form of Yankee identity, or *Yankee mystique*, which implies both a set of real attributes and an aura of ostensible aspirations or goals. Whether one's viewpoint is that of a native New Englander or an outside observer, there has always been the reality of those who live like a good Yankee and the perception of *Yankeeness*; the reality and the perception invariably overlap but

---

1. George Quintal Jr., *Patriots of Color, "A Peculiar Beauty and Merit": African Americans and Native Americans at Battle Road and Bunker Hill* (Boston: Boston National Historical Park, 2004), documents thirty-four Blacks and Indians in combat (tallies, p. 260), and names a further sixty-eight who had enlisted in companies that mustered in the vicinity, a proportion of which it is fair to assume would have engaged in combat; for a discussion of Poor, see Quintal, p. 70.

rarely coincide. Attributes of Yankeeness, with their Puritan underpinnings, fall into three broad categories: First, a physical bearing or presence that is upright, dignified, unpretentious, reserved, and purposeful. Second, an approach to work, leisure, and social interaction that should be self-disciplined, honest, sober, frugal, industrious, stubbornly independent, and restlessly creative or inventive. Third, an introspective philosophy—more Unitarian or even Deist than Congregationalist—that respects God's bounty, takes what God has given but then strives to improve those gifts, and presumes that the path to acceptance into God's eternal kingdom is inwardly moral, not outwardly material. Innovation, whether with things or ideas, has always been a Yankee trait, a necessarily amateurish yet often effective "tinkering," to use historian Robert Bruce Mullin's term. Willard's career represents one of U.S. history's most pronounced concurrences between the lived reality and the perception of Yankeeness, whereas the BHMA's directors exhibited—and struggled to overcome—a profound disjunction between the two states, which is why they needed Willard, and why Willard was able to leave his stamp on the Monument.[2]

Willard's Election to Architect and Superintendent

Solomon Willard was born 26 June 1783 at Petersham, in central Massachusetts, to Katherine and William Willard. Katherine Wilder was from Lancaster, thirty odd miles nearer to Boston, and William was from Biddeford, near Old Orchard Beach in the District of Maine, ninety miles north of Boston. Solomon had ten siblings, all but one of whom were older, and of which two died in infancy. Histories recall nothing of the women in the family, and little of the men. Solomon had a great-grandfather who was a trader and probably a smuggler in Jamaica; a brother who was a preacher sent blind, supposedly, by alcoholism; and, more auspiciously perhaps, an uncle, Rev. Joseph, who was Harvard College's twelfth president. William's father—also a minister—died when he was a youngster and Joseph was two, leaving the family destitute, which explains the Willard propensity for hard work and self-advancement. To support the family, William apprenticed as a carpenter, and Joseph went to sea, where he learned navigation; Joseph's ability in math attracted the notice of a local schoolmaster who helped him win a scholarship to Harvard. After William arrived in Petersham in the early 1760s, when the population was seven hundred, he became the town carpenter and served as deacon to the minister. Katherine would have run up credit at the general store, which William paid off with produce that he bartered for carpentry work. For 1781–84, by which time Petersham's population had doubled, William's peers elected him to the position of town clerk, notably so because prior to the War of Independence the Willards were Tories. Solomon Willard worked mostly as a farmhand, helped his father in the shop, went to school in the slack winter months, and pored over whatever books he could find, including Euclid's geometry. A weekly high

2. Robert Bruce Mullin, *The Puritan as Yankee: A Life of Horace Bushnell* (Grand Rapids, MI: William B. Eerdmans Publishing Company, 2002), pp. 4, 16–17, 258; also see Chard Powers Smith, *Yankees and God* (New York: Hermitage House, 1954), esp. pp. 292–93, 419–21.

point would have been the arrival of the post-rider, who brought a local newspaper like the *Barre Gazette* or *Worcester Intelligencer* and maybe a letter, as well as all the gossip he had gleaned since leaving town. In October 1804, a few months after turning twenty-one, Willard left home for Boston. It was an exciting time of transition. New England's yeoman farmers were switching from cereals to beef production, cash was replacing barn-raisings and barter, canals were reducing the exorbitant costs of inland transportation, and merchant capital in cities like Boston would soon be financing industrialization.[3]

There would have been plenty of work for an unskilled though aspiring carpenter, for Boston's maritime commerce and related industries were booming, at least until President Thomas Jefferson's ill-conceived Embargo Act of 1807 against Napoleonic France. Willard found work with a contractor, Pond & Gale, fitting piles into a wharf with a broad axe for fifty cents a day, including room and board. Given that lodgings in Boston were typically $1.50 a week, Willard's first job was worth $4.50 ($360) for a six-day workweek, although paltry wages never seemed to worry him, as long as he was busy and improving his mind. By January 1806, he had earned enough to buy his own tools, a few books, take a stagecoach home, and lend his father $200. Over the next few years, he enrolled in an academy to learn draftsmanship, and—according to his biographer—attended occasional lectures or perhaps night classes in French, chemistry, anatomy, and geology, but, for the most part, Willard taught himself. His carpentry skills and self-confidence had advanced to a point by 1808 that he took the job of installing a complicated multi-story staircase in the new Exchange Coffee House. But it would be in woodcarving where Willard found his niche in Boston's artisan milieu, fabricating and installing the Ionic capitals for the white-painted wooden columns of the Greek Revival churches that were then in vogue. By 1809, when he was twenty-six, he had enough work to employ two journeymen, and sufficient money to rent a room in the center of town on Somerset Street. He then progressed to carving a five-foot eagle for the pediment of the Custom House, and figureheads for ships, including a Tartar for a vessel of the same name, an Arab for the schooner *Caravan*, and a bust of the president for the 74-gun USS *Washington*, for which he charged a hundred dollars.[4]

There are no paintings or engravings of Willard, nor are there accounts describing his appearance, other than to mention he was tall, stocky, slow moving, and favored a grave expression. A "mantle of thoughtfulness always seemed to cover him," wrote his

---

3. William W. Wheildon, *Memoir of Solomon Willard: Architect and Superintendent of the Bunker Hill Monument* (Boston: Bunker Hill Monument Association, 1865), pp. 21–25; Sheldon S. Cohen, "Joseph Willard," *American National Biography Online* (February 2000), http://www.anb.org/articles/01/01-00973.html (accessed June 2008); Mabel Cook Coolidge, *The History of the Town of Petersham, Massachusetts* (Petersham, MA: Petersham Historical Society, 1948), pp. 50–51, 324. For weekly post-riders, see for instance Sidney Willard, *Memories of Youth and Manhood* (Cambridge, MA: John Bartlett, 1855), vol. 1, pp. 241–42. Maine became the twenty-third state during the Missouri Compromise of 1820. Population of Petersham (incorporated 1754): 1765, 707; 1790, 1,560; 1800, 1,794; 1810, 1,490; 1840, 1,775; 1900, 853; in *Vital Records of Petersham, Massachusetts* (Worcester, MA: Franklin P. Rice, 1904), p. 5.

4. Wheildon, *Solomon Willard*, pp. 27–30. Either Wheildon exaggerated or Willard quickly became sufficiently skilled to earn a substantial pay raise, for even if Willard had saved his entire wages he would only have had $180 to lend to his father.

biographer. He never married and, according to legend, he never drank, although this probably meant he did not imbibe spirituous liquors. As with other American towns, Boston's water was far from potable, so alternatives were expensive coffee, unpatriotic tea, fermented drinks like cider or ale, or water with antiseptic whiskey or rum mixed in. His abstinence—and probably his mantle of thoughtfulness—kept him aloof if not quite friendless, but also solvent, enabling him to make three trips to the South by sailing packet, in 1810, 1814, and 1817, when he would take his bag of carving tools and solicit commissions. Toward the end of the third trip, he made a model of the United States Capitol for its architect Charles Bulfinch. From 1818 to his involvement with the BHMA in 1824, the ever-industrious Willard teamed up with a Boston mechanic, Daniel Safford, on a design for a coal-fired hot air furnace for public buildings, gave drawing and sculpture lessons, and moved from wood to stone carving, preparing five marble panels for the granite façade of a Beacon Street mansion (now the Somerset Club) designed and built by Alexander Parris for David Sears, a wealthy merchant turned property developer, one of the BHMA's most generous early benefactors, and, by June 1825, a BHMA director.[5]

Books on Boston's architectural development from colonial town to modern metropolis typically give a few lines to Willard, sometimes one or two pages, which describe him as an architect, credit him with designing the Bunker Hill Monument, and usually mention various civic buildings, executed in granite, for which he was the architect and/or builder. Walter Muir Whitehill and Lawrence W. Kennedy's *Boston: A Topographical History* (2000) lists Willard and Parris as co-architects of St. Paul's Church on Tremont Street. Jan Holtz Kay's *Lost Boston* (1999), states that Willard was in "the design profession" and designed the Monument. Walter H. Kilham's seminal *Boston After Bulfinch* (1946) describes Willard as the "true artist and all-round genius" who co-designed St. Paul's and designed the Monument. Justin Winsor's *Memorial History of Boston* (1881) says, "In conjunction with Alexander Parris he [Willard] built St. Paul's." In fact, Willard neither designed nor built St. Paul's, although he did carve the four Ionic capitals that still sit atop its four plain freestone columns, and he assuredly watched as teams of laborers under master masons Gridley Bryant and John Redman—with Parris's supervision—worked out how to build the granite façades of the Sears mansion and St. Paul's Church.[6]

For a civic building today, architects are those who—after six-plus years of intensive training—sketch designs, draw up detailed plans and specifications, conduct engineering analyses, satisfy building codes, hire contractors, and oversee all aspects of construction; site managers, surveyors, and engineers then liaise with teams of

---

5. Wheildon, *Solomon Willard*, pp. 259, 34–47.

6. Walter Muir Whitehill and Lawrence W. Kennedy, *Boston: A Topographical History* (Cambridge, MA: Harvard University Press, 2000), p. 316; Jane Holtz Kay, *Lost Boston* (Boston: Houghton Mifflin Company, 1999), p. 130; Walter H. Kilham, *Boston After Bulfinch: An Account of its Architecture, 1800–1900* (Cambridge, MA: Harvard University Press, 1946), pp. 28–30; Charles A. Cummings, "Architecture in Boston," in *The Memorial History of Boston, Including Suffolk County, Massachusetts, 1630–1880*, ed. Justin Winsor (Boston: James R. Osgood and Company, 1881), vol. 4, p. 477. For Willard's contribution to St. Paul's, see Edward Francis Zimmer, "The Architectural Career of Alexander Parris (1780–1852)" (PhD diss., Boston University, 1984), pp. 376–77, 621–23.

contractors who carry out the work. Most architects in Willard's day were little more than those who could draw to scale a plan, a section, an elevation, and a perspective, thereby reproducing on paper the classical elements of Greco-Roman styling, or perhaps the design of an artist like Horatio Greenough. Superintendents were those charged by building committees with buying materials, keeping accounts, and supervising the work. Master masons and carpenters, whose experience and management abilities surpassed that of skilled artisans, were the ones who took what were frequently quite basic and inaccurate drawings and figured out how to execute them. There were exceptions, Alexander Parris being the most notable in New England, for he had apprenticed to a master housewright, built houses himself, was an artistic designer, a professional architect in the modern sense, and capable of superintending large-scale construction projects. Parris was a different kind of architect than Charles Bulfinch, say, who was Harvard educated and had toured Europe, but relied on master builders like Parris to implement his designs. By the time Parris settled in Boston in 1810, he had ten years of experience as the builder, superintendent, and architect of banks, churches, and even the Portland Harbor forts, under the direction of Henry A.S. Dearborn, who would be Parris's longtime benefactor and a BHMA director.[7]

Willard certainly wanted to be an architect like Parris, although in 1825 he had little direct experience of a major construction project, and his expertise was in carpentry, not granite masonry. How was it, then, that he came to be the Monument's official architect and superintendent, and credited by historians as its designer?

This question is a difficult one, as the principal sources are the obfuscatory histories by George Washington Warren and William Wheildon, which promote Willard's role. At the meeting on 7 June 1825 when the directors voted for an obelisk, Dearborn's report included sets of plans, along with estimates, for both designs under consideration. Parris provided the plans for a column; Willard provided the plans for an obelisk; and Gridley Bryant made the estimates for both options. Parris's role in the Monument's genesis was greater than either Warren or Wheildon were prepared to acknowledge. He had submitted a design for the competition in the spring, which, like Robert Mills's monument at Baltimore, was a replica of Trajan's Column, with a fluted shaft and a smaller entrance hall than Mills's. After the 17 June ceremony, the BHMA paid him $467.48 ($37,400) for the special document box, the sliver plaque, the cornerstone, and his work in preparing "plans and estimates." At the ceremony, Parris acted as the official architect, the silver plaque stated that he was the Monument's architect, and he submitted a second bill of $50 for his services on 17 June, which the BHMA also paid. Why did the BHMA reward Parris so handsomely for plans it rejected yet pay Willard nothing for plans it accepted? On one hand, Dearborn expected the directors would accept his recommendation for a column, Dearborn was Parris's patron, and Dearborn could pull the purse strings, in part through the influence of

---

7. In 1808 Henry A.S. Dearborn was an attorney in Portland, and his father, Henry Dearborn, was U.S. Secretary of War.

Edward Everett and Thomas Perkins, both column advocates who were not at the fateful meeting of 10 June 1825 when directors voted for an obelisk. On the other hand, Willard steadfastly refused to accept compensation, maintaining throughout his life that the Monument was the finest of patriotic endeavors, and that charging for his services would tarnish its shining image. Yet it was also the case that Parris, Bryant, and Willard were informal business partners, so what was good for one was good for all.[8]

These issues aside, it would not be until 5 July that the BHMA's Building Committee finalized the obelisk's dimensions. Loammi Baldwin Jr. chaired this committee, and rightly so, because he was a civil engineer with twenty years' experience using granite blocks in the construction of canals and other public works, whereas his fellow members—artist Washington Allston, lawyer Samuel Swett, doctor Jacob Bigelow, professor George Ticknor—had no knowledge of construction. Baldwin made accurately scaled card-stock cutouts of obelisks with different profiles, took his committee to the Mill Dam directly across the Charles River estuary from Charlestown, and attached the cutouts to a fence. By squinting at the cutouts, or perhaps making frames with their fingers, the committee settled on a shaft with a base of thirty feet on a side tapering to fifteen feet, with a pyramidal tip whose faces sloped at ninety degrees. Whatever plans existed prior to 5 July would, therefore, have needed redrafting to suit these final measurements. Baldwin's report provided comprehensive dimensions and specifications of the kind that a civil engineer would produce at the commencement of a project, with a recommendation that the directors hire a "skillful architect" to "make and prepare the detailed and working plans," and an "experienced stone-mason" for the superintendence of all construction. He called for a well to test ground conditions, discussed the depth and characteristics of the foundations, described the interior newel around which the stairs would spiral, the slit windows and viewing landings, and he even allowed for geomancy, by specifying that the sides of the obelisk face each compass point (a stricture, oddly enough, from which Willard deviated by 15°).[9]

There is only one extant plan (fig. 11), which occurs in slightly different forms in a number of publications, including G. W. Warren's history and an 1843 cost study by Willard. At first sight, it appears to be a working drawing, and may actually have been that, although it has a number of peculiarities: it carries a scale that corresponds to ten-foot intervals but has fifteen-inch subdivisions; the dimension across the top of the column is 17.4 feet when the specification—and size of the finished structure— was 15.0 feet; its tip has seven courses of stone at a sixty-degree angle, whereas the actual monument has five courses at ninety degrees; and the figures in its table are not an estimate of the quantities of stone required, rather they are the final quantities, written in as the construction proceeded. Willard probably drew this plan, although

---

8. George Washington Warren, *The History of the Bunker Hill Monument Association During the First Century of the United States of America* (Boston: James R. Osgood and Company, 1877), pp. 165, 137; Wheildon, *Solomon Willard*, p. 86.

9. Warren, *Monument Association*, pp. 182–88. It is difficult to explain why Willard canted the Monument's north face 15° west of true north; maybe he aligned the east face with the wall of the redoubt that took the redcoat assault, or he set the Monument at 45° so two faces met the rising sun on 17 June, or he had no compass and made an inspired guess.

it might be Parris's work, as it shares a stylistic similarity with a plan Parris drew for the Sears mansion. Similarly, Willard may have drafted plans for Parris, depending on who was the busiest at any given time. In 1834 when Parris opened a new design office in Boston, Bryant's son, Gridley J.F. Bryant, worked for him as an assistant architect, and Parris collaborated with Willard on the design of a new county courthouse.[10]

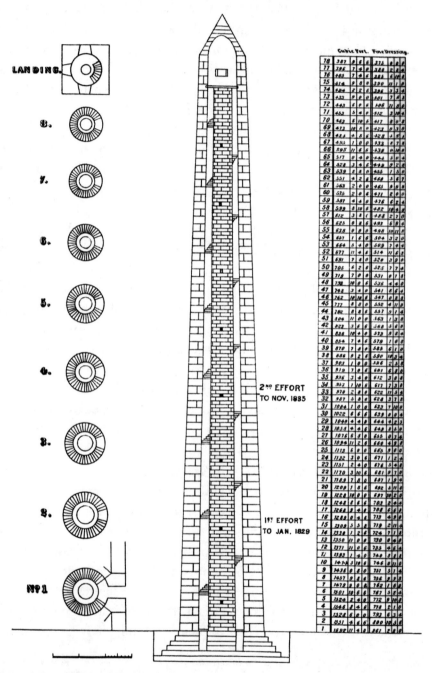

fig. 11: Monument, elevation and sections, probably by Solomon Willard, ca. 1845

10. Without examining further sets of plans drawn by both Willard and Parris, I would not want to push the point of stylistic similarities too far, but the method of drawing the staircases is identical and both plans use clean, simple pen strokes, whereas many draftsmen of the time depicted walls with shading or solid areas.

Based on the foregoing, this is a plausible summary of the design process, which was ultimately a collaborative effort: Horatio Greenough provided the inspiration for a plain Egyptian obelisk. Willard drew up the plans, probably with assistance from Parris. Bryant contributed construction details, and made the estimates. Baldwin verified the feasibility of Willard's plan and Bryant's estimates, supplied additional engineering parameters, and finalized the specifications. Sometime after 5 July, and perhaps not until December 1825, Willard redrew his plan to Baldwin's final dimensions and specifications. Underlying this scenario are business connections, which Yankees of the Early Republic established so readily between themselves. Bryant worked closely with Parris as his master mason on the Sears mansion, St. Paul's Church, and Quincy Market, and he had already developed a similar working relationship with Willard; in 1827, Parris and Baldwin formed a design-and-build partnership to handle lucrative construction projects at the Charlestown Navy Yard. Baldwin and Parris were both forty-five in 1825, Willard was forty-two, and Bryant was thirty-six.

BHMA directors, especially Dearborn, had expected that Parris would be the architect and superintendent. It is not clear why he pulled out, although he certainly did not need any more work; in addition to contracts for shops and housing in Boston, and a wall in the Navy Yard, he was busy supervising Quincy Market, his best-known building, and the centerpiece of downtown Boston today. When the directors rejected his stylish column in favor of a plain obelisk, Parris no doubt lost enthusiasm for the project. His experiences of working with the directors may also have hastened his departure. While they could spend lavishly on events such as the cornerstone ceremony, when it came to something as mundane as construction they were remarkably parsimonious. An indication of the ill will they could engender came in August 1825, when they insisted that Building Committee members would be personally liable for any cost overruns. Flabbergasted, Baldwin resigned and refused all entreaties to re-enlist, writing that not even in the dozens of commercial contracts he had made over the years had he ever experienced "such severe terms of service," let alone when he was providing his services free for a public good. With Parris and Baldwin gone, the directors had few trustworthy candidates for what they must have realized by then would be a thankless if not impossible task. Willard was beginning to look like their best and perhaps only hope.[11]

Even though the directors had upset Willard at the outset of the design phase in November 1824, by the end of May 1825 they had patched up the quarrel, in part because of his enthusiasm for the Monument. Wheildon wrote that, "It seemed at once to seize upon his imagination and feelings." Perhaps after hearing Daniel Webster's oration, Willard had become a believer in the Monument's manifold social virtues. "He did not look upon it simply as a work of art, which might be supposed to be his stand-point," noted Wheildon, "but regarded it as a high patriotic duty, sacred to the best and noblest sentiments of our nature." Willard's inexperience counted against

---

11. Warren, *Monument Association*, p. 193.

him, but the directors had heard about his recent involvement with the construction of Boston's new U.S. Branch Bank, a gloomy Greek Revival structure in Chelmsford granite on State Street (fig. 12). On 7 October, they solicited a letter of recommendation from Daniel P. Parker, a shipping magnate, who was either one of the bank's directors or the building's owner. Parker stated that Willard, as the architect, had built a model, drawn the plans, and provided advice to the bank's building committee, although the committee had made all the contracts and managed the project. (Bryant and James McAllister were the construction contractors.) Parker regretted he was unable to say whether Willard was qualified to "take the sole superintendence of an important public work," but stressed that Willard was "strictly moral and sober, and of indefatigable industry." It was his "extreme modesty and reserve," Parker felt, that had prevented a wider appreciation of his real merit. Duty, sobriety, morality, industry, and modesty were all archetypal Yankee characteristics that would have endeared Willard to the directors.[12]

fig. 12: U.S. Branch Bank, State Street, Boston

On 31 October 1825, a newly constituted Building Committee, with the personal liability clause removed from its charter, met at the home of its chairman, Dr. John C. Warren. It comprised state district attorney George Blake, Boston militia commander William Sullivan, merchant-investor Amos Lawrence, and Dearborn. Also there for dinner were the BHMA's president, vice president, and secretary, Daniel Webster, Judge Joseph Story, and Edward Everett respectively, which in G.W. Warren's estimation, meant that a "more select company of distinguished characters, eminent for intellect, wit, high attainment, and a genial flow of converse, could hardly be gathered in any city." They had not invited Willard, for whom wit and a genial flow of

12. Wheildon, *Solomon Willard*, p. 58; Warren, *Monument Association*, pp. 200–201; Wheildon, *Solomon Willard*, p. 44, mentions that Willard provided "a plan and model," which may have been the extent of his contribution. Developers replaced the bank, which was at the corner of State and Devonshire Streets, with the old Merchants' Bank building.

conversation was a perpetual struggle, but they talked about him. He was not a native of Boston, neither was he Harvard educated, but Willard was born in Massachusetts, and there was even a hint of pedigree through his uncle, Joseph, who had been president of Harvard when several of them were undergraduates, and, three generations before Joseph, through Rev. Samuel Willard, minister of Groton during King Philip's War in 1675. There was the issue of his inexperience, yet his reputation and character were exemplary. After due deliberation, they decided that the "'offices of superintendent and architect'" would henceforth "'be united in the same person,'" and unanimously elected Willard to the position.[13]

Willard's Yankee Mystique

More than simply guarding his reputation, Willard cultivated a mystique, which is probably why he never sat for an artist, and explains the encomium of contemporaries like Daniel Parker and historians such as Walter Kilham, who wrote that Willard "needed no incentive beyond 'the joy of working.'" Willard was the sober Puritan his ordained brother never was. He was the successful artisan his father had failed to be, supporting him with a substantial loan within two years of leaving home. By not marrying, he avoided the expense and heartaches of large families, which had so worn down his parents and brothers; through his unusual celibacy, seriousness, and devotion to the mechanic arts he could also create a priest-like aura. And perhaps through his unstinting endeavors to erect a patriotic monument he assuaged any guilt still lingering from his family's pre-1775 Tory allegiance. It is now difficult, if not impossible, to disentangle the real Willard from the Willard of his friend and booster William Wheildon, and from the historiography that has relied for 160 years on Wheildon's biography. Yet the issue here is to understand the legend and recognize its power, a legend of quintessential Yankeeness fostered by Willard himself at the time, exploited for all it was worth by BHMA directors and publicists, and elevated to an almost godlike level by Wheildon. Willard was the poor farm boy who came to the big city, worked hard, studied in his spare time, saved every penny, was honest to a fault, and consequently made good. In the hands of Wheildon, he became a paragon of Yankee virtue: his "habits were exemplary; his indulgences, even in innocent enjoyments, were very few"; he found it difficult to be frivolous, and "sought at all times the development and cultivation of his intellectual nature." Willard's industry arose "not in the hope of reward, not in the austerity of the bigot, not from any vain show or pretence of goodness, but from principle." Like his biblical namesake, "Solomon, builder and king," Solomon Willard "sought wisdom as the highest good." He was the kind of Yankee that the BHMA's directors wanted the world to think they were; he was the kind of Yankee that granite workers hoped to become themselves. For all of them, Willard lived the American Dream.[14]

Today, counselors would say that Willard was a role model, someone whose example one can choose to follow to make one's own life more fulfilling. In addition,

---

13. Warren, *Monument Association*, pp. 199–200.
14. Wheildon, *Solomon Willard*, pp. 257–58.

Americans tend to be especially enamored of larger-than-life characters like Willard, because they demonstrate how a particular facet of the Dream can become a reality. When asked to name their favorite role model, American high school students commonly pick figures such as Michael Moore for his courage of conscience, Tiger Woods for his work ethic, Hillary Rodham Clinton for her gritty determination, or Bono, even though he is not a U.S. citizen, for his humanitarian outreach.[15] These examples embody noble social attributes, yet it is also apparent that they are all children of blue-collar or middle-class families who have become rich and successful. Role models, of course, are just as prone to bursts of temper, disloyalty, jealousy, conflicts of interest—the failings of human nature—as anyone else, although the myth that grows around them provides a forgiving buffer, a measure of protection from public scrutiny. Admirers of a particular personality would sooner not dig too deeply, lest they destroy an image that they have tried to emulate.

Collective identities, whether of communities, tribes, or nations, rely by definition on a strong sense of difference or *otherness*, but in large measure they are also the sum of formative or founding myths, and the development of those myths over time. These myths give substance, give meaning, and especially give credence to national identity. As international relations scholar David Campbell has argued, the English and Dutch colonists who settled New England had an especially weak and fragile sense of identity. Independence from Britain proscribed Britishness, added an increasing number of competing local identities—Vermonters and Mainers, Federalists and anti-Federalists—and created a new, overarching American identity, which at the outset had little, or at least a problematic, meaning. This only made Americans more uncertain and anxious about who they were. As late as 1815, to define their nationalism in concrete terms, Americans could point to little more than a shattered economy, a disastrous foreign policy, a defeated navy, a burnt out capital, a cracked Liberty Bell, and a crinkled Constitution, which albeit was acquiring almost Biblical significance. Americanism has consequently depended—more so than other national ideologies—on the mythicized events, legendary figures, and moral claims of its formative years. Inherent to Americanism is therefore the paradox of integrity, for citizens and outsiders alike hold American values—freedom of speech, fairness, openness, rugged individualism—in high regard, and yet the history supporting those values is one of received wisdom if not outright falsehood, while social opprobrium awaits anyone who dares to question the myths.[16]

BHMA directors understood this paradox, Daniel Webster better than most. When the debate over the validity of Henry Dearborn's charges of delinquency against Gen. Israel Putnam was at its most acrimonious in 1818, Webster called the parties to order in a *North American Review* article. It was irrelevant, Webster seemed to say, where Putnam was on the battlefield on the afternoon of 17 June 1775, or even

---

15. I questioned respondents in 2009, before news of Woods's marital infidelity.

16. David Campbell, *Writing Security: United States Foreign Policy and the Politics of Identity* (Minneapolis: University of Minneapolis Press, 1998), pp. 110–13, 12, 3. This fragility may also explain Americans' need for a strong state and propensity for militarism.

whether he was actually a coward, as Dearborn's account implied. What mattered was that no one challenged the heroic myth, for "the characters of its great men are the real treasures of the country." What else did Americans have, he asked, except the characters of their great men? Upon what other themes could poets and orators draw? "What, but these, for the examples of its emulous youth?" Those who would expose the myths, Webster was saying, evinced a "strange disregard to the highest subjects of national interest." Patriotic Americans must hold the character and fame of their founding heroes in sacred trust. They owed a debt of gratitude to men like Putnam, and were "bound to defend and protect this trust against all *posthumous* enemies." For Americans, then as now, the myths of battles like Bunker Hill and the legends of heroes and role models like Warren and Willard were essential to the legitimacy of their republican mission.[17]

Early Granite Production

Boston's colonial-era houses and shops were generally oak framed with pine floors and clapboard siding. Fire being an ever-present problem, builders might apply a rendering of pebbles, broken glass, or shells. As the colony's wealth increased so did the use of brick facings. Because there was an abundance of high-grade timber, builders reserved limited supplies of stone for warehouses, forts, and the occasional church or mansion. Building stone falls into two basic categories: facing stonework can be relatively weak, even pliable like certain limestones, providing it has the properties of workability and esthetic beauty; structural masonry, while it can be visually uninteresting, must be longitudinally strong and free of flaws. During the colonial period, builders shunned granite as a facing material owing to the difficulties of splitting blocks to a uniform dimension, although it was their preferred option for lintels to bridge windows and doorways, and for wells, wharves, cellars, and in-ground posts. So scarce was building stone that towns such as Braintree passed ordinances regulating its use within the township and prohibiting its export to another town without a license from the selectmen.[18]

Seventeenth- and eighteenth-century granite production was a labor-intensive affair, when the technique required setting a brushwood fire around a surface boulder, waiting while it heated through, and then pummeling it with an iron ball, or *beetle*, dropped from a wooden derrick until the boulder cracked and split. Stonecutters had the onerous task of sizing and shaping the pieces. First, they chipped a groove along the surface with an axe-shaped hammer to induce a crack, although depending on the physical properties of the stone they had little control over the direction the split would take. Each resulting block required hewing, which meant long hours of further chipping and hammering to produce a rough face of relative flatness and at least four

17. Daniel Webster, book review of *An Account of the Battle of Bunker Hill*, by Henry Dearborn, and *A Letter to Major General Dearborn*, by Daniel Putnam, *North American Review and Miscellaneous Journal*, 7:2 (July 1818), pp. 232, 231, emphasis original.

18. Arthur W. Brayley, *History of the Granite Industry of New England* (Boston: National Association of Granite Industries, 1913), vol. 1, p. 13.

corners that were approximately square. Suitable granite occurred in large surface boulders at Westford and Tyngsborough, near Chelmsford, thirty miles north-west of Boston, and in boulders and a few ledges at Quincy (pronounced QUIN-zee) and Braintree, ten miles by water to the south. Sloops and barges transported the light-gray Chelmsford granite down the Merrimack River, and the darker Quincy granite down the Neponset River or via Braintree's Mill Cove. Prior to 1805, there were few granite structures in Boston, most notably Hancock Manor on Beacon Street (1737), King's Chapel on Tremont Street (1754), a powder house near Pinckney Street (1774), and a lighthouse on Beacon Island (1793).

Three developments during the early 1800s increased the availability and drove down the cost of hewn granite. First, in 1798, in anticipation of hostilities with Napoleonic France, the federal government ordered the fortification of Boston Harbor's Castle Island, which served as the Massachusetts state prison. Lieutenant-Governor Edward Hutchinson Robbins, the commissioner of prisons, decided to build a substantial new facility at Lynde's Point in Charlestown, two hundred feet by forty feet, on four floors, with walls of granite because, in the days before Portland cement and reinforced concrete, inmates had a propensity to carve, whittle, or dig their way out of lesser structures. Probably because his hometown of Milton was adjacent to Quincy, Robbins specified Quincy granite. Soon after ground-breaking, it became apparent that supplies of finished granite blocks were as inadequate as they were expensive, and construction slowed.[19]

Second, in 1803, stonecutters in the Quincy area began splitting granite blocks using metal wedges. According to a story that may be apocryphal, Robbins happened to be traveling through Salem in a chaise, when he spotted a newly constructed building that had a granite basement. Stopping to investigate, he noticed unusual gouges in the face of each stone at six-inch intervals, and after asking the builder where he had purchased the stone, Robbins tracked down a mason by the name of Tarbox in Danvers, a few miles up the Porter River from Salem. Tarbox explained how he first made a line of small holes in the granite with a hardened iron plug drill (rotated in one hand while struck repeatedly with a hammer in the other; figs. 13, 20), then he pounded pairs of tiny metal wedges into the holes until the block split, horizontally along the line of holes, and vertically following the ninety-degree angle of the holes. Realizing the significance of this innovation, and with the construction of the prison so far behind schedule, Robbins bought the impoverished Tarbox some clothes and carted him off to Quincy, where he passed on his skill. Legend or not, Josiah Bemis, Michael Weld, and George Stearns began using metal wedges at their small quarries in West Quincy, and the price of dimensioned granite fell from $4 to $2.50 a perch (about twenty-four cubic feet, and typically three to six blocks, or say from $90 to $60 today for a rough-faced block thirty-six by eighteen by eighteen inches).[20]

---

19. Lynde's Point merges today into landfill, but approximates to the western end of the Bunker Hill Mall in west-central Charlestown, opposite the Bunker Hill Community College.

20. Brayley, *Granite Industry*, vol. 1, pp. 18–19.

fig. 13: a nicely split block (7 x 4 x 3 feet) of Quincy granite, showing lines of drill holes

Third, in 1803, Loammi Baldwin, a civil engineer, Revolutionary War hero, and father of the BHMA's Loammi Baldwin Jr., opened the Middlesex Canal, which connected the Merrimack River (by the later mill town of Lowell) to the port of Boston, with a termination near Charlestown Neck. Because Baldwin specified granite for the canal's twenty locks and eight aqueducts, his contractors gained experience in granite masonry, and the production of rough granite blocks and stones from surface boulders in the Chelmsford area increased. Once the Massachusetts State Prison in Charlestown opened, these three developments combined to further increase the supply and decrease the cost of hewn granite for masonry construction. Nineteenth-century convicts paid for their food and incarceration through hard labor, the principal component of which at Charlestown became—quite logically—the production of hewn granite. Stonecutters in the Chelmsford area, eager for new markets now that the canal was finished, could send roughly dimensioned blocks by barge to the prison for hewing. Quincy stonecutters could similarly maximize profits and eliminate the toil of hammering by shipping rough blocks to Charlestown.

Cellars, wharves, and structures like Boston's harbor island forts typically consisted of large, irregularly shaped blocks of granite, which masons fitted together as best they could with the minimum of on-site chipping; they might bed the blocks in mortar or fit them dry, as with the pillars for Baldwin's aqueducts. With a few exceptions, such as rough or *rusticated* granite basements, whenever masons employed granite as a facing material, they laid it in ashlar courses of twelve to eighteen inches in height. In ashlar construction, stonecutters split the thinnest slabs they could from large blocks by drilling and wedging. Stoneworkers then hewed one face to the required smoothness and squared off the edges. When the slabs arrived at the work site, masons matched the slabs by size, planned how to fit them together with the minimum of dressing, and finally cemented the slabs onto a structural wall of smaller stones or bricks. This method meant that the cheapest materials formed the mass of the walls and the granite slabs were of a manageable weight. To ensure rigidity and improve aesthetics, masons used solid blocks for cornerstones or *quoins*.

Hewing and squaring a stone as hard as granite without electricity or compressed air demanded brawn as well as skill. Tools had to be of hardened iron, and they needed frequent sharpening, to the extent that in 1804 stonecutters persuaded a blacksmith to open a forge where they worked at West Quincy. After the War of Independence, as well as the French and Indian War, stoneworkers from Hesse—former mercenaries and their relatives—settled in New England, some at what would become Germantown in Quincy. These workers introduced specialized masonry tools and techniques, such as long-handled, two-handed, heavy iron sledgehammers with one side of the hammerhead ground to a blade, which were useful for rough chipping and grooving without recourse to a chisel. Moving into the 1810s, the supply of and demand for hewn granite in the Boston area gradually rose, propelled by the influx of skilled labor, iron wedging, and especially Charlestown's convicts.

Light-gray Chelmsford granite, split by wedging from surface boulders, constituted the ashlar façades of Boston's Court House (1810), New South Church (1814), Congregational House (ca. 1815), Parkman House (ca. 1815), University Hall, Cambridge (ca. 1815), Massachusetts General Hospital (1816), Dedham Jail (1817), a block of houses on Brattle Street (1818), as well as the basement of the Exchange Coffee House (1808), and the pillars of the General Hospital and some stores in Cornhill (1817). As stonecutters began to exhaust the supply of surface boulders, a few quarrymen began turning to exposed ledges, primarily at West Quincy, and later at Rockport, situated right on the coast thirty-six miles by water north of Boston, where they would split blocks in situ, then winch them out with a derrick. A particularly light shade of Quincy granite formed the façades of the David Sears mansion (1819) and St. Paul's Church (1820). Impressive though this list seems, before the 1830s granite buildings were as prohibitively expensive as they were rare, quarrying was a cottage industry, and supply could be restricted to the winter months, as at West Quincy, when oxen dragged sleds over the snow-covered ground to a wharf in the town.

Each of these buildings, nevertheless, required thousands of perches of hewn granite, and hewing was a tough way to make a living. A momentary lapse of concentration or fatigued muscles and the hammer would slip, splitting a nail, crushing a thumb, or bruising a joint; leather gloves offered protection but they were clumsy and made hands sweaty. Stone chips or metal splinters occasionally punctured an eyeball. Maneuvering massive blocks could cause hernias or a ruptured disc, while a block that toppled unexpectedly could break toes or worse. Less immediate health hazards included back strain, respiratory issues, and tendonitis of the hands or elbows. So tough was the work that a handy solution was to farm it out to convicts, and such was the spiraling demand for hewn granite for churches, mansions, banks, courthouses, and hospitals that granite production at the State Prison became big business. Granite blocks arrived at the prison by barge down the Middlesex Canal or by sloop from Quincy. Convicts hammered and dressed the stone. Superintendents and master masons paid Warden Gamaliel Bradford for the finished product. After Bradford had paid his overseers and purchased scanty provisions for the convicts, the profits went back into state coffers, so legislators could fund more buildings with dignified granite façades and Greek Revival pillars. From 1824 to 1826, Bradford made the state a profit of $20,000 ($1.6 million).[21]

To boost production and increase profits, Bradford used a carrot-and-stick approach, paying substantial bonuses to Samuel R. Johnson, his overseer of the granite department, a portion of which Johnson used to reward industrious convicts who exceeded their hammering quotas, a practice called *overstint*. Prison reformers—Bradford being one—believed that adults turned to crime because they were lazy, so a regimen of hard labor that taught convicts the value of work, as well as useful skills, would rehabilitate them as productive citizens. In theory, the reform movement had merit, though in the case of granite production at the Massachusetts State Prison it is hard not to conclude that reformers were perpetuating a corrupt, pernicious system that was slavery by another name. On 12 April 1823, convicts refused to leave the mess hall and return to work, claiming that their ration did not support their labor, a valid complaint, because Bradford only gave them ten ounces of bread and two ounces of molasses a day, or about 960 calories. To avoid starvation, convicts had no choice but to overstint so that they had money to buy food from the prison commissary, whose proprietor turned a profit of $400–$500 ($32,000–$40,000) a year. Convicts who worked especially hard could afford tobacco. Conversely, convicts subjected to solitary confinement, a common punishment, could not earn overstint and would therefore starve.[22]

There is a contemporary engraving (fig. 14) of granite hewing in the prison factory, which depicts seventeen convicts at work in a well-lit, airy building; their uniform looks neat but none wear gloves; only one of them appears to be Black, although about a third of the prison population at the time was African American. Conditions in the prison may have been relatively benign, yet on 12 March 1824, there was a mutiny. Whether because they were not hammering enough stone, or for other forms of disobedience, three convicts were in solitary confinement awaiting a public flogging in the prison yard. When an officer entered one of the cells, the convict overpowered him, took his keys, and released his two friends, although they failed to coerce the

21. Profit, from Larry Goldsmith, "'To Profit By His Skill and to Traffic on His Crime,' Prison Labor in Early 19th-Century Massachusetts," *Labor History*, 40:4 (1999), p. 452.

22. Goldsmith, "'To Profit By His Skill,'" pp. 452, 455. Molasses = 120 calories/ounce; stone-ground bread = 72 calories/ounce.

officer into assisting them with a jailbreak. As the alarm sounded, several dozen convicts armed themselves with "hammers, chisels, and every weapon attainable," forming—according to Justin Winsor's history of 1881—"a band whose strength, vileness, and reckless daring could hardly be equaled." Marines soon arrived from the Navy Yard, their commander lined them up inside the prison, and he gave them an order to kill any convicts who had not surrendered inside five minutes. So desperate were the mutineers that it seemed as if they preferred death to stone hammering, but one by one, their resolve weakened until the last man had capitulated.[23]

fig. 14: hewing granite, Massachusetts State Prison, Charlestown

All that was required to keep the system running was a steady supply of tractable convicts. Any suggestion that Boston's judges passed sentences with the intention of boosting granite production would be impossible to prove, and yet the temptation existed. Half of the BHMA's directors were involved in making or enforcing the law in Suffolk County (Boston). Warren Dutton, Stephen Gorham, Benjamin Gorham, Thomas Perkins, William Prescott Jr., and William Tudor were justices of the peace. George Blake and Dexter Franklin were district attorneys. Isaac P. Davis was a State Prison Visitor, and Theodore Lyman Jr. was president of the Prison Discipline Society. In its annual report of 1826, Lyman's society noted that hewing granite was "laborious and healthy," there was "great demand for the work," the business was "profitable to the institution," and the art of hewing stone was "very useful to the convicts after they leave the prison." At minimum, it is clear that BHMA directors were enthusiastic participants in a system geared to the production of state-subsidized hewn granite through convict labor. At worst, their scheme was a conspiracy. On 24 February 1825, Governor William Eustis signed an act authorizing the BHMA to receive ten thousand dollars

23. George Henry Preble, "The Navy, and the Charlestown Navy Yard," in *Memorial History of Boston*, ed. Justin Winsor, vol. 3, p. 351.

worth of free granite, "hammered and prepared to be used, at the state prison in Charlestown," to whatever specifications "the Directors of said Association may request." Gen. William Sullivan had drawn up the bill and Senator Seth Knowles had shepherded its passage, both of them BHMA directors; Edward Everett wrote letters to representatives of both houses, lobbying for the bill and stressing its patriotic intent. Nonetheless, the bill did meet resistance in the lower house and represented a compromise, for the original bill stipulated that all the granite for the Monument would be free.[24]

Bunker Hill Quarry

Solomon Willard's first and most critical challenge as Monument architect and superintendent was to secure a supply of granite. Inside the Monument, there would be a hollow newel of six feet diameter and 147 courses, around which the stairs would wind, and, facing into the stairwell, the inner blocks of the outer wall (see fig. 22); all this internal granite could be of the type produced at the state prison. Still, from his observations of construction at St. Paul's Church, the Sears mansion, and the U.S. Bank, Willard had seen the difficulties of master masons John Redman, James McAllister, and Gridley Bryant as they struggled to cope with the unpredictable supply and variable quality of a product produced by disaffected convicts. Then there was the issue of granite for the outside, which was another matter entirely. Courses of between two and three feet high, as Loammi Baldwin Jr. had specified, and blocks ten or twelve feet long, would minimize the length of joints exposed to the weather as well as increase structural stability. Building a gradually tapering obelisk meant that each block would need a slight yet precise taper on three sides. Fitting such blocks together with minimal gaps required prime quality stone, and the finished faces, from ground level to capstone, had to be of uniform appearance. This meant that all the external granite—a third of the 9,000-ton total—should come from a single source, which ruled out surface boulders. Willard needed a quarry. Yet one of sufficient size did not exist, and anyway, Willard knew that quarrying at that time was "in the hands of those who had neither the means nor the skill which is necessary for conducting business in a proper manner." Locating a suitably large site and then managing the resource directly was the obvious solution.[25]

According to a story told by BHMA director Amos Lawrence in 1849, Willard journeyed as far as Hallowell, thirty-six miles up the Kennebec River near Augusta, Maine, and hiked some three hundred miles around the hills of coastal Massachusetts, before settling on a site in the Blue Hills at West Quincy. It was one of Willard's "most laborious undertakings," wrote his biographer, "and he was indefatigable in its accomplishment." Further elements of the Willard legend, of which Lawrence's story forms a part, hold that the BHMA paid the bargain price of $325 for what would become the

24. Prison Discipline Society of Boston, annual report, cited in Goldsmith, "'To Profit By His Skill,'" p. 452; Everett's lobbying, and the Act itself, are in Warren, *Monument Association*, p. 94.

25. Solomon Willard, *Plans and Sections of the Obelisk on Bunker's Hill with the Details of Experiments Made in Quarrying the Granite* (Boston: Chas. Cook's Lithograph, 1843), p. 6.

Bunker Hill Quarry. Willard then developed the quarry, managed the production of the stone, and supervised the entire building project over an eighteen-year period for a $1,000 fee, which he promptly contributed to the Monument's building fund. All of this was true. Missing are the parallel stories of Willard's partners and associates, as well as the way that the BHMA's directors and historians appropriated Willard's Yankee mystique, ensuring the legend's survival.[26]

fig. 15: Bunker Hill Quarry, ca. 1910, sixty years past the end of its working life

In June 1825, Gridley Bryant purchased four acres of rough woodland at West Quincy from farmer Frederick Hardwick for $250 ($20,000). Bryant signed the deed on 9 June, just after the directors at the 7 June meeting had voted to erect an obelisk to Willard's plans and Bryant's estimate. Bryant borrowed the capital from John C. Warren, nephew of hero Joseph Warren, and the director whose change of heart probably swung the vote in favor of the obelisk. Given that Bryant had to collect the money and then take a three-hour carriage ride over the rough track from Boston to Quincy, he could hardly have arrived any sooner. Perhaps Willard had walked three hundred miles before he and Bryant worked out a deal with Hardwick, but the foregoing months were especially busy for both men, with Bryant working simultaneously on Parris's Quincy Market and Willard's U.S. Branch Bank, and Willard consulting "daily" with the bank's building committee, according to committee member Daniel Parker. Once the BHMA had appointed Willard as architect/superintendent on 31

26. Statement by Amos Lawrence, August 1849, in Wheildon, *Solomon Willard*, p. 108.

October, Bryant offered to sell the BHMA the right to sufficient stone to build the Monument for $325. To give the appearance of fairness to potential vendors, Warren, in his new capacity as building committee chairman, solicited competitive tenders in three Boston newspapers for three thousand tons of "best Quincy Granite of uniform color." Not surprisingly, as Willard later wrote, "no proposal was offered, except by one individual, who offered to furnish a part at a price three times the estimated cost." Warren then exercised the right, leaving Bryant with a guaranteed customer for however much granite the Monument required, $75 ($6,000) of working capital, and he still had the same four acres of quarry-able land.[27]

Bryant had bought an exposed portion of a vast seam of high-grade riebeckite-aegirine granite, rising in places to a height of three hundred feet, but extending down as far as opencast quarrying techniques allow, some two hundred feet below sea level. To historians, North America represents the New World, but for geologists it is more ancient than Europe. Its granite is one of the oldest types of igneous rock, an extrusion of molten magma during the Precambrian period. Some 440 million years ago, at the onset of the Silurian period, the Blue Hills erupted from a volcano astride the Boston Basin's southern fault line. At the time of the geologically recent Quaternary ice age two-and-a-half million years ago, New England's coast extended fifty or sixty miles eastwards and its granite mountains were hundreds of feet higher. At Quincy, the Blue Hills were about two hundred feet taller, even though they lay pressed down beneath massive ice sheets three to five thousand feet thick. As temperatures increased, the sheets rumbled and cracked their way seaward, grinding down the underlying granite, and leaving the reprofiled rock buried under dozens of feet of debris. Retreating glaciers produced so much ground-up material that, upon melting, they left behind new hills and dumped rounded islands into the ocean; such drumlins occur near Quincy at Houghs Neck, Wollaston Hill, and Forbes's Hill. Relieved of its colossal ice burden, the earth's pliable crust then bobbed up, only to sink slowly back down into the equilibrium position in which it exists today. Even though the Blue Hills are a sorry remnant of once-mighty mountains, hiking them offers windy views of fifty or more miles.[28]

Quincy granite has an even grain of medium to coarse size, comprising about 60 percent feldspar, 30 percent quartz, and 10 percent hornblende, three of the hardest constituents of rock with values of 6–7 on the Mohs scale (hardened steel has a Mohs value of 7–8). Quarrymen called it syenite, after the granites from Syene (Aswan) in Upper Egypt, because it contains hornblende instead of glittery though soft mica. Medium gray to a dark bluish gray for the most part, it has spots that appear black but are actually green- or blue-black. There is variety too, most obviously in Gold-Leaf

27. When Bryant bought the land, four independent entrepreneurs—Jackson Field, Josiah Bemis, William Packard, and William Wood—were operating small quarries at West Quincy. Wheildon, *Solomon Willard*, pp. 109–10; Warren, *Monument Association*, p. 200; *Independent Chronicle & Boston Patriot*, 16 November 1825, p. 3, and in *Boston Commercial Gazette* and *Columbian Centinel*; Willard, *Plans and Sections*, p. 19.

28. Irving B. Crosby, *Boston Through the Ages: The Geological Story of Greater Boston* (Boston: Marshall Jones Company, 1928), pp. 43–52.

Quincy, the lightest shade, which contains yellowish specks of iron oxide. Because of the stone's absence of mica, it takes a high and lasting polish, and the stone is virtually frost proof. Most importantly, it is geologically *massive*, meaning that it lacks a directional grain. While this massive character does complicate quarrying, for blocks do not easily split away from the face, wedging results in straight, predictable fractures, and finished blocks have great structural integrity. As soon as Bryant and Willard had worked out how to develop their Bunker Hill Quarry, it would not only furnish high quality granite for the Monument at a bargain price but it would also facilitate a granite building boom in Boston, which made fortunes for several BHMA directors and their business partners.[29]

Granite Railway

Once they had fulfilled their commitments in Boston, Bryant and Willard took lodgings in West Quincy and turned to the business of quarrying full time. Willard had originally expected to quarry the granite in the warm months, drag the blocks over snow-packed ground on sleds pulled by oxen to the coast at Quincy, and then ship the blocks to Charlestown Prison for hewing before final squaring and surfacing at the Monument. Now that farmer Hardwick had cleared the quarry site of trees and they had reconnoitered the area, Bryant had an idea for a new plan. He would build a railway to take the blocks to a wharf on the Neponset River. Historians like to credit Bryant's Granite Railway with being the first railroad in the United States, which it was not, although the claim adds yet another memorable element to the Monument's popular legend. References to the Granite Railway and the Monument often appear together, as in *A Popular History of American Invention* (1924): "The first railway to be built in America was . . . constructed to bring heavy blocks of granite from the Quincy quarries to Boston for the Bunker Hill Monument." Tourist guides, such as Susan Wilson's *Boston Sights and Insights*, still attribute the "'first commercial railroad in America'" to Bryant. Bryant's engineering was as inventive as it was bold, his railway did perform as intended, and, in many respects, his Yankee sensibilities were on a par with those of Willard's. Yet there was precedent for Bryant's anachronistic design, while its originality, experimental nature, and exorbitant construction costs ensured it would do little to advance U.S. railway engineering.[30]

From his classical studies, Willard might have alerted Bryant to the wagonways of the ancient Greeks and Romans, such as the grooved stone tracks used to transport boats five miles across the Isthmus of Corinth in the sixth century BCE, or for quarrying in Malta. Another precedent, albeit as original as Bryant's railway would be, was the Haytor Granite Tramway of 1820, which moved granite ten miles across Dartmoor

29. James W. Skehan, *Roadside Geology of Massachusetts* (Missoula, MT: Mountain Press Publishing Company, 2001), pp. 52, 183–88.

30. For a contemporary example, see for instance, Emerson Davis, *The Half Century* (Boston: Tappan and Whittemore, 1851), p. 205, "The first railroad in the United States was constructed at Quincy, Massachusetts." Waldemar Kaempffert, ed., *A Popular History of American Invention* (New York: Charles Scribner's Sons, 1924), vol. 1, p. 7; Susan Wilson, *Boston Sights and Insights* (Boston: Beacon Press, 1994), p. 34.

to a canal on south-west England's Devonshire coast along L-shaped granite rails. Steam locomotives had been operating commercially in Britain since 1812, and the Darlington–Stockton service that opened in September 1825 carried forty tons of coal along twenty-six miles of T-section iron rails bedded on stone sleepers (ties). Americans could not travel by steam train until 1830, although the Leiper Railroad began moving granite for Philadelphia's curbstones in 1811, fourteen years before Bryant's Granite Railway. Thomas Leiper, a no-nonsense Scottish-American, simply used existing British railroad technology, which consisted of the kind of iron rails on wooden sleepers that would look familiar today; a single oxen walking between the rails easily pulled a loaded wagon downhill from Leiper's quarry to a wharf a mile away, then tugged the empty wagon back up to the quarry.

fig. 16: Gridley Bryant, ca. 1834

To fund the undertaking, Bryant approached Thomas Handasyd Perkins, by far the wealthiest of the BHMA's directors at that time, and one of the most entrepreneurial. Like his fellow director Amos Lawrence, Perkins was eager to increase his investments in what he knew would soon be America's booming industrial revolution, and here was a marvelous opportunity. He could tell that for Bryant and Willard their motivation was not any desire for profit but rather the challenges of the engineering, the creativity of their craft, and the fulfillment of what historians would later call the American Dream. If the quarry contained as much top-quality granite as Bryant intimated, if Willard could assemble a skilled workforce to process it, and if there was an efficient way to ship it to Boston year round then Perkins might be able to corner Boston's growing market for building stone. On 5 January 1826, Perkins; Lawrence; William Sullivan, an BHMA director; David Moody, who owned the Boston Iron Company and gristmills at the Mill Dam; Willard; and Bryant petitioned Massachusetts

General Court for a charter to establish the Granite Rail Way Company. Perkins owned the bulk of the shares, and later acquired all the capital. Willard and Bryant would have owned 1 or 2 percent, as it was common practice to make part of the remuneration for architects, engineers, and supervisors contingent on the project's success.[31]

Also on 5 January, canal developers presented a proposal to the General Court, drawn up by Loammi Baldwin Jr., to connect Boston Harbor to the Hudson River, the latter being navigable to the Midwest via the recently completed Erie Canal. Baldwin's ambitious scheme called for a canal tunnel in the Berkshires (where the Hoosac railroad tunnel opened in 1875 after long delays) to connect North Adams to the Deerfield River, and it highlights the commercial rivalries between states during the Early Republic. Senators were in favor of establishing a railway, and they passed the bill for engrossment on 18 February, but it met stiff opposition in the House, primarily from members with stakes in the Middlesex Canal. So new and unsettling was the concept of rail transportation (newspapers could not decide whether it was a rail way, a rail-way or a railway) that legislators split into rival parties. Suddenly excited by a technology they had previously ignored, the railway party was soon dreaming of a statewide network of granite rails, while the canal party worried they would lose investors for their canal expansion projects. After Representatives David Simmons, John Taylor, and Nathaniel Denny drew up an amended version on 25 February, and Perkins lobbied hard for its passage, the bill passed by a slender majority on 28 February.[32]

An indication not only of the capital that men like Perkins were prepared to risk in the Granite Railway but also of the profits they intended to make, is that over the next year Bryant would spend $100,000 ($8 million) to construct three miles of track furnished with rolling stock and build a wharf. Instead of running his railway east, past existing quarries, to Brackett's Wharf in the town of Quincy, Bryant chose a somewhat more practical route running due north to the Neponset River, which also meant that the other quarrymen would not benefit. As soon as it was warm enough for construction to begin, a gang of 150 workers began clearing and grading the route, and laying the tracks. After descending a steep inclined plane below the quarry (fig. 18), the track would fall gradually, until it reached a 1,500-foot wharf, which another gang of workers was building at an elbow in the Neponset, just upstream of the present-day Granite Bridge. Bryant's system incorporated stone sleepers, spaced eight feet apart and laid on foundations deep enough to be frost proof, which supported pine rails (Bryant later replaced these with granite rails) one foot thick and six inches wide, set to a five-foot gauge. On top of the rail went a two inch oak capping, and a strap-iron strip three inches wide and a quarter of an inch thick, secured in place by

---

31. Wheildon, *Solomon Willard*, p. 114; Brayley, *Granite Industry*, vol. 1, p. 42. Moody co-owned the iron company with Horace Gray and Samuel Dow Jr.

32. Petition, *Boston Commercial Gazette*, 9 January 1826, p. 4, House, id., 27 February 1826, p. 2, and 2 March 1826, p. 2; *The First Railroad in America: A History of the Origin and Development of the Granite Railway at Quincy, Massachusetts* (Quincy, MA: Granite Railway Company, 1926), p. 10.

counter-sunk iron nails. Gravel spread between the rails provided a firm purchase for draught animals.[33]

fig. 17: Bunker Hill Quarry, with the Granite Railway running to the Neponset River, ca. 1827

Bryant designed a wooden and iron car with a built-in lifting engine (fig. 19), which Boston mechanic Phinehas Dow supplied for $718 ($57,700) apiece. Four wheels six-feet tall with flanged iron rims to fit the rails ran in iron bearings bolted beneath a stout timber frame. An integral winch could raise or lower four chains attached by eyebolts to the corners of a detachable wood and iron skid. With the skid on the ground, workers lifted a granite block onto it with a derrick, backed the car over the skid, attached the chains, and then winched up the block so that it just cleared the ground. This arrangement would safely carry a six-ton load, while two cars coupled together doubled the capacity. Additional cars with smaller wheels, hitched

33. William Churchill Edwards, *Historic Quincy, Massachusetts* (Quincy, MA: City of Quincy, 1957), pp. 129, 131.

to the end of the train, held blocks that workers could manhandle; an entire train typically carried ten to fifteen tons of granite. Because the downhill grade was never less than thirteen feet to the mile, when Bryant conducted a test run on 7 October 1826, he found that a single horse could pull three cars carrying sixteen tons of granite—an all-up weight of twenty-one tons—the three miles to the Neponset River. Two or three horses were necessary to haul the empty train back up the final steep sections where the grade was sixty-six feet to the mile, and a full team of eight for the 315-foot-long inclined plane, which rose the last eighty-four feet to the quarry itself.[34]

fig. 18: the inclined plane, as it appeared in 1924, adapted for a truck; Bryant's original rail bed, with central channel for the endless chain and its guide pulleys, is to the left of the new track

By the time he declared the railway operational on 27 March 1827, there were stables for the horses, cottages for the workers, a blacksmith's shop, and sheds for stores and equipment. Bryant had designed and installed a turntable at the foot of the quarry, a counterbalanced swing platform to tip the cars onto the inclined plane, and an endless chain mechanism that ran around the inclined plane to brake descending and ascending cars. He would later add a branch line to another quarry connected by a set of moveable points (a switch). Yankee inventiveness, it seemed, could surmount every technical hurdle. Given that he worked everything out from scratch and had to produce his own rolling stock, it was a remarkable achievement to complete the project inside twelve months. Bryant, Willard, and their workers even found the time and energy to erect a celebratory forty-foot-high granite obelisk at the top of the quarry.[35]

---

34. Ibid.; test run, in *Boston Daily Advertiser*, cited in the *Baltimore Patriot*, 13 October 1826, p. 2.
35. *First Railroad*, pp. 13–14.

fig. 19: replica of the railway car designed by Bryant and built by Dow

In June 1827, two hundred members of the Massachusetts legislature, in the company of the Granite Railway and BHMA directors, embarked from Boston at 3:00 AM aboard a steamer for a tour of the new railway. Even though the dignitaries had to hike several miles when a bridge over the Neponset River blocked the steamship's passage, newspapers could still report that, "the excursion was highly interesting and gratifying." Over the following months, so many sightseers came to marvel at Bryant's achievement that an enterprising tavern keeper opened a lodging house close to where the railway tracks crossed the road from Boston. Daniel Webster came to inspect the railway, but was unable to grasp its physics, believing for many years that railways could never be a practical proposition in New England because frost on the rails would render them useless. Throughout his life, Webster retained an ambiguity about technological progress. He lobbied the federal government to invest in the South Carolina Canal and Railroad Company, and by the late 1830s he was using trains routinely to speed his trips to the Capitol, yet he complained to friends that "the clatter of railroads" disturbed the quiet of the countryside. Webster might have lacked Bryant's mechanical touch, yet both men seem to have appreciated that innovation was a fundamental adjunct to Yankee industriousness.[36]

---

36. *Essex Register*, 11 June 1827, p. 3; Webster at Quincy, in *First Railroad*, p. 16; and railroads, in Claude Moore Fuess, *Daniel Webster* (Boston: Little, Brown, and Company, 1930), vol. 1, p. 362, vol. 2, pp. 28–29; "clatter," from

A satisfying life, Bryant maintained, required the development of "skill, industry, and energy." As related in a third-party memoir, his story—like Willard's—was poor boy goes to the big city and, through hard work, honesty, and thrift, makes good. From his birthplace at Scituate on the coast south of Quincy, where he was "generally at the head of the young urchins," he apprenticed at age fifteen to a leading Boston builder. Within four years, he took charge of the builder's business, and in 1819 aged twenty-one, started on his own, winning his first major contract to build St. Paul's Church. Granite construction fascinated him, as it did Willard, probably because there could be no more difficult a stone to work and handle. While building the U.S. Bank in 1823, Bryant invented a portable derrick to maneuver the massive blocks into place. Believing that innovations should be for the greater good of society, Bryant never took out any patents. Proud that he spent his life "constantly and usefully employed upon works, in which self was always subordinated to the public good," in old age Bryant was nevertheless bitter that he would die in debt.[37]

Yankee Industry, Yankee Pride

When Bryant opened the railway in March 1827, it was not a day too soon for Willard, who was frustrated by what he saw as avoidable delays. Eager to lay the Monument's first blocks in spring 1826, he had been in two minds about the railway, to the extent of advising the BHMA to take no part in the scheme. Nevertheless, Bryant's railway proved to be of crucial significance. Apart from the fact that Willard could blame the Railway Company for any delays, now that the railway was running reliably it would dramatically expedite deliveries. Most importantly, the interval gave Willard the chance to experiment with hewing and finishing the blocks at the quarry prior to shipment. As with the BHMA's directors, Willard seems to have had no qualms against using prison labor to hew granite, and he probably agreed with the prevailing view that hard labor reformed unproductive citizens. Rather, his issues with the prison were over the reliability of supply and the quality of the product for the price charged, which he suspected was inflated.

For someone who moved slowly—according to legend, he never ran—Willard had been as industrious on the quarrying side of the business during 1826 as Bryant had been with railway construction. He had purchased $2,000 ($160,000) of tools and equipment, including hammers, bars, wedges, ropes, blocks, derricks, and jacks, along with several items that mechanics had fabricated to his own design. On cleared ground adjacent to the quarry, he had built a boarding house for the men, and various outbuildings. Work crews had graded access roads and carted away the topsoil from the quarry site. Once he realized the quarry's potential to yield top-quality stone, he settled on seventy-eight courses for the shaft of the obelisk (about 2.6 feet per course), and the longest block size possible to give a geometrically pleasing effect, which meant

---

Clarence Mondale, "Daniel Webster and Technology," *American Quarterly*, 14:1 (Spring 1962), fn. 13, p. 45.

37. C.B. Stuart, *A Brief Memoir of Gridley Bryant, Civil Engineer* (Boston: Henry W. Dutton & Son, 1871), pp. 4, 3, 12. Bryant died in 1867, aged seventy-seven, in his Scituate hometown.

that the corner blocks for the lowest courses would be 12.0 x 2.6 x 2.6 feet (81 cubic feet), and weigh about seven tons. As the summer dragged into fall, and the railway was obviously far from finished, Willard erected a large, open shed to provide shelter, and trained a crew to dress the stones on site.[38]

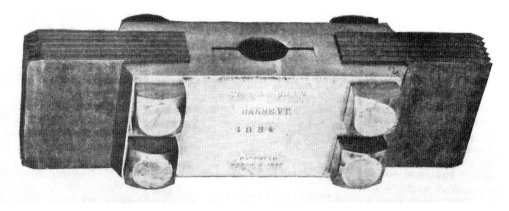

fig. 20: Trow & Holden patented bush hammer, No. 2, 9 lb, 6-cut, $5.50

For each block, Willard drew an accurate, three-dimensional plan, from which a patternmaker made wooden templates set to the exact angle for each face. A combination of derricks, wooden rollers, and iron pulling and lifting jacks maneuvered the rough, oversized block to the workplace, and raised it off the ground at a convenient height. Blows from a long, two-handed peening hammer gradually chipped away major irregularities; further work with a lump hammer and chisel brought the block closer to the template. To dimension the block, and begin the work of smoothing the external face—or faces, for corner blocks—the hammerer took an iron straight-edge (a strip fifteen feet long and four inches wide, with a knife-edge filed straight to an engineer's reference plate) and by chiseling a groove, gradually let it into the surface of the block, corner-to-corner, until the straight-edge met a mark on the template. Repeating this process across the other diagonal and at right angles every foot or so, created a grid of grooves, all set to exactly the same depth. A tool called a bush hammer, the head of which consisted of a grid of pyramidal points (resembling a meat tenderizer), smoothed the surface by crushing the crystal structure of the stone. Working in between the demarcated areas, the hammerer struck rhythmic blows—heavy at first, then lighter as the work progressed—leaving the surface striated yet increasingly flat and smooth, until the grooves just disappeared. Bush hammerheads came in varying grades of coarseness depending on the finish required. A patent hammer (fig. 20), invented around 1830, improved on the basic bush principle; a stack of metal blades sandwiched between clamps formed the hammerhead, which made regular sharpening far more convenient, while varying the number and thickness of blades changed the fineness of the finish. There were various techniques for coarse buffing, if required, such as rubbing wet beach sand over the granite with blocks of hardwood (the only practical way to

38. Wheildon, *Solomon Willard*, pp. 180–82.

polish granite being by machine). It took one of Willard's skilled hammerers about a day and a half to dress one of these large blocks.[39]

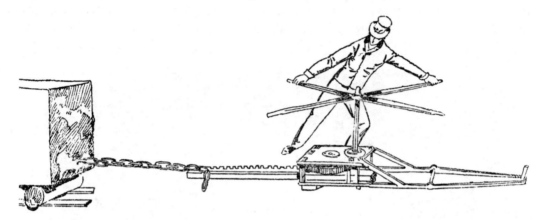

fig. 21: pulling jack

Willard conducted experiments to ascertain the cost per finished cubic foot of stone, which he found to be 9.5¢. Even after adding 10¢ a cubic foot for transportation—the Granite Railway's fee, plus shipping to Devens's Wharf and cartage from the wharf to the Monument—the cost of 19.5¢ per cubic foot, or $15.80 ($1,260) for one of the big blocks, was still a quarter of the going commercial rate for stone from Charlestown Prison. Eager to fulfill his commitment to the contract that Perkins had made with the BHMA to supply thirty tons of granite each working day to the wharf in Charlestown, Willard began hiring and training more workers. He set up five departments, three of which were at the Quincy end of the operation: for quarrying, there was one master quarryman, five common hands, three capstan men, and one blacksmith. For hammering, there were thirty hammerers, two blacksmiths, and a patternmaker. There is no record of the personnel for the carrying department, but over and above the Granite Railway's staff, there were probably two or three workers at Quincy for moving blocks from the quarry to the hammering shed, and then supervising the safe handling of the blocks on and off the rail cars, making a total workforce at the quarry of about forty-five men.[40]

Sloops of eighty or so tons, with oversized deck timbers and uprated cargo booms, handled inter-coastal stone delivery. Weighted down with a cargo of granite blocks, their gunwales were so close to the waterline that they had to scuttle to port at the first sign of stormy weather. Whenever Perkins's Granite Rail Company sold granite out of state, as it would do increasingly in the 1830s, it relied on commercial sloops, but for its Boston trade, it stuck to its vertical-integration business model by investing in the latest technology. Perkins spent $2,000 for a pair of barges, ideally suited for moving granite blocks loaded by shore-mounted derricks, and, to pull the barges, he paid

39. For an account of traditional stone working, see Harley J. McKee, *Introduction to Early American Masonry: Stone, Brick, Mortar, and Plaster* (Washington, DC: National Trust for Historic Preservation, 1973), chap. 1.

40. Wheildon, *Solomon Willard*, p. 152. Workforce at its peak in November 1827; numbers for July 1827 were twenty-seven men at the Quincy end of the operation.

$6,500 ($520,000) for *Robin Hood*, a steamboat, probably of the center-wheel type. *Robin Hood* gave reliable service, despite killing Jacob Lowell Jr., its captain, who in 1829 was below deck checking on the engine when some change slipped out of his pocket; as he bent down to retrieve the money, the crank of the main shaft crushed his skull. Early steamers were crude and troublesome affairs. When *Robin Hood* needed a refit in 1830, Perkins contracted towing to the owners of *Ousatonic*, a ninety-ton steamer. A few days later, while her crew slept at a mooring in Boston Harbor, a leaky cooking stovepipe started a fire. Firefighters managed to save her from total destruction, but only a year after a rebuild, another fire, this time from the boiler, proved terminal.[41]

Once a block had arrived at Devens's Wharf in Charlestown, a derrick swung it from the barge to a sturdy wooden cart, which multiple teams of oxen pulled over a paved road that zigzagged up Breed's Hill to the work site. Willard had two more departments, of hoisters and masons, to build the Monument. Working under Almoran Holmes, a seaman turned master mechanic, were three common hands, a foreman, and a rigger, who employed a combination of jacks, winches, derricks, and shears to maneuver the blocks. To lift the blocks into position, Holmes, devised a hoist that fitted into the Monument's center cavity (fig. 22). Its fifty-foot gaff covered a hundred-foot circle yet could lower an eight-ton block—as Willard put it—"with ease and grace." Before the industrial production of steel wire in the mid-1830s, lifting heavy weights with pulleys depended on the quality of rope spun from manila, hemp, or sisal fibers. A new, dry, two-inch manila rope with a thirteen-ton breaking strain would safely lift ten tons, but the same rope when old and wet might pose a danger at three tons. In practice, ropes for granite work were from four to six inches in diameter, and even when oversized to such an extent, there was always a high degree of subjective danger. Thick ropes, one at each corner, kept tension on the central shaft of Holmes's hoist, and served to stabilize the staging (fig. 23); anchoring these ropes as the obelisk rose, were large granite blocks. Staging consisted of wooden planks, but while there appears to have been a guardrail around the inner shaft, there was nothing to protect workers from falling over the face. In September 1828, E. Wetherall, a forty-seven-year-old father from Pembroke, tumbled off the staging to his death. Holmes himself would not live to see the Monument finished. Four years after Wetherall's fall, he was supervising the use of a diving bell suspended from a derrick to recover granite blocks from a collapsed section of Boston's Long Wharf. As he tested the bell for air tightness, its six-inch rope snapped, breaking the leg of an assistant, toppling the derrick onto an elderly bystander, and taking Holmes to the seabed. Earlier, when someone had asked him if he was not concerned for his safety, he explained that the rope would bear a far heavier weight.[42]

---

41. For sloops, see Barbara H. Erkkila, *Hammers on Stone: A History of Cape Ann Granite* (Gloucester, MA: Peter Smith, 1987), pp. 27–38. Brayley, *Granite Industry*, vol. 1, p. 55; Lowell, from *Newport Mercury*, 2 May 1829, p. 2; *Ousatonic*, from *Salem Gazette*, 27 April 1830, p. 2, and 1 July 1831, p. 3.

42. Willard, *Plans and Sections*, p. 23; Wetherall, in *Christian Watchman*, 9:37 (12 September 1828), p. 147; Holmes, in *Farmers' Cabinet*, 28 September 1832, p. 3, and *New Hampshire Sentinel*, 4 October 1832, p. 2. E.H.

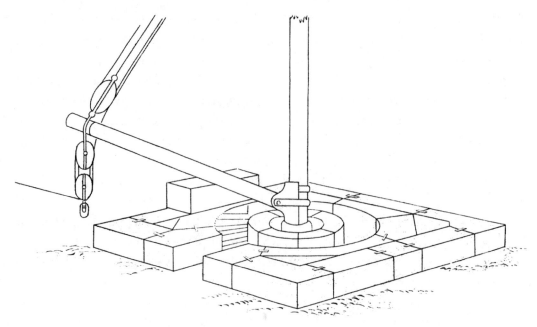

fig. 22: Holmes's hoist installed in the first course; note method of construction

Willard's primary contractor was James Sullivan Savage, under whom served master mason Charles Pratt, three journeymen, an apprentice mason, a blacksmith, and a tender. Savage and his department of eight had spent much of 1827 digging out the Monument's foundations to a depth of about fifteen feet, pounding a thick bed of crushed granite and gravel into the underlying glacial hardpan, and setting out six courses of massive granite blocks, twelve feet below grade. When one of the facing blocks arrived at the hill, they would rectify any transit damage, verify the block's dimensions, and sit it in position to check and adjust its alignment with a theodolite, water levels, and setting wedges. They would then install it on a bed of mortar, and tie it to the adjacent blocks with fourteen-inch-long flat iron straps with turned down ends, let into the granite about half an inch (visible in fig. 22). Similar in attitude and temperament, and with a shared vision of the Monument's republican purpose, Savage and Willard strove for perfection in every aspect of the construction. Instead of using straight lime mortar, they mixed in Springfield hydraulic cement, a recent invention; slag (from iron smelting), which reacts with water to impart strength over time; and iron filings, which oxidize as the mortar cures thereby removing air bubbles, strengthening as well as waterproofing the mortar. Because they wanted the Monument to stand for eternity, which meant worrying about earthquakes, they originally specified—in addition to the iron straps—iron dowels, or Lewis clamps, to lock the blocks vertically as well as horizontally, but after the first four courses they abandoned these as excessive. By the end of 1828, they had installed fourteen courses of stone, and the Monument stood at thirty-seven feet four inches. In under thirty-six months, using only hand tools, Willard's workforce that reached fifty-nine men at its peak had

Cameron, "Of Yankee Granite: An Account of the Building of Bunker Hill Monument," *Technology Review* (June 1952), p. 438, suggested that the four tensioning/stabilizing guys were of chain rather than rope.

quarried about 5,000 tons of granite, hammered 4,400 square feet to a smooth finish, and erected 2,287 tons at the site. They had, moreover, built their own facilities, developed their own equipment, and taken every technical challenge in stride.[43]

Whether from the scale of its challenge, the simplicity of its design, or the heroic patriotism it represented, the Monument embodied the soul of Yankeeness. For Willard, especially, its essential purity fired his imagination to the point that it became an obsession. Its lines had to be perfect, its faces unblemished. Its executives, he wrote in one report, ought to be "competent managers, who were zealous," preferably to the extent of "performing the service gratuitously," as he had done. When the BHMA's directors insisted on paying him $1,000 for his services, he gave the check to the Monument fund. Money for the Monument, he believed, should be from Bostonians, and freely given. Willard "always disliked the plan of sending to foreign places," such as "Southern cities," to "beg subscriptions," because doing so would expose "our own meanness," thereby "disgracing the work on which we are engaged." Above all, those who created the Monument had to be as moral as they were thoroughly American. Willard, and Savage who was also a teetotaler, forbade the drinking of alcohol by anyone working on the Monument. Willard did advocate paying top wages for the best men—common hands earned $1.50 a day, and even apprentices earned $1, about twice the going rate—although in return he had high expectations. He was proud that he had employed "no graduate of the penitentiary, or foreigner." All his workers were thoroughgoing "Americans," by which he meant they were old-stock locals, or at worst, "natives of neighboring states." Some were relatives of veterans of the Battle of Bunker Hill and had therefore inherited "a genuine spirit for the work." In those few instances when a master had sought to "tyrannize" a subordinate, Willard had issued reprimands, for they were engaged in a "work of patriotism, where all should be on equal terms." There was an "uncommon degree of harmony among them," he wrote, a "spirit and economy" about their work. Harmony, spirit, and economy were central elements of the Yankee mystique that seemed to flow from Willard through all those involved in the quarrying, hammering, and installation of granite blocks for the Monument, which is perhaps why they gave of their best.[44]

Willard's essential Yankeeness left its mark on the physical presence of the Monument in two important respects: First, there is no plinth. Horatio Greenough's original design included a pedestal twenty feet high. While the Board of Artists judged this excessive, they always had the expectation that the shaft of the obelisk would sit on some sort of architectural feature. Quite naturally, therefore, Loammi Baldwin's report of July 1825 specified a "platform" four feet high, extending twenty feet from each face, "of broad, well-hammered stones, resting on foundation walls" six feet deep, with a line item in the estimate of $10,900. Yet from the outset of his tenure as

43. Construction details, from George E. Ellis, *History of the Battle of Bunker's (Breed's) Hill, on June 17, 1775* (Boston: Lockwood, Brooks, & Company, 1875), p. 140; Ellis listed cinders rather than slag; for the benefits of iron filings, see Cameron, "Of Yankee Granite," p. 438.

44. Wheildon, *Solomon Willard*, pp. 184–85, 145.

architect and superintendent, Willard seems to have intended that there would be no such platform. Admittedly, Baldwin stated that construction of the platform should occur after completion of the obelisk, and the ground does slope gently away from the level of the lowest course, so it would have been possible to install a platform to Baldwin's specifications. Still, Willard made no provision for the platform's foundations when he laid out the foundations for the obelisk itself, and the natural plane of the hill matches the base level of the obelisk, not the proposed base of a four-foot plinth. All his other designs, furthermore, demonstrated the same inherent simplicity, as with the U.S. Branch Bank and the Suffolk County Court House (1836), where the columns stood directly on the flat entryway or stylobate, as in Athenian temples. Second, the size, fit, and finish of the blocks. Once he realized the quality of Quincy granite, Willard specified the largest possible block size, meaning that the longest blocks for the lower courses were thirteen feet long. He then insisted on the utmost precision for dimensioning the blocks, so that they abutted perfectly with minimal joint gaps, and he inspired a level of perfection among the hammerers that resulted in blocks with a beautifully flat surface.[45]

fig. 23: construction in progress, with staging, rigging, and hoist

45. Baldwin specified three steps—meaning there would be four rises—with a rise of eight inches topped by a granite slab, making "1 foot for top," in Warren, *Monument Association*, p. 189. Greenough to Morse, ca. April 1832, in *Letters of Horatio Greenough, American Sculptor*, ed. Nathan Wright (Madison: University of Wisconsin Press, 1972), p. 114.

Because of these two features of Willard's design and construction, the Monument appears to be a solid shaft of stone rising up out of the earth, as if a hidden organic force were impelling it. Indeed, Greenough was appalled when he first saw the finished product, writing to Samuel F.B. Morse that it started "sheer from the dirt like a spear of asparagus." From a distance, the Monument has a unity of form, a harmony that becomes sublime once a close inspection has revealed its composite structure. What Willard had created, perhaps unconsciously, was so basic, so elemental that Greenough failed to appreciate the brilliance as well as the power of its symbolism. In the hands of the Yankees who built it, the Monument exemplified the singular character of American republicanism—*E pluribus unum*, out of many, one—it became, as G.W. Warren put it so well, "a fit type of the national unity." Through the selfless force of their own labors, Willard, Bryant, Savage, and their Yankee work crews adapted and harmonized its many separate blocks, so that its "grandeur as a single object" far exceeded the sum of its parts.[46]

And yet, those same blank granite walls seemed to be an affront to another pillar of Americanism: individual expression, which is probably why an artist like Greenough condemned what was after all his own concept. An object so monstrously contrived from a material so impossible to manipulate as granite was just unnatural. Willard had defined the physical form of the Monument for the generations to come, but simply because he had made it so invitingly plain, disparate groups of Americans during periods of sociopolitical change would seek to possess it as their own. Possession might involve marking the Monument—typically in a figurative sense, although in one case by projecting photographs and in another by spraying graffiti onto its surface—or duplicating its image elsewhere, whether on paper, in film, or as a physical copy. Possession has inevitably meant appropriating the Monument's existing symbolism, as well as adding new meaning. Would-be possessors have had to reconcile the Monument's republican message with its austere appearance: Does it represent a *tabula rasa*, a blank slate primed to absorb—and reflect back—the rich, diverse experiences of an enlightened nation of immigrants? Do its rigid, almost brutal lines demand a strict conformity to predetermined national values? If the latter then what might those values be and from where do they derive their moral authority? Was the Monument a man-made, skyward pointing beacon of the directors' achievements, or did it operate in reverse, like a celestial antenna, beaming down Providence's guiding hand? Before the Monument was even finished, indeed, because the BHMA's directors became incapable of finishing it, Americans began arguing over these questions, at the heart of which was the issue of national identity: just who were they, these citizens of the Early Republic? Sarah Josepha Hale, the woman who was primarily responsible for raising the funds to allow its completion, was confident that she knew the answer.

---

46. Warren, *Monument Association*, p. 376.

3. SARAH HALE: BIBLICAL NATIONALISM

Edward Everett's fundraising circular of September 1824 had promised a classical column of Chelmsford granite that would be the tallest in the world at 220 feet, and he had estimated "with great accuracy" a price of $37,000. At that time, none of the Bunker Hill Monument Association (BHMA)'s directors even knew if what they proposed was feasible, let alone what it would cost. There was no heavier construction material than granite, no material harder to form into blocks, and no precedent for lifting such blocks to a height of two-hundred-plus feet. Not even the columns of first-century Rome—Trajan's or Marcus Aurelius's, built with the assistance of thousands of slaves from relatively soft marble—had exceeded 125 feet. Roman engineers employed huge wooden lifting towers, whose size increased exponentially with height, and they erected their columns on thick foundations of concrete, a material that awaited the reinvention and industrial-scale production of Portland cement in the 1840s. Pervading the directors' thinking was an astonishing self-assurance, as if once men of their caliber had decided on a particular enterprise then it must happen, and that was the end of it. Even more remarkably, Solomon Willard's team had embarked on the impossible task, raising the Monument to a height of thirty-seven feet with what appeared to be consummate ease. A strange, self-reinforcing calculus had somehow balanced the disparate halves of the equation. Separated from the day-to-day realities of manual labor by an unfathomable gulf, the directors took the building process for granted; for their part, Willard, Gridley Bryant, Almoran Holmes, James Savage, and their crews were professional artisan-mechanics whose Yankee pride would not let them fail. With each course the Monument rose, directors and builders alike received proof that they were right all along. What made the equation work was the physical presence of the Monument, and yet the achievement was hubristic.[1]

By the fall of 1828, the BHMA had raised an impressive $54,400 in subscriptions and received a grant of $7,000 from the General Court in lieu of stone hammered at the State Prison. Of this $61,000, they had spent $24,000 to buy the battle site and $5,400 on the grand ceremony to lay the cornerstone. Willard had invested $10,000 in construction equipment and facilities at the Bunker Hill Quarry, and he had paid out $46,500 for wages, transportation, and materials. To fund the shortfall, the BHMA had borrowed $22,400 ($1.8 million) against a lien on the land. Subscriptions then slowed to a trickle, and the Suffolk Bank refused to advance any more cash. At a meeting in January 1829, the directors formally suspended quarrying and, after their annual meeting on 17 June, they discharged Willard. A fair assessment, in consideration of the work hidden below ground in the foundations, the development of the distant quarry, and so forth, would have been that the project was over half way toward completion. Subscribers as well as directors were nonetheless confused and disillusioned.

1. George Washington Warren, *The History of the Bunker Hill Monument Association During the First Century of the United States of America* (Boston: James R. Osgood and Company, 1877), p. 113; Lynne Lancaster, "Building Trajan's Column," *American Journal of Archaeology*, 103:3 (July 1999), pp. 419–39.

To the eye, a sixth of the Monument sheltered forlornly under rough timber cladding, the BHMA was deep in debt, and critics were snickering. A squat pile of stones made stubbier by a wooden cover was hardly a symbol of male potency, a fact not lost on other groups eager to challenge old-stock elites for their control over the new nation. Willard would eventually complete the obelisk, yet in order to overcome the nadir of 1829, as well as a worse crisis during the economic Panic of 1837, the directors had to accommodate other viewpoints.[2]

Those who fought over the unfinished Monument were part of a nationwide struggle to decide what it meant to be an American. While the War of 1812 had given a boost to American nationalism, it had also exposed national weakness, whether in transportation, fiscal policy, or military planning. It had demonstrated, moreover, that Jeffersonian producerism—an ideology centered on contented yeoman farmers producing small surpluses for export—was too dependent on European markets; perhaps government-subsidized factories protected by steep tariffs were necessary for the survival of the republican experiment. Debates over the decentralization of government, the inviolability of corporate charters, and the extent of democratization brought Andrew Jackson to the White House in 1828, ending single-party consensus politics and the so-called Era of Good Feelings. In Boston, BHMA directors bore the brunt of bad feelings. Their Federalism, as typified by Daniel Webster, exposed them to the Jacksonian populist critique of corrupt power and cronyism. Their close alliance with Freemasonry ensured they would be the natural target of Evangelical Presbyterians and the Anti-Masonic Party, despite Anti-Masonry's opposition to Jackson's Democratic Party. By constituting the BHMA as a gentlemen's club that held its meetings in taverns, they alienated women, reformers, and newcomers who sought inclusion in the American republic. A range of sociopolitical challenges, therefore, ensured that the directors would spend much of the 1830s refighting the Battle of Bunker Hill.

Yet when writer-editor Sarah Josepha Hale entered the contest for control of the Monument, and assembled the all-women group that ultimately raised the money to complete it, her motivation was not that of a feminist excluded from a man's world. On the contrary, she thought it was only fitting that the BHMA's directors were all men. Rather, Hale believed that women were the conservators of morality, so if the Monument was unfinished then it was because the men who were responsible for its construction had lost their way. Specifically, they had lost God's way, for Hale's morality came from the fire-and-brimstone prophecies of the Old Testament. Americans were latter-day Israelites in the Promised Land. They were increasing in numbers and prosperity because God had a mission for them, just as failure awaited them if they sinned. With her stress on education, harnessing of print culture, and promotion of the Monument's unifying spirit, Hale in many respects was a modern nationalist. And yet, she imagined her nation much as she thought Isaiah experienced the Kingdom of Israel 2,500 years earlier. A *biblical nationalism* infused her writings, just as it did the

---

2. Warren, *Monument Association*, pp. 113, 121, 165, 189, 198, 215.

speeches that Edward Everett and Daniel Webster, the leading orators of the Early Republic, gave in support of the Monument. Hale's father had fought in the War of Independence, a steady diet of romanticized war stories had nourished her childhood, and she had an eye for opportunities through which women could claim the moral high ground of Yankee society. These were all factors in Hale's preoccupation with finishing the Monument, although, for her, its greater significance would seem to have been in the Providential messages that she thought it could transmit to the developing nation.

Battling for the Monument

Since its convocation in 1823, BHMA directors had maintained their association's exclusivity, aligning its interests with the top tier of Bostonian society, and confining its fundraising to the immediate area. Even as they broadcast an appeal for funds that reached beyond the wards of the city via regional newspapers in February 1829, they projected a confident superiority as unshakable as the Monument's granite. It was on Bunker Hill, they claimed, that the Revolution was "really achieved," and that achievement had created "the only free government founded on the rights of the people" in the world. It was only proper, therefore, that they should erect "the temple to liberty" on the consecrated "holy ground" of Bunker Hill. Once complete, their monument would be "*the highest of the kind in the world*," they stressed, and "only below the height of the Egyptian Pyramids." So tall would it be that no traveler would ever again have to ask directions to the famous battleground. Built of "our Quincy granite," their monument would "endure until the foundations of the earth itself are shaken." Their descendants would have before them a "perpetual memorial" to the "virtues and valor of their ancestors," an ever-enduring reminder of the "price and the value of liberty." Yet despite knowing it would take over $60,000 ($5 million) to finish the job, their appeal for funds was as lacking in urgency as it was unpersuasive. Men of their status, they seemed to say, should never beg for money; their role was to explain the Monument's centrality to the national interest, after which contributions would arrive as if by their own volition. Contributions did not arrive; "there was no response," the BHMA's historian G.W. Warren admitted.[3]

Once the directors had accepted that the methods on which they had relied were no longer working, they began to understand the seriousness of the dilemma they now faced. Every month the Monument remained unfinished meant another interest payment to Suffolk Bank and another round of taunts from detractors. Broadening the scope of their fundraising, perhaps even to the extent of accommodating some of their critics, meant relinquishing the control they had guarded so closely for the prior six years. They also discovered that experimenting with alternative fundraising strategies was not necessarily the answer, as each innovative new effort only seemed to bring criticism from unexpected quarters. Attacks on and claims for possession of their

---

3. Published in several editions (for instance, the *New Bedford Mercury*, 20 February 1829, p. 1), cited in the *Salem Gazette*, 27 February 1829, p. 1, emphasis original; the full report is in Warren, *Monument Association*, pp. 235–37.

unfinished monument came from all sides, especially from abolitionists, Protestant moralists and pacifists, temperance advocates, nationalists, Irish Catholics, and Anti-Masons.

Abolitionists questioned in the simplest of terms how BHMA elites could celebrate liberty while ignoring slavery. Shortly after the cornerstone ceremony, L.D. Dewey wrote a letter to the *New-York Observer* on the plight of Haitians. "An extraordinary apathy," Dewey could not help but observe, existed in the minds of his fellow citizens. How could Americans "celebrate the great anniversary of our liberty, erect a Bunker Hill monument, feel the patriotic fire," and, like Daniel Webster, shout, "'Our country, our whole country, and nothing but our country,'" yet not blush at the fact that "two millions of our countrymen are slaves." A letter-writer to the *Genius of Universal Emancipation* (Mount Pleasant, Ohio, which William Lloyd Garrison was helping to edit), hypothesized the arrival from Haiti of a Black Marquis de Lafayette, who led American slaves to "glory, liberty, and independence," and then began erecting a monument to commemorate a great battle in which they had killed hundreds of whites; would Christian newspapers consider it a "'beneficent object,'" as they did the Bunker Hill Monument, and help to raise funds for it? Social activists who disagreed with the Monument's message sometimes threatened to carve—whether physically or metaphorically—their own agenda on its surface. An abolitionist writer in the *Boston Centinel* thought that if the Monument were to convey to future generations the correct views of "liberty, philanthropy, and glory of our country," then it should bear an inscription reading, "Fifty years subsequent to the Battle for Liberty, the Inhabitants of the United States were a FREE PEOPLE, Excepting TWO MILLIONS of Slaves, Whose condition had excited little sympathy, and for whose emancipation no national effort had ever been made!"[4]

Protestant moralists and pacifists, whose varied concerns all boiled down to the promotion of Christian ethics, were one of the most vocal groups to attack the Monument or seek to control its symbolism. An editorialist in the *New-England Magazine* cited the Monument to advance an argument for building more so-called common schools, which were ostensibly multi-denominational but in reality inculcated Protestant values. "Where religion did not supply the motive," the writer stressed, all initiatives were doomed to failure, just like Charlestown's Monument that "goes up very slow" because it was too "secular." Writing in the *Christian Register*, "B" heaped castigation on the Monument, beginning with the inroads made on the "sober and industrious habits of the community" by the "public relaxation and excitement" of the cornerstone-laying celebration. There could scarcely be imagined a "greater instrument of public demoralization than political holidays." Idleness was the mother of vice, "B" reminded his readers. An occasion of such "dazzling influence of military pomp," with so much "temptation to sensual indulgence," would irresistibly corrupt

---

4. Dewey, in the *Christian Watchman* (Boston), 6:33 (22 July 1825), p. 130; "Consistency," writing from Minot, Maine, *Genius of Universal Emancipation*, 1:6 (September 1830), p. 84; *Centinel*, cited in the *Christian Register* (Boston), 4:34 (27 August 1825), p. 138.

"congregated multitudes." Children, carried to the parade by their mothers, had witnessed "scenes of fascinating riot" and delighted in "sensual pleasure," so they would consequently grow up with a love of indolence, show, and sensuality. Celebrating such a "decided defeat" as the Battle of Bunker Hill would expose Americans to the derision of the world; monuments, moreover, wasted money that should go instead to bible societies, missions, schools, and hospitals. "B" leveled much of his ire at the martial spirit that he thought the Monument symbolized, along with actual fortifications, navies, and military establishments, which were all "glaring violations of Gospel precepts, provokers of renewed hostilities, fruitful nurseries of impiety, violence, and vice." By renewed hostilities, "B" meant the War of 1812, in which "it pleased Divine providence to chastise us" with another defeat.[5]

"Reflector," in a letter to the *Christian Register*, similarly argued that the Monument was "inconsistent with the genuine spirit of Christianity," because it "perpetuated unfriendly prejudices" and exulted in feats of bloodshed. All those who fell at Bunker Hill, "Reflector" observed, were "brethren of the same nation." Redcoats faithfully discharged their duty by obeying the orders of their superiors, just as the rebels thought they were doing their duty by killing their redcoat brothers. Such was "the power of military delusion." There were also pacifist critics who implicated their fellow Christians in "war-degeneracy." Rev. William Allen, president of Bowdoin College, looked back in 1840 at the failure of numerous fundraising schemes to complete a monument to commemorate "mutual butchery between nominal Christians," and which was "part and parcel of the war-system," a "system of blood" sanctioned by church members and ministers. Allen was pleased because the Monument's unfinished state demonstrated "a reproach to a waning spirit of war."[6]

Temperance advocates, as did many groups hoping to claim the Monument, exhibited mixed feelings. On one hand, there were newspaper reports of hedonistic BHMA directors quaffing numerous toasts at celebratory dinners, while on the other hand Willard and Savage were ascetic Yankees who only hired so-called total abstinence men. In 1828, when directors realized they had to widen their appeal, they advertised that their fundraising would henceforth be by "the fruits of entire abstinence," which thrilled the editor at Utica's *Western Recorder*. *Fessenden's Silk Manual and Practical Farmer*, an innovative though short-lived Boston publication by an abolitionist legislator and friend of Daniel Webster, reprinted a proposal that would solve the BHMA's financial difficulties: at every celebration in New England, the usual toast, "To the Heroes of Bunker Hill," would be drunk with "pure sparkling spring water," and a plate passed round for donations that could not be more than one dollar. Still, temperance, as well as the Monument, could be the butt of jokes, as when popular

---

5. "Common Schools," *New-England Magazine* (September 1832), p, 204; "B," "Bunker Hill Monument," *Christian Register*, 4:25 (25 June 1825), p. 100.

6. "Reflector," *Christian Register*, 5:21 (27 May 1826), p. 82; William Allen, "War-Degeneracy of the Church: American Examples," *Advocate of Peace* (Washington), 3:25 (3 October 1840), pp. 199–200, also in the *Liberator* (Boston) and the *Christian Reflector* (Boston).

actor Henry J. Finn in a performance at Boston's newly opened but always loss-making Greek Revival-style Tremont Theatre asked, "Why is the Bunker Hill Monument like a Temperance Committee?" Because, he answered, "it is not allowed to get high."[7]

Nationalists seized on the Monument's unfinished state to question the manliness and honor of New Englanders, and to argue, by extension, that the Monument should be a national rather than a local endeavor. Cincinnatians, the increasingly confident beneficiaries of westward expansion, new canals, and earlier land grants to Revolutionary War veterans, probably agreed with the *Cincinnati Mirror*'s editor in 1836, when he called the Monument "the folly of its projectors—and a disgrace to the citizens of New England, in general, and of Massachusetts in particular." From Buffalo, the *Literary Inquirer* observed that "our Yankee brethren" had been "less persevering and energetic" in building the Monument than the "general character" of Yankees implied. At the *Southern Rose Bud*, Charleston, South Carolina, a sarcastic editor could not understand all the rush and "nervous anxiety" of northerners to complete the Monument. St. Peter's Basilica, after all, had taken 120 years to finish. "Why not let a century put forth its prospective hand, and lay stone after stone upon its noble base?" A leisurely approach would ensure the Monument would be "more the work of the people," and less a product of "the forcing system," an allusion to northern bankers and industrialists. "Literatus," a writer for the *Southern Literary Journal*, also of Charleston, referred to the unfinished Monument as a "pile," efforts to resuscitate its construction as a "'Forlorn Hope,'" its half-erect profile as an "impotent conclusion," and considered that "an air of ridicule" had soured the whole affair.[8]

New Englanders, like a writer in Boston's *American Monthly Magazine*, were acutely conscious of southerners' "reproach." Bostonians felt the shame of a once-proud city, and they especially felt "the shame of the Pilgrim land" in which they all reverently thanked God that they were born. Yet the fame of Joseph Warren, the writer insisted, was the inheritance of all. Sectional divisions, the writer wanted Americans to understand, were undermining national greatness, so "the reproach must be national." It was of no concern to Britons whether Lord Nelson died in northern or southern seas; nor did the deaths in exile of Themistocles or Napoleon make them any less Greek or French. Americans owed everything—their very essence as Americans—to the Revolutionary War. They must honor heroes like Warren because they were "the first martyrs, in the holiest of human causes." Completing the Monument was not about perpetuating the spirit of war but rather "the spirit of religious and civil freedom." Ages hence, the writer assured all Americans, whenever wanderers from any clime approached "these Pilgrim shores," their first association would be the Monument. From afar, they would see "the sunshine lingering upon its lofty summit," they would

7. *Western Recorder* (Utica, NY), 5:200 (29 April 1828), p. 70; *Fessenden's Silk Manual and Practical Farmer* (Boston), 2:3 (July 1836), p. 37; *Spirit of the Times* (New York), 8:31 (15 September 1838), p. 248.

8. *Cincinnati Mirror, and Western Gazette of Literature, Science, and the Arts*, 5:15 (7 May 1836), p. 114; *Literary Inquirer* (Buffalo, NY), 1:15 (16 July 1833), p. 116; *Southern Rose Bud* (Charleston, SC), 2:7 (12 October 1833), p. 26; "Literatus," "Modern Improvements," *Southern Literary Journal and Magazine of Arts* (Charleston, SC), 1:4 (June 1837), p. 320.

see sunlight "playing among the folds of its starry banner," and they would remember those who fought for liberty and those who built the Monument as Americans, united as one. Still, there were plenty of New Englanders, particularly those with the most fervent religious convictions, who found the new spirit of nationalism disturbing. A writer to the *Boston Recorder and Religious Telegraph* argued that the Monument would foster an ungodly national pride in warmongering instead of a "proper remembrance of our fathers' valor, and the favor of God to our country." Just as the unfinished Monument focused debate on how nationalistic Americans ought to be, so it also raised the question of who was actually included within the new nation.[9]

Boston's burgeoning Irish Catholic community was engaged in an especially fierce struggle for inclusion. After the Napoleonic Wars, European cereal prices plummeted, so to maintain profitability Irish landlords raised rents and farmers began switching to livestock production, which pushed bankrupt crofters and unemployed laborers off the land. Attracted by opportunity and a common language, 125,000 Irish emigrated to America during 1825–30; despite hostility from old-stock Protestants, some settled in Boston, increasing the Irish Catholic population to 8,000 by 1830, or 13 percent. In their bids for acceptance, a favored tactic by Irish community leaders was to emphasize a shared heritage of rebellion against English oppression, which made the Monument a natural symbolic marker in debates over the legitimacy of Irish-American citizenship. In May 1834, Boston's *The Jesuit* was thrilled to reprint a report from the *Boston Courier* that an Irish immigrant to the seaport town of Thomaston, Maine, had contributed $5 to the Monument fund. It should be a matter of "some reproach," the *Courier* chastised its readers, that asylum seekers fleeing the "despotism and tyranny over which our fathers triumphed" had stronger feelings of national pride than native New Englanders. "We hope the example of this worthy son of Ireland may be emulated by every true-born Yankee." But there were plenty of Bostonians who thought Irish Americans were positively unworthy. Three months later, a mob of fifty or sixty laborers, most of whom were Scots-Presbyterian bricklayers, first looted and then burned down Charlestown's Ursuline Convent, which had been educating girls from elite Protestant families. A malicious rumor that nuns were holding a novitiate against her will was the proximate cause, although the underlying issue was that growing numbers of Irish immigrants were taking the laborers' jobs. More perhaps from a dread of riotous behavior than from a concern for religious toleration, elites, including the BHMA's Judge Joseph Story who served on the investigating committees, found the violence appalling; legislators agreed in principle to pay compensation, although no money was ever forthcoming. During an attempt by the BHMA to raise funds in 1838, Boston's Catholic press jumped on the still festering episode.[10]

---

9. "Bunker Hill Monument," *American Monthly Magazine* (Boston), 2:4 (July 1830), pp. 250–53; "Bunker-Hill Monument," *Boston Recorder and Religious Telegraph*, 15:9 (3 March 1830), p. 84.

10. For the growth of Boston's Irish population, see Thomas H. O'Connor, *Bibles, Brahmins, and Bosses: A Short History of Boston* (Boston: Boston Public Library, 1991), pp. 146–47; *The Jesuit; or, Catholic Sentinel*, 5:25 (21 June 1834), p. 197; for a surprisingly balanced account of the riot, see *The Jesuit*, 5:34 (23 August 1834), pp. 267–68; bricklayers, from Jenny Franchot, *Roads to Rome: The Antebellum Protestant Encounter with Catholicism* (Berkeley: University of

Sixty-three years ago, the *Boston Pilot*'s editor noted wryly, colonists felt so "grievously oppressed by the Mother country" that they fought a battle for "liberty of speech, thought and religion" on a mound in Charlestown called Bunker Hill. One Thomas Jefferson wrote a declaration of independence, setting forth a doctrine that all men were equal and entitled in the sight of their Creator to enjoy equal rights. Americans then began erecting a granite shaft on the mound to celebrate victory in the first contest for freedom. As the Ursuline Convent burnt to ashes, its light "flashed brightly" on the still unfinished edifice. No wonder that Americans' zeal for the Monument had flagged. Catholics should now ensure that the Monument reached up to the clouds, where it would stand as a "continual reproach to those who have departed from the faith and practice of their free-souled ancestors—the Hancocks, the Warrens, the Jeffersons." With the Monument finished, the contrast of the ruined convent would add to the effect, providing a quaint "memento of persecution and illiberality so near to the tower of liberty." Even Protestant editors found the irony irresistible. Hartford's Baptist *Christian Secretary* printed a rumor that Catholics were petitioning Massachusetts legislators for the granite for the Monument so they could rebuild the convent, and if legislators refused then Catholics would donate the ruined stones of their convent to the Monument's noble cause.[11]

Anti-Masonry provided the context for the first of two major battles for the Monument. Freemasonry's stress on an individual's belief in the Supreme Being ensured its popularity among America's Enlightenment-era Founding Fathers, but its secret rituals, elitist membership, and closed-door paternalism seemed anachronistic in the Evangelical, reformist atmosphere of the 1830s. Two factors fueled a crusade against Freemasonry, which culminated in the short-lived single-interest Anti-Masonic Party of 1831–37, centered on New England and New York. First, the abduction and suspected murder of William Morgan, a disaffected Mason who published an exposé of Freemasonry in 1826, led to talk of a conspiracy when trials of his kidnappers handed down minimal sentences. Second, political opponents of Jackson's administration—Whiggish northerners such as John Quincy Adams and newspaper editor Thurlow Weed—exploited the fact that he was a Mason. A man of principle who harbored grudges, Adams stood out from his fellow Yankees for his long-standing disapproval of the Monument, which would be difficult to explain were it not for his dislike of Webster. An early foray in the Anti-Masonic Party's campaign was against the BHMA.

Only ten of the BHMA's thirty directors bothered to attend the annual meeting on 17 June 1831, and they were not expecting any of the general members to put in an appearance. Officers were standing for reelection unopposed, there was little new business to discuss, and perpetual shortfalls in fundraising had left them unusually apathetic. They were therefore surprised and initially encouraged by the attendance of

California Press, 1994), p. 136.

11. Cited in the *Catholic Telegraph* (Cincinnati), 7:46 (25 October 1838), p. 362; *Christian Secretary* (Hartford, CT), 1:45 (25 January 1839), p. 3.

thirty of the newer members but, on tallying the ballots for officers, they realized they were victims of a coup, which under the democratic rules of their constitution they were powerless to reverse. With the exception of longtime treasurer Nathaniel P. Russell, whose position no one coveted, Anti-Masons replaced the entire board, as well as eleven directors. All the old board could salvage was an adjournment until 25 July to decide the fate of the remaining directors. There was uproar in Boston when the news broke. Proclaiming his previous neutrality on the issue, the *Boston Centinel's* editor felt that the Anti-Masons' "persecution" against men of "spotless purity and exemplary lives" compelled him to speak out, and warn Bostonians about this "dangerous combination of fanatics who disturb the public peace, for the purpose of their own political aggrandizement." After cataloguing the leading usurpers—Dr. Abner Phelps, John D. Williams, George Odiorne, and William Marston—the editor of the *Boston Daily Advertiser* noted how the previous directors had "written, spoken, toiled, and given their best hours, and their money" to raise the honorable Monument. "Who, after this, will doubt what anti-masonry means?" he asked rhetorically. Anti-Masons were builders too, he conceded, but they "must demolish before they can erect." Now it was up to those who were neither Masons nor Anti-Masons to "demolish the enemy of the public peace!"[12]

Demolition, in a sense, was to be the physical validation of the Anti-Masons' moralist agenda. By gaining control of the BHMA, they intended to "tear the disgraceful plate from its proud resting place," by which they meant the silver plaque, with its Masonic "inscriptions of vanity," prepared by Alexander Parris for the cornerstone ceremony in June 1825. They seem to have understood that tearing out the plaque would have meant removing the cornerstone and probably toppling the Monument, because their alternative plan was to install a new plaque, "so that the *truth* may be handed down to future ages." With the new plaque installed, they could take possession of the Monument. They would give it a new meaning, a new truth, and they would banish everything they loathed about the Masonic directors who had begun the project. As their magazine made clear, until they had exorcised the evil of Masonry from the Monument, it would symbolize the idolatry of Egypt, the sorcery of Chaldea, and the conceit of Babel. Masons borrowed their mystical virtues from the Rosicrucians (a secret society of seventeenth-century German occultists), their magic from the Necromancers, their morals from the Jesuits, and their "horrid oaths" from their "own bowels." Freemasonry was un-American. Its "'love of good cheer, the profusion, the lengthening out of the feast, the intemperate drinking,'" all these gross practices followed the taste of the English nation, and it was the duty of American Anti-Masons to banish them "'*to the taverns of London, to which they legitimately belong.*'" Did Americans not realize that *latomi*—the Latin name for their "heaven born order"—were not proud craftsmen but rather degenerate "*slaves and vagabonds condemned to the quarries*" of ancient Rome? Such was the "genuine wit of the Mother Lodge of Freemasons"

---

12. Cited in the *Boston Masonic Mirror*, 3:1 (2 July 1831), p. 3; cited in the *Salem Gazette*, 21 June 1831, p. 3.

in England. As long as the Masonic plaque remained under the cornerstone, so would England exercise a right over the Monument, the same "right which a parent has over his offspring." Until they repossessed the Monument, the Anti-Masons were saying, and installed a plaque that told the truth about Yankee virtue, Americans would be nothing more than debauched, idolatrous English children.[13]

Other than mentioning that a grand master mason had laid the cornerstone, there was, in fact, nothing Masonic about the silver plaque; it bore no hieroglyphics, Greek letters, secret designs, or inscriptions. Yet as this incident demonstrates so well, in an anxious society that relied on myth for national meaning, superstition the more easily assumed the power of fact, and conspiracy theories attracted staunch believers.[14]

Debate between supporters and opponents of Masonry was especially intense in Maine. A week after the Anti-Masonic takeover of the BHMA, John H. Sheppard, a Boston lawyer and Masonic official, journeyed to Wiscasset, fifty miles north of Portland, for a St. John the Baptist's Day celebration, John being the patron saint of Freemasons as well as French Canadians. After a parade through town streets lined with hecklers, Sheppard delivered an address at the Lincoln Lodge, which the *Boston Masonic Mirror* serialized over its next three editions. Masonry, Sheppard made explicit, could not be anti-Christian, because it was a "religious Institution" whose "very foundation" was the Bible. Neither was it hedonistic, for lodges had been the "earliest movers in the cause of temperance." Most importantly, Masonry was "decidedly and totally republican." Qualification for office was by merit alone, there was a written constitution, and Masonry's government was elective; in terms of its operations and principles, a lodge was actually a "miniature republic." How could Masonry be an anti-republican secret society, Sheppard asked, when Presidents Washington, Jefferson, Madison, Monroe, and now Jackson had all been Masons? How could it be a canker worm eating out the tree of liberty when founding statesmen like Patrick Henry, Benjamin Franklin, George Clinton, John Marshall, and Henry Clay were Masons or when the author of the Declaration of Independence was a Mason? If those who waged the "war of antimasonry," which was raging "like an epidemic," still doubted Masons' republicanism, then they should visit Boston, where Grand Master Mason Joseph Warren was one of the first to rock the cradle of independence. They should remember the jubilee that witnessed Master Mason Lafayette lay the cornerstone of the Monument. Sheppard observed—in a footnote to the printed address—how a "sly meeting of a *secret society* of antimasons" had "suddenly and unexpectedly crept in" to the BHMA's annual meeting, overpowering a few patriots who were not expecting a nefarious plot. Now the Monument was "in the hands of Goths and Vandals." There

---

13. Except "vanity," which is from a report published by Anti-Masons, cited in Warren, *Monument Association*, p. 247, quotations are from "History of Freemasonry," *Anti-Masonic Review and Magazine* (New York), 1:11 (1 November 1828), pp. 340, 337, 339, 346, 351–52, emphasis original, and double quotes from J.L. Laurens, *Essais sur la Franche Maconerie* (1805).

14. "Fac-similie of the Silver Plate deposited under the Corner Stone of the Bunker Hill Monument in 1825," *Proceedings of the Bunker Hill Monument Association, at the Fifty-Fifth Annual Meetings, June 17, 1878* (Boston: Bunker Hill Monument Association, 1878), inset fp. 1.

was a strange sound in the wind, as if its "Corner Stone would give place to a stone without a corner."[15]

So many supporters of the BHMA's old-guard directors rallied for the 25 July adjournment that the chosen venue could not accommodate them. At a further adjournment on the afternoon of Monday, 1 August at Faneuil Hall, members packed the floor and spectators lined the galleries. Pro-Masonic members could do nothing to evict the Goths and Vandals, but 582 of them did at least manage to vote back most of the ousted directors to fill eighteen vacant positions, and they modified the BHMA's constitution to hamstring the Anti-Masonic executive. With power divided between the executive and the board, and insufficient funds to restart construction, the 1831–32 year was a stalemate. For the following general meeting, the BHMA again hired Faneuil Hall, and ensured the attendance of 455 members, who chose "in harmony"—as historian G.W. Warren would have his readers believe—the old familiar names to the executive and rescinded the restrictive bylaws. This episode, Warren asserted, was "the first and only attempt ever made to identify the Association with a political party," but it was rather the first of several discordant, politicized struggles for possession of the Monument. In what was to be the second major battle for the Monument, women were not only the leading actors but also the ultimate victors.[16]

Hale's Biblical Nationalism

When their traditional fundraising through membership contributions had failed in 1829, the BHMA's directors had reluctantly decided to reserve a plot 600 feet by 400 feet (5.5 acres) for the Monument and sell off the excess land. Willard drew up a plan that divided the 9.5 remaining acres into roads and building plots the sale of which the directors expected would pay off the Suffolk Bank loan as well as provide funds for a resumption of work on the Monument. This sensible expedient met with an outcry from BHMA members and Bostonians at large who saw the entire battle site as sacred, so the directors abandoned the sale. For their next fundraising experiment, the directors settled on a lottery, for which there was plenty of precedent. To fund Baltimore's Washington Monument, the Maryland General Assembly had organized six lotteries over fifteen years starting in 1811, and the City of Washington's corporation had run lotteries since 1822 to pay for government buildings and infrastructure. Townsfolk of Groton, Connecticut, ran lotteries in the late 1820s with $4 tickets and a $10,000 first prize so they could erect a 127-foot granite obelisk to commemorate a valiant but unsuccessful militia defense at the Battle of Groton Heights (1781). Locally, Harvard College had resorted to a lottery some years earlier to fund a new hall. BHMA director George Blake, who was also a state representative, met with the organizer of the Baltimore lotteries, J.K. Casey, and worked out the details of a lottery to raise $50,000. Lotteries in Massachusetts needed state authorization, so in December 1829 the BHMA

---

15. John H. Sheppard, "Address, Delivered Before Lincoln Lodge, Wiscasset, Maine," *Boston Masonic Mirror*, 9:16 (23 July 1831), pp. 18, 33–34, emphasis original, and parade, ibid., 24 June 1831, p. 11.

16. Report of the meeting in the *Boston Centinel*, reprinted in the *Salem Gazette*, 5 August 1831, p. 1; Warren, *Monument Association*, pp. 246–47.

petitioned the General Court. Immediately, the complaints poured in from moralizers. Perhaps the surge in religious revivalism since Harvard's successful petition was the cause, or maybe it was the pro-Masonic sentiments of the directors. A widely reprinted editorial in the *Christian Register* wondered what the effect would be of selling $2 million of tickets, roughly the amount necessary to raise $50,000. "Undoubtedly to excite the spirit of gambling among the laboring classes," which the editor was certain would lead laborers to "idleness, intemperance, and ruin." Better the state pay a million dollars in direct taxation; better the Monument remain forever unfinished. "Nay," it would be better if "every stone of it should be buried in the ocean, than that the morals of the state should be sacrificed for its completion." Any reader who was also an BHMA member must lobby the directors to abandon the "scandalous proposal," which would only bring "shame and disgrace" on the Monument.[17]

Another charge that the lottery was an appeal to the "avarice and gambling propensities of the people," just as it was "humiliating, even degrading to the character" of Massachusetts' citizens, came in "The Worth of Money," a seven-page essay by Sarah Josepha Hale in the *Ladies' Magazine*, a literary journal recently launched in Boston, of which she was the founding editor. Through a talent for identifying issues with resonance for women, she attracted a national readership for what would later become *Godey's Lady's Book*, the most popular women's periodical of the nineteenth century. Hale became famous for her nursery rhyme to promote schooling, "Mary Had a Little Lamb," and for convincing President Abraham Lincoln to make Thanksgiving a national holiday. Along with her involvement in the Monument, these were all nationalistic endeavors, as a brief account of her early life and first book will begin to explain.[18]

Her father, Gordon Buell, from Killingworth, Connecticut, had fought in the War of Independence, reaching the rank of captain, but soldiering left him wounded, poor in health and resources. After Buell married Martha Whittlesey from nearby Saybrook, west of New London, his grandfather, a deacon, gave the newlyweds four hundred acres of unimproved land in Newport, in the center of southern New Hampshire, which the grandfather bought from a veteran who drew it in a lottery. In the 1780s, Buell's farm was hardly the frontier, but whenever his family gazed across its hilly meadows to the Sugar River snaking through the valley, or watched him clear its timber and bring its thin soils into cultivation, it would have seemed as if they were living in the wilderness. Martha bore him four children, two of whom died in their teens. She gave them an elementary education at home, and when a boys-only common school opened nearby she enrolled Horatio, her second son, who would graduate from Dartmouth College in 1809. Self-reliant and competitive, Sarah, born in 1788,

---

17. Warren, *Monument Association*, pp. 233–34; copies of the petition appeared in many newspapers and journals, such as the *Masonic Mirror*, 1:26 (26 December 1829), p. 207; "Bunker Hill Monument Lottery!" *Christian Register*, 8:49 (5 December 1829), p. 194, in, for instance, *Salem Gazette*, 11 December 1829, p. 1. Groton Heights Monument: cornerstone laid in 1826 on 6 September, the day of the battle; dedicated in 1830; height increased to 135 feet for a centennial celebration in 1881.

18. Sarah Josepha Hale, "The Worth of Money," *Ladies' Magazine and Literary Gazette*, 3:2 (February 1830), p. 54.

borrowed her brother's textbooks so that she could educate herself. When Sarah was ten, she read David Ramsay's *History of the American Revolution* (1795), which, she later recalled, "'deeply engraved on my heart'" the "'love of country.'"[19]

Ramsay's account of the Battle of Bunker Hill told how 1,500 Americans inflicted 1,054 casualties on a British force of 3,000 through bravery and the quality of their marksmanship. "The dexterity which by long habit they had acquired in hitting beafts, birds and marks, was fatally applied to the deftruction of British officers." Ramsay reserved special praise for the "noble facrifice" of Joseph Warren to the cause of liberty, which Warren espoused from the "pureft principles." To the "virtues of domeftic life, the eloquence of an accomplifhed orator, and the wisdom of an able ftatefman," Warren had added "the pureft patriotifm and moft undaunted bravery." Warren had taken such an active part in the "defence of his country, not that he might be applauded and rewarded for a patriotic fpirit, but because he was in the beft fenfe of the word, a real patriot." With Warren's purest patriotism engraved on her heart, Sarah determined from an early age "'to do something for my own country.'"[20]

Her first opportunity came at age eighteen, when she began teaching in a local private school, a position she held for seven rewarding years because the school enrolled girls as well as boys. Sarah could never understand why a society educated boys in preference to girls, when mothers were the originators of their sons' moral character. In 1810, Buell sold the farm and moved to town, where he opened the Rising Sun Tavern. It was at the tavern where Sarah met David Hale, a prosperous local lawyer and Freemason, whom she married in 1813. For nine years, they enjoyed a close companionate marriage, until an event that underscores the fragility of existence before antibiotics. Returning in his gig from a meeting with a client, David ran into a late September snow squall; chilled and damp, he came down with pneumonia and died a few days later, leaving Sarah to support five children. Sarah Hale tried needlecraft, but then turned to writing, publishing a book of poetry with an advance from the Newport Masonic lodge, and a novel, *Northwood, a Tale of New England*, which became a best seller on both sides of the Atlantic.[21]

Northwood served to transport the reader to Hale's ideal nation. A young British visitor, Mr. Frankford, traveled with his friend Sidney to the New Hampshire farmstead of James Romilly, Sidney's father, arriving the day before Thanksgiving. In setting the stage, Hale described the carved eagle over the mantelpiece, "his head powdered with stars, his body streaked with white and red alternately," gripping in his talons an olive branch and a bundle of arrows, signifying that "although he loved peace, he was prepared for war," while his beak held a scroll "inscribed with the talisman of American liberty and power—*E pluribus unum*." Hale used Frankford's

19. Cited in Sherbrooke Rogers, *Sarah Josepha Hale: A New England Pioneer* (Grantham, NH: Thompson & Rutter, 1985), p. 13.

20. David Ramsay, *The History of the American Revolution*, (Dublin: William Jones, 1795), vol. 1, pp. 181–82; "'do something,'" cited in Rogers, *Hale*, p. 13.

21. Rogers, *Sarah Josepha Hale*, pp. 20–21.

puzzlement as a stranger to emphasize the qualities of American society. Why did Romilly never lock the farmstead door? Because "'the pride of character infused by our education and cherished by our free institutions,'" Romilly explained, meant there were no vagabonds. What was Thanksgiving? It was "'the exponent of our Republican institutions, which are based on the acknowledgement that God is our Lord, and that as a nation, we derive our privileges from Him.'" All Americans, Romilly advocated, should observe Thanksgiving, rather than just New Englanders as was the custom, for then it would be a "'grand spectacle of moral power and human happiness, such as the world has never yet witnessed.'"[22]

fig. 24: David and Sarah Hale, ca. 1820

Next day, Romilly—whose name rhymes conveniently with *homily*—took Frankford to church, where the preacher "industriously" searched the Bible before choosing Isaiah 26:15, "'Thou hast increased the nation, O Lord, thou hast increased the nation,'" for the sermon. Escaping the persecutions of the Old World and braving the perils of the New had endowed the first Pilgrims with a special character, which they passed to their descendants. These settlers had then fought a war of revolution against oppression, which they won because the Lord was on their side. Members now of a "'nation whom God increased,'" Americans created "excellent institutions," based on a foundation of "intelligence and public virtue," thereby "securing the liberty and happiness of the people." With God on their side, the preacher was confident that

---

22. Sarah Josepha Hale, *Northwood, a Tale of New England* (Boston: Bowles & Dearborn, 1827); Hale republished it with an additional chapter on abolition, as *Northwood, or Life North and South: Showing the True Character of Both* (New York: H. Long & Brother, 1852), from which I have cited here, pp. 60, 71, 68.

Americans could draw on "unparalleled and almost inexhaustible resources" and continue to experience the "increase, power, and glory" of their nation.[23]

When Rev. John Lauris Blake read *Northwood* he was so impressed that he offered Hale the editorship of his forthcoming *Ladies' Magazine*. An Episcopalian headmaster of the Cornhill School for Young Ladies in Boston, Blake shared Hale's belief that improving the female mind would further God's plan for Americans. Leaving her four oldest children behind with relatives, Hale moved to Boston for the January 1828 launch, and soon built up the magazine's circulation through twinned strategies: First, she targeted home-bound women readers, capturing their imagination with informative articles—many of which she wrote herself—in lively prose, on American themes. As she explained in the debut edition's introduction, *Ladies' Magazine* was "national"; all its poems, letters, sketches, and tales would be "descriptive of American scenery, character, and manners." Although Hale was not averse to including articles by men, she ensured that every contributor was American, in contrast to other literary journals that borrowed material freely from British publications. Second, she marketed subscriptions to the husband, whose duties compelled him to "leave the partner of his fortunes in a solitary home," but who would "rejoice" that he could afford his spouse "the means of agreeably beguiling the interval of his absence." Husbands could rest assured that an educated wife would not "usurp the station, or encroach on the prerogative of the man," but rather "lend her aid to the moral and intellectual character of those within her sphere." Three dollars ($240) for a year's subscription was a small price, Hale was saying, to ensure a rational companion, virtuous children, and an improved nation.[24]

In February 1830 when the BHMA's directors announced their lottery scheme, Hale pounced on it as the latest evidence of the selfishness of increasingly rich men whose morality was in a state of decay, in large part because mothers had forgotten their role as teachers of God's righteousness. Here was the perfect opportunity to boost circulation, engage women in civic activism, and do something for her country. Hale's opening salvo in the *Ladies' Magazine*, "The Worth of Money," noted that Americans lived in an "age of economy," an age of "speculative plans and practical exertions to improve the condition of the world." Her essay's premise was that men faced a choice: they could accumulate wealth for "pleasure, fame and power," or employ their property "in elevating and refining the social, mental and moral character" of mankind. History afforded no better example of the sin of avarice than the Spanish, for whom South American gold, which Spaniards coveted for selfish enjoyment, became a burning curse. Could not the "free people of our Republic" be the first to shake off this "dominion of selfishness," and make "moral and mental excellence" their ambition? But without education, even Americans would fail, and here the

---

23. Hale, *Northwood*, p. 83. Hale was using the Authorized King James Version (1611), which continues: "thou art glorified; thou hadst removed it [the nation] far unto all the ends of the earth"; the American Standard (1901) Holy Bible makes this meaning of the last phrase clear: "thou hast enlarged all the borders of the land."

24. Sarah Josepha Hale, *Ladies' Magazine*, 1:1 (January 1828), pp. 1–3.

responsibility lay with women, those who "first awaken the moral feelings," and through whom "the moral sentiments are directed, and the habits which finally stamp the character, fixed." "Mothers," Hale implored, "can you not teach your children the art of doing good?" Evidently not, she concluded from the unfinished state of the Monument, for which a lottery would only compound Americans' moral degeneracy.[25]

After five pages of sermonizing, Hale revealed her plan: there could be no better way to demonstrate to husbands the true worth of money, nor to show degenerate Spaniards that God favored Protestant Americans, nor for mothers to teach their children morals than for the women of Massachusetts to raise the $50,000 to complete the Monument. For the plan to have full moral effect, every dollar must come solely from the "industry, economy or self-denial" of ladies. They must not importune their husbands, fathers, or brothers, and they must be scrupulously careful not to infringe "feminine propriety" when "coming before the public." Wives could prove their patriotism and virtue by donating their allowance for ornaments, just as Roman women had contributed jewelry to pay the ransom demanded by Gauls who had captured their city. Mothers could encourage their children—of both sexes, providing the boys were younger than twelve—to donate pocket money otherwise intended for toys or sweetmeats, thereby exciting them to emulate the goodness that they had heard their elders eulogize. What an opportunity to awaken in children's "hearts the love of country, of liberty, of social order and the refined enjoyment of doing good"; what an opportunity to imprint on children's "souls the deeds and virtues of those worthy men," like Joseph Warren, that Americans should hold in everlasting remembrance. Yes, here was the chance that might never again occur for these wives, mothers, and daughters of Massachusetts to render "a public tribute of respect to virtue, valor, and patriotism."[26]

By April 1830, Hale could report that ten ladies had taken up her challenge and formed a Ladies' Society, headed by a suitably named Committee of Correspondence, reminiscent of the committees established in the 1760s to fight British efforts to raise taxes. All ten were daughters of or had married into elite Bostonian families, including Mary Sheldon Lord, wife of John Pierpont, an abolitionist educator and the maternal grandfather of banker J.P. Morgan; Sarah Preston Everett, Edward's sister, and wife of Nathan Hale, a lawyer and editor of the *Boston Daily Advertiser*; Lucretia Orne Peabody, wife of Alexander Hill Everett (Edward's elder brother), who had just returned from an ambassadorship at Madrid and had taken over the editorship of the *North American Review*; and Katherine Bigelow, wife of Abbott Lawrence, then the speaker of the Massachusetts House of Representatives and later the founder of the mill town of Lawrence. Having received the BHMA directors' enthusiastic—if somewhat skeptical—approval of their "exalted motives" and "generous zeal," the ladies began their campaign.[27]

---

25. Hale, "The Worth of Money," *Ladies' Magazine*, 3:2 (February 1830), pp. 49, 52.
26. Ibid., pp. 54–55.
27. "To the Women of New England," *Ladies' Magazine*, 3:4 (April 1830), pp. 171–73.

As with any fundraising endeavor, they quickly encountered the gulf that exists between a good idea and its successful implementation. How would they reach sufficient donors, especially when they imposed a limit on donations of one dollar? Where would donors deposit their contributions? Should they send thank-you notes, and would the cost of stationary and postage exceed the value of small donations? Compounding this problem of praxis was their limited access to a public system circumscribed by men, particularly when they themselves—as respectable ladies—were so intent on maintaining the separation of men's and women's spheres. They must never "usurp the station, or encroach on the prerogative of the man," Hale had insisted since the first edition of *Ladies' Magazine*, scrupulously retaining their self-made mores of feminine propriety when coming before the male public. One tactic that Hale adopted was an appeal to newspaper editors to print an advertisement calling on storekeepers to volunteer their premises as collection points, which prompted several editors to voice objections to women fundraisers. She responded by quoting Exodus 35:22, wherein Moses gladly accepted contributions from women to help build God's tabernacle: "'And they came, both men and *women*, as many as were *willing-hearted*, and brought bracelets and ear-rings, and rings, and tablets, all jewels of gold.'"[28]

A surprising discovery for Hale was that *Ladies' Magazine* readers responded best not to pleading articles but to poetry. One of two poems that particularly caught readers' sympathies was Hale's "The Last of the Band," a lamentation by the last living veteran of the Battle of Bunker Hill. "Yes, here is still the Mountain Grave— / But where's the Pile, they said should rise, / . . . A Beacon far o'er land and sea— / Signal and Seal of Liberty?" Despondent in old age, the veteran had "felt my cherished dreams depart, / And found my idols were but clay— / But then Hope whispered— 'more remain.'" It was "then I saw that Pile begun— / And prayed to live till it was done!" A second poem, "The Obelisk," anonymously by Lydia Huntley Sigourney, was even more redolent with the Monument's "citty upon a hill" imagery. "Rise, lofty Column!—in thy simple grace, / And to the stranger-bark that patient braves / Yon boisterous ocean, point the *pilgrims' land*." Charlestown's obelisk would "Teach awestruck Egypt . . . of Tyranny," but—Sigourney implored—"be *thou* true, / Recording Column!—to thy sacred trust, / And the blest memory of that glorious race / Who sought no guerdon [repayment] save their country's weal, / Transmit to unborn ages."[29]

When their campaign lost momentum in August 1830, Hale and her fellow Ladies' Society members would be bitterly disappointed that they had only collected $2,225.38 ($178,000), which was not enough to warrant recommencement of quarrying and the rehiring of construction teams. For the most part, men reacted with condescension toward the endeavor, as in the sarcastic lines of Grenville Mellon's

---

28. "Introduction," *Ladies' Magazine*, 1:1 (January 1828), p. 2; Exodus, *Ladies' Magazine*, 3:3 (March 1830), p. 135, emphasis added by Hale.

29. Sarah Josepha Hale, "The Last of the Band," *Ladies' Magazine*, 3:4 (April 1830), p. 174; Lydia Huntley Sigourney, "The Obelisk," *Ladies' Magazine*, 3:5 (May 1830), pp. 216–17, emphasis original. Sigourney, of Hartford, CT, was one of the most popular women poets in nineteenth-century America.

poetic rejoinder, read to the Phi Beta Kappa Society in Cambridge: "With wide material at her quick command / To new forms springing from her plastic hand, / In each event incalculably brisk, / Now builds a Monthly, now an Obelisk; / And with a glowing ardor panting still, / Fights for new victory on Bunker Hill!" Yankee women could be disparaging too. Katherine Augusta Ware, editor of the *Bower of Taste*, a Boston competitor of the *Ladies' Magazine*, thought it absurd that a society of women in such a "goodly city" as Boston were soliciting "*sugarplum* money" to "*build our national Monument!*" "The proper sphere of woman," Ware bellowed, was "where she may exert her *influence* with *propriety*," and that she could never do "when she encroaches upon the *prerogatives* of man." Criticisms aside, the money represented the contributions of more than three thousand women and children, which was two or three times the number of New Englanders who had contributed directly to the BHMA's fund during the previous seven years. In addition to an appreciation of how tightly husbands controlled the family budget, Hale had also gained operational experience that would later prove invaluable.[30]

Place, Memory, Identity

Once they had ousted the Anti-Masonry Party politicians, and with barely $3,000 collected, the bulk of it by the Ladies' Society, the BHMA's directors amid a growing sense of desperation appealed for funds to the Massachusetts Charitable Mechanic Association. Several directors were honorary members of this prestigious organization, formed by artisans through Paul Revere's influence in 1795 to provide aid to members fallen on hard times and as a forum for technological advancement, which by the 1830s was becoming more of a manufacturers' networking club. Mechanic Association president Joseph T. Buckingham, a state representative and editor of the *Boston Courier*, hired Faneuil Hall for a public meeting on 28 May 1833. After an introductory speech by Col. Charles Gordon Greene, who had recently founded the *Post*, Boston's largest circulation daily until the 1940s, Edward Everett delivered the keynote oration to a capacity audience. It was Everett's first speech in Faneuil Hall, and one of the finest of his career. He begged leave to exercise his "birthright as a Yankee" to answer a common question posed by objectors: what good would the Monument do? "What good does any thing do," he wondered prosaically, "What is good?" Mechanics, he expected, knew what good railroads or canals did: why, they facilitated intercourse, opened markets, and increased the wealth of the country. And what good did that do? Well, individuals prospered and became rich. Was mere wealth—"gold and silver, without an inquiry as to their use"—a good thing? "Certainly not." There had to be some higher moral goal, Everett's Yankee birthright told him. Surely, there must be feelings—"generous and patriotic sentiments"—that were "good,

---

30. Warren, *Monument Association*, pp. 238, 293; Grenville Mellon, "The Age of Print," from *Christian Examiner and General Review*, 9:2 (November 1830), p. 233; Ware cited in Lawrence Martin, "Women Fought at Bunker Hill," *New England Quarterly*, 8:4 (December 1935), p. 470, emphasis original. I am discounting fundraising through collection plates passed round at specific events, or other group fundraising activities, of which there seem to have been few.

humanly speaking, of the highest order," sentiments that had prepared Americans like Joseph Warren to fight and die for their country. But why bother to build a monument to perpetuate a remembrance of such events, objectors had asked him, when a history book would serve just as well.[31]

To answer this objection, Everett considered the relationship between place, memory, and identity, and his observations were as deep as his opening remarks had been deliberately banal. As a classical scholar, he had read all about Achilles and the siege of Troy, about the fall of Leonidas at the pass of Thermopylae, about Hannibal's overthrow of the Roman consuls at Cannae. Yet after wandering around the Hellespont, the foothills by the Gulf of Malis, and the plains of Apulia, he could find no markers of the original sites, nothing that might inform the senses or fire the imagination, nothing to warm and elevate the heart. He had no doubt that history books would similarly preserve the story of Bunker Hill, but history alone, without "sensible monuments," could not sustain what he called the "knowledge of the identity of the spot." Something visceral happened when you stood on the exact spot. There was "an original element in our nature,—a connection between the senses, the mind and the heart,—implanted by the Creator for pure and noble purposes, which cannot be reasoned away." When you tired of reading and talking about history, you could step on the spot of some great exploit and immediately "your heart swells within you." Reason played no part in this process; it was pure feeling, it was the "inspiration of the place." As cold philosophy vanished, your instinct was to slip off your shoes and feel the holy ground. That was why they must complete the Monument. "It speaks to the heart." No American deserving of the name could stand on that spot with indifference.[32]

Everyone in the hall, Everett was certain, could place himself "in imagination" on the Monument's summit, looking out on the "unsurpassed loveliness, that spreads before him, by land and sea." From the summit, one could marvel at the united features of town and country: long rows of buildings lining city streets, the sweep of the surrounding countryside checkered with prosperous villages, on one side the towers of city churches and on the other a long succession of rural spires. Rivers flowing to the sea, the harbor, the bay dotted with verdant islands, a hundred ships dancing over the waves, warships keeping guard at the foot of the hill, upon which, amid venerable trees and the ashes of the great and good warriors of 1775, stood "the noble obelisk, rising to the heavens." Who among them could not look on this scene with his mind's eye and fail to contribute to the Monument's completion. And yet, Everett's was much more than a clever fundraising speech. Having explained the spiritual link between place and memory, he was now making the metaphysical leap that a monument—providing its design and location were apropos—had the power to build national identity

---

31. Solomon Willard was a full member; honorary members included Daniel Webster, Theodore Lyman, Thomas H. Perkins, and Joseph Story, see *Annals of the Massachusetts Charitable Mechanic Association, 1795–1892* (Boston: MCMA, 1892), p. 14. Warren, *Monument Association*, pp. 261–65; speech in Faneuil Hall, 28 May 1833, in *Orations and Speeches on Various Occasions by Edward Everett* (Boston: American Stationers' Company, 1836), pp. 335–36.

32. *Orations and Speeches . . . by Edward Everett*, pp. 337–39.

through symbolism, which in turn drew its representational values from the place–memory nexus. Who among them, Everett was suggesting, could not see that a plain granite obelisk rising toward the heavens from the redoubt where Warren fell would demonstrate that God smiled favorably on the Puritans' vision of a united republic, productive farms, urban culture, regular worship, seaborne commerce, and a strong defense, all of which had happened as a consequence of Warren's martyrdom on Bunker Hill.[33]

fig. 25: Edward Everett

To close his address, Everett recalled the closing words of a speech by Warren on the "memorable anniversary of the 5th of March." Everyone present presumably knew that Everett was referring to Warren's Boston Massacre Oration of 5 March 1772. After depicting the "labors, hardships, and sacrifices endured by our ancestors, in the cause of liberty," Warren had broken forth in the "thrilling words, 'the voice of our fathers' blood cries to us from the ground!'" Many of the Mechanic Association members would have recognized this paraphrase of God's rebuke of Cain, in Genesis 4:10, after Cain had killed his brother Abel: "the voice of thy brother's blood crieth unto me from the ground." On the heights of Charlestown, Everett continued, Warren himself became the first great martyr in the American cause of liberty, struck down with a band of kindred spirits, "the gray-haired veteran, the stripling in the flower of youth," all of those who had stood side by side on that dreadful day and fallen together, "like the beauty of Israel, on their high places!" Everett was conjuring up the blood of Abel,

33. *Orations and Speeches . . . by Edward Everett*, p. 340.

the world's first shepherd who died at the hand of a tyrannical brother; the blood of the Boston Massacre victims; the blood of Warren and the patriots who died with him; and the blood of the Children of Israel. In a brilliant stroke of biblical nationalist rhetoric, Everett then took all this accumulated blood and staked it through the hallowed ground of Bunker Hill with an obelisk, a plain yet ancient and mysterious Egyptian obelisk that had the symbolic power to commune with God. "From the summit of Bunker-Hill *the voice of our fathers' blood cries to us from the ground.*" It must have been a graphic moment. "Let us hear that awful voice; and resolve, before we quit these walls, that the long-delayed duty shall be performed; that the work *shall be done, shall be done!*" Newspapers reported that the address had somehow been different from Everett's usual eloquent deliveries; there had been "such a strain of argument and feeling" as Bostonians had not "before witnessed in that or any other hall."[34]

fig. 26: Amos Lawrence

Amos Lawrence, who had been the leading advocate of an approach to the Mechanic Association, judged it the best speech that Everett ever delivered. On his copy of the oration, Lawrence wrote, "If I had been in health, I would have had the whole thing done, so far as collecting fifty thousand dollars would have done it, in forty-eight hours after the adjournment of this meeting." In 1830, Lawrence had become a principal investor in the establishment at Lowell of a model textile mill, but the following year he contracted a stomach disorder that left him so enfeebled that he decided to retire and devote the rest of his life to philanthropy. Deeply religious and a believer in Yankee virtue, Lawrence would make the Monument one of his greatest

---

34. Ibid., pp. 341–42; cited in the *New-Hampshire Patriot* (Concord), 3 June 1833, p. 2.

causes, in part to honor the memory of his father, Samuel, who had fought in the redoubt with Col. William Prescott. When Lawrence wrote to caution his eldest son in Paris in 1828 not to adopt French habits but remain, "as long as you live, a well-bred, upright *Yankee*," he mentioned that it would be "the pride of your father" to lead the Marquis de Lafayette to the top of the Monument. In a will he drafted in 1833, Lawrence considered that Bunker Hill was the "most interesting [spot] in the country." But instead of striking "while the iron is hot," as Lawrence hoped, officers of the Mechanic Association first dawdled, then encouraged wealthier members to pledge large sums contingent on the total subscription reaching the $50,000 necessary to finish the Monument; when it became clear in December, nine months after Everett's oration, that contributions only amounted to $14,000, many members withdrew their pledges. Boston's wealthy mechanics behaved no differently to other groups interested in the Monument: they were prepared to donate substantial sums but only if they could make the Monument their own. Contributions tapered off at $19,000 ($1.5 million), although along with the Ladies' Society fund this was sufficient to bring Solomon Willard's construction teams back to Bunker Hill. When Willard exhausted the money in November 1835, the Monument stood at eighty-five feet.[35]

With the U.S. economy plunging into the deepest recession of its history, BHMA directors struggled through five desperate years. During the Panic of 1837, the Suffolk Bank, being one of America's largest financial institutions, operated like a central bank to assist smaller banks through the crisis. Consequently, it demanded from the four directors who had made personal guarantees an immediate payment of $8,000 in outstanding interest payments on the loan secured by the battle-site land; this would have bankrupted them were it not for a temporary facility of $5,000 from Amos Lawrence. There were serious proposals to reduce the height of the Monument to 160 feet, and mounting criticisms of the directors' conduct over the prior fifteen years.[36]

An editorial in the *New-Hampshire Patriot* shortly after Everett's Faneuil Hall oration provided a catalogue of typical complaints. First, the "Boston Aristocracy" squandered huge sums on officers' salaries and an expensive parade without accomplishing anything. Next, the "Boston Ladies tried their pretty hands at monument building"; they "simpered, talked enchantingly and looked ineffably," but similarly achieved nothing. Regular Bostonians, who were as "obstinate as Maj. Noah's Jews," pointed out that they had already given the Aristocracy more than enough to complete the Monument, and they were not about to be "fleeced again." Finally, the Mechanic Association had commenced a "regular fire of *speeches* upon the Monument," yet these would fail too. Speeches and loud talk would never raise a monument. If the time spent speechmaking had been employed in working on the Monument then it would

35. William W. Wheildon, *Memoir of Solomon Willard: Architect and Superintendent of the Bunker Hill Monument* (Boston: Bunker Hill Monument Association, 1865), p. 170; *Extracts from the Diary and Correspondence of the Late Amos Lawrence, with a Brief Account of Some Incidents in his Life*, ed. William R. Lawrence (Boston: Gould and Lincoln, 1855), pp. 83–84, 171, emphasis original; Wheildon, *Solomon Willard*, pp. 170, 188.

36. Warren, *Monument Association*, p. 280.

now be "peering to the skies instead of groveling in the dust." If only Everett would just "take off his gloves, tuck in his ruffles, and *work*" until the sweat started from his brow, then he would set before the mechanics a good example. A particularly scathing attack came from H.F.H. in the *Ladies' Companion*, a New York rival to Hale's *Ladies' Magazine*. Although H.F.H. was Henry F. Harrington, he wrote from the perspective of women who "blush when we name Bunker Hill" and felt disposed to skulk away, "out of the sight and the cognizance of men." How could BHMA directors have blundered so badly? They had evidently forgotten the Bible's injunctions, in particular: "'Who of you would build a [tower] and sitteth not down and first counteth the cost?'" Either they had not counted or they had expected to draw from a limitless treasury by exploiting Americans' patriotism. Now this half-built tower was worse than a shame, it was "a bitter, accursed thing!" "*Women of America*, take up this cause! Be you the avengers of your country's honor! Wipe you away the stain that is upon us! Plead, implore, *weep!*" H.F.H.'s appeal of November 1838 may have shamed women readers but it did not raise contributions.[37]

Selling Kisses

When Sarah Hale read the BHMA's annual report of June 1840, she was in no mood for its pessimistic comment that the present generation would not live to see the Monument completed. In 1836, her *Ladies' Magazine* had merged with *Godey's Ladies' Book*, published by Louis Antoine Godey of Philadelphia, and under her editorship its circulation had since climbed above 140,000. It was a presidential election year. There were signs the economy was recovering. And, in part through confidence gained as organizers of the abolition movement, Yankee women were increasingly asserting their equal place in the American republic. Surely, 1840 should be a year of resolve. But how to raise the huge sum of $50,000 ($4 million) to complete the long-overdue project? There had been major campaigns in 1824, 1829, 1830, and 1833, all of which, aside from minor differences in style and target donors, had relied on voluntary subscriptions and consequently petered out short of the mark. Hale had learned from her own initiative of 1830 that even wives of wealthy husbands had only small amounts of discretionary cash. Since then, in 1833, she had formed the Seaman's Aid Society, begun as a ladies' sewing circle but which had quickly expanded to include a clothing store stocked by seafarers' wives; to fund the store, Hale had organized a fair that netted over a thousand dollars. Among other precedents for—if not a trend toward—charitable fairs provisioned and run exclusively by women was a June 1840 "Ladies' Fair" in Charlestown town hall to raise funds for a new Episcopal church, which promised a "beautiful display of useful and fancy articles" produced by those who were "always engaged in labors of kindness, and love." Hale would also have noticed the food, clothing, and curio stalls proliferating around Boston Common, most of which

---

37. *New-Hampshire Patriot* (Concord), 3 June 1833, p. 2, emphasis original; *Ladies' Companion*, 10 (November 1838), p. 41. Harrington would seem to have been quoting from memory, as he wrote *house* instead of *tower*. "For which of you, intending to build a tower, sitteth not down first, and counteth the cost, whether he have sufficient to finish it," Luke 14:28.

had female proprietors. Through these experiences and observations, no doubt, Hale developed what would be the winning strategy. Just as she had learned that Boston's ladies had little disposable income, she had found them to be natural organizers, with an array of manual skills and plenty of free time: could they not crochet and knit, bake and decorate, paint and craft?[38]

fig. 27: Judah Touro

Adding impetus to Hale's idea for a huge ladies' fair, was the extraordinary generosity of two men, Amos Lawrence, who guaranteed a $10,000 ($800,000) donation once the Monument fund had reached $30,000, and an identical pledge from a less likely benefactor, Judah Touro, a New Orleans merchant, who happened to be born on 16 June 1775. Sentimentality, his biographer claimed, was Touro's only motivation; his birth "was contemporaneous with that of the United States" at Bunker Hill, which made him "a proud, worthy and patriotic son." Perhaps it was, but by matching Lawrence dollar for dollar the gift was also a perfect opportunity to demonstrate how a first generation Jewish American could be every bit as successful and philanthropic as an old-stock Bostonian, while claiming a piece of the Monument for Judaism. Neither was Touro without connection to Yankee high society, for his wife was the sister of Michael Moses Hays, a Boston merchant and close friend of BHMA mainstay Thomas Handasyd Perkins. And in important respects, Touro was a practiced exponent of Yankee virtue, making a point of never borrowing money, conducting business honestly, working hard (his biographer noted he was always the first to

38. *Bunker-Hill Aurora*, 6 June 1840, p. 2; Seaman's Aid Society, in Rogers, *Hale*, pp. 53–58; Finley, *Lady of Godey's*, pp. 70–71.

open his store and the last to close in the evening), living frugally, drinking rarely, practicing humility, fighting for his country's expansion, which he did literally at the Battle of New Orleans (1815), and always walking in God's sight.[39]

At a special directors' meeting on 25 June 1840, G.W. Warren, who was the BHMA's secretary for 1839–47, presented a proposal for a ladies' fair. Even though in his history of the Monument Warren mentioned how "several ladies" held the opinion that a fair would prove successful, he implied the initiative was his. His fellow directors were skeptical, as the most that a fair in Boston had ever raised was about $3,000. But what had they to lose, and anyway, none of them had any better idea. Indeed, at their annual meeting the week before, Warren noted with hindsight how "gloom" had overhung the BHMA "like the last thick cloud before the clearing up of the sky." Clearly desperate, yet still hoping to claim some credit should Hale's fair actually work, the directors voted to authorize an all-women committee to organize the event. They set the opening date for 8 September, to coincide with the week-long Massachusetts Whig Convention that would be assembling not only in Faneuil Hall but also on Bunker Hill, thanks to lobbying by the predominantly Whig directors, two of whom—Franklin Dexter and Warren—were Whig central committee members. And for a venue they booked Quincy Market, conveniently adjacent to Faneuil Hall. This meant there were only ten weeks in which to prepare, although Hale's executive team had the right connections. It comprised: Catherine G. Prescott, wife of William H., a historian and grandson of Col. William; Susan P. Warren, wife of John C., the surgeon and nephew of Gen. Joseph; Abby Wales, wife of Thomas B., a ship owner; Sarah Darracott, wife of George who, among other civic ventures, was a proprietor of the Boston Public Garden; and Lucinda Chapman, wife of Jonathan, Boston's thirty-three-year-old mayor who was also a BHMA director. They networked through a plethora of women's organizations such as the Seaman's Aid Society, printed broadsheets, sent announcements to newspaper editors, and delivered a circular to every house in Charlestown as well as most homes in Boston.[40]

As the circular shows, gentleman directors and lady organizers interacted within tightly demarcated social roles—or spheres as they called them—of their own making. Instead of the circular being a call to action from the organizing committee to other ladies, it was a decree by the directors to "such gentlemen as would voluntarily co-operate with them," that they all should "solicit the aid and co-operation of the Ladies of New England, and especially of Massachusetts." Hale was particularly conscious of

---

39. Morris A. Gutstein, *Aaron Lopez and Judah Touro: A Refugee and a Son of a Refugee* (New York: Behrman's Jewish Book House, 1939), pp. 70, 96–97, and for character traits, passim, but esp. pp. 78–79; for Hays, see Alexander Walker, "Judah Touro," in *Lives of American Merchants*, ed. Freeman Hunt (New York: Office of Hunt's Merchants' Magazine, 1856), p. 446.

40. Warren, *Monument Association*, pp. 295–96. Directors may have discounted a three-day fair at Faneuil Hall on 1 May 1833 for Thomas Handasyd Perkins's fund for the Asylum for the Blind, which raised $10,000, because contributions accounted for a large proportion, *Boston Courier*, 1 May 1833, p. 2 and 3 May 1833, p. 2. Whig central committee members, including Dexter and Warren, decided to site their convention on Bunker Hill at a meeting in Worcester on 17 June, so it is logical that Hale would have learned this from her newspaper (or from her Whig friends) at the same time as the pessimistic report of the directors' annual meeting, making it clear to her that the timing was propitious for a successful fair.

the need for propriety, for this was not some church bazaar but an effort by women to complete a failed undertaking by men to build the nation's principal battle monument. Among other precautions, she drew up a set of rules to govern conduct at the fair. Ladies must be behind their tables at all time s, and be forthright in furnishing change; there must be no raffles, games of chance, party emblems, or any device suggesting political affiliation; two male marshals hired by the committee would monitor each table; ladies were responsible for the "order and decorum" of their table; most importantly, perhaps, their desire to see the Monument completed should not induce them "to use importunity, or any other means of increasing our funds inconsistent with the respect we owe ourselves." Even with the lengths to which Hale went to ensure that stallholders would behave with "high and honorable character," as Warren put it, the gentlemen viewed the fair with paternal condescension. Before admitting that the course now proposed by the directors was necessary, and agreeing it was "fitting that woman, the pride and ornament of creation should now be invited to participate," the *New Bedford Mercury*'s editor wondered nonetheless how "humiliating" it must be, "especially to the *sons* of our Revolutionary sires," to resort to women fundraisers. An article in Charlestown's *Bunker-Hill Aurora* by its editor William W. Wheildon entitled "Appeal to the Ladies," noted the establishment of a committee to "ascertain what may be expected from the Ladies of Bunker-Hill." Wheildon judged it "unnecessary to state that much will be expected from them," and provided a list of men with their home addresses where ladies could bring articles for sale.[41]

fig. 28: Quincy Market, 1830

---

41. Circular, see for instance, *Barre Gazette*, 24 July 1840, p. 2; rules, Warren, *Monument Association*, pp. 299–300; *New Bedford Mercury*, 17 July 1840, p. 2, emphasis original; *Bunker-Hill Aurora*, 18 July 1840, p. 2.

Bunker Hill's ladies, along with women across Massachusetts who already knew what they expected of each other, needed little encouragement and were soon busy sewing, embroidering, cooking, bottling, and crafting. Four thousand visitors toured the fair on its first day, intrigued to see what the "ingenuity and skill, aided by the patriotism and perseverance, of *woman*" could accomplish; according to the *Boston Courier*, they found the spectacle to be "the most splendid and tasteful" ever exhibited in New England. After buying a 25¢ ticket (50¢ on opening day), fairgoers climbed a specially erected staircase to Quincy Market's second-floor hall, 380 feet long with 18,000 square feet of space (figs. 28, 29). A panorama of the Charlestown Navy Yard, complete with models of the vessels then at anchor, and "the rising Sun just greeting the *now*-unfinished monument with its brilliant rays," was the first spectacle. Other wonders included an eighteen-foot scale model of the finished Monument; a concert piano that attracted a bid of $400 ($32,000); a "*splendid moorish cushion*, wrought by a Moorish Lady for an English physician," in gold and silver brocade on a velvet background; a "genuine fac simile" of Gen. Warren's handwriting; and a model of the house where Warren was born. Spread across forty-three tables, staffed by several hundred women from Nantucket to Northampton, were antique porcelains, japanned stools, cigars, canes, cutlery, bags, hats, gloves, dolls, fairies, aprons, tapestries, lithographs, glassware, coral baskets made of red sealing wax, scrimshaw dolphins, smoking caps, silk vests ornamented with gold figures, along with all manner of books, clothing, flowers, fruits, baked goods, preserves, toys, and candies.[42]

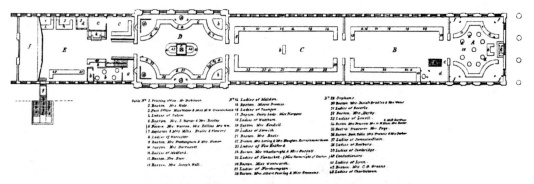

fig. 29: tables at the Ladies' Fair

To keep fairgoers informed of special events and musical performances, such as those by the Brigade Band that played in the evenings, as well as to promote Monument-related poetry and sell advertisements, Hale produced a daily newspaper, *The Monument*, which a Boston printer and typefounder, S.N. Dickinson, printed in the hall on the latest rotary press. Another revenue-generating innovation was the Bunker Hill Post Office, which in addition to handling regular mail sold personalized letters in stamped envelopes that appeared to have arrived from Fairyland. So great was the fair's popularity, that Hale's committee decided to keep it open an extra week. Ticket

---

42. *Boston Courier*, 8 September 1840, p. 2, emphasis original; fair items primarily from the *Courier*, 8, 9, 10 September 1840, all p. 2.

receipts came to $9,885, indicating there were 35,450 fee-paying visitors. Contributing to total net income of $30,035 ($2.4 million) was $556 from *The Monument*, $552 from the Post Office, $869 in homemade confectionery, and $200 for the model Monument, purchased on Judah Touro's behalf by visitors from New Orleans. One of the most popular tables, though at $606 only the seventh highest in sales, was Medford's, which the *Courier*'s reporter praised for the "beauty and chasteness of the articles, as well as the lady-like deportment of its fair assistants." Irked no doubt by the fair's astonishing success, and perhaps troubled by a growing female assertiveness, Yankee gentlemen sought opportunities to slur the ladies' achievement.[43]

Boston newspapers made much of an "amusing incident," initially reported in the *Salem Observer*. On the fair's first full day, a "noble-hearted, jolly tar" came to the table of "a lovely and rich young lady." Turning to his friend, Jack murmured, "'I swear, I would give *twenty dollars* to kiss that girl.'" "'You may,' said the young lady, timidly stepping forward, and receiving a kiss." Jack willingly handed over the money, feeling he had made a good bargain. Newspapers reprinted the story in full, even as they went to inordinate lengths to deny its truthfulness, to the extent that the *Courier*'s editor (correctly) dated its origin to a ladies' fair held at Faneuil Hall in May 1833 to raise funds for the New England Asylum for the Blind. Yet despite demonstrating that the tale was apocryphal, the editor nonetheless wrote that it "probably" never happened, which left the door open to the idea that it did, with the insinuation that attractive girls at the fair were happily selling kisses. Retelling the story, and then embarking on a lengthy evaluation of its authenticity, was a device through which the editor could emphasize the ideal societal mores that differentiated virtuous Yankee ladies and honorable Yankee gentlemen. Salem was "a distant place," the *Courier*'s editor explained, where reporters did not appreciate the "delicacy and propriety of deportment" that was such a "distinguishing characteristic of the ladies" at the fair. To suggest that a lady would ever kiss a sailor in public was "insulting and injurious to the ladies, whose purity of character" was equal to their patriotism. Feigning surprise that the *Transcript* could have printed such an "odious lie"—even though he had just done the same thing himself—allowed the *Courier*'s editor to point out that his counterpart at the *Transcript* had previously been "proverbial" for his "chivalry in all that relates to the purity and delicacy of the female character." Still, reactions to the amusing incident were essentially tongue-in-cheek compared to the furor that erupted two weeks later.[44]

Shows of solidarity with and support for Hale's fair came from ladies' initiatives in and out of state, although contributions were generally small. A notable exception was the proceeds of a performance at Boston's Tremont Theatre on 1 October 1840 by the beautiful Austrian ballerina Fanny Elssler, who had already turned heads in Manhattan with her tango-like Cachucha in Rossini's *The Lady of the Lake*. So

43. Warren, *Monument Association*, pp. 300, 305–6; *Boston Courier*, 10 September 1840, p. 2.

44. *Boston Courier*, 15 September 1840, p. 2, emphasis original. For the original story, in which the sailor paid $10 for the privilege of staring at the lovely lady, see for instance the *New-Hampshire Patriot*, 27 May 1833, p. 3. Salem is fifteen miles from Boston.

enthralled were Bostonians at the prospect of seeing her dance that one aficionado paid $502 ($40,000) for the Tremont's choicest box. Yet when Elssler presented the BHMA with a check for $569, her earnings for a single night, Yankee editors took umbrage.[45]

"*General La Fayette* laid the corner stone," fumed the *Boston Recorder*, "and a *Theatre dancing girl* finishes the structure—What a humiliating contrast!" It was disgraceful, chimed the *Christian Observer*, that the "shameless arts of a public dancer" should raise a monument to American patriots. "Newspapers, from one end of the country to the other," had "launched their shafts of scorn and irony": "*the money must be returned.*" As did several other journals, the *Observer* compared Elssler's gift with Phryne's offer to rebuild the shattered walls of ancient Thebes providing they bore an inscription, "destroyed by Alexander, restored by Phryne the courtesan." Even the Athenians, noted one editor, "a people that made no pretence to the morality of the gospel, but yet had some remains of a sense of national dignity," declined to accept. Boston's *Weekly Magazine* questioned whether the BHMA's directors—and all those who adored "'the divine Fanny'"—had more respect for "their wives and daughters, or a French dancer." "The wages of obscenity," the editor warned, must never "mingle with and pollute the free-will offering of New England daughters." Bostonians must not allow a monument to their fathers' and their country's glory to "go up stained with the proceeds of an exhibition fraught with indecency." Out-of-state editions were no less blistering. New York's *Observer and Chronicle* ranted that the honor of crowning the Monument had fallen into the hands of an "imported hireling female, who disgraces, not herself, that were impossible, but her sex, for so much a night." There could be no "possible palliation for such an insult to the nation." Should the directors accept the donation, the editor hoped that "the lightning of Heaven" would raze the Monument to its foundations. By comparison with the "antics of a shameless, half naked Dutch dancer," the "naked hill on which so many brave men bled and died for their country, and for mankind," was the most solemn and patriotic sight.[46]

Irony abounded in the Elssler affair, as it inevitable does in matters of national honor. As Joseph Buckingham, the BHMA's president and editor of the *Courier*, one of only two Boston newspaper's along with the *Transcript* to defend Elssler, pointed out, if Bostonians were thrilled to have a foreigner—Lafayette—lay the Monument's cornerstone then surely they could accept a contribution to the Monument's completion from a foreigner. Americans at that time had a president whose first language was Dutch, and his son, John Van Buren, had been Elssler's escort and dinner companion while she was in New York. When attacking Elssler, editors boasted of the "noble example" set by Bostonians in the "full flush of refinement and civilization," who were

45. *Boston Transcript*, 9 September 1840, p. 2, 2 October 1840, p. 2, 8 October 1840, p. 2, 10 October 1840, p. 2; regular seats sold for $3 ($240 today).

46. *Boston Recorder*, 25:42 (16 October 1840), p. 167, emphasis original; *Christian Observer*, 19:43 (22 October 1840), p. 171; Phryne, from the *Baptist Advocate* (New York), reproduced in the *Christian Secretary* (Hartford), 3:33 (30 October 1840), p. 2; *Boston Weekly Magazine*, 3:4 (10 October 1840), p. 31; *New York Observer and Chronicle*, 18:41 (10 October 1840), p. 162.

the "free citizens of the most high-toned, moral, and intellectual" state in the Union. Yet these editors were too ignorant to learn that Elssler's nationality was Austrian, calling her French or Dutch at random; there could have been few events of a more refined or civilized nature than a performance by a world-class ballet dancer of an opera by the leading Italian composer; and there was little that was high toned or free spirited about slandering a professional female artist for a cultural activity promoted and patronized by society's male elites. In the event, an embarrassed Hale sided with the critics, and a puzzled Buckingham banked the money.[47]

Lying at the heart of this hidebound affair, as with all the other internecine struggles for possession of the Monument's soul, were the mounting external threats to the parochial world inhabited by old-stock Yankees. Theirs was an insular and oddly anachronistic milieu, which their ancestors had created and they were determined to maintain, based on a selective interpretation of a history first compiled by tribes of nomadic shepherds halfway around the globe some three thousand years earlier. They were anxious and defensive, these Yankees, even as their own wealth and power grew exponentially, albeit through a pattern of economic booms and busts. Challenges of a technological, ideological, and cosmopolitan nature swept across the Atlantic with every sailing ship, and were proliferating among inquiring immigrant minds within their own hemisphere. Yet even as they enthusiastically incorporated many of these developments into their culture, most notably in railroads, mass media, firearms, and finance, they relied increasingly on their founding myths, Yankee mystique, and biblical nationalism to define who they were.

As "The Bible," an article reprinted from the *Hartford Courier* on the *Bunker-Hill Aurora*'s front page by William Wheildon (Solomon Willard's biographer), demonstrates so well, it was the Old Testament that laid out the principles of Yankeeness in 1840. "A nation must be truly blessed"—as, of course, the American nation patently was—"if it were governed by no other laws than those of this blessed book; it is so complete a system, that nothing can be added to or taken away from it." It provided instruction and council for a senate, as well as authority and direction for a magistrate; it cautioned a witness, and required an impartial verdict from a jury. It "sets the husband as lord of the household, and the wife as mistress of the table; tells him how to rule, and how to manage." It "entails honor to parents, and enjoins obedience upon children." It limited the sway of sovereigns, prescribed the authority of masters, and promised God's protection for all those who walked by its rules. It gave directions for weddings and burials, and laid out the tenets of marriage and inheritance. It defended the rights of all people, just as it revealed vengeance to the defrauder, the over-reacher, and the oppressor. It was both the first book and the oldest book in the world, comprising the choicest material, the finest instruction, and the most pleasurable and satisfying revelations. "It contains the best laws and profoundest mysteries that ever were

47. *Boston Courier*, 7 October 1840, p. 2, and 22 October 1840, p. 2; "noble," *Christian Observer*, 19:43 (22 October 1840), p. 171. In 1843, the Free Church Baptists bought the Tremont Theatre, which they renamed the Tremont Temple.

penned." It resolved all debates, eased the mind and conscience of any scruples, and it revealed the only living and true God. It exhibited life and immortality and showed the way to everlasting glory.[48]

Biblical nationalism was as rooted in Yankee ideology as it was persistent. Forty years later, as part of a grand celebration to mark the 250th anniversary of Boston's founding, Mayor Frederick O. Prince began an evening of oratory in Faneuil Hall by confining his introductory remarks to Boston's Puritan heritage. He need not remind the assembled Bostonian elites—although that was of course what he was doing—of the hardships and sufferings of those first settlers, of their fortitude and heroism, and especially of their "piety, and godliness, and religious devotion." Everyone knew the Puritans' story, which was "as familiar as household words," and rightfully so because Bostonians were indebted to the Puritans for the blessings they all enjoyed. "They sowed, we reap." Under Puritan tutelage, Boston had grown from a single inhabitant to a "great and prosperous city, containing a large and an intelligent, thrifty, and happy population." It was in Boston that Puritans had erected America's first church, its first schoolhouse, and its first printing press, "those mighty agents in the progress of civilization." Bostonians were the first to proclaim man's capacity for self-government, and the right to education at public expense, because they understood how ignorance bred disorder. There could be no doubt that John Winthrop's landing in 1630 was a momentous event, for it had "kindled the vestal flame of liberty, civil and religious." Since then, "Watched by Puritan care, and protected by Puritan valor," that flame had become "the beacon of hope to all oppressed nations of the earth."[49]

G.W. Warren, former mayor of Charlestown, municipal judge, state representative, and the Monument's historian, was the evening's closing speaker. Turning to Mayor Prince, Warren reiterated that Winthrop's first objective had been to form a church, so as to secure the "free, unmolested worship of God," and this first work of Winthrop's had "lasted to this day." Charlestown's First Church, where Warren worshipped, had exactly the same covenant, in precisely the same words, as the one signed by Winthrop in 1630. "Whatever change and progress may be brought about by material things," Warren was confident that there would be "no change in the expression of Christian fellowship." Winthrop's great work, Warren had no doubt, was the "founding of a Christian commonwealth." All the good influences that Massachusetts had exerted, and would surely continue to exert, were directly traceable to the "good seed" brought by Winthrop and planted in Boston. *Sicut patribus sit Deus nobis* (may God be with us, as he was with our fathers) emblazoned on Boston's city seal and flag (and its motto still) was "an official acknowledgement of the providence of God, and

---

48. *Bunker-Hill Aurora*, 6 June 1840, p. 1.

49. "Remarks of the Mayor, Frederick O. Prince," *Celebration of the Two Hundred and Fiftieth Anniversary of the Settlement of Boston, September 17, 1880* (Boston: City Council, 1880), p. 32. A Bostonian, John Cotton, did establish the first public school in colonial America, Boston Latin, in 1635, and the wife of Rev. Jose Glover installed the first printing press at Harvard College in 1635, but credit for the first church belongs to a primitive fort in Plymouth that doubled as a meeting house for the First Church of Christ, in 1622, if not an earlier shed in Plymouth that burned down soon after construction.

a perpetual prayer for its continuance." For as long as Bostonians devoutly recognized the providence of God, "in church, and in school, and in daily life," so God would bless their endeavors.[50]

Finishing the Monument

Since the directors published their gloomy report in June 1840, there had been a dramatic turnaround in the BHMA's finances. Sarah Hale's Ladies' Fair, which generated $30,000, had guaranteed $10,000 apiece from Amos Lawrence and Judah Touro. There had been Fanny Elssler's contribution of $570, and various other donations amounting to $4,550. Sale of the extra land surrounding the Monument for property development had more than paid off the loan from the Suffolk Bank. After repaying the debt to Lawrence, and the rent for Quincy Market of $400, the accounts stood at $47,190. Instead of paying the contractor and work crews by the hour, as Solomon Willard had done, the directors bowed to public pressure and signed a fixed-price contract with James Savage for $43,800 to finish the job by 1 October 1843. Willard, ever parsimonious, always maintained that this represented a premium, but at least it satisfied the critics and assured the project's completion.[51]

Because a fixed contract gave Savage the chance to make a profit, it encouraged innovation and efficiency, with little risk of sacrificing quality, as the directors made sure to retain Willard's services as architect and supervisor. Savage had soon purchased a six horsepower steam engine to drive the hoist, arranged a wire-operated bell so that masons at the apex could communicate with riggers at the engine, and it is likely that by 1842, if not earlier, Savage switched from hemp to the latest iron ropes, manufactured at a factory in Saxonburg by German immigrant John A. Roebling. "It was a novel sight," Warren wrote, to watch immense blocks of stone "gracefully moving upward to their places," propelled only by the "mysterious and newly adopted force" of steam. For every extra course that Savage's men laid, so the degree of difficulty multiplied. Ropes were longer, the engine worked harder and wore out quicker, wind gusts grew stronger, the workspace became more constricted, and laborers had many more stairs to climb to the worksite.[52]

Especially tricky were the last seven conical courses, for while they comprised smaller, lighter blocks, it was no longer possible to use Almoran Holmes's center-mounted hoist. Riggers had to install wooden staging to friction-fit around the cone as it rose toward the capstone, and, on the ground, they had to erect shears to lift the blocks, materials, and workers, and then remove the staging when the job was complete. There are no extant drawings of the shears, but they were probably similar to the system used to complete the 101-foot Commemoration Column at Devenport, England, in 1827 (fig. 30). Riggers would first have erected a substantial post fifty or

50. "Address of Hon. G. Washington Warren," ibid., pp. 60–62.

51. Warren, *Monument Association*, p. 311; contract completion date from *Boston Courier*, 6 November 1840, p. 2.

52. Steam engine and bell, E.H. Cameron, "Of Yankee Granite: An Account of the Building of the Bunker Hill Monument," *Technology Review* (June 1952), p. 422; Warren, *Monument Association*, p. 303.

sixty feet high, made from quartered Douglas-fir trunks banded together with heat-shrunk iron hoops, stepped on the foundations, braced with backstays, and lashed to the Monument at intervals with suitable spacers.

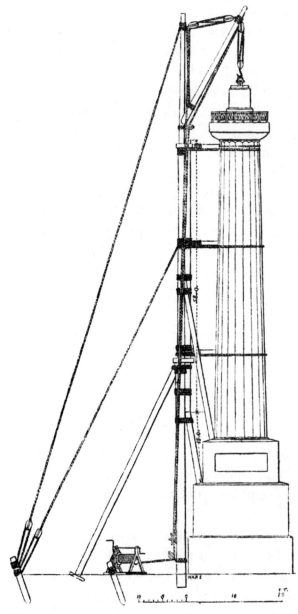

fig. 30: lifting shears installed on the Commemoration Column, Devenport, England

Using Holmes's hoist, they would then have winched up a second post, socketed it into the first post with an iron collar, and similarly lashed it to the Monument. Three or four further sections would have brought them close to the apex, where they could then install the lifting shears. Wire or rope guys would provide additional bracing. With the Navy Yard being so close to the work site, it would have been economical to use salvaged masts for the five or six sections. It was a testament to Yankee ingenuity

that there were no accidents during this last phase of construction. Savage felt sufficiently confident about the reliability of the shears that he sold rides to the top in a
bucket for 20¢.[53]

Steam was up in good time on Saturday, 23 July 1842. With the first chime of the
town clock at 6:00 AM, Charlestown artillery fired a signal gun, Savage opened a valve,
and the engine began to lift the capstone, a pyramid of polished granite three feet six
inches high and weighing two and a half tons. Riding the stone was Col. Charles R.
Carnes, the Monument's chief rigger and a native of Charlestown, gripping the rope
with one hand and a large American flag with the other. For sixteen minutes, the directors and several hundred locals craned their necks and no doubt perspired slightly
with anxiety as Carnes and the flag approached the apex. He appeared to be "mid-
way," as one newspaper put it, "between heaven and earth." Just after 6:30, masons
finished cementing the capstone in place, and the artillery let loose with a twenty-six
gun salute, one shot for each state in the union.[54]

Although there is little evidence to suggest they did, Bostonians may have known
that for ancient Egyptians, obelisks symbolized the great sun god Ra. There is something visceral about an obelisk—like the arm of a giant sundial—that prompts such a
conclusion. References to the sun and its rays abounded in Monument discourse.
With evident pride as well as relief, the *Boston Courier*'s editor wrote, "The column has
risen to its projected height. The sun greets it at his rising from the ocean," and "the
last beams of departing day linger and play on its summit." "Long may it stand," the
editor hoped, as a memorial to the patriots of '75, and as a "lesson to light posterity
on the path to glory, honor, and entire national independence." There would have
been many a celebration that night at the Warren Tavern in Charlestown, and perhaps
even Savage and his crew broke their pledge of abstinence.[55]

Blessing the Capstone

With the capstone in place, the BHMA's directors could at last plan a celebration
for the next Battle of Bunker Hill anniversary—17 June 1843, a Saturday—to dedi-
cate the finished Monument. After everything they had been through to complete the
project, there would inevitably be an air of anticlimax about the proceedings; there
would be no Lafayette, few of the veterans of the battle were still living, and now great-
grandsons of those who fought would be present, for whom the events of 1775 were
that much less immediate. Yet in most respects, the dedication turned out to be as
grand an affair as the cornerstone laying ceremony of 1825. Following a cold, rainy

53. Thomas Grissell, "Account of the Scaffolding Used in Erecting the 'Nelson Column,' Trafalgar Square,"
Discussion 667, *Institution of Civil Engineers*, 3 (1844), pp. 209–10. John Foulston designed the column in honor of the
Plymouth Dock Town Hall, which itself signified George IV's recognition of the new town of Plymouth. Freestanding
shears would have been possible but highly problematic in the days before steel, requiring a huge mass of timber for the
back stays as well as the load-bearing center post and hinged gaff arm, which would have needed to be about 240 feet tall.
Dismantling the shears would also have been tricky; Savage's riggers probably attached guy ropes at intervals, ran these
around a system of pulleys anchored through the obelisk's viewing windows, unlashed the post, and then paid out the
ropes so that the whole contraption toppled and fell to the ground in a controlled manner.

54. *Boston Courier*, 25 July 1842, p. 3. In 1842, Congress fixed the official national salute at twenty-one guns.

55. Ibid.; also in many local editions, such as *Farmer's Cabinet*, 29 July 1842, p. 2.

Friday, the *Boston Courier* could report that the day was "cloudless and serene," mirroring the weather pattern of eighteen years earlier by a "remarkable coincidence." A continuous display of "flags, banners and streamers of all nations and of every hue and shape" lined the route, and draped the rigging of the 2,700-ton battleship USS *Ohio*, revenue cutter USS *Hamilton*, and other vessels in the harbor. An escort of militia, comprising twelve companies of artillery and forty-eight companies of riflemen, led the parade, which took an hour to pass. President John Tyler waving from an open barouche came next, followed by other dignitaries including what amounted to Tyler's entire cabinet, and then a dozen carriages bearing 107 veterans of the War of Independence (thirteen of Bunker Hill), of which the oldest was ninety-seven and the youngest seventy-four. There were thirty marching bands, contingents of Freemasons, and delegations from a range of societies and all parts of the country. Two hundred policemen kept back the dense crowds, whose cheers were most "deafening" when the veterans passed. Deafening too would have been salutes from the guns of the Navy Yard as the head of the procession crossed the Warren Bridge, and from Charlestown's artillery when it reached Bunker Hill at 12:30 PM, an hour and three-quarters after leaving the State House.[56]

Down-slope from the Monument overlooking the Mystic River, upwards of fifty thousand Americans—all of them standing during the proceedings, except for a few hundred ladies privileged to have reserved seating—ringed a pavilion for the dignitaries and speakers. Rev. George E. Ellis, pastor of Charlestown's Unitarian Church, gave the blessing, and Buckingham introduced the orator. Jaded, disconsolate even, after two decades of public service and five weeks retired as Tyler's Secretary of State, it was a different Daniel Webster from 1825. He had just walked from Ellis's rectory having sunk a tumbler-full of brandy, which would not have been his first drink of the day. A breeze came past him from the hill, and a sea of bodies soaked up his usually powerful waves of sound. As he droned on about all those who had made the Monument possible, some of those straining to hear must have wondered how this could be the declaimer of legend. But once into the meat of the speech, perhaps warmed by the brandy and with the wind backing around, his old genius became apparent.[57]

Speaking "slowly and with great deliberation," as one spectator later recalled, Webster proudly exclaimed, "The Bunker Hill Monument is finished. Here it stands," infinitely high in its objects and purpose, rising over the land and over the sea, visible from the homes of 300,000 citizens of Massachusetts. This was no mere memorial or

---

56. *Boston Courier*, 19 June 1843, pp. 1–2; the *Courier* provided a detailed description of the various displays, including mention of the flags and a model ship hanging from the British consulate. Warren, *Monument Association*, pp. 318–20. Secretary of the Treasury John C. Spencer, Secretary of War James M. Porter, Postmaster General Charles A. Wickliffe, and Secretary of the Navy Abel P. Upshur; Atty. Gen. Hugh S. Legare had arrived with Tyler's entourage but he fell sick and died on 20 June; Webster had just retired as Secretary of State and Tyler did not reshuffle his cabinet until July, moving Upshur to State and appointing David Henshaw to the Navy; Tyler had replaced the deceased Harrison, so there was no vice president.

57. Several newspapers reckoned the crowd at 100,000, although Webster's estimate of 50,000 seems more likely. More precisely, Ellis ran the Harvard Universalist Society. Claude Moore Fuess, *Daniel Webster* (Boston: Little, Brown, and Company, 1935), vol. 2, pp. 130–32; Daniel Webster, *An Address Delivered at the Completion of the Bunker Hill Monument, June 17, 1843* (Boston: Tappan and Dennet, 1843), pp. 1–4.

work of art. It had a purpose, a purpose that enrobed it with "dignity and moral grandeur," a purpose that gave it character. Indeed, the words they were hearing at that moment came not from mortal lips but from the very soul of the Monument: it was "the orator of this occasion." It was a plain shaft. It bore no inscriptions. "Fronting to the rising sun, from which the future antiquarian shall wipe the dust," it stood silent. And yet, at the sun's rising and setting, in the noonday blaze and the "milder effulgence of lunar light, it looks, it speaks, it acts, to the full comprehension of every American mind." In its blank anonymity—Webster was explaining—lay the Monument's oracle-like purpose, "its silent, but awful utterance." On that day, it happened to be speaking to them through Webster, just as it would speak to them in future oratories through successive generations of Americans, as they rose up before it and gathered around it. Because of its special character, its message, he predicted, would always be "of patriotism and courage; of civil and religious liberty; of free government; of the moral improvement and elevation of mankind." For theirs was a civilization founded on solid science, informed by knowledge of nature and the arts, stimulated by moral sentiment, and purified by the truths of Christianity.[58]

fig. 31: Daniel Webster, ca. 1852

Webster spent much of the oration, which was longer than in 1825 at 116 minutes, comparing Spanish colonizers with Puritan settlers. Because there was no liberty in Spain, there had been none to transmit to the Spanish half of the New World.

---

58. George Frisbie Hoar, *Autobiography of Seventy Years* (New York: Charles Scribner's Sons, 1903), vol. 1, p. 135; Senator Hoar, a Harvard freshman in 1843, had first walked three and a half miles from Cambridge to Boston, marched with his classmates in the Harvard contingent from the State House to Bunker Hill, and then stood for the speech. Webster, *Address*, pp. 5–6.

Greedy for gold and power, Spanish conquerors behaved as they did at home, robbing, destroying, and enslaving the native peoples. Standing armies acting in the king's name acquired territory by fire and sword, killed thousands by fire and sword, and even attempted conversion to Christianity by fire and sword. Under the "Providence of God," by contrast, the English had been fitting themselves for self-governance, and the "great work of introducing English civilization, English law, and what is more than all, Anglo-Saxon blood, into the wilderness of North America." Social equality prevailed among the Puritan settlers. They were of the "middle, industrious, and already prosperous class," and brought with them Bacon and Locke, Milton and Shakespeare, but most of all they brought the Bible, a book of faith and doctrine that had taught them individual responsibility, dignity, and equality. England's Puritan settlers were consequently "industrious individuals, making their own way in the wilderness, defending themselves against the savages, recognizing their right to the soil, and with a general honest purpose of introducing knowledge as well as Christianity." "Behold, then, fellow citizens," Webster implored them, his arm no doubt outstretched to the Monument, the difference resulting from the operation of the Spanish principle and the Puritan principle. "Here, to-day, on the summit of Bunker Hill, at the foot of the monument, behold the difference!" Americans' inheritance was liberty, "secured and regulated by law, and enlightened by religion and knowledge," whereas South America's legacy was "power, stern, unrelenting, tyrannical, military power." Look around, he gestured, to the fields, "verdant and beautiful, well cultivated," and at that moment "loaded with the riches of the early harvest." Look at the thousands of vessels filling the harbor. Look at the fair city, the abode of so much happiness, so much independence, so much knowledge. Look at the hundred churches, where citizens worshipped God in peace. "Everywhere there is order; everywhere there is security." And over all this, Webster emphasized, "hovers liberty, that liberty which our fathers fought, and fell for, on this very spot."[59]

Whether from the shifting direction of the wind or a lift in his delivery, by the end of his address "great organ tones"—as one spectator recollected years later—were reverberating around the declivity of Bunker Hill. Webster had them now, these Yankee descendants of John Winthrop. They had deserted their ancestors' homeland, skirmished constantly with Amerindians up and down their western frontier, fought a crippling war for independence from King George III, blundered through the War of 1812, and puzzled their way out of a three-year economic slump. Now their farmlands were fertile, their harbor bustled with commerce, and their finished Monument—"by its uprightness, its solidity, its durability"—could proudly proclaim their forbearance and rectitude to the cruel Spanish New and corrupt European Old Worlds alike. One of the greatest living orators in their language was reminding them that the blessings they enjoyed were dependent on the duties and obligations they must perform. He was enjoining them to remember that it was only their religion, their morals, and their knowledge that could keep them respectable, happy, and free. He was urging

---

59. *Boston Courier*, 19 June 1843, p. 2; Webster, *Address*, pp. 13, 11, 16, 13, 17, 13, 14, 15–16.

them to elevate and improve, to look to their children's future, so that love of country would grow with equal fervor in the hearts of their descendants. "And then, when honored and decrepid age shall lean against the base of this monument," there would rise from every youthful breast, "the ejaculation—'thank God, I,—I also—am an American.'" Webster's innuendo may have been unintentional, yet he could hardly have constructed a more vivid metaphor to link the now fully erect Monument with the upright morals and virile forcefulness of the Yankee character, even among Americans of advancing years.[60]

fig. 32: "Here it stands"

Those sufficiently important to have invitations assembled at Faneuil Hall for dinner at 6 PM. Colored streamers cascaded from the center of the ceiling to the pillars. Placards between the pillars carried the names of the nine previous American presidents, as well as Benjamin Franklin and Robert Fulton, developer of the paddlewheel steamer. Either side of the hall's permanent sculpture of an American eagle hung signboards bearing the names of Judah Touro and Amos Lawrence (but not Sarah Hale or

60. Hoar, *Autobiography*, vol. 1, p. 136, borrowed from Fuess's research; Webster, *Address*, pp. 19–20.

Solomon Willard). On prominent display was a sign in honor of "Agriculture, the Mechanic Arts and Commerce." It must have been a grand occasion, as well as a rare one, for there have been few times when every functioning member of a president's cabinet has met outside the Oval Office for a public event. Notable by his absence, though, was former president John Quincy Adams, who was at home in a pique, and not, as Webster had said in his oration, too ill to attend. "What a name in the annals of mankind is Bunker Hill! What a day was the 17th of June 1775!" Adams wrote in his diary, but "what a burlesque upon them both" was "an oration upon them by Daniel Webster, and a pilgrimage by John Tyler and his cabinet of slave-drivers." There was venom in Adams's pen that day. "And then a dinner at Faneuil Hall in honor of a President," he added, "hated and despised by those who invited him to it, themselves as cordially hated and despised by him." Adams not only detested Freemasons and Whigs in general, and Tyler in particular, but he had also sneered at the Monument since its inception, despite his strong biblical nationalist sentiments.[61]

After the meal, which included sampling two confectionery representations of the Monument, came the standard thirteen toasts. To mollify prohibitionists, Buckingham toasted Tyler with water, although—according to the historian and Massachusetts Democrat George Bancroft—Tyler was surreptitiously ducking under the table during the evening to imbibe on a flask of brandy. Tyler toasted his former Secretary of State Webster with a reference to Webster's stand against Britain's policy of searching ships suspected of carrying contraband. In a portent of U.S. foreign policy to come, Webster gave his toast to "The rights of American Commerce, everywhere to be protected, at any expense of blood and treasure." And Secretary of War James Madison Porter toasted, "The monuments erected by the Pilgrims and their descendants—The first of *morals* and the second of *granite*—may they be as coeval in duration as matter can be with mind." Porter hailed from Norristown, Pennsylvania, but as orators like Everett and Webster had suggested, when Americans of any state in the Union planted their feet on the exact spot where the immortal Warren fell, they would absorb the special character of Winthrop, the Revolution's heroes, and all their Yankee forebears. When they rose up and gathered round the Monument to speak, a special message of biblical nationalism would flow into them: they would talk of Puritan morality and toast their granite-like Yankee character.[62]

"Know this is the place," Puritan settlers assured themselves in 1628 before sailing from England, "where the Lord will create a new Heaven, and a new Earth," and they could build "new Churches, and a new Common-wealth together." Those first Yankees knew from their Bibles (Isaiah 65:17–23) that God had promised them he would

61. *New-Hampshire Patriot*, 22 June 1843, p. 3, from the *Boston Advertiser*. From Penn's Hill near his Quincy home, Adams, aged seven, and his mother Abigail, had watched the smoke from burning Charlestown and heard the rumble of the distant cannon. Other occasions were the dedications of the Emancipation Memorial (1876, Washington, DC), the Washington Monument (1897, Philadelphia), and the Comte de Rochambeau statue (1902, Washington, DC), and the Memorial Day ceremony of 2007 (Washington, DC). *The Diary of John Quincy Adams, 1794–1845*, ed. Allan Nevins (New York: Longmans, Green and Co., 1928), 17 June 1843, p. 550.

62. For Tyler's drinking, see Fuess, *Daniel Webster*, vol. 2, p. 134. *New-Hampshire Patriot*, 22 June 1843, p. 3, from the *Boston Advertiser*, emphasis original.

"create new heavens and a new earth," where bad things would be forgotten and there would be rejoicing. In this new place, he would "create Jerusalem," where they would "build houses, and inhabit them," where they would grow crops and eat of the bounty. They would not labor in vain in this new place, for they were "the seed of the blessed of Jehovah." Boston was a special place, where they would follow God's word, tread in his footsteps, work hard for his glory, and covenant between themselves and with God to keep their end of the bargain. As they could see by the speed at which Boston grew into the Commonwealth of Massachusetts, Providence looked favorably on their endeavors: assuredly, they were God's elect and this place was the New Jerusalem.[63]

Webster similarly understood the God-given specialness of *place*. He was a pious believer who worshipped every Sabbath, told his household shortly before dying "that there *is* a God, all must acknowledge," and once surprised a dinner party by confessing, "The most important thought that ever occupied my mind was that of my individual responsibility to God." When he orated at Plymouth Rock on 22 December 1820 to commemorate the first settlement of New England, he said, "There is a local feeling, connected with this occasion, too strong to be resisted; a sort of *genius of the place*, which inspires and awes us." They could all feel that they were "on the spot" where Puritans laid the first hearths and the first altars of New England, "where Christianity, and civilization, and letters made their first lodgment, in a vast extent of country, covered with a wilderness, and peopled by roving barbarians." Because the Rock, that special spot "on which New-England received the feet of the Pilgrims," was beneath their feet, "reverence and admiration" filled their hearts and elevated their character.[64]

Faith in God's plan also explains the Monument's obelisk form. As he stated in a series of lectures on art, the Monument's designer Horatio Greenough based his abhorrence of "embellishment" on the hypothesis that "there is one truth, even as one God, and that organization is his utterance." Only the purest, "organic" forms, therefore, conveyed God's organization and infallible artistic taste. When it came to monumental architecture, there could be nothing more organic than an obelisk. An obelisk, moreover, had "a singular aptitude, in its form and character, to call attention to a spot in history." A plain, unembellished obelisk "says but one word, but it speaks loud." If Greenough understood its voice correctly, "it says, Here! It says no more," and that was why he designed an obelisk for Bunker Hill. Solomon Willard, who was of a mind with Greenough, labored to ensure that the joints were tight, the faces flawless, and the angles precise; Willard even dispensed with Greenough's single accoutrement, the plinth. An unembellished obelisk, constructed of smooth granite blocks,

---

63. Capt. Edward Johnson, *Wonder-Working Providence of Sions Saviour in New-England* (London, 1654), in William Frederick Poole, ed. (Andover, MA: Warren F. Draper, 1867), p. 3; Authorized King James Version (1611), Isaiah 65:17–23.

64. Fuess, *Daniel Webster*, vol. 2, pp. 408–10, emphasis original; Fuess, who acknowledged that "Webster's conduct was not always that of an ascetic," was nonetheless convinced Webster was no cynic when it came to Christian faith (p. 411). Daniel Webster, *A Discourse, Delivered at Plymouth, December 22, 1820, In Commemoration of the First Settlement of New-England* (Boston: Wells and Lilly, 1821), pp. 11–12, emphasis original, and "character," p. 8.

rising sheer from the ground, was a pure organic form. It said, "Here I am—I mark the spot—I convey God's purpose," and nothing more. Such was the Monument's indefinable yet uncompromising genius of place.[65]

fig. 33: harbor, State House, and Monument, from across the Mystic River, ca. 1845

For the God-fearing Yankees like Greenough, Willard, Hale, and Webster who designed it, quarried its granite, raised funds for its completion, and orated in its shadow, the Monument inspired and it awed. When they stood on the very spot where Warren fell—overlooking the improved farms, church steeples, industrious city, and bustling harbor where Winthrop landed in 1630—they felt the genius of the place. When they planted their feet on Bunker Hill, the moral character of their Puritan ancestors filled their hearts. When they gathered beneath the Monument, marveling at its perfectly smooth, tightly fitting blocks of granite, they remembered the battle of 17 June 1775 and the origins of their unique republicanism. As they squinted at the sunlight glinting off the polished capstone high above, a powerfully compelling biblical nationalism crept into them too. Webster's vigorous diplomacy had resolved the Canadian border dispute with Britain (the Webster–Ashburton Treaty of 1842), which in turn freed President James K. Polk to concentrate on westward expansion. Webster was one of many who thought Polk's Mexican adventure foolish, yet the discovery of gold in California in 1849 quickly convinced thousands of doubters that colonizing North America from sea to shining sea was their manifest destiny.

65. Horatio Greenough, "Independent Beauty," and "Aesthetics at Washington," in *A Memorial of Horatio Greenough*, ed. Henry T. Tuckerman (New York: Benjamin Bloom, 1853), p. 135, "his taste infallible," p. 143, "Here!" p. 82, and see Greenough's extended footnote explaining why "fractional" columns made unsuitable monuments.

4. THOMAS HANDASYD PERKINS: SHINING CITY

A mutually reinforcing combination of belief and evidence created an assumption held by many Americans that they and their country were not merely different but exceptional. Had not the Puritans covenanted that as long as they were industrious, frugal, moral, and God fearing, Providence would guide their destiny? Had not the civilizing virtues of unique republican institutions facilitated a rare combination of population growth, territorial expansion, economic productivity, and social stability? When Wellesley College professor Katherine Lee Bates thought about her country in 1895, she conjured a vision of a gleaming alabaster city, undimmed by human tears. "America! America!" she cried exultantly, "God shed His grace on thee," and crown thy good with brotherhood, "from sea to shining sea." Whether of hammered stone or gilded metal, a *shining city on a hill* has been symbolic of American exceptionalism ever since John Winthrop's colonists settled the slopes of Boston's Trimountaine and their sons began pushing inexorably west.[1]

Appropriately enough, the phrase itself originated in the Gilded Age, coming into print in "A Towered City," an 1890s poem by Gardiner L. Tucker dedicated to his alma mater, the University of the South at Sewanee, Tennessee: "A shining city, set upon a hill / Above the world, to send forth truth and light." Prior to this, there were two related yet distinct metaphors, both inspired by the New Testament. On one hand, there was a holy *shining city*, to be a magnet to first draw, then house and fortify the faithful. "And the city had no need of the sun, neither of the moon, to shine in it," promised Saint John the Divine in the Book of Revelation 21:23, "for the glory of God did lighten it, and the Lamb is the light thereof." To English Christians like John Bunyan this meant a shining city not only in heaven but also as an earthly paradise for God's elect. "We will build him a Golden shining City," preached Bunyan in the 1660s, "the Joy of all the World." On the other hand, there was an exemplarist *city on a hill*, to be a beacon of hope to the rest of the world. When Winthrop addressed his fellow Puritans on the *Arbella* in 1630, he drew from Matthew 5:14–16, Jesus' Sermon on the Mount. "Let your light so shine before men," Jesus told his disciples, "that they may see your good works, and glorify your Father which is in heaven." Because they were "the light of the world," they were as a city upon a hill, and "A city that is set on an hill cannot be hid." On Boston's hills, Puritan settlers and their Yankee descendants would both build and become that city—a shining city of granite buildings and upright souls—which would combine the spiritual nourishment of Bunyan's "New-Jerufalem" with Winthrop's example-setting moral beacon.[2]

Cognizant of its biblical resonance and patriotic meaning, political elites across the centuries have chosen aspects of the metaphor's coded rhetoric to promote

1. Katherine Lee Bates, "America the Beautiful."

2. For Gardiner's poem and a discussion of its provenance, see *New York Times* (*NYT*), 1 March 1942, p. BR31; John Bunyan, *The Holy Citie: Or, The New-Jerufalem* (London: Francis Smith, 1665), p. 153, "fhining" in the original; Authorized King James Version (1611). For exemplarism, see H.W. Brands, *What America Owes the World: The Struggle for the Soul of Foreign Policy* (Cambridge: Cambridge University Press, 1998), esp. pp. 1–4 and chap. 5.

progressive agendas and nurture national consciousness. Delivering a Fourth of July oration in 1821, Secretary of State John Quincy Adams told Washingtonians that they and their Declaration of Independence stood alone, "a beacon on the summit of the mountain, to which all the inhabitants of the earth may turn their eyes for a genial and saving light." They must bless God "for the bounties of his providence" and "renew the genuine Holy Alliance" of the Declaration's principles, recognizing them as "eternal truths." Unveiling Manhattan's Simón Bolívar Monument in 1921, President Warren G. Harding told New Yorkers that the New World was a "miracle" of the divine plan, an "inevitable part in the supreme scheme for developing civilizations." America's constitutional republican system was a "gift to mankind," a "beacon fire," a "model" after which were fashioned the "fundamental laws of the world." Few presidents have seemed as convinced of Providence's guiding hand as George W. Bush, who as Republican nominee in 2000 told a B'nai B'rth convention, "Our nation is chosen by God and commissioned by history to be a model to the world." President Barack Obama, whose speeches frequently referred to America as a beacon, told a gathering at the Pentagon Memorial on 11 September 2010 how Muslims who destroyed the World Trade Center "sought to demoralize us, divide us, to deprive us of the very unity, the very ideals that make America *America*—those qualities that have made us a beacon of freedom and hope to billions around the world." Few presidents deployed the metaphor's power better than Ronald Reagan, who also appreciated the symbolic properties of granite. Perhaps he had heard the legend that settlers named New Hampshire's White Mountains after seeing sunlight sparkling from their mica-rich granite summits. "How stands the city on this winter night," Reagan asked the nation in his farewell address of 1989. "She still stands strong and true on the granite ridge," he answered, "And she's still a beacon, still a magnet for all who must have freedom." Yet just as exceptionalism has defined Americans' sense of self and lent purpose to their lives, so too has it also created anxiety.[3]

How was small-town colonial Boston, with its clapboard row houses, gray granite warehouses, and cows grazing its bucolic Common able to grow so rapidly during the Early Republic, becoming not merely a thriving metropolis but also a physical New Jerusalem, a shining city on a hill with gilded domes and glinting skyscrapers? Wharves still jutting into Boston Harbor from Atlantic Avenue, though occupied now by upscale condominiums, suggest the logical answer, of trade with European partners just 3,000 miles away on favorable winds. Roads running behind Atlantic Avenue with names like Pearl Street, East India Row, and Canton Street provide clues to a more exotic explanation, lying far distant across the Pacific Ocean. By the 1840s, Atlantic

3. John Quincy Adams, *An Address Delivered at the Request of a Committee of Washington; on the Occasion of Reading the Declaration of Independence, on the Fourth of July, 1821* (Washington, DC: Davis and Force, 1821), p. 22; Warren G. Harding, speech, Simón Bolívar Monument unveiling, *NYT*, 20 April 1921, p. 2; Bush cited in *NYT*, 29 August 2000, p. A19; as of February 2011, Obama had given at least a dozen speeches referring to America as a beacon of hope or a beacon of freedom; Obama cited in http://obama-speech.org/transcript.php?obama_speech_id=3633 (accessed 28 January 2011), emphasis added; "Transcript of Reagan's Farewell Address to American People," *NYT*, 12 January 1989, p. B8.

trade was indeed fundamental to Boston's commerce, but the capital for that commerce and the export-led textile industry burgeoning behind it accrued during the Old China Trade of the prior two decades, in particular, from the smuggling of Turkish opium to Canton by a single merchant, Thomas Handasyd Perkins.

For Bostonians of the early nineteenth century, a forest of rigging and a flapping of canvas were daily reminders that without mercantile trade there would be no prosperity. Still, regular business profiteering provides only a partial explanation for the swift accumulation of capital during the 1820s that fueled the Massachusetts miracle.[4] Merchant families found turning a profit from common trade to be a competitive, hardscrabble business. They also had learned over the generations that their unique geopolitical situation offered boundless possibilities for lucrative contraband trade, which the more astute of them conducted on a surprisingly global, transoceanic basis. Churchmen and reformers fretted about smuggling, although proud Yankee merchants, bankers, shipwrights, and insurers disowned the word. Instead, they worked collectively to project an exemplary image of their upstanding character. They legitimated their status by erecting granite edifices, just as they assuaged their consciences with generous acts of philanthropy. For anxious Yankee elites, granite was always far more than a practical building material. Quarried locally by devoted artisans who charged little for their labors, it was affordable—frugal. Impervious to frost, it was durable—incorruptible. This hardest and heaviest of stones was special—exceptional. Its installation demanded industry and ingenuity—work in God's sight. Rough, smooth, or polished, it was sober, rather than glitzy like marble—yet seemingly it could reflect the sun.

Custom House: Granite Icon

At the Bunker Hill Monument's completion in 1843, its superintendent Solomon Willard published a treatise to prove why, far from being exorbitantly expensive as detractors charged, it was actually a bargain. Instead of paying the 90¢/foot market rate for stone, Willard had supplied top-quality Quincy granite for just 20¢/foot. Whereas granite for the $102,000 Monument had totaled $70,000, of which $35,000 was for transportation, Willard estimated that Boston's Custom House then under construction would contain a similar volume of granite but cost over a million dollars. Important benefits, moreover, had accrued from his quarrying endeavors. He noted how a new industry was developing at Quincy that had already generated over three million dollars ($240 million), and the stone-working and installation techniques he pioneered to successfully erect the Monument had led Boston's architects to adopt granite as their preferred medium of construction. In claiming to have "established the credit of a new building material," Willard was perhaps too modest. For two decades, granite was his life—he had become its devoted apostle. In addition to super-

---

4. My use of the term, here, is ahistoric but apropos; Governor Michael S. Dukakis liked to take credit for the so-called Massachusetts Miracle of the 1980s, which saw the rise of technology companies such as Digital Equipment Corporation and Wang Laboratories along Route 128 and the concomitant transformation of the local economy.

intending the Monument and several downtown granite building projects, from a gateway for the Granary Burying-Ground to the Bowdoin Street Congregational Church (1830) and the Suffolk County Courthouse (1836), Willard sold at prime cost all the finished stone his Quincy quarry workforce of a hundred or so men could produce. Ignoring complaints from other quarry owners that he was destroying their livelihoods, Willard argued that by furnishing the highest quality stone at the lowest possible price he was creating a market where none had previously existed, so all would benefit. Commensurate with his work, Willard observed that there had been a "strongly marked improvement" in "the style of building, and the taste in architecture." He was thinking in particular of three massive Greek Revival edifices by local architects Isaiah Rogers and Ammi B. Young, for which his quarries supplied the granite.[5]

Rogers designed and supervised two similar Merchants' Exchange buildings, one on New York's Wall Street (1842), the other on Boston's State Street (1842). For the New York exchange, Willard arranged for the owners to buy what became the Wigwam Quarry at Quincy, contracting his services to them for $5 a day. At the height of this project, Willard employed ninety drillers, riggers, and hammerers who cut and finished $256,000 ($20 million) worth of granite, including fifty blocks of over twelve tons, and eighteen fluted columns of thirty tons each. After splitting the last two columns from a single eighty-foot slab, Willard reported that his crew had "the greatest hoorah and throwing of caps that ever was in Quincy!" Upon hoisting the last block onto a Manhattan-bound schooner, they fired three rounds from an old cannon that they affectionately called the Yankee. New York's exchange sprouted a second story in 1910 and is today a historic landmark. Boston's, which sported Doric rather than Ionic columns and featured a carved granite panel of an eagle astride the globe, withstood the Great Fire of 1872 only to make way for the Boston Stock Exchange (1891) by Peabody & Stearns, the magnificent granite Romanesque Revival façade of which still graces the east elevation of forty-story Exchange Place (1984).[6]

For what would be one of the most expensive public buildings yet constructed in America, architect Ammi B. Young specified granite as the sole structural material for Boston's Custom House (1847), not only for the walls and floors but also for the domed roof. Its thirty-two Parthenon-like fluted columns, cut by Willard's crew from the Granite Rail Quarry, were thirty-two feet high and weighed forty-two tons, making them the largest monolithic stone elements in the country. It took combined teams of fifty-five yokes of oxen and twelve horses to drag them all the way from Quincy on sixteen-wheeled wooden cars. Many of the blocks in the lower courses, which masons set at four feet five inches, were fifteen and a half feet long; at just under three feet thick, these weighed fifteen tons apiece. Few structures could have projected mercantile solidity and bolstered civic pride quite like Young's brooding, iconic

5. Solomon Willard, *Plans and Sections of the Obelisk on Bunker's Hill, with the Details of Experiments Made in Quarrying the Granite* (Boston: Chas. Cook's Lithograph, 1843), pp. 19, 20, 21; prime cost, in William W. Wheildon, *Memoir of Solomon Willard: Architect and Superintendent of the Bunker Hill Monument* (Boston: Bunker Hill Monument Association, 1865), pp. 233, 228–29.

6. Wheildon, *Willard*, pp. 233–34.

Custom House. Struggling to convey its enormity, a reporter for the *Boston Post* could only say it was "imposing in its dimensions, harmonious in its proportions, impressive in its solidity, and beautiful in its strength." Less sympathetic commentators were more verbose.[7]

fig. 34: Custom House, ca. 1880

In a *North American Review* article so scathing that the U.S. Treasury commissioned William W. Wheildon to publish a rebuttal pamphlet, Arthur D. Gilman judged the Custom House to be "so incongruous and absurd a pile" that he could scarcely enumerate its "deformities" and "reckless squandering." From the outset, the architect had "gratuitously violated" every Grecian standard of taste. "Extravagantly *large stones*" destroyed all proportion; monstrous columns—"excrescences" requiring complete removal—shut out the light and emphasized the "harsh nakedness" of the wall behind; apertures in the elevated stylobate (to access the basement) were "beyond the reach of reasoning, irony, and invective"; unrelieved by architrave, the windows were "mere holes in the wall," while windows between the frieze's triglyphs were "barbarisms"; and "the *dome*—its last and crowing absurdity"—defied all reason. At least its aspect was "sufficiently gloomy and forbidding," Gilman mused. He expected that its cramped office space and "ill-digested arrangement of the principal apartments" would prove, like the sullen caves of the necromancer Domdaniel, inconvenient for the transaction of business.[8]

7. Walter H. Kilham, *Boston After Bulfinch: An Account of Its Architecture, 1800–1900* (Cambridge: Harvard University Press, 1946), p. 30; William Churchill Edwards, *Historic Quincy, Massachusetts* (Quincy, MA: City of Quincy, 1957), p. 122; *Boston Post*, 18 August 1847, p. 1.

8. William W. Wheildon, *Strictures, on an Article in the* North American Review, *for April, 1844, entitled*

Gilman was right about its aesthetics. A Roman dome ill suited a Doric colon-nade, the basement access doors and windows in the frieze were incongruous (the black rectangles below and above the six windows to the right in fig. 34), and the over-all execution was heavy-handed, with the solidity of the finished product belying the fine lines of the architect's proposal. But as a Grecian temple to honor the god of trade it was nonetheless a masterstroke, even if, as an office building, it had outstripped its utility before opening day. Then again, the demand for more floor space by a growing army of federal inspectors, weighers, gaugers, and desk clerks was as much a product of Boston's burgeoning mercantile trade. Boston's first house-sized custom house on Red Lion Wharf sufficed for forty-eight years; its second, on Exchange Street, lasted thirty eight; its third, on Custom House Street, twenty-nine; and its fourth, at the head of Long Wharf, overflowed its bounds within ten years. Once it had recovered from Thomas Jefferson's ill-conceived trade embargo and the War of 1812, Boston's seaborne commerce expanded substantially. Vessels arriving in Boston Harbor from foreign ports rose from an average of 569 and 610 per year during the 1790s and 1810s respectively, to 787 and 1,336 per year during the 1820s and 1830s respective-ly.[9] Tonnage entering the port rose from 140,000 in 1826 to 194,000 in 1835 and 309,000 in 1845, a year when 564 ships over 100 tons and eighty-three over 500 tons bore Boston registrations.[10] From 1824 to 1836, the value of Boston's official foreign trade—imports plus exports, as tallied by Custom House clerks—doubled, from $17.9 million to $34.4 million ($2.7 billion today).[11] Until the Civil War, excise duty, levied by customs officials at ports of entry, was the principal source of federal govern-ment revenue, accounting for 92 percent by the 1840s, or $27.5 of the $30 million total. To put it another way, taxes on imports at Boston Harbor paid for one sixth of the federal government's entire budget. Through their trade journals, Boston's com-mercial elites proudly advertised their huge contribution to the national treasury, iron-ic though that was, given their parents' rationale for fighting the War of Independence. It was as if the weight of the granite Custom House was stamping a fiscal imprimatur on decades of illicit profiteering.[12]

Imported goods were subject to excise tax at rates from 5 to 100 percent, with 30 percent being the most common duty. Regular Bostonians had always chafed against

---

"*Architecture in the United States*" (Boston: W.D. Ticknor, 1844); Arthur Delavan Gilman, "Architecture in the United States," *North American Review*, 58:2 (April 1844), pp. 440–44, emphasis original.

9. "Commercial Statistics," *Merchants' Magazine and Commercial Review*, 6:2 (1 February 1842), p. 184. Extant sources present data unsystematically; here, the tonnage for the 1830s is an average of 1,199 for 1830–35 and 1,473 for 1835–41.

10. "Progressive Wealth and Commerce of Boston," *Merchants' Magazine and Commercial Review*, 15:1 (1 July 1846), p. 36, rounded from 139,609, 194,420, and 308,943; registrations, "Commercial Statistics," *Merchants' Magazine*, pp. 83–88.

11. "Progressive Wealth," *Merchants' Magazine*, p. 39; these figures do not include the bulk of Perkins's trading activity, conducted in large part as that was through the Port of New York.

12. *Historical Statistics of the United States*, "Federal Government Revenue, by Source, 1789–1939," ed. John Joseph Wallis (Cambridge University Press, 2009, online), table Ea588–93; in 1848, Boston's merchants paid Custom House collectors $4.9 million ($392 million) on $21.2 million ($1.7 billion) worth of dutiable goods, see *Niles' National Register*, 75:25 (20 June 1849), p. 389, and Wheildon, *Strictures*, p. 20.

these taxes. William Lloyd Garrison, publisher of the anti-slavery *Liberator*, was furi-ous when the collector charged him $60 on a China tea service valued at $180 ($14,400), which liberationists in Edinburgh had sent as a gift in recognition of his activism. Merchants passed import duties on to wholesalers, so they could accept them as an inevitable cost of doing business, although as pragmatists they sought workarounds, ranging from trading abroad then banking the cash proceeds, to various forms of smuggling. When a country institutes a price control, tariff, or outright ban on the import or export of a particular good, and then two traders collude to circum-vent the regulations, the good becomes contraband and the traders become smugglers. While the word is pejorative, circumstances often paint the crime as victimless, or even cast smugglers as popular heroes. Moralistic Bostonians naturally pooh-poohed any insinuation that their shining city might somehow be a smugglers' den. Indeed, they frequently elevated practitioners of the art to storied patriots and worthy philan-thropists, a tradition that U.S. historians have perpetuated. Boston's leading role in the radicalism of the 1770s made this ironic double standard possible.[13]

Revolutionary War history allowed Boston's citizens to gloss—or deny—their smuggling roots, and its merchants to justify the activity as a patriotic endeavor. They knew that their mid-eighteenth-century counterparts—particularly the wealthiest ones—cheated on their half of the mercantilist marriage with Britain, which required them to trade exclusively with the mother country in return for advantageous pricing and a range of colonial benefits, from naval protection to jurisprudence. Historians have shown that during the late colonial period, three-quarters of the tea and a quarter of total imports were contraband, though they prefer to reject charges that Boston pa-triots such as John Hancock were "Notorious Smuggler[s]." Still, it seems odd that legitimate traders would have led a boycott against their own goods. Neither was it logical for the likes of Hancock to don Mohawk costumes and claim that tipping 342 chests of British East India Company (EIC) tea into Boston Harbor was a patriotic act when the EIC was actually making tea cheaper by selling it directly to the colonists. Unless, that is, Hancock and his fellow rabble-rousers understood that Parliament's Tea Act of 1773 had obviated their lucrative smuggling business. At the time of the Tea Party, Hancock lived in the grandest mansion in Boston, built on Beacon Hill of Quincy granite by his merchant uncle, Thomas, with profits from trade with Britain as well as illegitimate trade with Holland and the Dutch East Indies, smuggling, that is, in contravention of Parliament's Navigation Acts.[14]

13. Tax rates, *Niles' National Register*, 75:25 (20 June 1849), p. 389; "Grateful Acknowledgement," *Liberator*, 17:31 (July 1847), p. 122.

14. For smuggling, see Carole Shammas, "How Self-Sufficient was Early America?" *Journal of Interdisciplinary History*, 13 (1982), pp. 247–72, and esp. Wim Klooster, "Inter-Imperial Smuggling in the Americas, 1600–1800," in *Soundings in Atlantic History: Latent Structures and Intellectual Currents, 1500-1825*, eds. Bernard Bailyn and Patricia L. Denault (Cambridge, MA: Harvard University Press, 2009), pp. 141–80. A particularly forceful denial that Hancock was a smuggler is O.M. Dickerson's "John Hancock: Notorious Smuggler or Near Victim of British Revenue Racketeers?" *Mississippi Valley Historical Review*, 32:4 (March 1946), pp. 517–40; for a discussion of the unlikelihood that Hancock personally boarded the ship to destroy the tea but was nonetheless urging others to do so, see Alfred F. Young, *The Shoemaker and the Tea Party: Memory and the American Revolution* (Boston: Beacon Press, 1999), pp. 55–57; for an analysis of transatlantic misunderstandings and the raising of the Tea Party mob, see John Ferling, *A Leap in the Dark: The*

Capital that had accrued by 1775 from colonial-era smuggling had dissipated by 1783, but wharves, shipbuilding, and attitudes survived the War of Independence, as had distant contacts in foreign markets. Boston's merchants were soon afloat again, eager to rebuild their capital by exploiting new niches, the most profitable of which required smuggling, at first with the French colony of Saint-Domingue and the Spanish colonies of South America, and then, after the Haitian Slave Revolt, increasingly through Canton, the only Chinese port open to trade with foreigners. Estimating the macroeconomic contribution of an illegal activity is necessarily problematic, although extant materials can sometimes be sufficient to document a micro study that illuminates the bigger picture. Such is the case for Boston, and its leading smuggler-merchant, Thomas Handasyd Perkins. Perkins, in company with his network of Brahmin relatives and associates, accounted for so much capital—and so much philanthropy, including donations to the BHMA—that it is hard to look across the harbor toward Boston, with its glinting granite skyscrapers and shining State House dome, without acknowledging the contribution of the Old China Trade in general and smuggled opium in particular.

Most remarkable about the three-cornered trading model that Perkins pioneered between Boston, Smyrna (Izmir) on the Turkish Aegean, and Canton is not the scale of the profits, nor the model's sophistication or complexity, nor even the boldfaced alacrity with which Perkins implemented it.[15] Rather, Perkins was the director of a transnational conglomerate, operating at a supra-governmental level, 170 years before Theodore Levitt coined the term *globalization*. When Perkins sent the aptly named brig *Bocca Tigris* across 39,000 miles of blue water to a subsidiary's warehouse at Smyrna, then to the Bocca Tigris or Tiger's Gate at the mouth of Canton's Pearl River to transship cargoes, then to the Port of New York with luxury goods before banking the proceeds in Boston, he was setting the open-access, open-ocean ground rules that underwrote American free-market capitalism.

Perkins's Shining City

When he turned twenty-one in 1785, Perkins was ready for a mercantile career. His maternal grandfather, Thomas Handasyd Peck, had been New England's principal trader of otter pelts, his father had just begun trading furs and wine when he died prematurely in 1773, his widowed mother ran a Boston store, and Perkins himself had worked in a merchant's countinghouse for five years. He began shuttling between a Boston warehouse and Le Cap François in Saint-Domingue, where, in partnership with his brother James and Walter Burling, an older man who had Caribbean experience, he traded commodities such as salt cod, flour, horses, coffee, and slaves on commission. All this business was illicit because French mercantilist regulations stipulated that colons could only trade with the mother country and must transport their goods

---

Struggle to Create the American Republic (Oxford: Oxford University Press, 2003), pp. 94, 104–6.

15. In terms of physical trade, New York, the port through which Perkins sold the imported goods, rather than Boston would be more accurate, but he ran the operation from his Boston headquarters and it was to Boston that the profits flowed.

in French vessels. But Perkins the entrepreneur equated risk with opportunity, and the profit he made proved his premise. "There are so many dangerous consequences," Perkins explained to one Salem merchant to justify his steep charges, adding with a hint of sarcasm that, "smuggling is a heart-rending business." At a time when a 150-ton schooner changed hands for $8,000, it is noteworthy that a healthy male slave could fetch $2,300 at auction in the Caribbean, a sale that yielded Perkins a $60 ($4,800) commission. Saint-Domingue's planters welcomed the goods that American smugglers offloaded to droughers or sneaked into port—as Perkins preferred—"under cover of night," no more so than after the slave revolt in August 1791 when they became a lifeline. Perkins, Burling, & Co., along with other U.S. merchant houses, supplied the bulk of the French soldiers' food, supplies, and ammunition. They fought too. Burling sustained a leg wound in battle against former slaves, and James and a third brother, Samuel, commanded a guardhouse at Le Cap. Having amassed at least $10,000 in profits, James pulled out of the doomed island in May 1792 to form J. & T.H. Perkins Co. with his brother Thomas, although the partnership continued slaving, at least into 1793, including voyages by the *Delight* and the *Willing Quaker* to Cuba and Jamaica with as many as 147 slaves.[16]

After a voyage to Canton in 1789 as supercargo (trading officer) for a Salem merchant, Thomas Perkins had his eye on the far greater profits of the China trade, to which end he developed a calculated risk-taking strategy that within thirty years would make him one of America's wealthiest men.[17] He speculated, tapping into the latest commodities at their cheapest source, starting with sea otter pelts from the Northwest Coast. Gambling that illegal activity drove away competition, he sought opportunities for contraband trade despite the hazard of seizure or fines. At the same time, he spread risk, apportioning his capital across multiple vessels, pooling investors for each voyage, and insuring cargoes. He entrusted captaincies to friends, account books to his brother, and commerce at ports-of-call to relatives, establishing branch offices with caches of specie and storage facilities at Canton, London, and Smyrna. Even bad times rewarded his boldness. Perkins Co. shipped sugar and flour to starving Parisians during the Terror of the French Revolution, and, toward the end of the War of 1812, Perkins fitted out a privateer, the 500-ton *Jacob Jones*, which captured two EIC ships off Malaysia loaded with gold and opium.[18]

---

16. Perkins to William Gray, 16 December 1787, J. & T.H. Perkins Co. letterbooks, compiled by James Elliot Cabot, Thomas Handasyd Perkins Papers (hereafter cited as THPP-L), Massachusetts Historical Society, Boston, reel 6, p. 16 (hereafter 6:16); at an auction in September 1786, Perkins sold one slave for Samuel Proctor for $2,300 and another, being lame, for $1,600, THPP-L, 6:11; "under cover," THPP-L, 6:13; Samuel G. Perkins, "Insurrection in St. Domingo," *Proceedings of the Massachusetts Historical Society* (April 1886), esp. pp. 319–21, and p. 334, where French soldiers, Perkins noted, "had been fed principally by the American merchants at the Cape"; Timothy M. Matthewson, "George Washington's Policy Toward the Haitian Revolution," *Diplomatic History*, 3:3 (Summer 1979), p. 325. *Delight*, THPP-L, 6:42–44; due to the imprecise language of the letterbook extracts, the intended destination of all 147 slaves specified is unclear.

17. In the early 1820s, there may have been only three richer Americans: Philadelphia banker Stephen Girard, New York landlord Stephen Van Rensselaer, and New York fur trader John Jacob Astor.

18. France, May–August 1793, THPP-L, 6:45, 48–49; *Jacob Jones* sailed under a letter of marque, capturing an EIC ship and a brig at Pontian (Johor, Malaysia), THPP-L, 6:223, 6:228–29, 6:232.

Transatlantic shipping, from West Indian coffee to Dutch woolens, was steady business but Perkins was after the high profits of 70–130 percent from landing China teas, luxuriant silks, and brightly colored, hand-printed nankeen cottons at New York, where the population had trebled in twenty years and the postwar economy was booming. He had efficient transportation, ready capital, dependable wholesalers, and, at Canton, not only his own factory but also the trust of Houqua, the most astute of the thirteen *hong* merchants licensed by the Qing government to conduct business with foreigners.[19] Aside from the hazards of a 34,000-mile round trip, his only difficulty was in supplying Houqua with sufficient funds to buy the cargoes.[20] With the Chinese largely self-sufficient in commodities and luxury goods, Canton was a challenging market for U.S. exporters, excluded as they were from India's specialty spices and opium by the EIC, and now that they had over-culled the Northwest sea otter and the Antarctic fur seal. When there was still no national currency, U.S. bank notes were problematic tender in Atlantic ports and useless in China, while acceptable specie— Spanish silver dollars or gold doubloons—was in short supply, commanding a premium of 5 percent just as its purchasing power in Canton was falling due to inflation. Perkins's solution was to experiment with innovative exports, particularly quicksilver (mercury) and Turkish opium, as illustrated by the first voyage of the brig *Bocca Tigris* in the 1818 season. This voyage was by no means the first to carry these cargoes, in which Perkins had been dabbling since 1811, and neither was it typical of the dozen or more that Perkins ran to Canton each season, primarily for the tea trade.[21] But it is ideal for demonstrating how he was able to finance trade in steady commodities like tea without excessive recourse to specie, particularly because it is also one of the few voyages for which extant account ledgers, blotters, and letters, combined with newspaper reports, allow for an accurate reconstruction.

For bulky cargoes of tea, Perkins favored ships, small ones, similar to the 360-ton *Astrea* on which he had sailed to Canton in 1789, but brigs half that size could be advantageous for mixed cargoes. Launched by Sprague & James of Medford in 1816, *Bocca Tigris* was typical of the efficient brigs built for under $10,000 by the father-and-son shipwrights whose yards lined the tidal banks of the Mystic and North Rivers. At eighty-five by twenty-two feet and with an eleven-foot draft, the 180-ton *Bocca Tigris* could reach ten knots and carry 250 tons, yet sail over sandbars and beach with safety for cleaning or repairs; with no superstructure save a low-slung wheelhouse, she could sail close to the wind or ride out a storm. A captain, two mates, and six or

---

19. For New York's burgeoning economy, see Paul E. Johnson, *The Early American Republic, 1789–1829* (New York: Oxford University Press, 2007), p. 62. Foreign traders found *Houqua* easier to pronounce than his Chinese name, Wu Bingjian.

20. Sailing directly to Canton and back, via Cape Horn and the Pacific, was roughly 17,200 miles each way, but, in practice, most of Perkins's voyages included other ports, often in Europe, to either transship cargoes from Boston or New York, buy specie or goods for sale in Canton, or to sell China teas on the return leg; a voyage that included the Mediterranean was closer to 40,000 miles than 34,400.

21. For Perkins's first experiments in quicksilver and opium, see Perkins to J.W. Langdon, supercargo of the ship *John Adams*, "If your terms [for selling nankeens at the best price] cannot be had there [Gibraltar], you may carry them [the nankeens] to Malta and there exchange them for Opium or quicksilver," November 1811, THPP-L, 6:203.

seven seamen could handle her two square-rigged masts and a gaff off the main, making few demands on cargo space and costing little in wages. Most importantly, in
Canton, where EIC or Dutch ships of 800–900 tons were the norm, Perkins's diminutive craft attracted little notice and may have been able to sidestep some of the costly,
arcane procedures imposed by Qing officials to regulate trade with foreigners.[22]

fig. 35: Thomas Handasyd Perkins

Under Capt. Samuel Conant, *Bocca Tigris* left Boston Harbor in October 1817
bound for the Mediterranean with flour, coffee, Havana cigars, pepper, Chinese sugar,
and Chinese cinnamon (cassia), the latter items being transshipments from prior cargoes. Arriving at Smyrna in mid-November, Conant consigned the cargo to Woodmass
& Offley. Edward Woodmass was one of a dozen merchants organized through the
Levant Company of London, along with relatives George and John Perkins, Loyalist
refugees who had fled Massachusetts in 1775, and who constituted Perkins Brothers
of Smyrna. After loading 40,000 pounds (300 chests or piculs) of Turkish opium,
Conant left for Leghorn (Livorno), where he added 250,000 pounds of quicksilver

22. *Bocca Tigris*, from Hall Gleason, "Old Ships and Shipbuilding Days of Medford," *Medford Historical Register*,
32:1 (March 1929), p. 12; L. Vernon Briggs, *History of Shipbuilding on North River, Plymouth County, Massachusetts*
(Boston: Coburn Brothers, 1889), gives prices for several vessels, including the 317-ton ship *Foster* that sold in 1819
for $10,057 (p. 324); for life aboard a similar brig, see Richard Henry Dana Jr., *Two Years Before the Mast: A Personal
Narrative* (1840; repr., Boston: Houghton Mifflin Company, 1912), in the *Pilgrim*, 180 tons, 86.5 feet, built in 1825 by
Bryant, Sturgis & Co.; Conant's total disbursements during the three months he was at Canton were a steep $7,455 but
given the array of potential fees (pilotage, comprador, linguist, tolls, chops, port) and import/export duties—as detailed
in Paul A. Van Dyke, *The Canton Trade: Life and Enterprise on the China Coast, 1700–1845* (Hong Kong: Hong Kong
University Press, 2005)—Perkins's vessels seemed not unduly troubled by the strict, complex regulations imposed by the
Qing government, even though small vessels paid proportionally higher port fees (ibid., pp. 105–7).

from the mines of Monte Amiata, contained in clay or iron flasks holding seventy-five pounds and in smaller leather-lined wooden boxes. Perkins presumed that Canton's sudden spike in demand was from dyestuff makers who converted quicksilver into vermilion, but, as he learned later, domestic mines had tapped out, leaving refiners of precious metals scrabbling for mercury amalgams. Conant also took aboard 104,978 Spanish dollars, which cost Perkins $109,283 at a 4 percent premium. From Gibraltar, where Conant loaded 860 pigs of lead, bought charts, and restocked his provisions including six barrels of salted beef landed from another Perkins Co. vessel, *Bocca Tigris* followed the trade winds, south, to skirt the Doldrums. Even in the vastness of the South Atlantic, mariners could find company on popular sea lanes. Thirty-seven days out, at lat 21º 56′, long 27º 30′, Conant exchanged messages with a home-going vessel before heading east to catch the Roaring Forties and clear the treacherous Cape of Good Hope. From Madagascar and Mauritius, he cut across the Indian Ocean to Java Head, and then passed the Malay islands to Portuguese Macao.[23] During the three months he was in the Pearl River Delta, Conant sold the opium directly to smuggler-traders in multi-oared sampans (*fast crabs* or *scorpions* in Chinese), before proceeding to Whampoa, the anchorage below Canton proper, where he discharged the lead, mercury, and silver and took aboard 245 tons of return cargo.[24] Her crew rested and her stores replenished, *Bocca Tigris* left Canton on 7 October 1818, tying up at a New York wharf 117 days later, completing the 17,200-mile journey at an average speed of 5.3 knots.[25]

Newly affluent New Yorkers were eager purchasers of the brig's luxury Chinese goods. Manhattan auction house J. & P. Hone & Co. immediately sold 688 cases of silks and 35,400 of the best-quality yellow, white, and blue cotton nankeens for $327,718. Merchants Carnes & Rhodes bought 40,000 yellow nankeens. Other merchants purchased crepe shawls, delicate blue and green sarcenets, nankeens, and camphor, an aromatic distillate used in antiseptic liniments. Peter Remsen, who was acting as Perkins's agent, transshipped star anise to London, sent portions of the cargo to Boston, and took debentures on the balance, which included 50,500 nankeens and 200 cases of camphor. Over a year later, when all the sales invoices had arrived at Perkins's Boston counting house, extant account ledgers show that the cargo yielded $495,577 ($39.6 million), a large sum for a small boat.[26]

---

23. Voyage details synthesized primarily from Perkins's ledgers and letterbooks, esp. THPP-L, 6:262, 6:291; there is some background on the historical usage of mercury in China for embalming and the production of stamp ink, mirrors, and cinnabar ware in Leonard J. Goldwater, *Mercury: A History of Quicksilver* (Baltimore, MD: York Press, 1972), pp. 62, 79–80; lat 21º, in *Baltimore Patriot*, 6 January 1819, p. 2; as Nathaniel Bowditch's *New American Practical Navigator* (New York: Edmund M. Blunt, 1826), pp. 269–70, shows, there were well-plotted routes that captains could follow from the Atlantic to Indian Oceans en route to Canton; at Canton, *Mercantile Advertiser*, 16 January 1819, p. 2.

24. It is beyond the scope of this project to disentangle from the incomplete yet labyrinthine ledgers Houqua's involvement in trading Perkins's opium (direct or otherwise, some or all); a running ledger covering 1819–22, entitled "Perkins & Co. & Houqua Opium A/C [Account]," for instance, contains balancing "To Houqua" and "By Houqua" entries of $26,335, suggesting that Houqua was drawing a commission or handling connivance fees.

25. *New York Daily Advertiser*, 1 February 1819, p. 2.

26. "*Bocca Tigris*, P&L Estimate: First Voyage to Smyrna and Canton, 1818 Season," spreadsheet, compiled by author (available on request), from blotter and ledger entries, THPP, reels 9, 11, as well as prices published at the time.

Detailed blotters and summary ledgers allow for accurate computation of the outbound cargo's Mediterranean purchase price and the inbound cargo's New York sales revenue, as well as the voyage's costs, but there are no figures for sales or purchases at Canton, so the net profit requires estimation. *Bocca Tigris*'s specie would have sold into an inflated market for a loss of about $9,500, but demand for quicksilver allowed Houqua to mark it up by 150 percent—40/100 as Perkins wrote it—from its purchase price of $0.45 per pound to $1.13, yielding $169,000.[27] In his eagerness to corner the market and price out competitors, Perkins paid too much for his first bulk purchase of Turkish opium, at $3.57 per pound, and it sold at a discount in Canton to the EIC's Bengal and Malwa opium, but, in 1818, traders were still paying $5.43 a pound for Turkish, for a profit of some $74,000.[28] Adding in sales of the lead, a consignment of glassware and cotton, and the modest profit on the cargo from Boston to the Mediterranean of $16,000, the outbound cargo on this basis generated $239,000, after Houqua's 5 percent commission. While Perkins invariably failed to sell his inbound cargoes at retail price (100/100), paying at minimum a 5 percent commission and sometimes selling teas at 75/100 into a glutted market, he generally bought in Canton at less than 50/100, sometimes as low as 15/100 in the case of corals. For the premium blue nankeens that Hone auctioned for $1.50, Houqua—given his connections and bulk buying—no doubt paid under $0.75, which is also in the $0.60–0.90 range quoted by contemporary sources. On this conservative basis, the inbound cargo cost $269,000 at most, a net outlay over the outbound cargo of $30,000 rendered small by the high-profit sales of quicksilver and opium. After deducting New York customs duties of $64,157, cargo insurance of $7,509, Hone's auction charges of $19,921, the voyage's overhead of $15,882, various commissions and other costs of $9,585, and $5,000 for depreciating 50 percent of the *Bocca Tigris*'s value, the net profit was $344,000 ($27.5 million).[29]

Profit from this first voyage of the *Bocca Tigris*, which eclipsed that of the ten other Canton voyages during the 1818 season by Perkins's ships, requires qualification. Italian quicksilver and Chinese silks fetched premium prices at their ports of destination. Conant was an astute trader who captained an exemplary voyage. Teas that constituted the bulk of the other ships' cargoes sold into a more competitive market. And there were, of course, loss-making voyages, such as the *Bocca Tigris*'s third in March 1820, when a storm off Ostend drove her aground, drowning Benjamin Hector, an African American of Providence, Rhode Island, who was probably the brig's cook. It is also important not to exaggerate profits from opium, at least during Perkins's initial

27. Perkins to Paine, November 1819, THPP-L, 6:302.

28. Perkins to Paine, mid-1817, THPP-L, 6:285. Carl Seaburg and Stanley Patterson, *Merchant Prince of Boston: Colonel T.H. Perkins, 1764–1854* (Cambridge, MA: Harvard University Press, 1971), point out that the price of opium doubled (p. 296), reaching $10 a pound in 1821 (p. 298), but they underestimate the weight of a picul (a chest of opium bags) at 125 pounds rather than 133; while I doubt Perkins & Houqua ever netted much more than $7 per pound, Perkins's figure of $5.43 that I have used is safely conservative.

29. For nankeen prices, see for instance, Andrew Ljungstedt, *Historical Sketch of the Portuguese Settlements in China; and of the Roman Catholic Church and Mission in China* (Boston: James Munroe & Co., 1836), p. 314. "*Bocca Tigris*, P&L Estimate," estimated numbers rounded.

forays. While opium accounted for a third of *Bocca Tigris*'s outbound cargo, it represented just 22 percent of the voyage's net profit, contributing 7 percent to a company-wide profit of $1.05 million ($84 million). Still, at least one other Perkins vessel carried opium to Canton in the 1818 season, a cargo of six hundred chests—double the *Bocca Tigris*'s—of high-grade Persian that shipped from the Gulf and sold at a 25 percent premium to Turkish. Windfall opportunities like quicksilver succumbed within a season or two to competition and market saturation, whereas demand for opium at Canton kept increasing. As specie became scarcer, Perkins increased his reliance on Turkish opium, to the point where it was fundamental to the success of the sophisticated, transoceanic business model that he was developing.[30]

An indication of the growing scarcity of specie in the United States was that in 1818 and again in 1820 Perkins sailed for London in an effort to locate new supplies. Specie, anyway, was a dead-weight cargo, attractive to thieves and pirates, which cost premiums to buy and insure. Substituting opium generated a substantial profit through the hands of eager Chinese traders, while cargo insurance and Canton's steep port taxes were irrelevant to contraband. For sure, there was greater risk as well as the need for bribes or connivance fees, but Perkins relished those prospects as costs of doing business that raised the barrier to entry for other traders. "From the intention of the Chinese to be very strict about opium, the competition you fear," Perkins explained to his Leghorn agent Fred W. Paine in March 1818, "we think will not exist." Indeed, there was "no one but Astor we fear." Perkins, though, had an advantage over his New York rival John Jacob Astor. Once the Levant Company had satisfied European demand for some 50,000 pounds, Perkins's Smyrna operation of Woodmass & Offley and Perkins Brothers could offer him preferential terms on the remainder of the Turkish crop, typically around 100,000 pounds, a figure that would soon rise once farmers across the Ottoman Empire responded to demand by planting more poppies. "We shall be glad," he told Paine, "to have as large a proportion of the crop as we can compass," and he set about establishing a monopoly.[31] For the 1819 season, Perkins instructed Woodmass & Offley that, presuming the Turkish opium crop would be 150,000 pounds, "and 1/2 of it is wanted for Europe, we should have no objection to taking the remainder, at 2-3/4 dollars," meaning 75,000 pounds for 25 percent less than he paid for the 1817 crop.[32] With experience and economies of scale came increased margins.

---

30. Perkins insured the cargoes of eleven ships returning from Canton—*Alert, Augusta, Canton Packet, Cordelia, Levant, Nautilus, Ophelia, Orozimbo, Thomas Scattergood, Unicorn, Zephyr*—but I suspect that one of these sailed in the 1819 season rather than the 1818 season; storm, in *New York Daily Advertiser*, 19 April 1820, p. 3. Deciphering the multiple ledgers of Perkins & Co.'s double-entry bookkeeping system is problematic, in part because they are incomplete but also because they run continuously; years 1818 through 1824 typically show a profit carried forward in excess of $1 million, such as $1,429,030 carried forward from 1823, in folio 483; Profit & Lofs ledger, folio 169, for 1820, carries forward $1,052,676 from the 1818–19 ledger, which is the figure I am using here, so it represents an approximation for the full year; all in THPP, reel 11.

31. Perkins to Paine, 24 March 1818, THPP-L, 6:289, 6:291; Charles C. Stelle, "American Trade in Opium to China, Prior to 1820," *Pacific Historical Review*, 9:4 (December 1940), pp. 425–44, provides useful background, despite noting incorrectly but with apparent relief, "the facts that American exploitation of Persian opium was of brief duration and that there is no evidence of repetition of the Perkins' successful venture [of the *Bocca Tigris* opium shipment]," p. 441.

32. Perkins to Paine, 24 March 1818, THPP-L, 6:291.

Historians have rather ignored Perkins, concentrating instead on glamorous merchant-princes like Astor, but in 1821, when a House of Lords inquiry into securing Britain's foreign trade worried about the growing volume of U.S. business at Canton, the only name that popped up was Perkins's. "Would you be surprised at hearing," Lord Lansdowne asked EIC official James Goddard, that "the house of Perkins and Co. in conjunction with Howqua [Houqua] the Hong merchant" had an agreement to supply "nearly a million sterling" in goods of English manufacture per annum? "Certainly not," Goddard replied, for he knew that Perkins had been trading English goods for some years, though he seemed unaware it was Perkins Brothers of Smyrna and another relative Samuel Williams in London who helped him circumvent mercantilist regulations. What did Goddard estimate total U.S. exports to Canton to be? "I conceive them to be upwards of 7,000,000 of dollars." "Should you be astonished," rejoined Lansdowne, "were you to hear that they were ten"? Asked why he thought Americans like Perkins were outperforming the EIC, Goddard identified their government's lack of restrictions and the nimbleness of their small vessels. Despite data showing the collapse of U.S. fur exports, from 270,000 pelts in 1804 to 84,000 in 1818, the Lords could see that the total value of U.S. trade with Canton had more than doubled over the same period, in large part from increased sales of quicksilver, lead, and opium, with the EIC's data for contraband goods naturally being gross underestimates. Reports also showed that U.S. merchants had increased their silk purchases tenfold and tea by 30 percent, with large cargoes going to European ports. Had the reports listed ships by owner, they would have seen that of 22,138 tea chests landed in 1819 at Hamburg, 13,171 were Perkins's, just one piece of his transatlantic trade that would double again over the next five years, largely because he turned to Turkish opium to buy Chinese tea.[33]

Perkins consolidated his operation during the 1820–23 seasons, anchoring a storeship—the *Cadet*—off Lintin Island, forty-five miles from the eyes of Chinese officials at Whampoa, and from where he could ride out periodic gluts in the market. His opium running peaked in the 1825 season, when six ships brought 177,837 pounds (1,337 chests), and remained close to that level into the 1830s when it accounted for at least half the Turkish crop. Over the course of the EIC's early attempts to drive Americans like Perkins out of business by flooding the market and until the Qing government's later crackdowns, a season's profit varied, but assuming an average of $430,000 on top of the first years' efforts gives a yield of some $4.6 million ($368 million) for the thirteen seasons by 1830, a year when Perkins puffed to his Canton office that the trial balance of his profit-and-loss ledger recorded $1,127,432. A measure of

---

33. Seaburg and Patterson's chatty and less than rigorous account is the only book-length study, and there is little else except Thomas G. Cary's contemporary biography, "Thomas Handasyd Perkins," in *Lives of American Merchants*, ed. Freeman Hunt (New York: Office of Hunt's Merchants' Magazine, 1856), pp. 33–101. *Report (brought from The Lords, 7 May 1821) Relative to the Trade with the East Indies and China*, in *British Parliamentary Papers: Select Committee Reports on the East India Company and Trade with China, 1821–31*, China, vol. 36 (Shannon: Irish University Press, 1971), pp. 19–20, 17, 50, "surprized" in original; importation into Hamburg and Altona by *True American, Ophelia, Canton Packet,* and *John and Hannah*.

the working capital Perkins was accumulating at his various offices around the world—London, Isle de France, Gibraltar, Leghorn, Smyrna—was that when his cousin and then partner James Perkins Jr. died from alcoholism in 1828 and Perkins was mulling semi-retirement, he wrote to his nephew Thomas T. Forbes in Canton, "If you ship to the amount of 1500 m dollars [$1.5 million], you will have yet a million [on hand] to supply your demands."[34] Given such vast sums made from trade in a proscribed drug, it is as tempting as it is easy to pass judgment.

fig. 36: Houqua

It is easy to cast Perkins as a ruthless capitalist whose fortune came at the expense of millions of impoverished Chinese peasants, without accepting that it takes two to trade. Chinese merchants made every bit as much money as their Western counterparts. Indeed, if it seems absurd that in 1829 Forbes's factory was holding seventy-six tons of silver (2.5 million Spanish dollars at 0.969 ounces each) then it is of note that Houqua's net worth rose to some $26 million ($2.08 billion); when a fire gutted his Canton factory in 1822, a river of molten silver flowed into the street. Sales of silk and tea at high prices to eager foreign buyers provided a better livelihood for millions of Chinese producers who were otherwise isolated from international trade. Because of the rudimentary state of domestic banks and capital markets, Chinese businesses, moreover, relied on loans from foreign merchant houses.[35]

It is easy to blame Perkins and his cohort of Western merchant-princes for the advancing decrepitude of the Qing Empire and Chinese people's national humiliation

34. Charles C. Stelle, "American Trade in Opium to China, 1821–39," *Pacific Historical Review*, 10:1 (March 1941), p. 64; 1820-23, 140,000 lbs @ $3.50 / $5.75; 1824-30, 160,000 lbs @ $3.40 / $6.10; THPP-L, 6:345, 6:324; *m* was shorthand for *mille*, meaning a thousand.

35. Hong merchant Finqua's obituary of Houqua put his net worth at $25 million, even after he had given an $800,000 ransom to the British in 1840 to save Canton from shelling during the Opium War, *New-Hampshire Patriot and State Gazette*, 23 May 1844, p. 4; for capital markets, see Van Dyke, *Canton Trade*, p. 160.

after the first Opium War of 1839–42, without recalling that rulers during the later Qing period (as during the Ming) tried to quarantine China from foreign influence even though high taxes from the Canton trade were a primary source of revenue. When the Daoguang Emperor sent Commissioner Lin Zexu to shut down the opium trade in 1839, his government's concern was not the immorality of opium smoking but rather the consequences of corruption inherent to the opium trade's illegal nature. Six years earlier, English anti-monopolist reformers had successfully lobbied Parliament to end the EIC's privileges. But this well-intentioned lifting of the EIC's monopoly did more than wreck the complex though balanced Canton system that for 130 years had been funding the Qing court's extravagances. It prompted British traders to call in their loans to several of the more indebted hong merchants, making public knowledge of the vast sums involved and embarrassing the Qing government, not least because it was technically liable for them as the guarantor of any loan made by a public official.[36]

It is easy to judge Perkins as a heartless narcotics trafficker who poisoned Chinese society, without acknowledging that opium had become as central to what it meant to be a Chinese man as beer, wine, peach brandy, tobacco pipes, or Havana cigars had to English, French, American, or Spanish men. Opium was both an important medicine, particularly for treating intestinal infections and as a painkiller, and, at the outset of the nineteenth century, a luxury recreational drug that was crossing from elite to mass consumption as the price fell and availability rose. Poorer Chinese sought the same pleasures and markers of status that fashionable aristocrats enjoyed. Qing rulers and officials who claimed to be regulating its use were opium smokers. When the Qing government reiterated its ban in 1810 declaring, "Opium is a poison undermining our good customs and morality," its heir-apparent Daoguang was writing poetry in a smoky haze: "Sharpen wood into a hollow pipe, / Give it a copper head and tail, / . . . Inhale and exhale, fragrance rises, / . . . Mountains and clouds emerge in distant sea." And for a majority of long-term users, opium was neither particularly addictive nor harmful, arguably less so than alcohol or tobacco. Empress Dowager Cixi (1835– 1908) was a regular evening smoker who advocated moderate use by retirees.[37]

None of this is to suggest that Perkins had no sense he was doing anything immoral. Indeed, his enthusiasm for the Bunker Hill Monument stemmed in part from a troubled conscience, though not because he was selling opium per se. Two decades before ministers and reformers began railing against drug abuse, opium had a romantic allure, as illustrated by the popularity of Thomas de Quincey's anonymous *Confessions of an English Opium-Eater* (1821), which U.S. reviewers presumed to be the work

---

36. "The Judge's and Treasurer's Report Respecting Hing-tae's Debts," 29 December 1837, noted that one Hong merchant, Hingtae, owed over $2,320,000 ($184 million), and one British trader, William Jardine, had lent at least $1,700,000, in *Correspondence Relating to China: Presented to both Houses of Parliament, by Command of Her Majesty, 1840* (London: T.B. Harrison, 1840), pp. 272–73: I am grateful to Stephen Watson for his research into alternative explanations for the Opium War.

37. For the counterpoint on Chinese opium use, see particularly Zheng Yangwen, *The Social Life of Opium in China* (Cambridge: Cambridge University Press, 2005); Qing decree of 1810, in *A Documentary Chronicle of Sino–Western Relations, 1644–1820,* ed. and trans. Fu Lo-shu (Tucson: University of Arizona Press, 1966), vol. 1, p. 380; Dauguang cited in Zheng, *Social Life*, p. 57; Cixi, in ibid., pp. 161–62.

of Samuel Taylor Coleridge, one of a coterie of English Romanticists who relied on opium to enhance their creativity. Rather, Perkins became wealthy because he broke laws, smuggling by definition being an illegal activity. He knew full well, as did his Boston Brahmin peers, that the Qing government had appealed to U.S. merchants to respect its opium ban. Newspapers carried the 22 September 1817 address from the hong merchants' council, the co-hong, to U.S. consul Benjamin C. Wilcox, stressing that opium was "a prohibited dirt for smoking" and its importation constituted a "crime." Perkins, along with the Cabot, Cushing, Forbes, Russell, and Sturgis relatives who staffed his offices, banked his profits, shared his dinner table, and took over his mercantile operations when he retired, lived with the knowledge that their wealth was a product of deceit. And yet, these elite Bostonians proclaimed that their hometown was a guiding light, an exemplarist shining city on a hill. They therefore sought to sanctify their success and legitimate their privilege through high culture, church worship, public service, acts of philanthropy, and particularly by building the Bunker Hill Monument, a granite beacon of virtue. Perkins, moreover, had a double motive for his backing of the Monument project: more members of the Perkins clan than he cared to admit were Loyalists in 1776, two of whom were sourcing his Turkish opium. What better way to demonstrate his patriotism than by playing a leading role in the BHMA.[38]

Turkish Opium and Greek Independence

Perkins's enthusiasm for opium smuggling and Bostonians' dependence on the profits he created led to an odd—and understudied—episode in the history of U.S. foreign relations, which exemplifies the pragmatic, ad hoc nature of foreign policy-making during the Early Republic as well as the praxis underscoring the inherent ironies of American ideology. In October 1823, at the height of Perkins's efforts to monopolize Turkish opium production, Edward Everett mounted a campaign to support Greeks who were fighting for independence from the Ottoman Empire. Everett's was not the first such effort by Americans, all of which lagged campaigns in England and France, but it carried the highest profile. A more worthy champion the Greek cause in the United States could hardly have found. For five years, Everett had been professor of classical Greek at Harvard, he had toured Greece in 1818 as a guest of Ali Pasha—a pitiless ruler—through an introduction from Lord Byron, he published regularly in newspapers and literary journals, he was one of America's finest orators, and he had the right social connections. Bored with teaching though only twenty-nine, he was considering a run for office to the U.S. House of Representatives, so his activism was as much political as ideological.[39]

Everett's first initiative was a salvo in the widely read *North American Review*. Under the pretext of reviewing a new edition of A. Coray's primer on Aristotelian

38. For an early reference to opium as a "destructive vice," see for instance, "Opium Smoking in Penang," *Chinese Repository*, 11:11 (November 1842), p. 587; "Did Coleridge write this book?" asked a reviewer for the *United States Literary Gazette*, 1:3 (15 May 1824), p. 38; address, published widely but cited here in the *National Register*, 5:9 (28 February 1818), p. 139.

39. Paul Revere Frothingham, *Edward Everett: Orator and Statesman* (Boston: Houghton Mifflin Company, 1925), p. 59.

ethics, he built a passionate case for a virtual crusade, in what was "emphatically a war of the crescent against the cross." Even though the real revolutionaries were every bit as brutal and inhumane as their Turkish adversaries, Everett cast the "civilized, enterprising, industrious" Greeks not only as kindred spirits fighting for independence from tyranny but also as fellow Christians, "bowed beneath the yoke of barbarous infidels." They were fathers and mothers, "condemned to see their children torn from them and doomed to the most cruel slavery." They were proud men, bereft of the bounties that providence had lavished on Americans. "Unaided, single-handed, at perilous odds," Greek fighters were waging a "war of extermination against tyrants" who denied them "not only the blessings of liberty, but the mercies of slavery." Everett challenged Americans to make the Greeks' cause their own, to imagine "an overwhelming force of barbarians, speaking another language, following a strange faith," let loose on Boston or New York, putting its men to the sword and selling "its matrons and virgins in the open market." Just as Europeans had supported them in their war against British oppression, so Americans should raise funds to supply matériel, and petition Congress to dispatch a commissioner as a precursor to recognizing an independent Greece. As he suggested in a letter to Secretary of State and fellow Bostonian John Quincy Adams, Everett was hoping to be that commissioner.[40]

His second initiative was to recruit Congressman Daniel Webster (F-MA). Twelve years his senior at forty-one, Webster was a fatherly mentor who, like Everett, drew his political power and social prestige from a self-aggrandizing network of Bostonian elites tied by marriage and patronage. Having just returned to Congress after a seven-year hiatus, Webster was eager to reaffirm his leadership of the former Federalist contingent. He was therefore happy to harness himself to Everett's Greek chariot, though rather from the opportunity it afforded for an authoritative oration on a popular issue than from any personal interest in or sympathy for the cause; it was not until mid-November that he picked up Everett's *North American* article. After canvassing House and cabinet colleagues who assured him of their support, particularly former House speaker and now Secretary of War John C. Calhoun, Webster prepared a motion for the appointment of a commissioner to Greece. He confided to Everett that he had used one of those colleagues to recommend Everett to President James Monroe as the ideal candidate, although Calhoun, no doubt the unnamed colleague, had actually given such a recommendation three months earlier, so Webster was probably currying favor. To work into what would be his maiden speech to Congress as representative of Massachusetts's 1st District, he asked Everett to prepare research material, because "my real difficulty," he confessed to him on 28 November, was "ignorance." But he could also confide that Monroe's annual message to Congress four days hence "would contain strong expressions of sympathy for the Greeks.[41]

40. Edward Everett, "Coray's Aristotle," *North American Review*, 17:2 (October 1823), pp. 420, 400, 422, 423; Everett to Adams, 30 October 1823, The Adams Papers, Massachusetts Historical Society, "Letters Received and Other Loose Papers," microfilm edition, reel 463.

41. Everett's relationship with Webster was the "closest and most influential friendship of his life," according to biographer Frothingham, *Edward Everett*, p. 60. For Calhoun, see John Quincy Adams, *Memoirs of John Quincy Adams*,

Emboldened by Monroe's message stating, indeed, that Greek independence was "the object of our most ardent wishes," and by an outpouring of public sympathy, dubbed Greek Fever by historians, Webster submitted his motion on 8 December, only to postpone his supporting speech for six weeks, a tactic that further heightened anticipation.[42] At the Adams family Christmas dinner table, "the subject of Greece," noted Charles Francis Adams, "created some conversation as Mr. Webster is about to come out in his most powerful manner." An hour before the House commenced its proceedings on 19 January 1824, Pennsylvania Avenue was a throng of carriages. Senators and ambassadors packed the visitors' gallery to hear Webster deliver an impassioned two-hour oration, made the more authoritative with copious historical references supplied by Everett. In proposing that Congress appoint a commissioner to Greece, his motion was a product of "our own character, and called for by our own duty."[43] "Contending with ruthless oppressors," the Greeks turned their eyes to Americans. "By their ancestors, by their slaughtered wives and children, by their own blood, poured out like water, by the hecatombs of dead they have heaped up as it were to heaven, they invoke, they implore us"—Webster exclaimed—as the earth's great republic, "for some cheering sound, some look of sympathy, some token of compassionate regard." By their common Christianity, Greeks asked whether "we can forget that they are struggling, as we once struggled, for what we now happily enjoy." Webster did not know whether the Greeks would succeed. But even if he heard tomorrow that their "last phalanx had sunk beneath the Turkish scimitar," that the flames of their last city had flickered out in its ashes, and that naught remained "but the wide melancholy waste where Greece once was," then he would reflect that he had petitioned Congress, in the name of seven million freemen, to grant the Greeks "at least the cheering of one friendly voice."[44] Members of the House could surely not resist the pathos of such a noble fight for independence. They could not fail to discharge their duty, after which they could leave the rest "to the disposition of Providence."[45]

---

ed. Charles Francis Adams (Philadelphia: J.B. Lippincott, 1875), vol. 6, p. 173, entry for 15 August 1823; Webster and Calhoun had both served in the House during the 13th and 14th Congresses; Webster to Everett, 28 November 1823, Edward Everett Papers, Massachusetts Historical Society, "Correspondence," ed. Frederick S. Allis Jr., microfilm edition, reel 2.

42. For Greek Fever, see Myrtle A. Cline, *American Attitude Toward the Greek War of Independence, 1821–1828* (Atlanta, GA: Higgins-McArthur Company, 1930), esp. pp. 55–62, Stephen A. Larrabee, *Hellas Observed: The American Experience of Greece, 1775–1865* (New York: New York University Press, 1957), p. 65, and Michael B. Oren, *Power, Faith, and Fantasy: America in the Middle East, 1776 to the Present* (New York: W.W. Norton & Company, 2007), pp. 109–10; James Monroe, "President's Message," 2 December 1823, *Annals of the Congress of the United States*, 18th Cong., 1st Sess. (Washington, DC: Gales & Seaton, 1856), p. 22.

43. Charles Francis Adams, 25 December 1823, DCA01d059, in *Founding Families: Digital Editions of the Papers of the Winthrops and Adamses*, ed. C. James Taylor (Boston: Massachusetts Historical Society, 2007); after graduating from Harvard, Charles Adams studied law under Daniel Webster's tutelage. *Rhode Island American*, 27 January 1824, p. 3; this report, from the *New York Statesman's* Washington correspondent, put the speech at over two hours, meaning that Webster's delivery would have been relatively slow, at less than 115 words per minute for the roughly 13,900-word total. Webster's "The Revolution in Greece" speech published in the congressional *Annals* and in newspapers at the time is significantly different from later collected editions; this passage is from *The Writings and Speeches of Daniel Webster* (Boston: Little, Brown, & Company, 1903), Speeches in Congress, vol. 5, p. 90.

44. These passages are from *Annals of the Congress*, 19 January 1824, p. 1099, and the almost identical full text of the speech in the *Rhode Island American*, 27 January 1824, p. 3.

45. "Disposition," *Writings and Speeches of Daniel Webster*, p. 90.

Yet resist they did. Despite backing from other congressional heavyweights like Henry Clay (DR-KY), Webster's resolution struggled through a week of debate, dwindled under amendment to little more than an offer of sympathy, and, even thus watered down, still succumbed 131:0 to a tabling vote. Webster made no further effort to revive his motion, preferring to see it languish on the table rather than suffer the ignominy of an overwhelming show of nay votes.[46]

Historians have puzzled over why Webster so quietly acquiesced. In the most cogent analysis, Lawrence S. Kaplan argues that the principal backers of a sympathy vote for the Greeks moved into alignment with John Quincy Adams's position on non-entanglement with the Old World, particularly when Monroe's December address had just propounded his doctrine for diplomatic separation of the hemispheres. Following from this explanation is that for the likes of Webster and Clay Greece was simply an opportunity to build political capital through alliance with a popular republican cause, for which they appreciated that anything more than rhetoric required federal expenditure and tipped at war. Indeed, in his biography *Daniel Webster* (1883), Henry Cabot Lodge noted how days before delivering his speech Webster "became aware that Calhoun had misled him" over the Monroe administration's ardor for Greek independence. Adams "considered Everett too much of a partisan" and was "wholly averse to any action" in support of the Greeks. With Adams in essence being the administration's foreign policymaking arm, Webster therefore appreciated that "an adverse vote [was] certain," so his best strategy was to exploit the speech as a public relations platform and then sidestep a vote.[47]

Still, if Adams's primary concern was to avoid entangling European alliances in light of the Monroe Doctrine's promulgation in December then it is surprising that his antipathy to aiding the Greeks was just as strong four months earlier.[48] It is odd, too, that the committed activist Everett would back away from his call to arms of October 1823, even to the extent of abandoning a humanitarian fund-raising drive through a committee he organized in Boston in December—unless some other factor had emerged to upset the calculus. That factor was a growing awareness of the magnitude and importance of Perkins's trade in opium with the Ottoman Empire.

At what happened to coincide with the height of Perkins's efforts to monopolize Turkish opium production, Everett embarked on a third Greek initiative: a committee of Boston elites to raise funds and petition Congress. It was the second week of December 1823, so given Webster's decision to delay his speech until mid-January, the action-oriented Everett may have doubted Webster's level of commitment as well as

46. *Annals of the Congress*, 26 January 1824, p. 1214.

47. See, for instance, Paul A. Varg, *Edward Everett: The Intellectual in the Turmoil of Politics* (Sclinsgrove, PA: Susquehanna University Press, 1992), p. 33, and Robert Vincent Remini, *Daniel Webster: The Man and His Time* (New York: W.W. Norton, 1997), p. 218, both of which side with Webster's own explanation that the obstacle to the motion's passage was Adams, essentially the Monroe administration; Lawrence S. Kaplan, "The Monroe Doctrine and the Truman Doctrine: The Case of Greece," *Journal of the Early Republic*, 13:1 (Spring 1993), p. 19; Henry Cabot Lodge, *Daniel Webster* (Boston: Houghton Mifflin Company, 1883), p. 135.

48. *Memoirs of John Quincy Adams*, vol. 6, p. 173, entry for 15 August 1823.

been frustrated by the slow train of events in Washington. He knew that New York's Philhellenic society had launched a fundraising drive, suggesting rivalry was another consideration. Forming a committee was, anyway, a natural step for Everett, who served on many and understood their utility. Just five months earlier, with John C. Warren, William Tudor, and Perkins, he had cofounded the BHMA, his secretaryship of which was already acting as a vehicle to advance his prospects ahead of the 1824 congressional elections. Oblivious of the importance of Turkish opium to the local economy, Everett naturally asked his friend and fellow BHMA director Perkins, along with several other associates who happened to be merchants or did business with them, to serve on the Greek committee.

A shake of the head and a wry smile must have characterized Perkins's receipt of the notice for the inaugural meeting, scheduled for 19 December at the palatial Exchange Coffee House, probably in the same room as the BHMA's inauguration.[49] Good food, fine wine, and the conviviality promised by a select gathering at an establishment like the Exchange was the kind of social opportunity he rarely passed up, and he enjoyed Everett's intellectual company and respected him an indefatigable organizer. In this case, though, his friend's well-meaning activism threatened catastrophe. Were Congress to aid the Greeks, Perkins feared that the Ottomans would retaliate by embargoing their trade with U.S. merchants. If he could no longer buy opium at Smyrna then he would have to fall back on increasingly scarce specie and the profitability of his new trading model would collapse. Unfortunately, the historical record is silent on whether Perkins had already interceded with either Webster or Adams, both of whom he knew well and saw frequently, so it is unclear how concerned he was over the stirrings in Washington on the Greeks' behalf prior to December. But he certainly took Everett's committee proposal seriously. Everett made for a formidable champion, of the Greek cause or any other, and those slated to serve on the committee were some of the most powerful men in Boston, such as Justices Warren Dutton and Thomas L. Winthrop, District Attorney George Blake, former U.S. Congressman Benjamin Gorham whose seat Webster had just won, and Boston Mayor Josiah Quincy.[50]

Stuck between the bounds of friendship and the forces of business, Perkins tackled his dilemma, on one hand, by apologizing to Everett that he was feeling too unwell to attend and, on the other, by writing a letter to the *Boston Daily Advertiser* signed "A Merchant," although his authorship soon became common knowledge. After agreeing that "people who are fighting for their freedom" from the "tyranny of the Turks" deserved the "sympathies of all Christendom," he argued that forwarding money to the Greeks for the purchase of matériel in England would "put at hazard" "the liberty of our own citizens," because Turkey would not only "let loose her corsairs upon our commerce in the Mediterranean" but also "induce all the Mahomedan powers" to do

49. Some days earlier, probably the previous Friday, 12 December, Everett had held a working meeting to discuss the formation of a committee, see *Christian Register*, 26 December 1823, p. 79.

50. In August 1818, Perkins had met Everett in Southampton, where he persuaded Everett to visit Stonehenge, Salisbury, and Wilton with him, Frothingham, *Edward Everett*, p. 56; *Christian Register*, 26 December 1823, p. 79; Gorham, a Democratic-Republican, won back the seat in 1827.

the same. This was a pointed reference to the Barbary Wars eighteen years earlier, when American crew held for ransom and lurid tales of captains' wives sold into harems had outraged Bostonians. In the style of the times, Perkins's letter was as circumspect as it was light on specifics, making mention of neither trade nor opium. He stopped short of giving full account of the number of American seamen whose lives indignant Mohammedans could put in jeopardy, or the "amount of property which would be put at hazard," because he trusted that he had already said enough "to call the subject to the serious consideration of the citizens at large," and the signature, *A Merchant*, underscored the reality of the unnamed subject.[51]

When a Brahmin of Perkins's stature loosed a broadside in the press, however discreet and anonymous, it challenged the consensus on which the ruling establishment depended for its authority. After the 19 December dinner meeting, its joviality overshadowed by A Merchant's admonition in that morning's paper, Everett returned by carriage to his Cambridge home. Before turning in for the night he wrote a letter to Perkins, pleading with him to bring his "influence, zeal, & liberality into the camp." There had been not a word said of recognizing the Greeks' independence, "nor any of building vefsels of war & shipping arms & munitions to them," but merely of raising a contribution for the relief of sufferers in the war. "It would truly rejoice y'r affectionate and obliged Friend," he implored, if Perkins could bring himself to cooperate with the committee.[52]

Everett's plea and unbridled enthusiasm for the Greek cause made clear to Perkins that the committee, and by extension "citizens at large," had failed to take his hint that the Smyrna trade was a critical component of Boston's maritime economy, which action in support of that cause threatened. To quench the Greek Fever he had now of necessity to pour out a full account of the property that the Philhellenists were hazarding, which meant talking about opium. His prior reticence, though, was not from any societal proscription, this being a time when opiates were gaining popularity as the active ingredient in patent medicines. Rather, Perkins cared for no one—from competitors to tax collectors—to know his business. Still, there was potential for moral stigma, because since 1818 newspapers had publicized the Qing government's edicts threatening prosecution for any American merchants caught smuggling opium in contravention of its 1810 decree.[53]

In his second and far longer letter from "A Merchant," which took him two days to prepare, Perkins reiterated "the interest we feel in the Greeks working out their own salvation from the oppression of the Turks," but stressed again that it was not in Bostonians' interests to go any further, whether to "send commissioners to spy out the

---

51. See Robert J. Allison, *The Crescent Obscured: The United States and the Muslim World, 1776–1815* (Chicago: University of Chicago Press, 1995); "A Merchant," *Boston Daily Advertiser*, 19 December 1823, p. 2.

52. Everett to Perkins, 19 December 1823, THPP, reel 2, "Correspondence."

53. See, for instance, *National Register*, 28 February 1818, p. 139, and *Niles' Weekly Register*, 21 December 1822, p. 249; these accounts generally made light of the matter, like the *New England Palladium & Commercial Advertiser* of 17 February 1818, p. 1, which noted how "the use of opium for smoking in China can be traced back for ages," and the latest fuss was merely a governmental effort to promote "internal tranquility."

state of affairs, or raise money to aid them in their war." He mounted a rebuttal of an attack by the *Evening Gazette* on his first letter, which had stated that not even with Sweden did America have less business dealings than insignificant—and of course Mohammedan—Turkey, and had suggested that sending arms to the Greeks would not compromise U.S. neutrality because Christian laws did not apply to "the Infidel," particularly when Washington had no diplomatic relations with Istanbul. Yet surely, Perkins countered, not having diplomatic relations made any resolution of the Greek problem harder, not easier. After accepting that there were fewer Americans resident in Turkey than many European countries, Perkins then laid out the magnitude of U.S.–Turkish trade. Far from aggravating the Ottomans by aiding the Greeks, this indicated that the establishment by Congress of a full embassy in Istanbul ought to be an immediate priority.[54]

With so much of the Ottoman trade going through his own firm, Perkins could speak with authority. There were figs, fruit, bulk wool, wine, lubricating oil, and carpets that came direct from Turkey, although, with the exception of carpets, these cargoes were of inferior quality and, he acknowledged, of little value. But there was one cargo of great worth. For the past three years, the opium crop had averaged "one million dollars, and at least the one half of the last crop will have been exported from Turkey for *American account*." This was "no small item!" "Great amounts in Specie"— Bostonians should understand—had consequently "come to the United States" through the expanded trade with Canton, and this, he could have added, was a far cry from just five years before, when large amounts of specie were leaving the country. "I affirm," he said, that "the capital employed in the trade with Turkey" was greater than with any other European country, Britain excepted; indeed, American trade with France, Holland, Spain, and Russia combined was less than the trade he was conducting from Turkey to Canton, en route to America. "Shall we then go a crusade in favor of the Greeks," he concluded ominously, "and hazard the liberty of our citizens and [so valuable a trade?]" Americans were a Christian nation, so, yes, the Greeks deserved their sympathy. But aiding Greeks with small contributions would only mock their distress, while "*according to the principles of the Constitution*," congressional "*interference with Foreign Nations*" may be dangerous.[55]

At Everett's next committee meeting on Monday evening, 22 December 1823, Perkins was conspicuous by his absence, as were merchant John Welles, congressman Gorham, and mayor Quincy, all of whom had showed up for the inaugural meeting. Press reports did their best to paper over Everett's embarrassment. There had been only an "apparent delay" in forming the committee, while those who "declined the appointment" did so "for reasons assigned by them." Still, the reports could not disguise the fact that the committee had to contend with the "doubts of individuals on the tendency of measures" slated for discussion. Once he had filled the committee's

---

54. "A Merchant," which Perkins dated 20 December but did not submit for two days, *Boston Daily Advertiser*, 23 December 1823, p. 2, unnecessary emphasis removed.

55. Ibid., emphasis original.

vacant seats, Everett called a succession of further meetings. There is no record of the proceedings, though Perkins's onslaughts in the press and the abstentions by Welles, Gorham, and Quincy evidently dampened the crusading zeal among the remaining members.[56]

When they delivered their petition to Congress on 5 January 1824, two weeks before Webster's speech, it was predictably effusive in its sympathies with the "contest of an oppressed and enslaved people for the invaluable blessings of self-government, and of a Christian people for the enjoyment of religious liberty." Missing no opportunity to stress how Americans' own "successful struggle in the cause of civil liberty" had advanced "the condition of the whole civilized world," the committee saw the "erection of a new independent Christian State" as a momentous event in the "progress of human affairs and especially deserving" of Congress's attention. And yet, as Perkins had advised, "deserving attention" was as far as the petitioners would go in their support of the Greeks. Not only did they sidestep their original intention of raising funds in Boston—let alone calling on Congress for an appropriation—but they also adopted the closing point of Perkins's second "A Merchant" letter, recommending noninterference as the rationale for Congress to table any further considerations. "In common with their fellow-citizens, generally," committee members felt the "just weight and obligation of that policy which hitherto has prohibited an interference with the internal concerns of any of the Powers of Europe." They felt an obligation, in other words, to uphold President George Washington's injunction in his Farewell Address of 1796 to avoid entangling political alliances, and to back the separate hemispheres ideology promulgated the month before in the Monroe Doctrine.[57]

Despite their clash over Greece, Everett remained Perkins's friend, a tribute to the close kin relationships between elite Bostonians and to a social culture that stressed the importance of building consensus. They were public figures and merchants, politicians and capitalists, supplicants and patrons, and they depended on each other for business as well as socializing. Two years later, Everett would write from Washington to ask if Perkins could extend a hundred dollars through his office in Smyrna to a constituent of Everett's, a young doctor who had exceeded his income while practicing medicine in Greece. Everett promised to repay the money, but Perkins would have understood the loan to be a political contribution.[58]

There is no correspondence to indicate that Perkins lobbied Webster or any other congressional representatives prior to his "A Merchant" letters, nor does it seem as if he did subsequently, preferring rather to let the import of his disclosure of the Smyrna trade filter through to Congress on its own merit. On 20 January, the first session of debate following Webster's speech, Henry W. Dwight (F-MA) rose to support his fellow Federalist, and touched on the issue of trade. "It may be said that we shall

56. *Columbian Centinel*, 25 January 1824, p. 1.

57. "Sympathy For the Greeks," memorial (petition) to Congress, *Annals of the Congress*, vol. 2, app., 5 January 1824, pp. 3107–9, and *American State Papers, Class 1, Foreign Relations* (Washington, DC: Gales & Seaton, 1858), vol. 5, pp. 261–62.

58. Everett to Perkins, 27 December 1826, THPP, reel 2, "Correspondence."

sacrifice our trade with Smyrna," Dwight conjectured, but members had only to examine the Treasury's official returns to "see how small will be the amount of that sacrifice." America's entire trade with Turkey, Dwight stressed, did not "exceed the value of a single cargo in the India trade," a "pitiful advantage" purchased by the "humiliating concession of suffering an American citizen to reside at Smyrna." From Dwight's vantage point as representative of Stockbridge, 130 miles from Boston Harbor in western Massachusetts, official statistics told the story he chose to believe. He knew enough to appreciate the immense value of the "India trade" but was apparently ignorant that one, crucial leg of it ran directly from Smyrna to Canton and hence was invisible to the official figures. Two days later, when Henry Clay rose in support of Webster, he memorably belittled the trade with Smyrna as "a miserable invoice of figs and opium." "What shall it profit a nation," Clay emphasized, paraphrasing Matthew 16:26, to save "a wretched commerce, and lose its liberties?"[59] Dwight and Clay had evidently not read Perkins's second "A Merchant" letter, or if they had then they chose to ignore its substance. Then, on 24 January, Timothy Fuller, also of Massachusetts, challenged Dwight and Clay's dismissal of trade with Smyrna by wondering if it was really so miserable then "why have we now a squadron engaged in the protection of it?" "That trade," Fuller insisted, was "highly important," and sending a commissioner to Greece would alienate the Ottomans, imperil the trade, and likely provoke a war. Fuller's constituency was Cambridgeport, where his home was a few blocks from Pacific Street and in line-of-sight across the Charles River estuary with the wharves where Perkins's brigs returned from Canton. Even so, Fuller's stand on trade, and his rhetorical question mentioning the role of the Mediterranean Squadron that was inside knowledge, does not—in of itself—demonstrate a link to Perkins's lobbying.[60]

In the speech he delivered to Congress on 19 January, as printed in congressional proceedings and newspapers at the time, Webster dismissed "the result to our trade should Smyrna be blockaded," suggesting, in the event of trouble, that a commissioner would make it easier to acquire information with which to broker a settlement.[61] It is significant that for subsequent publications Webster altered this passage to include a pointed reference to Perkins: "the greater our trade may happen to be with Smyrna, a consideration which seems to have *alarmed some gentleman*, the greater is the reason . . . to be accurately informed of those events which might affect its safety." This later version, which Webster no doubt adapted to rationalize his acquiescence in tabling the motion, even implied that the risk of a trade embargo lay with the Greeks, who had "declared the Turkish coasts in a state of blockade."[62] After the tabling vote, former New Hampshire senator Jeremiah Mason penned a note of consolation to Webster, pointing out that "he [Webster] had nothing to regret," having acquired "all

59. *Annals of the Congress*, 22 January 1824, p. 1175.

60. Editors routinely copied articles from other newspapers, which circulated freely in the mail without charge, so, although I have been unable to locate an "A Merchant" letter in the newspapers circulating in Washington, Dwight could still have seen one, and he may have used a clipping service. *Annals of the Congress*, 24 January 1824, p. 1198.

61. *Annals of the Congress*, 19 January 1824, p. 1099; *Rhode Island American*, 27 January 1824, p. 2.

62. *Writings and Speeches of Daniel Webster*, p. 91, emphasis added.

the credit the subject & occasion were capable of giving." "Indeed, the impression on the public mind," Mason assured Webster, would be no less positive than had the resolution passed "by a lean majority." In his reply, which gave no hint of enthusiasm for the cause at stake, Webster pointed to "Mr. *Adams'* opposition" as "the most formidable obstacle" to the resolution's passage, but, at the same time, credited "certain reasons, which the Public will never know, & which I will not trouble you with now." There are extant letters from Perkins to Webster either side of the Greek debate—the first of 23 December enclosing a petition for a uniform bankruptcy law, the second of 26 January urging Webster to do his utmost to block pending legislation to raise tariffs—and neither mention trade at Smyrna nor Webster's speech, remarkable omissions given both men's stake in the debate. Still, the subject was one that Perkins habitually guarded, so the "certain reasons" may well have been at Perkins's behest. Webster was also a supplicant of Perkins's patronage, periodically borrowing money from him at preferential interest rates, loans that Webster seemed to regard as political favors. In March 1819, Perkins converted a $1,000 loan of July 1816 to a new one of $3,000 ($240,000); Webster had paid neither principal nor interest on the initial loan, although George Sullivan—a mutual friend, New Hampshire attorney general, and a relative of another BHMA director William Sullivan—at least gave Perkins the $1,000.[63]

Ultimately, as Ichabod Bartlett (DR-NH) reminded the House, supporters of Webster's motion had to contend with the opinion of Secretary of State Adams, as expressed in a letter to the provisional Greek government of August 1823 and just furnished to Congress, that there were no grounds for recognizing independence, sending matériel would compromise U.S. neutrality, while dispatching the fleet, as urged by former treasury secretary and minister to France Albert Gallatin, constituted an act of war. Yet as much as Adams was intent on avoiding entanglement abroad, this opinion was more a technical expediency to cover his unerring promotion of trade.[64]

Two decades later in a lecture to the Massachusetts Historical Society, Adams defended British action in the Opium War as necessary to force the Chinese, with their "arrogant and insupportable pretensions," to engage in trade on "terms of equality and reciprocity." Working from Lockean principles that in a state of nature man was at peace, the pursuit of happiness was a natural right, and the source of that happiness was the right to property resulting from the two sources of occupancy and labor, Adams adduced that the right of barter—commerce—necessarily followed. By the "Christian precept to love your neighbor as yourself," there was "no other way by which men can so much contribute to the comfort and well-being of one another as

63. Mason to Webster, 1 February 1824, in *The Papers of Daniel Webster*, ed. Charles M. Wiltse (Hanover, NH: University Press of New England, 1974), correspondence, vol. 1, p. 351; Webster to Mason, 15 February 1824, ibid., p. 354, emphasis original; Perkins to Webster, 23 December 1823 and 26 January 1824, ibid., pp. 343–44, 348–50. Because Sullivan contributed $1,000 and the interest was $168.12 at 5 percent, Perkins gave Webster $1,831.88 of the new loan; blotter, 25 March 1819, THPP, reel 11. Webster continued to borrow from Perkins, as in the summer of 1836, when he accepted drafts for $8,000, see Evelyn H. Puffer, "A Great Business Lawyer," *Bulletin of the Business Historical Society*, 16:3 (June 1942), p. 61.

64. *Annals of the Congress*, 22 January 1824, p. 1154, and Adams's letter of 18 August 1823 to the self-styled envoy of the provisional Greek government, Andreas Luriottis, who was then in London, ibid., 20 January 1824, pp. 1109–10, and see *Memoirs of John Quincy Adams*, vol. 6, p. 172.

by commerce or mutual exchange of equivalents." For Adams, trade was not only a natural right but also a duty of all civilized Christians. At Smyrna, there was a trade that Adams saw as his duty to protect and grow, and it was in Adams that the loudest echoes of Perkins's lobbying reverberated.[65]

In 1819, the year the *Bocca Tigris* discharged her cargo of nankeens and silks at the Port of New York, Adams quietly sent lawyer Luther Bradish to Constantinople to negotiate a favorable trade treaty. This attempt failed, so Adams tried again in April 1823, through the mediation of George Bethune English, a Harvard graduate and Arabist who presented himself as a Turkish Muslim. In the fall of 1823, when English similarly had not delivered a treaty, Adams settled with appointing David Offley as U.S. consul at Smyrna, Offley being half of the Woodmass & Offley partnership through which Perkins traded. These were all illogical moves by a secretary of state to safeguard a miserable invoice of figs and opium, at a time when European allies were at war with the Ottomans, and for a Christian, albeit a Unitarian. Unless, that is, Adams was fully cognizant of the importance to Boston's economy of the Smyrna opium trade and of Perkins's efforts to monopolize it. Timothy Fuller, who spoke out against Dwight and Clay in the debate, met Adams twice on 17 January to discuss Webster's motion, and then a third time for dinner, which explains why Fuller knew to mention in his speech the squadron that Adams had stationed in the Mediterranean to protect Perkins's Smyrna trade. In as much as they furthered their goals through third parties, favored discretion over bluster, and preferred decision making to debating, Adams and Perkins were kindred spirits.[66]

Perkins must have been pleased with the outcome of his lobbying. Boston, after all, enjoyed the reputation of being not merely the Cradle of Liberty but also the Athens of America, the latter being a term coined by BHMA director William Tudor who also served on Everett's committee. To defeat an initiative in support of liberty-seeking Athenians by Edward Everett, professor of classical Greek at Harvard and an orator second only in rhetorical power to Congressman Daniel Webster, was a victory as consummate as it was ironic. Congressional initiatives to aid Greek independence continued into Adams's presidency, culminating in a resolution of 2 January 1827 by Edward Livingston (D-LA) to provide $50,000 in federal aid, against which the House voted 2:1 against, on the same grounds proposed by Everett's committee in 1824 and favored by Adams: the avoidance of European entanglement. As president, Adams appropriated $20,000 to negotiate a most-favored-nation treaty with Turkey, which led to the establishment of a U.S. embassy in Istanbul during Andrew Jackson's presidency, satisfying Perkins's wish for formal diplomatic relations. Perkins showed his gratitude by extending beneficial share offerings in factory stock to Adams. It might seem

65. John Quincy Adams, "Lecture on the War with China, Delivered Before the Massachusetts Historical Society, Dec. 1841," in the *Chinese Repository*, 11:5 (May 1842), pp. 288, 281, 276–77.

66. For background on English, see Richard H. Popkin, *Disputing Christianity: The 400-Year-Old Debate over Rabbi Isaac Ben Abraham of Troki's Classic Arguments* (Amherst, NY: Humanity Books, 2007), pp. 31, 233–38; a critic of Christianity and a scholar of Judaism, English read the Quran in Arabic, the Old Testament in Hebrew, and spoke those languages as well as Turkish in the vernacular; and for both Bradish and English, see Oren, *Power, Faith, and Fantasy*, pp. 107, 111–12.

ironic too that Adams, on one hand, would abandon Christian Greeks while, on the other, encourage Perkins's trade with Muslim Ottomans. Yet as much as Adams scorned "Mohammedan nations" for "their duty to propagate their religion by the sword," his duty was to propagate the "moral obligation of commercial intercourse between nations," founded solely—as he explained later to Massachusetts Historical Society members—on "the Christian precept to love your neighbor as yourself." A pious Unitarian, Adams believed in God's divine plan, and that no doubt extended to pragmatic, ad hoc foreign policymaking in support of Perkins's burgeoning Boston–Smyrna–Canton opium trade.[67]

Boston's Brahmin elites did not go a crusade against Mohammedan Turks, and their valuable overseas trade prospered—indeed, their wealth increased to the point where they could afford to capitalize New England's industrial revolution. When Perkins substituted scarce specie with saleable opium, he converted a 5 percent loss into a 100 percent gain, transforming not only the profitability of outbound cargoes but also the logistics and hence the efficiency of his entire trading system. His monopolistic hold on Turkish opium gave him an essential edge over competitors. As the first voyage of the *Bocca Tigris* shows, trading patterns were complex, with mixed cargoes going from Boston to Smyrna plus Leghorn and Gibraltar, then out to Canton and returning to New York with further transshipments from there; at all these ports, commission brokers, auctioneers, merchants, and tax collectors took their cut. But net proceeds far above those that accrued from legitimate trade ultimately accumulated in the brig's home port—Boston—in the hands of shipwrights, chandlers, sailors, insurers, bankers, co-investors, and particularly Perkins & Co. It was at the height of his opium smuggling of the mid-1820s that Perkins, now New England's wealthiest citizen, began throwing capital at anything that echoed the clatter of Britain's mature industrialization: lead mines, canals, textile mills, and the Granite Railway at Quincy. Some of his ventures were costly failures, such as the Monkton Iron Company in Vermont. Perkins nevertheless supplied much of the capital that enabled other enterprising Bostonians such as Nathan Appleton, Francis Cabot Lowell, and Amos and Abbott Lawrence to jumpstart industrial-scale manufacturing, which in turn fed back into foreign trade, creating further profits.[68]

Whereas, in 1820, Americans exported some $6.3 million in specie to Canton and imported 3,135,000 nankeens, by 1843 the drain in specie was negligible and they were exporting to Canton half a million pieces of cotton cloth produced in the water-powered mills of Waltham and Lowell. Throughout the 1820s and 1830s, Boston's foreign trade incurred an annual specie deficit of $800,000, but in the 1840s

---

67. On 11 January 1827, the House voted 109:54 against, 2nd Sess., 19th Cong., *Register of Debates in Congress* (Washington, DC: Gales & Seaton, 1829), vol. 3, pp. 577, 654; for MFN treaty, see James A. Field Jr., *America and the Mediterranean World, 1776–1882* (Princeton, NJ: Princeton University Press, 1969), pp. 147–50; Adams to Perkins, 3 October 1827, THPP, reel 2, "Correspondence"; Adams, "Lecture on the War with China," pp. 275, 277; For Adams's piety and Providential belief, see, for instance, Paul E. Teed, *John Quincy Adams: Yankee Nationalist* (New York: Nova Science Publishers, 2006), p. 112.

68. See, for instance, accounts for the Monkton Iron Company, 1819–20, folio 172, and Marble Quarry, 1827, folio 87, in THPP, reel 11.

that reversed to an annual surplus of $3.2 million ($256 million). Thereafter, as industrial production mounted, the China trade's contribution to the economy dwindled, remaining important only to optimists' imaginations. Two New England products, cotton cloth and ice, provide a guide for the mid-1840s: 40 percent and 38 percent respectively shipped out to foreign ports such as Rio de Janeiro, Valparaiso, Amsterdam, and London, but only 8 percent and 7 percent respectively went to Canton and Hong Kong. Nevertheless, the trade had been crucial in facilitating the capital accumulation that encouraged Perkins—along with his relatives and associates—to risk huge sums, first on industrial infrastructure such as canals and railways, and then on factories. From 1810 to 1845, Boston's wealth (personal estate plus real estate) increased seven-fold, from $18.5 to $136 million, and the taxable value of the average citizen's estate doubled, from $546 to $1,188 ($95,000). Liquidity soared; deposits held by the Suffolk Savings Bank increased from $33,000 in 1834 to $545,000 in 1845. In 1845, twenty-four Boston banks held $18 million ($1.4 billion) in capital and paid average dividends of 6.3 percent; sixteen insurance companies capitalized at $4.6 million paid an average dividend of 13.9 percent. What made this rapid—and sustainable—growth possible was the extra seed capital that flowed into Boston's industrializing economy from Perkins's Turkish opium business.[69]

Despite several blind-alley investments, Perkins was an astute reader of transatlantic industrialism, turning his attention with dexterity from the China trade to infrastructure, to mining, to textile manufacturing. He appreciated progressive social currents too. From provincial if not downright rusticated roots in small-town Boston of the 1770s, Perkins passed swiftly through mercantile adventuring and world traveling to emerge wealthy and—in common with his Brahmin cohort—with an excited, even exaggerated need for cultured urbanity. In addition to the Bunker Hill Monument, Perkins sponsored a range of charitable and philanthropic causes that are Bostonian institutions today. He cofounded and made several donations to the Massachusetts General Hospital, including one for $5,000 ($400,000) in 1820; he supported the McLean Asylum (the McLean Hospital today) for homeless psychiatric patients; in 1832, he gave his downtown mansion to the New England Asylum for the Blind (now the Perkins School for the Blind); and he was a director of and principal contributor to the Boston Athenaeum and to its art gallery, which matured into the Museum of Fine Arts. All these projects were collaborative, with Perkins serving on advisory boards constituted from the same tight-knit group of relatives and Brahmin friends, and they were invariably competitive, with Perkins offering $5,000 or $8,000 on condition that another benefactor put up a matching contribution.[70]

69. Specie and nankeens, "The China Trade," *Merchants' Magazine and Commercial Review*, 12:1 (1 January 1845), pp. 49, 51; "Boston Imports and Exports of Specie," *Merchants' Magazine and Commercial Review*, 18:2 (1 February 1848), p. 202; cotton and ice, "Progressive Wealth and Commerce of Boston," *Merchants' Magazine and Commercial Review*, 15:1 (1 July 1846), pp. 40–41; taxable value and wealth, ibid., pp. 46–47; liquidity, banks, and insurance companies, ibid., pp. 42–43.

70. For instance, Mass. General Hospital, blotter, 8 April 1820, THP, reel 9; during the 1820s, James Perkins, Thomas Perkins, and James Perkins Jr. gave $40,000 ($3.2 million) to the Athenaeum, see Ronald Story, "Class and Culture in Boston: The Athenaeum, 1807–1860," *American Quarterly*, 27:2 (May 1975), p. 182; Perkins made an $8,000

fig. 37: Massachusetts General Hospital

A culture of philanthropy grew from these shared endeavors, simultaneously necessitating and legitimating more wealth-creation, which further accelerated Boston's transformation from a provincial port to a vibrant city. Whereas in 1810, Boston was little more than half as big as its mercantile rival Salem, by 1840 Boston was six times larger, and over ten times the size by 1870. Salem's harbor silted up, and its civic buildings and captains' mansions were of brick or clapboard. Wharves bristled from every inundation of Boston's dredged shoreline, against a backdrop of granite edifices. Boston's shining skyline is unimaginable today without acknowledging two Yankees whose gritty ambitions intertwined with the construction of the Bunker Hill Monument: Solomon Willard's obsession with granite provided the look, while Perkins's infatuation with smuggling footed the bill.

Charlestown's Beacon of Hope and Reconciliation

Until the 1900s, by which time steamships had replaced the last of the packet sailing vessels and when the first office towers began to sprout skywards, masts and church steeples defined Boston Harbor's cityscape while, then as now, the Bunker Hill Monument four miles due north of Boston Common in Charlestown topped its skyline. As a monument to memorialize a battle for independence from the British Empire by thirteen Anglo-Protestant but nonetheless culturally and doctrinally distinct colonies, it enshrined a paradox central to American exceptionalism: it was a shining beacon of liberty yet it also symbolized an unyielding bond of union. Its polished capstone glinting in the sun shouted, "Come hither and live free," just as its immovable, tightly-fitting blocks of dull, hammered granite murmured, "But, never forget, there is no life

---

donation to the Athenaeum's Academy of Fine Arts, conditional on the trustees raising a like sum from other subscribers.

apart." In as much as social man craves unity, consensus, and order—even orders— the Enlightenment's promise of limitless freedom is too unsettling, the "dizziness of freedom" as described by Danish philosopher Søren Kierkegaard is too prone to creating an unbearable angst, as we stare dumfounded into a vortex of infinite options, infinite temptations. Yankee descendants of Puritan separatists were a restless lot. Never satisfied, they were always tinkering, whether with some new technology, commercial venture, financial vehicle, administrative system, or social reform. But this fidgeting all too easily created arguments, often heated ones that on too many occasions led Yankees into conflict, even outright warfare, after which their cognitive dissonance sought a harmony-restoring consensus. So it was that the Monument came to stand not only as a beacon of hope but also as a tower of reconciliation. It stood for rebonding bonds, for cementing back together the granite-like blocks of traditional American society that morally troubled Yankees maybe should never have sundered, first with their British brothers across the Atlantic and then with their Confederate neighbors south of the Mason-Dixon Line.[71]

Albert Edward, Prince of Wales, was just eighteen when, in the fall of 1860, he became the first British royal to visit the United States—and the last until George VI in 1939—creating a sensation from the moment he landed in Detroit from Canada. In contrast to the obsessive security and choreographed public appearances of twenty-first-century state visits, Albert's was refreshingly impromptu if not laughably slap-dash. Crowds pressing forward as Albert left the gangplank pushed one aide into the Detroit River, from where he was lucky to escape with minor injuries after the still-rotating paddlewheel hit him. Later, at a grand society ball that New Yorkers hoped would be the climax of the prince's trip, the specially constructed wooden dance floor collapsed in mid-waltz. With New Yorkers and Bostonians vying to see who could roll out the best reception, this embarrassing snafu tilted the rivalry in the latter's favor. Judging by welcome speeches and newspaper reportage, Americans read the royal visit as an exercise in reconciliation, so with provenance for the opening shots of 1775 undisputed, Boston may anyway have been the tour's talking point.[72]

Boston, newspapers reported, "was literally running over with people," as many as 100,000 of whom flocked to the Common to watch the young prince review militia regiments. So conservative were Bostonians "in all [their] traditions of the old country," *The Times* of London's reporter noted with bemused irony, that some of the companies wore uniforms from the days of George III, as "old and quaint-looking as the soldiers in the pictures of the victories of Wolfe [at Quebec]." An earthquake that morning set bells a-ringing in church steeples up and down New England but Bostonians engrossed with the royal visit scarcely noticed. From flagpoles around the city, most conspicuously at the State House and City Hall, the Union Jack fluttered next to the Stars and Stripes. At the Massachusetts Historical Society, its president

---

71. Søren Kierkegaard, *The Concept of Anxiety: A Simple Psychologically Orienting Deliberation on the Dogmatic Issue of Hereditary Sin*, ed. and trans. Reidar Thomte (1844; repr., Princeton, NJ: Princeton University Press, 1980), pp. 41–42, 61; Leon Festinger, *A Theory of Cognitive Dissonance* (Stanford: Stanford University Press, 1957), esp. pp. 4–21, 50–51.

72. Detroit, *The Times* (London), 10 October 1860, p. 8; New York, London *Times*, 30 October 1860, p. 9.

Robert Charles Winthrop—former U.S. Senator, seventh-generation descendant of Massachusetts's founder John Winthrop, and who was also the BHMA's president—showed Albert two swords worn during the Battle of Bunker Hill, the one by Royal Navy Capt. John Linzee whose sloop-of-war *Falcon* shelled the rebel redoubt, the other by Col. William Prescott the redoubt's commander. To emphasize that the War of Independence was but a ripple in the transatlantic special relationship, Winthrop explained how Linzee's granddaughter later married Prescott's grandson. Entertainment that evening was at the Boston Music Hall, its balconies bedecked for the occasion with alternating swaths of crimson and blue velvet trimmed with gold brocade, intertwined with British and American flags, altogether, in the eyes of *The Times* reporter, "rich, luxurious, and magnificent." On tiers that rose fifty feet above the orchestra, 1,200 choristers sang a special version of "God Save the Queen": "Lord, let War's tempest cease, / Fold the whole earth in peace, / Under Thy wings! / Make all Thy nations one, / All hearts beneath the sun, / Till Thou shalt reign alone, / Great King of Kings!" After retiring to lodgings at the Revere House, Albert received a visitor, Ralph Farnham, who was Albert's age when he fought with Prescott, making him 105 and the only surviving veteran. Such was the public praise for Albert that Farnham feared Americans had become royalists. Still, as one newspaper reported, he judged the prince to be "'a very nice young man'"—"'not proud at all.'"[73]

Newspapers made little comment about Albert's impromptu trip to the Bunker Hill Monument, which *The Times* of London described in passing as a "tall and rather ugly obelisk [that] looms over the city," although the Monument's historian G.W. Warren saw the visit as the symbolic climax of Albert's tour. Noting that the date was 19 October, the anniversary of Lord Cornwallis's surrender at Yorktown in 1781, Warren thought it a "Providential" omen of "permanent peace" between England and America. Winthrop directed Albert's attention to the Union Jack flying for the first time alongside the Stars and Stripes at the Monument's apex. "'This Monument was not erected to our glory,'" said Albert. "'True, your Highness,'" Winthrop replied, "'but it marks the birth of a kindred nation, which will ever own its affection for the mother-country.'" Prophetic of the special relationship during the coming century's two world wars, Winthrop added that, as an ally, the United States would "'prove as valuable as though she were still a part'" of Britain. Warren sent a memento to Buckingham Palace in the form of a reproduction of the Monument's visitors' book bearing Albert's signature. By the time this arrived, seven cotton states in the South had seceded from the Union. On Albert's behalf, Secretary of State for the Colonies Henry Pelham-Clinton, who had been on the royal tour, replied to Edward Everett with commiserations. "Time was, and that not long past, when you might have heard in every society jeers at the supposed failure of your institutions." But now,

---

73. Details of Albert's visit from the *Farmer's Cabinet*, 24 October 1860, p. 2, but similarly comprehensive coverage appeared in several regional newspapers; earthquake, in ibid.; swords, from George Washington Warren, *The History of the Bunker Hill Monument Association During the First Century of the United States of America* (Boston: James R. Osgood and Company, 1877), pp. 354–55; London *Times*, 6 November 1860, p. 6; Farnham, cited in *Maine Farmer*, 28:45 (25 October 1860), p. 2.

Pelham-Clinton assured Everett, there was an "all but universal" desire that the Union would prevail.[74]

Shocked to their Yankee core that the South's "excited leaders"—as Warren characterized them—had "torn in pieces" the flag of union, the BHMA's directors summoned the mystical power of the Monument in the Union cause. For the first anniversary of the Battle of Bunker Hill following the outbreak of the Civil War, they bolted a seventy-foot flagpole, topped appropriately by a gilded ball, to the Monument's upper courses. Before a crowd of dignitaries that included Massachusetts Governor John A. Andrew, the BHMA's president Winthrop declared that a "belief in a beneficent Providence" assured the North's ultimate triumph. "Order," Winthrop insisted, was "Heaven's first law." It followed, therefore, that because they had established "the best . . . system of law, of order, of culture, of progress and happiness," Heaven would not want to destroy the United States for the "wanton purpose of attempting new combinations." It would be as ridiculous, Winthrop suggested, to "batter down this Monument to its base, with the view of rearing from its disjointed materials a structure more firm, more appropriate, and more majestic," as it would be to dissolve the Union and construct multiple confederations, which would not last long enough to garner their own respect let alone that of the world. Winthrop passed the podium to Governor Andrew. "If this Monument needed a voice, if it does not now speak with silent but most mysterious and most eloquent organ, then let our country's flag, as it crowns the pinnacle of its loftiest height, speak for it." Andrew was taking a leaf from Daniel Webster's orations. "I spread aloft the blazing ensign of the republic, testifying for ever, to the last generation of men, of the rights of mankind, and of constitutional liberty and law." "Let it rise," he said—not as Webster did of the Monument at the cornerstone laying in 1825 but of the Stars and Stripes—"until it surmount the capital of the column; let it float on every wind, to every sea and every shore; from every hilltop let it wave; down every river let it run." Andrew tugged a rope that by some artifice of pulleys released the giant flag 260 feet above. "It was a spectacle worthy of Bunker Hill," Warren wrote, "and of her heaven-born mission—sublime and stirring enough to have fixed in loyalty any swerving Southern heart," if only Southerners had been there to see it.[75]

Next to the podium came Col. Fletcher Webster, commander of the Massachusetts 12th Regiment, who survived his father Daniel, as well as his brother Edward killed in the Mexican War. "I feel the inspiration which breathes around this spot," Webster said, invoking the rhetoric of both his father and Everett. "I feel the awful presence of the great dead, who speak to us out of this hallowed ground." Webster took his departure for the warfront from that spot, content in the knowledge that wherever his eyes closed they would turn north to the Monument, "gilded by the earliest beams of the

74. London *Times*, 6 November 1860, p. 6; Warren, *Monument Association*, pp. 353–54; Duke of Newcastle (Pelham-Clinton) to Everett, 8 February 1861, cited in ibid., pp. 356–57. Winthrop was also the great-great-grandfather of long-serving Massachusetts senator and 2004 presidential candidate John Kerry.

75. Warren, *Monument Association*, pp. 360–61; extracts of Andrew's speech of 17 June 1861 in ibid., pp. 362–63.

rising sun," and certain "that still departing day lingers and plays on its summit for ever." His eyes closed for the last time at the Battle of Bull Run a year later. It would not be until 25 November 1866 that the BHMA lowered the flag from the Monument's pinnacle, on the fourth Thanksgiving since Abraham Lincoln took Sarah Josepha Hale's advice and made it a national holiday, and on the first Thanksgiving for President Andrew Johnson as a day of atonement for a reunified nation. Historian Warren concluded that the flag-topped Monument had "fully served its purpose" of reuniting the United States. That purpose was no more apparent than during the lavish celebrations for the Battle of Bunker Hill centennial anniversary of June 1875.[76]

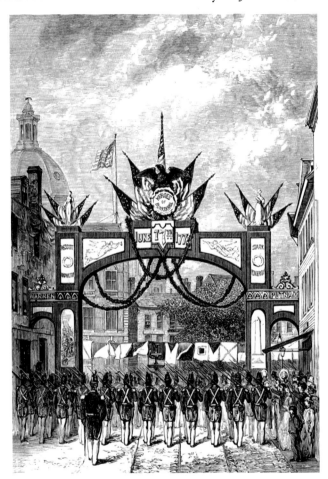

fig. 38: entrance to City Hall Square, Charlestown, 17 June 1875

Charlestown's residents became "wrought up to a high pitch of Revolutionary fervor," according to the *Boston Globe*, with nearly every house adorned with flags and bunting. Banners hung from trees across Boston Common. Downtown Boston's civic buildings were awash with patriotic decorations. Inscriptions identified points of historic importance for the events of 1775. Where the parade route entered Charlestown at City Square there was a triumphal arch, flanked by panels depicting the Monument and the battle for the redoubt, topped with liberty statues, flags, and the

76. Ibid., pp. 364, 368.

American eagle (fig. 38). At night, there were bonfires and firework displays, while limelights—rods of calcium oxide made incandescent with oxy-hydrogen flames and backed by metal reflectors—illuminated the domes of the State House, the Bunker Hill Monument, and Charlestown's City Hall, or rather old City Hall because the year before Charlestown had incorporated with the City of Boston. On the evening of 16 June, dignitaries gathered at the 2,500-seat Music Hall (renamed the Orpheum Theatre in 1906), including Vice President Henry Wilson, Gen. William Tecumseh Sherman, Senator Ambrose E. Burnside, Supreme Court Justice William Strong, the state governors of Massachusetts, Maine, and Michigan, and several former Confederate officers headed by Gen. Fitzhugh Lee of Virginia.[77]

fig. 39: reception in the Boston Music Hall, 16 June 1875

From a flower-festooned lectern emblazoned with the word *Peace* (fig. 39), Mayor Samuel C. Cobb welcomed the company, particularly the military contingents from the South, to Boston, the "sacred Mecca of the entire American people." He anticipated that fired by the inspiration of reunion the following day's celebrations would be a once-in-a-century red-letter day. Boston's spires and domes would shine with an unprecedented radiance, while a heretofore-unknown tide of life pulsed through the streets. Cobb painted a virile vision of the Monument. On Bunker Hill, its "granite

77. *Boston Daily Globe*, 16 June 1875, p. 1.

shaft will loom up many cubits taller into the sky," and its heart "will throb audibly beneath the tread and the acclaim of the gathering multitudes." But it was to the southerners—those from beyond the Kennebec and the Green Mountains, beyond the Savannah and the Tennessee—that he concentrated his address, exhorting them to "unite with us, and that right heartily," in commemorating the men and deeds of Bunker's Hill, and the way in which "an ever gracious Providence" had led them through peril to their "present height of greatness and prosperity." Cobb judged the omens propitious. Newly tested in civil strife and having prevailed, their national polity had passed the experimental stage. Tomorrow, they would dig the grave in which to bury any of the Civil War's lingering animosities. "Brave men love brave men," he assured the soldiers of both sides, "with the magnanimity that knows how to honor each other's courage." They had been "foemen in war" but they would be "brothers in peace," for that was the history of chivalry, in Boston as everywhere. Providence, which was wiser than their wishes, knew how to bestow benefits richer than those it withheld, so those southerners present should understand that "whatever was right and good in the lost cause" they had loved was "not finally lost, and that whatever was false or wrong in the winning cause cannot permanently triumph." In thrall to the Monument's unifying mystique and harkening to Cobb's Lost Cause rhetoric, only the hardest of former Confederate hearts could have resisted reaching for the olive branch of reconciliation.[78]

fig. 40: looking NNE up Monument Ave. from Main Street, 17 June 1874

78. *Celebration of the Centennial Anniversary of the Battle of Bunker Hill* (Boston: Rockwell and Churchill, 1875), pp. 28–32. Some accounts suggest that *Welcome*, formed from flowers, was the word on the lectern. For Lost Cause ideology as "a public memory, a cult of the fallen soldier, a righteous political cause defeated only by superior industrial might," see David W. Blight, *Race and Reunion: The Civil War in American Memory* (Cambridge, MA: Belknap Press of Harvard University Press, 2001), p. 38 and passim.

One of the earliest casualties of the secessionist argument had been Solomon Willard. Prior to breakfast on 27 February 1861, he learned from his newspaper that the Confederate States were seizing Federal forts and preparing for combat. Appreciating the military prowess of southern generals, Willard feared that the Confederate armies would triumph, march to Boston, and demolish the Monument, presumably because he understood its symbolism not only of union but also of Yankee hegemony over that union. Distraught at the thought that his life's greatest work would end as a pile of rubble, tears were on his cheeks. Before he could move his chair to the breakfast table, a fatal fit of apoplexy felled him. It was a tragedy that Willard died grief stricken over the Monument, which he loved like the first-born son he never had. Yet even in the angst of his death, he was true to his Yankee character. Only the day before, at age seventy-eight, he had been clearing granite boulders to make a new road to the estate of his Quincy neighbor Charles Francis Adams, son of John Quincy Adams. But if Willard could have risen from his grave in the 1980s then he would have been overjoyed to see not only his Monument still standing proud but also that granite was once again in vogue for downtown Boston's signature architecture.[79]

Granite's Coat of Many Colors

Throughout the last decades of Willard's life and into the 1870s, granite was the building material of choice for Bostonian architects, contractors, and clients. Even when cheaper sandstones or flashier marbles and then in the 1950s–70s concrete, pebble aggregates, and glass gained popularity, granite still had its adherents, primarily because the granite building boom of the 1830s–40s that Willard's pioneering endeavors ushered in had set the street-level standard for style and taste. By the 1880s nonetheless, granite had its Bostonian detractors, both on technical and aesthetic grounds. In evaluating the catastrophic damage caused by the Great Fire of 1872, safety inspectors realized that when fire hoses played cold water on hot granite walls, quoins and lintels could crack, sending the whole edifice crashing into the street. Structural granite's fire resistance would become a moot issue once builders adopted steel beams and reinforced concrete, although granite panels, like many other forms of cladding, can still pose a hazard for firefighters if they crack under extremes of temperature. Writing in Justin Winsor's classic *Memorial History of Boston* in 1881, Charles A. Cummings judged granite to be "one of the least admirable [materials for] any purposes of grace or luxury." Its color forbade "any agreeable play of light and shade, and its texture scarcely admits of clean-cut ornament except at great expense; and when all is done, the ornament is without effect." Perhaps if Cummings could have seen the golden colors, rich textures, and ornate carving in the granite of the Old Stock Exchange (1891, at State and Kilby Streets) then he would not have been so crotchety. Architectural critics have castigated the modern integration of the Exchange's magnificent Romanesque Revival façade into the black-glass towers of Exchange Place as "a species of false history," but, to a more forgiving eye, the combination makes for one of the most

---

79. Wheildon, *Willard*, pp. 252–54; it is my inference from Wheildon that he read this in his newspaper.

remarkable buildings to grace any American city (fig. 41). And 75 State Street (1988), clad in a Joseph's coat of five different colors of granite—from biscuit to russet—in both rough and smooth finishes, and trimmed with gold-leaf arrow-shaped flashes into a Jezebel of a building, would have left Cummings speechless (figs. 41, 42, 43).[80]

fig. 41: Old Stock Exchange (1891) and Exchange Place (1984), with 60 State Street (far left) in brown granite and 75 State Street (rear left)

Aside from masonry columns such as the Bunker Hill and Washington Monuments, high-rise construction was impractical until the coalescence by the 1890s of three sets of inventions: concrete, curtain walls, and the elevator. Concrete was actually a re-invention as it was the Romans who discovered the properties of hydraulic lime, most notably casting the dome of Rome's Pantheon (126 AD) in concrete. Industrial-scale production of Portland cement, and its use with aggregates of pebbles and sand to make concrete, began in the 1840s, and by the 1880s builders were learning how to cast structural concrete floors, pillars, and beams inside wooden forms containing steel reinforcing wire and ridged rebar.[81] Architect-engineer William Le Baron Jenney pioneered steel-frame construction, although at ten stories and 138 feet his Home Insurance Building (1885) in Chicago was hardly a skyscraper. Jenney's crew first erected a riveted steel and iron skeleton, and then attached the walls and floors to the frame,

80. Charles A. Cummings, "Architecture in Boston," in *The Memorial History of Boston, including Suffolk County, Massachusetts, 1630–1880*, ed. Justin Winsor (Boston: James R. Osgood and Company, 1881), vol. 4, p. 483; Naomi Miller and Keith Morgan, *Boston Architecture, 1975–1990* (Munich: Prestel-Verlag, 1990), p. 87. Exchange Place is at 53 State Street.

81. Sara E. Wermiel, "California Concrete, 1876–1906: Jackson, Percy, and the Beginnings of Reinforced Concrete Construction in the United States," *Proceedings of the Third International Congress on Construction History* (May 2009), pp. 1509–16.

which bore the bulk of the load, making the building a third the weight of all-masonry construction. Later refinements of the curtain wall system allowed builders to attach thin panels of stone, precast concrete, aluminum, or glass directly to the frame with brackets. A string of inventions made possible the electric elevators of the 1900s, beginning with wire ropes and Elisha G. Otis's safety brake (1853), to which in the 1890s another American, Frank J. Sprague, added variable acceleration, safety switches, and automated floor controls. Well into the 1960s, nevertheless, elevator cars traveled with a uniformed, white-gloved operator on a stool by the bank of buttons, adjusting the floor height at each stop and opening the crisscross lattice doors.

fig. 42: 75 State Street (center), with two more granite classics, Quincy Market (left) and One Faneuil Hall Square (center right), which is also clad in polychromatic granites

It was appropriate that Boston's first true skyscraper[82] would be an obelisk-like tower of light-gray granite sprouting from the Custom House, which by the 1900s was woefully inadequate to handle the Port of Boston's shipping transactions. Local architects Peabody & Stearns could ignore the city's height restriction of 125 feet because Federal buildings were exempt, so they decided on an ambitious forty stories with an elevation of 486 feet. So massive was Ammi Young's original construction that, with the dome removed and six caissons dug into the subsoil, the existing walls became the foundation. "Somehow the first thing that impresses you," wrote *Boston Globe* reporter A.J. Philpott at the tower's dedication in January 1915, "is its strength and solidity," as if it "would endure forever." To reach the windy viewing balcony, with its sixteen-foot forty-ton white Cape Ann granite eagles perched at its southwest and northwest corners, required riding the main elevator to the eighteenth floor, taking a

---

82. From a technical standpoint, the Ames Building (1893) was a skyscraper, although at only thirteen stories there were church steeples that dwarfed it.

second elevator to the twenty-fifth, and then ascending four flights of stairs, leaving another eleven left to reach the spire's last floor. But "what a view there is from the top of that tower!" Philpott said of the novel experience, marveling at the "toy wharves, part of a toy city" that jutted out into a toy harbor, plied by toy ships protected by toy lighthouses.[83]

fig. 43: street-level floors of 75 State Street

Appropriately, too, the Custom House Tower's history has been the stuff of legend. It had no company until the first John Hancock Building (1947) at 485 feet, and not until 1964 did the 749-foot Prudential Tower exceed its height—though never its beauty. Unopposed for so long, and with such a commanding presence downtown, the Custom House became a talking point as well as a comfortable friend, a sign for visitors that they had arrived and for travelers that they were home. It was a barometer of low cloud and unhealthy smog, a proving ground for the power of the Boston Fire Department's latest pumping engines, and on two occasions the departure point for suicides. During the Great War, a purported German spy created a bomb scare. In the late 1950s when, according to the *Globe*, one in five Bostonians owned a camera, it was the model for photography instruction, from figuring the focal length of telephoto lenses to shooting in low-light conditions. A peregrine falcon that made the upper reaches of the Custom House his home raised fifty chicks during his record-setting seventeen-year lifespan. And contrary to a myth that it is America's tallest building not to use a steel frame, general contractor Orlando W. Norcross employed the latest technology, with steel framing encased in concrete fireproofing.[84]

---

83. *Boston Globe*, 23 January 1915, p. 1; eagles, ibid., 4 July 1914, p. 8.

84. For cloud, see, for instance, *Boston Globe*, 26 September 1934, p. 16; for fire-fighting, *Globe*, 25 April 1927, p. 22; suicides, *Globe*, 11 September 1915, p. 14, and 13 September 1931, p. A7; bomb scare, *Globe*, 15 July 1915, p. 9; photography, *Globe*, 26 October 1958, p. A30, and 20 August 1961, p. A32; "Peregrine Falcon," Natural Heritage

fig. 44: Custom House Tower

Most legendary has been the unreliability of the tower's twenty-two-foot diameter, four-faced clock, making it the excuse for many a forgotten appointment. Pundits usually blamed an undersized electric motor, although after 1950 a conventional—albeit 144-lb—pendulum regulated the giant mechanism and electricity only served to wind the driving weights. One of the few repairmen prepared to work on the finicky clock was James J. Foley, who was deaf and had no phone so custodians requested maintenance visits by letter. There was trouble with plump, sleepy pigeons or winter's ice weighing down the eight already-heavy 150-pound hands, but Foley believed that high winds in this windiest of cities were the main cause, slowing the hands from eight to twelve and speeding them up from twelve to eight. What could he do to fix it,

and Endangered Species Program (December 2007), http://www.mass.gov/dfwele/dfw/nhesp/species_info/nhfacts/falco_peregrinus.pdf (accessed 19 June 2011); construction, Sara E. Wermiel, "Norcross, Fuller, and the Rise of the General Contractor in the United States in the Nineteenth Century," *Proceedings of the Second International Congress on Construction History* (2006), p. 3304.

asked a reporter? "'You have to shim the eight bushings which go in the hangar on the pole that operates the verge on the escape wheel,'" a frustrated Foley bellowed. "'I'm sorry I ever agreed to work on the thing.'" When Marriott International converted the tower into vacation condominiums in 1997, it could count on the expertise of David Hochstrasser, whose innovations included replacing the wooden hands with light-weight composite plastic. "'It's almost like a living organism,'" Hochstrasser commented in a *Globe* interview. "'Sometimes you hear it straining and creaking and groaning, and of course, hearing it tick is kind of like a heartbeat.'" Bostonians have a special attachment to the quirky clock of the iconic Custom House Tower, which is still the waterfront's signature building. As with the Bunker Hill Monument, stories that grew with the telling personalized the tower in local folklore, just as the tower's granite character became part of what it meant to be a proud Yankee citizen of the shining city.[85]

fig. 45: downtown from the northeast, with Custom House Tower at center, 17 June 2008

Boston's visitors today may notice glass monoliths like the John Hancock Tower, cast-concrete excrescences like the Le Corbusier-influenced, Brutalist-styled City Hall (1969), or the 614-foot aluminum-skinned louver door that is the Federal Reserve Bank and miss the prevalence of granite as a facing material. Of thirty-nine down-town high-rises featured in Naomi Miller and Keith Morgan's *Boston Architecture*,

85. Foley, *Boston Globe*, 11 June 1970, p 1; winds, *Globe*, 26 November 1974, p. 22; Hochstrasser, *Globe*, 7 January 2006, p. B1.

1975–1990, granite forms the cladding material of eighteen. All but four of the seventeen high-rise structures in fig. 45 have granite facings, most notably the magnificent rose granite cylindrical towers and 18-story annex of 46-story International Place (far left); the pink granite of 200 State Street (front-left of the Custom House); the rose granite in both rough-hewn and polished finishes of the Paine Webber Building (behind 200 State); the two-tone light-rose granite of 30-story 125 High Street (behind Paine Webber); the polished light-gray granite of 23-story 260 Franklin Street (right of the Custom House); 31-story 75 State Street with its beige and deep red granites set off by v-shaped gold leaf accents; the 37-story First National Bank Building in polished dark-brown granite (behind 75 State); and the brown granite of 38-story 60 State Street (far right). A style favored by Boston's architects and their clients, moreover, has been to employ granite to grace the lower floors of buildings that otherwise use cheaper stone or mundane artificial materials. Boston's first technical skyscraper, the Ames Building (1893), has ten upper floors of brick and sandstone but sets off its lower three floors with richly carved granite. Architects of the Edward W. Brooke Courthouse (2000) contrasted the Indiana limestone of the upper floors with a darker gray granite plinth, featuring rusticated arches. Several modernist towers in glass or pebble aggregate benefit by association with traditional granite buildings, such as the former Federal Reserve Bank (Langham Hotel) that nestles comfortably against the thirty-nine clinical stories of One Post Office Square.

fig. 46: Quincy Market, south plaza, 18 June 2011

When it comes to external beauty as well as internal elegance, few buildings in Boston, or any other major international city for that matter, can outclass 75 State Street, the fabulous, fairytale-like development adjacent to downtown Boston's Quincy Market (figs. 42, 43). "If this gold-leafed tower is glittery," the *New York Times*'s architecture critic Paul Goldberger remarked, "it is hardly vulgar." It used "decoration not as glitz but as part of a larger goal toward a civilized urbanity." Indeed, for a city that had always been "a curious mix of gentility and toughness, of refinement and bluntness," 75 State mirrored Boston's "complex character." Goldberger was paying tribute to designers Graham Gund and Adrian Smith, as well as to Boston's granite rootedness, when he realized how—brash though at first sight it appears—75 State takes its cues from its surroundings, fitting "neatly, even gracefully, into the complicated web of little streets," and had "much more in common" with "quirky, amiable buildings like the Customs House tower of 1915" than abstract modern architecture; these granite structures, he implied, were individualistic yet friendly. He thought the gold crowned top looked "splendid from the harbor" and made the building "vibrate on the skyline." Seventy-Five State's granite coat of many colors, he could have said, with its vibrating golden crest, epitomized Boston's continuing image into the twenty-first century as the shining city of Perkins's mercantile days.[86]

Boston's Granite Fengshui

When Paul Goldberger identified the "spirit" of amiable granite buildings like 75 State Street or the Custom House Tower he was not thinking about their geomancy, or *fengshui*. Yet it is surprising how many Western architects who dismiss fengshui as Asian mumbo jumbo actually employ its principles, no doubt because those principles derive from an organic sense of simply what feels right about a given design or its setting. Fengshui originated in Confucian China before the Ming Dynasty that popularized it as a method for regulating the *qi* energy that flows through all things, harmonizing qi in home and work spaces to ensure health, prosperity, and happiness. Qi (pronounced chee) is forceful and potentially disruptive, so it should first approach and then flow through a building by a sinuous rather than direct path. In the classic fengshui armchair configuration, a house sits on a mountain's south-facing slope for back support, with lower hills to left and right as armrests for side protection, and a low hill out front for a footstool; a river meanders around the footstool and, in front of the house, is an open space, a bright hall or *mingtang*. Just as evil spirits cannot see around corners, so the spirit wall that stands in the entryway deflects head-on qi energy. Inside the home, where windows and doors face into a central courtyard, geometric latticework, screens, potted plants, goldfish pools, and symmetrical surfaces painted in pastel greens and reds further regulate chi and harmonize the spatial elements. As exemplified by Beijing's single-story courtyard homes or *siheyuan* with their gently curving tiled roofs and carved stone doorways, these structures have an intricacy, a human-scale lowness that makes them as interesting as they are comfortably

86. *NYT*, 13 August 1989, p. H32.

intimate. But they are practical too: south-facing aspects are bright and warm; spirit walls and inward-facing windows facilitate privacy; irregular surfaces absorb street noise; and plants produce oxygen, while greens and reds naturally uplift the soul.[87]

fig. 47: granite sidewalk and, at center, 52 Broad Street

In the late-1960s under the modernizing rubric of destroying the Four Olds, Mao Zedong unleashed radical Red Guards to persecute intellectuals and purge every shred of traditional Chinese culture from memory. Fengshui not only escaped eradication but also blossomed, for it had crossed the Pacific, where in cities like San Francisco it developed a cult following, particularly among environmental activists and with-it homemakers. Hip Americans—intellectuals who enthused over *Quotations from Chairman Mao Tse-Tung* but, it is ironic to note, would have been the Red Guards' first victims had they lived in Beijing—hired interior designers brandishing compasses and trigrams and lo-shu squares from the *I Ching* to harmonize their living spaces,

87. "Spirit," in ibid. Accessible introductions are Sarah Rossbach and Master Lin Yun, *Fengshui Design: From History and Landscape to Modern Gardens and Interiors* (New York: Viking, 1998), and Stephen Skinner, *Feng Shui Style: The Asian Art of Gracious Living* (Singapore: Periplus Editions, 2003).

particularly by cutting the clutter that allowed qi to stagnate. Since the 2008 Olympics, with its lesson that there is nothing like nationalism to build pride and hence popular support, the Chinese Communist Party has eagerly appropriated cultural trappings—from calligraphy and herbal medicine to Buddhist temples and ethnic music—to legitimate its nationalist credentials. Now back in vogue, fengshui, with its adopted American characteristics, has re-crossed the Pacific.[88] Given the Puritan aesthetic for functional simplicity and order, as well as Bostonians' sympathy with Chinese culture derived from the Old China Trade, fengshui is an appropriate frame of analysis for Boston's Monument-induced granite geomancy.

fig. 48: Charlestown home, with granite basement, entryway, and sidewalk

Granite fengshui harmonizes Bostonians' Yankee qi on two spatial or experiential levels, first vertically, through feet down on the sidewalk and then via eyes up at the roofline. Many cities, for sure, have sidewalks edged in granite, a solid form against which to roll tar macadam roadways and tamp concrete pavement, and a durable defense against the gouging wheels of errant parkers. Yet it is far from ubiquitous, as is evident from the cast-concrete edgings of, say, Los Angeles or Phoenix to the steel-edged sidewalks of Manhattan. But in Boston it is not just that the edgings are granite—entire sidewalks are too. Dating back to the nineteenth century and patinated by the steel-tipped Florsheim of many a successful Yankee, these retain their original drainage grooves and the capped holes of basement coal chutes (fig. 47). Aside from

88. See Ole Bruun, *Fengshui in China: Geomantic Divination Between State Orthodoxy and Popular Religion* (Honolulu: University of Hawaii Press, 2003), pp. 242–46.

the fact that these slabs have paid for their installation a dozen times over, they—literally—connect pedestrians to their history. Around signature architecture like International Place, granite flows out of the buildings, descending the stairways, mounting the balustrades, and enriching the walkways. Downtown Boston's ground-level granite extends to public meeting places, like Quincy Market's plazas; other than the darker areas of red brick, the patios, seats, and buildings, both old and new, shown in fig. 46 are all granite. There are homes throughout Boston dating from the nineteenth century that have granite basements and entryways, a style particularly evident in Charlestown (fig. 48), and there, increasingly so the nearer the townhouse is to Monument Square, suggesting the influence of the Monument as well as the proximity of suitable building stone left over from the Monument's construction. Facing the Monument to its north and directly abutting the sidewalk on three sides is the old Charlestown High School (1848), built by Ammi Young from Quincy granite using techniques pioneered by Solomon Willard.

fig. 49: Custom House Tower, Two International Place, and Zakim Bridge

Moving the eye from basement to stairway to roofline is an equally rewarding experience in downtown Boston, where granite detailing can be at its best a dozen stories up, as with the intricate ninth-floor balcony and rooftop cornice alive with gargoyles at the Old Stock Exchange (fig. 41). Built in 1853 as a workaday gray-granite warehouse for the clipper ship trade with China, 52 Broad Street's architect endowed it nonetheless with a cornice of arched dentils topped by an elegant mansard, set off with dormers reminiscent of a Chinese roof (fig. 47). Whereas in so many cities, particularly in Asia, socialist High Modernism has demolished traditional forms—and Boston, too, has its share of Le Corbusier banality—it is important to consider why this building stands proud today: its original owner had built up sufficient capital from trading tea, and maybe from a relative who traded opium, to specify quality construction and elegant design; its resulting durability recommended refurbishment over replacement; its history caught the attention of preservationists; and its aesthetic won the praise of the Boston Society of Architects, whose members have made it their headquarters.

fig. 50: Leonard P. Zakim Bunker Hill Memorial Bridge, looking north on I-93

Boston's horizontal alignment of granite fengshui does not conform to a rigid north–south axis, as in Beijing, where a line runs from the Olympic Bird's Nest stadium in the north, over the Coal Hill back support, through the main hall of the Forbidden City, and on, to Yongdingmen, the central gate of the Outer City to the south. Neither did Boston's architects and city planners have fengshui principles in mind when they selected the style or location of particular buildings, as was the case in Beijing, from Kublai Khan's Dadu laid out by the Daoist architect Liu Bingzhong, to the Yongle Emperor's fabulous Forbidden City, through to the planning for the 2008 Olympic Games. It appears, nevertheless, that the Custom House Tower takes stylistic and spatial cues from both the white spire of the Old North Church and the conical tip of the Bunker Hill Monument, 0.7 and 1.4 miles due north respectively. More striking, is the alignment that greets visitors to Boston from the north on I-93, particularly when they exit at Charlestown. Although the shining, conical cap of Two International Place is fifty-two feet taller than the Custom House Tower, it lies 500 yards to the south, making a line that appears to run through the twin obelisks of the Leonard P. Zakim Bunker Hill Memorial Bridge (fig. 49). Visitors that stay on I-93 enter Boston by passing between the Zakim's giant legs, as if the Bunker Hill Monument had sired twin sons who had obligingly walked down to the Charles River to toy with the roadway (fig. 50).[89]

fig. 51: Charlestown's City Square Park, looking toward the Zakim Bridge

Uncanny yet visually satisfying granite alignments crop up all over north Boston and neighboring Charlestown. At City Square Park, pillars that would be obelisks were they not blunted with floppy granite leaves, line up with the Zakim, as does the granite obelisk that is the World War II Memorial, just visible in the trees at center-left

---

89. Old North is half a degree and the Monument roughly five degrees west of due north.

in fig. 51. And at the Old Navy Yard's granite Korean War Memorial, the forgotten war's unknown soldier stares out, past the columns bearing the names of his fallen local comrades, at the Bunker Hill Monument (fig. 52). Perhaps, like Fletcher Webster, he had left Charlestown for the Korean battlefront inspired by the faith that wherever his eyes closed they would turn east to the Monument, gilded by the first beams of the rising sun.

fig. 52: Korean War Memorial, looking toward the Bunker Hill Monument

5. James Duncan: American Dream

Boston had its storied elites, iconic Bunker Hill Monument and Custom House Tower, and imposing granite commercial buildings, whereas Quincy, eleven miles to the south, was a city of dusty workers, clapboard houses, gloomy saloons, and dangerous granite quarries. As Boston went up, it was as if Quincy went down. In Solomon Willard's day, quarrying, cutting, and surfacing granite blocks required a team of craftsmen who took pride in their work for high wages, and for many of whom there was neither attitudinal distinction nor practical barrier between hourly pay, subcontracting, and outright entrepreneurialism as stonemasons, builders, or quarry owners. But with the granite building boom that Willard unleashed, the rapid expansion of Quincy's granite tombstone business in the 1890s, and the introduction of compressed air drills and machine surfacing equipment, granite production changed from a cottage industry of craft workers to big businesses operated by wealthy owners. Nearly all these entrepreneurs, as well as those they employed, were European immigrants who arrived as journeymen and then worked their way up, first into a partnership and then to owner-operators by buying out their partners. What sustained the successive waves of Scots, Irish, Italians, Swedes, and Finns who blasted the seams, drilled the blocks, rigged the tackle, cut the slabs, and operated the polishing machines was a dream that through their efforts they, too, would one day be prosperous.

Asked to define the American Dream, respondents—from U.S. citizens to illegal immigrants to foreigners—readily provide an answer little changed from when James Truslow Adams coined the term in his *Epic of America* (1931), to mean "a land in which life should be better and richer and fuller for every man, with opportunity for each according to his ability or achievement." Some will mention Adams's caveat, that the Dream has not been merely of "motor cars and high wages" but also of "a social order," whereby everyone "shall be able to attain to the fullest stature of which they are innately capable," and receive recognition "for what they are, regardless of the fortuitous circumstances of birth or position." Interpretations of the Dream are otherwise as varied as the dreamers.[1]

For former President Herbert Hoover, who as a self-promoter of the hardworking self-made man did much to popularize the phrase, it meant the "immutable principles of ordered liberty" given to Americans "by the God of our fathers," and from which came personal independence, economic security, and prosperity. Perhaps because he sought to distance himself from Hoover, President Franklin D. Roosevelt rarely spoke of the Dream and then to mean "individual farm ownership." Kentucky's Governor Thomas E. Dewey believed that "a vital and necessary part" of the Dream was that "America shall, by her conduct and example, give leadership and inspiration to the world." Frank R. Equi stressed that "Home Ownership Is the American Dream," but then he was the president of Middlesex Homes. Columnist Dorothy Thompson

---

1. James Truslow Adams, *The Epic of America* (1931; repr., Boston: Little, Brown, and Company, 1939), p. 415.

acknowledged that it stood for "freedom, equality, and happiness," but she also worried that it encouraged "mediocrity—in high places and low." For Thompson, the Dream was "to be average, to temper the intellect and work to the common run, to denigrate and debunk the great, to 'get by with things,' to make pleasure and leisure the aim of life, to indulge in fatuous optimism, to be certain that in some way 'everything will turn out all right,' and to run screaming after scapegoats if it didn't." It was perhaps for newcomers and would-be immigrants that the Dream had most salience. Abraham A. Ribicoff's parents were Jewish immigrants from Poland. His father was a poor factory worker who nonetheless valued education, so Ribicoff excelled in the public schools of his New Britain, Connecticut, hometown and then took a part-time factory job to pay for university. When he enrolled in Chicago University Law School, he continued working for another branch of the same company, rising to a management position. In 1938 aged twenty-eight, he entered politics as a Connecticut congressman and, in 1955, he became governor of the state. "'I used to lie under a tree and dream the great American dream,'" Ribicoff told a *Boston Globe* reporter. He was living proof that in America "any boy or girl could dream and send those dreams as high as the sky." There was nowhere else on earth, the reporter emphasized, where immigrants could dream of high political office, with the opportunity that such office provided to serve fellow men, than the United States.[2]

Yet for every American who lived the Dream there were countless more who resigned themselves to Thompson's mediocrity or who settled instead into a work-a-day subculture at the bottom of the socioeconomic pyramid. Even before he presided over the burgeoning military-industrial complex following the Korean War, Gen. Dwight D. Eisenhower cautioned in 1949 that the Dream had become a "'nightmare'" of big government, turning the once independent American into "'the serf of institutions he creates.'" Slavery was always on the mind of civil rights activist Martin Luther King Jr., for whom "America is essentially a dream, a dream as yet unfulfilled." For most ethnic and religious minorities, the sky that Ribicoff was lucky or aggressive enough to reach was actually a low glass ceiling. There have been twenty-five Jewish state governors and eight Hispanic Americans but only one Chinese American (Gary Locke) and not yet a single Muslim; it was not until Keith M. Ellison (D-MN) in 2007 that there was a follower of Islam in the U.S. Congress. Many immigrants, moreover, have learned that what makes the Dream realizable is a necessary irony of U.S. citizenship. By comparison with most other nation-states, from Bolivia to Britain to China to Denmark, it is easy to become an American—a million immigrants do so each year— but this citizenship is, in reality, worth little. Education, health care, workers' compensation insurance, welfare benefits, and retirement pensions are not socialistic entitlements but expensive commitments that each citizen must pay for directly or through payroll and real estate taxes.[3]

2. Hoover at Fort Wayne, Indiana, cited in the *Boston Globe*, 5 April 1936, p. A20; Roosevelt to Congress, *Globe*, 17 February 1937, p. 32; Dewey, *Globe*, 9 September 1944, p. 3; Equi, *Globe* headline, 16 September 1956, p. A35; Thompson, *Globe*, 25 June 1940, p. 8, and *Globe*, 17 December 1941, p. 18; Ribicoff, *Globe*, 6 May 1956, p. C40.

3. Eisenhower, *Boston Globe*, 25 October 1949, p. 6; King, "The American Dream," Lincoln University, PA, 6 June

In addition to the ironies of mediocrity and citizenship, a more troubling paradox stalks the Dream's innermost chambers, as the case of Scottish immigrant, granite cutter, and union leader James Duncan in the context of Quincy's granite industry makes clear. While some immigrants came to the United States as eager entrepreneurs, others brought with them a belief, as powerful as scientific truth, in the socialism and trade unionism that was then sweeping Europe. Strike action—the threat behind collective bargaining—was only effective when all the workers of a given trade acted in unison, so, through the lure of higher wages or, when that failed, by intimidation, they drew their fellow workers together into an exclusive craft union. Their conviction that industrialization was destined to split society into antagonistic forces of capital and labor became a self-fulfilling prophecy, a trap that denied the possibility for upward mobility and achievement. But while brother unionists, as they called each other, sought solidarity after work in saloons and union halls, their employers donned tuxedos to socialize in Masonic lodges, further emphasizing the cultural divide. They were proud of their success, these newly rich businessmen, keen to prove they had made the American Dream come true. What better way to show their American-ness, therefore, than by emulating the mores of old-stock Yankees, which they then sought to impose on their employees, in part to reduce their own cognitive dissonance but also because industriousness, order, and sobriety boosted productivity. Fulfilling the American Dream, particularly in a unionized workplace, created a culture of division on one hand, while on the other, it furthered a culture of conformity that together stifled individual liberties and the ability to achieve, which were the Dream's promise.

Quincy's Granite Industry in the 1890s

Until the turn of the century, Quincy was a surprisingly pre-industrial city, partly due to a lack of waterpower but primarily because its work practices stemmed from labor-intensive granite production, associated tool sharpening, and the traditional leather trades. An 1865 survey listed 155 firms engaged in twenty-four activities with 1,258 employees, 472 of whom were making shoes, largely by hand, 368 were granite workers or shippers, 151 were farming, 77 were shipbuilders or sailors, 43 were tanning leather, and 36 were gathering firewood. Thirty years later, the picture had changed little, except that shoemaking was in steep decline because manufacturers in towns like Lynn on Boston's north shore were investing in electrically operated machinery. It would not be until the mid-1900s that Quincy began to industrialize, with the growth of the Fore River Shipbuilding Company, the Boston Gear Works, and the Tubular Rivet & Stud Company. Even then, Quincy manufacturers retained a craftworking ethos, as exemplified by the Avedis Zildjian Company, the world's largest cymbal maker, which opened its Quincy factory in 1928.[4]

While granite continued into the 1920s to constitute Quincy's "commercial backbone," as the *Boston Globe* put it, that was only because of a transformation in the

1961, in *A Testament of Hope: The Essential Writings and Speeches of Martin Luther King Jr.*, ed. James Melvin Washington (New York: HarperSanFrancisco, 1986), p. 208.

4. Helen F. Burke, *Quincy Industries, 1625–1943* (Quincy: City of Quincy, Massachusetts, 1943), pp. 12–14.

local business model. Going into the 1880s, four factors had conspired to knock the bottom out of Quincy granite as a building material: First, Boston's Great Fire of 1872 revealed an inherent weakness with all-granite construction for the taller commercial buildings then coming into vogue, whereby cold water from fire hoses played on hot granite caused cracks that undermined the structure. Second, Gilded Age clients seeking a showier aesthetic with less concern for durability turned to lighter-colored limestones and marbles. Third, competition increased, both from extensive new quarries in the United States, such as at Graniteville and Barre (pronounced BA-rri) in Vermont, and then from South America and even Europe, as the cost-effectiveness of shipping grew. Fourth, the profitability of quarrying at Quincy fell as larger seams tapped out, unionized workers demanded more pay for shorter hours, and quarry owners lacked capital to invest in machinery. What not merely saved Quincy's granite industry but boosted it from sales of $200,000 in 1880 to $3.3 million by 1920 was a switch to the production of cemetery tombstones, monuments, and mausoleums.[5]

fig. 53: polished memorial with gold-engraved lettering, by Benjamin Bishop, Quincy

As more New Englanders moved from producerist yeoman farming to join the manufacturing and service sectors, consumption for the resulting middle class turned from necessities to commodities to luxuries. Once newly affluent consumers had satisfied their needs for housing, furnishing, transportation, and leisure, they turned to burials, the last item on life's list. "Consumption beyond the home followed on from a new level of materiality first achieved in the domestic setting," and cemeteries, archeologist Harold Mytum suggests, "offered a new, and more public, arena for consumption." Additional demand factors, particularly in the New England states, included: the pietistic Third Great Awakening of the 1860s–90s with its stress on post-millennial theology; an urge by aging Civil War veterans to leave a public testimonial to their

5. *Boston Globe*, 18 March 1898, p. 7; J. Nelson Clifford, "Granite Industry of Quincy, Massachusetts," *Economic Geography*, 15:2 (April 1939), pp. 147–48.

rank and service; the effectiveness of advertising in the new mass media; the burial funds of fraternal organizations that could finance basic memorials for even the poorest of workers; and the cultural importance attached to burial sites by newly-arrived immigrant groups, especially Italians. Art historian Joseph J. Inguanti notes how Italian Americans extended their home-centric family life to the "domestication of the grave," arguing that for many poor apartment dwellers, a well-kept grave might have been "the only parcel in which the 'American Dream' of home ownership [was] most closely realized."[6]

fig. 54: Mount Wollaston Cemetery, Quincy, with fine examples of polished granite spheres

On the supply side of the memorial business's exponential growth during the last two decades of the nineteenth century was the availability of urban land for cemeteries and the willingness of town committees to provide burial grounds, the switch from hand to power tools for carving granite, and, in particular, the introduction of machine polishing, which in turn drove demand by endowing granite with a dark luster that showcased gold-engraved lettering. Granite had an appealing—and marketable—permanency that the cheaper sandstones and easier to work marbles lacked. Advertising by Quincy's Granite Manufacturers' Association featured a Pharaonic pyramid and the Sphinx set against the letter Q, ringed with the slogan, "Lasting Until Everlasting." A polished granite memorial like the one in fig. 53 found ready buyers at around $200 ($4,800[7]), but there was plenty of scope for far more extravagant displays of wealth and prestige. In 1900—twenty-seven years before he died—New York

6. Harold Mytum, "Popular Attitudes to Memory, the Body, and Social Identity: The Rise of External Commemoration in Britain, Ireland, and New England," *Post-Medieval Archeology*, 40:1 (2006), p. 103; Joseph J. Inguanti, "Domesticating the Grave: Italian-American Memorial Practices at New York's Calvary Cemetery," *Markers*, 17 (2000), p. 30.

7. Adjusting for inflation for the 1920s is especially tricky as there was inflation in the first years of the decade, then deflation, and then a return to inflation; this chapter adjusts to 2011 by applying a factor of 24, a geomean derived from "Inflation Data, 1921," spreadsheet, compiled by author (available on request), of price data, including categories for food, drink, apparel, toiletries, entertainment, travel, appliances, automobiles, accommodation, wages, and salaries.

brewer George Ehret ordered a domed mausoleum thirty-three feet square and forty-five feet high with a marble interior, the granite alone for which cost him $45,000 ($1.1 million).[8]

fig. 55: obelisk memorial to Mary E.B. (1851–95) and John R. Graham (1847–1915)

Supply factors no doubt exaggerated Quincy's own memorial boom, although the prominence of its cemeteries is typical of many a New England township. Consecrated in 1855, Mount Wollaston Cemetery was originally twenty-five acres but in the 1890s it doubled to fifty-seven acres of 30,000 lots. In addition, there are seven more cemeteries located within the city of 92,000 residents (in 2010): Hall, Hancock, St. Joseph's, Christ Church, two small sailors' cemeteries, and Pine Hill constructed in 1962 at fifty acres. Despite the growing popularity of cremation, Quincy is running out of burial plots, especially for those who wish to lie next to their kin. "'When the city . . . doesn't have any graves for its citizens,'" fretted veteran gravedigger Richard McNeice, "'that'll be a big wake-up call.'" Although it has few elaborate mausoleums, Mount Wollaston contains one of the best displays of grave art in the United States, most noticeably its Monument-like obelisks (fig. 55) and the polished granite spheres produced by the Lyons Granite Company and the Quincy Column & Turning Company (figs. 54, 62). Yet despite the inherent profitability of this boom, Quincy's granite industry would collapse in 1929 and never recover. Combined with two

8. See, for instance, *Quincy Granite: Lasting Until Everlasting* (Quincy, MA: Granite Manufacturers' Association, 1932); *Granite Cutters' Journal*, 23:278 (May 1900), p. 2.

other interlinked revolutionary changes—the introduction of steam and later compressed air for drilling and surfacing stone on one hand, and the restrictive demands of unionization on the other—the shift to memorials created a fatal disjuncture in the workplace.[9]

To quarry, dimension, and finish granite, whether as a building material or for memorials, was skilled work, but, as the alacrity with which convicts learned the trade indicates, it was easier to master than carpentry, stonemasonry, or bricklaying, and the process broke down into specific skill sets conducted at geographically separate locations. Riggers, blasters, and drillers typically worked at quarries around Quincy's western hills, tool sharpeners at nearby machine shops, and hammerers, polishers, and engravers at downtown factories. There were few barriers to entry for proprietors of the small quarries and finishing shops that proliferated at Quincy. Of at least eighty-nine granite businesses operating in 1897, 60 percent were partnerships or sole proprietorships, with just twenty-seven registered companies, nine operators of large quarries, and only eleven businesses that had invested in steam boilers to power cutting drills or finishing mills. It was easy enough for a father and son, a pair of brothers, or a couple of friends with a month's wages and a bag of hand tools to take over a small or nearly exhausted quarry or go into business carving and lettering tombstones. Still, their income depended on physical effort, their working environment was typically as rudimentary as it was insular, and they were unable to meet demand for the new fashion in mirror-finish memorials that only expensive polishing machines could produce.[10]

Once successful proprietors reached the stage of investing in a bigger quarry or in a steam boiler to power machinery, of necessity they quickly transitioned to managers of large businesses with invested or borrowed capital of $10–20,000 and an hourly-paid workforce. Their worries escalated from not bashing a finger or having a customer default on a payment to motivating workers, marketing product, and paying down bank loans. Equipment to generate steam or compressed air, and the machines to cut or polish granite slabs, were most efficient when in regular use. Further efficiencies came from vertically integrating machine cutting, surfacing, and polishing under one roof, fitted with sliding gantries for moving heavy stone. At the Henry C. Smalley Granite Co., expansion came by the simple if ugly expedient of building a huge shed to cover a yard between two existing sheds (figs. 56, 57). Undertakers and bereaving relatives ordered memorials at any time, if anything in greater numbers during the winter months, and that was when steam boilers used more fuel and sheds required heating as well as ventilation. Owners, therefore, were under pressure to maximize their turnover and regularize their workforce. Recent immigrants, particularly Italians with poor command of English, drew to the larger finishing shops, where they had few responsibilities and could socialize with compatriots in their own language. But immigrant stoneworkers arrived from Europe imbued with socialist, collectivist, and

9. McNeice, interviewed in the *Quincy Patriot Ledger*, 6 December 2008, p. 11.

10. *The Mine, Quarry, and Metallurgical Record of the United States, Canada, and Mexico* (Chicago, IL: Mine and Quarry News Bureau, 1897), pp. 498–99.

anarchist ideologies that were an uneasy fit with the principles inherent in the American Dream.[11]

fig. 56: Henry C. Smalley Granite Company, Quincy, with 32 employees, ca. 1910

fig. 57: Henry C. Smalley Granite Company, Quincy, with 64 employees, ca. 1920

With more men working together, and with more machinery powered by compressed air to kick up the dust, so granite workers' concerns turned to the size of their weekly pay packet and maintaining their health long enough to enjoy retirement. They understood that their employers depended on them to satisfy the order book just as they realized that their skill sets were narrowing to a particular piece of machinery; they wielded greater bargaining power and yet their jobs were more easily replaceable. Unionization seemed to offer the solution. Aside from its substantial periphery of craft-working owner-operators, Quincy's granite industry soon stratified into what unionists called "capital and labor." When the memorial business turned profitable in the 1890s and seemed set to grow indefinitely, local union leaders, emboldened perhaps by Quincy's reputation for the quality stone that built the Bunker Hill Monument, became even more strident in their calls for higher wages than the Granite Cutters' Union's new chief executive James Duncan might, with hindsight, have thought prudent.[12]

---

11. A running feud between Barre's Italian socialists and anarchists sometimes boiled over into violence, as when in 1903 socialist Alessandro Garetto shot and killed anarchist Elia Corti and wounded another at a political meeting; for background, see, for instance, Paul Heller, "Preaching the Gospel to Anarchists and Socialists: Baptist Missionaries in Barre, 1899–1916," *Vermont History*, 78:2 (Summer/Fall 2010), pp. 196–207.

12. "Capital and Labor," title of regular page two column in the *Granite Cutters' Journal* after mid-1900.

Duncan's American Dream

Across the Atlantic from Boston and twelve hundred miles nearer the Pole on Scotland's rocky northeast coast, lies another Granite City, Aberdeen, so named after its gray building stone quarried at Rubislaw, two miles west of downtown, which is today a vast, water filled hole 460 feet deep and 130 yards across. Over the years, Rubislaw Quarry produced some six million tons of granite and made the careers of hundreds of granite cutters, many of whom bought one-way passages on steamers to New York. One of them was James Duncan, born in 1857 to a farming family in Portlethen, a fishing village eight miles south of Aberdeen, to which he journeyed for school until thirteen or fourteen before apprenticing to a granite cutter. Other than a few letters in the American Federation of Labor (AFL) archive, his dry articles in the *Granite Cutters' Journal*, and boilerplate union committee minutes, Duncan contributed little to the historical record, so his reasons for emigrating as soon as he finished serving his seven-year apprenticeship in 1879 are unknown. A popular guidebook to Scotland begins its description of the city by citing the novelist Lewis Grassic Gibbons: "'One detests Aberdeen with the detestation of a thwarted lover,'" going on to explain that "while some extol the many tones and colours of Aberdeen's granite buildings, others see only uniform grey and find the city grim, cold and unwelcoming." Aberdeen's "tiresome" weather, its "cutting wind and driving rain," was the problem, even if that did "transform the buildings into sparkling silver." So perhaps it was the bleak climate where winter daylight lasts less than seven hours that drove Duncan away, or a rift with his parents' strict Presbyterianism, but, most likely, it was the promise of the American Dream.[13]

To New York, Duncan brought an activism and an aptitude for journalism in the tradition of Scottish immigrant Thomas Paine. Right after arrival, he attended a committee meeting of the local Granite Cutters' National Union (GCNU). Two years later, the committee's members elected him as their branch secretary. In 1882, he moved to Philadelphia where the local union appointed him to the same position. After a stint cutting stone in Richmond for the State, War, and Navy Building (now the Eisenhower Executive Office Building) in Washington, DC, he settled in Baltimore in 1885 and again became local union secretary. He was soon contributing articles to the *Granite Cutters' Journal* and active in the national trade union arena. He attended the AFL's inaugural convention of 1886, and then, in December 1894, he won election to the second-ranked vice-presidency of the AFL. In March 1895, by which time the GCNU had rotated its headquarters from Concord, New Hampshire, to Baltimore, Maryland, Duncan began his long editorship of the *Granite Cutters' Journal*. Two months later, the committee elected Duncan to national secretary and treasurer, posts he held for three decades.[14]

---

13. For Duncan, see footnote, below; *Scotland: The Rough Guide*, 4th edition (London: Rough Guides, 2000), p. 437.

14. Compiled primarily from: "Duncan Has Busy Office at Quincy," *Boston Globe*, 2 September 1907, p. 4; *Who's Who in America*, vol. 12, 1922–23 (Chicago: A.N. Marquis & Company1922), p. 978; "Minutes, National Union

fig. 58: James Duncan (seated left) at the Paris labor conference, 1919, with Samuel Gompers (foot on stool) and Frank Duffy, William Green, and John R. Alpine (back row, left to right)

Stolid and introverted, at least if the scant historical record is any guide, Duncan was a large, disciplined man who rose at dawn to walk four or five miles before breakfast. For thirty odd years as AFL vice-president, Duncan was a close confident of the AFL's seminal leader Samuel Gompers, who sent Duncan to the Budapest labor conference of 1911, to Moscow in 1917 as President Woodrow Wilson's diplomatic envoy, and who accompanied him to the Paris labor conference of 1919. Yet when Gompers wrote his voluminous autobiography *Seventy Years of Life and Labor* he could only find one thing to say about his friend. When complaining that John McBride, briefly AFL president during 1894–95, "shrank from hard work," Gompers mentioned that Duncan, who stepped in as acting president after McBride fell ill, "infused life and energy." What Duncan lacked in charisma he evidently delivered as a dependable, efficient, and energetic organizer with an eye for detail. And labor unions were nothing without organization.[15]

Immediately after becoming the GCNU's secretary, Duncan insisted on typed rather than handwritten committee minutes, a trivial change but one that set the tone for his leadership. He standardized record keeping, policed branch audits, and published

Committee Meetings, Granite Cutters' National Union," Granite Cutters' International Association of America Records, 1877–1978, series 1, box (b.) 1, Archives of the University of Massachusetts, Amherst (hereafter cited as GCNU-M), 1 May 1895, p. 319, and passim; *New York Times* (*NYT*), 18 December 1894, p. 10. At its inception in 1877, the GCNU was the Granite Cutters' International Union of the United States and the British Provinces of America; at its inaugural convention in Columbus, OH, the AFL began as the Trade and Labor Unions of North America.

15. *Boston Globe*, 2 September 1907, p. 4; Samuel Gompers, *Seventy Years of Life and Labor: An Autobiography* (1925; repr., New York: E.P. Dutton & Company, 1943), vol. 1, p. 372.

lists of members in default in the *Granite Cutters' Journal*, which, by 1899, had grown to an eight-page, newspaper-sized monthly. According to a reporter who visited it in 1907, the GCNU's office, with its "clerks, stenographers, typewriters, compositors and pressmen," was "a model one for any business house to copy." "So well systematized" had Duncan "got the details of his work" that he had "his hand on the pulse of every granite town in the country." Most importantly from the standpoint of his brother members, Duncan's GCNU was well worth its dues. Through a relentless campaign of strike threats and action, the GCNU won some of the highest daily wages of any craft union in the country. In addition to providing the usual union hall where members could socialize after hours and generous strike pay, the GCNU paid a burial benefit of $150, a fitting tribute for workers who carved headstones but it was one of the first unions to do so. Within four years of taking office, Duncan had multiplied the GCNU's membership to 4,800, and it was poised to become a leading force in the American trade union movement.[16]

In common with other craft unions, the GCNU's hundred-odd branches, forty-four of which were in New England with Maine accounting for 1,300 members, operated with relative autonomy under national jurisdiction. Once the national committee had recognized a branch, its local committee enrolled as many granite cutters as it could who were employed by quarries and shops within its designated territory, and gave each man a union card. Only master cutters—those who had completed an apprenticeship—were eligible. An initiation fee of five to ten dollars was typical for cutters new to the union, on the proviso that those who declined would face a twenty-five dollar fee for future membership. It then drew up a bill of prices, covering hourly, daily, or piecework pay scales for different categories of work, effective for twelve months, which it then had to persuade employers to sign, under implied threat of strike action. Once an employer was in contractual agreement, the local would collect union dues, usually from the employer as check-off, of seventy cents a month for each member in good standing. This represented about 1 percent of wages, reasonable given that it was the only deduction in an era before income tax, but considerably higher than the forty or fifty cents levied by most other unions. After renting a union hall and, in the case of larger branches, paying their secretary's salary, the committee sent the balance to national headquarters for its expenses and strike fund. In the event of a strike or lockout, members who answered the daily roll call drew a dollar, unless they participated in the strike committee, when they drew a dollar fifty per day. Members "in opposition" who continued to work incurred a twenty-five dollar fine. When in need, particularly during a strike, members could borrow up to ten dollars from the union or from other members; Duncan regularly published a list in the *Granite Cutters' Journal* of 500-odd members who carried unpaid loans dating back as far as ten years. Members who stopped working, left the area, or set up in business on their own accord requested a withdrawal card to prove later that they were in good standing. A

---

16. *Boston Globe*, 2 September 1907, p. 4.

typical GCNU-negotiated wage rate in 1899 was three dollars a day, more than double the wages of, say, German stonemasons and a third higher than most U.S. craft workers.[17]

High though his members' wages were, and with their nine-hour workday already an hour lower than trades like loom fixers, sawmill workers, and machinists, in 1900 Duncan launched his union on a crusade for an eight-hour day at no reduction in the daily rate. Despite its inherent inflexibility and impact on the efficiency of shops that had switched to steam-powered machinery, a shorter day was not without merit. Even with machinery, there were still plenty of tiring, repetitive tasks involving hammering or sanding, there was the issue of exposure to unhealthy dusts, and there were established precedents. Welsh reformer Robert Owen had sought a ten-hour day as early as 1810, and it was Owen who in 1817 propagandized the notion that eight hours for work, eight for recreation, and eight for rest constituted a natural regimen. Labor organizations in Europe, Australia, and the United States had been calling for an eight-hour day since the 1840s. At its 1888 convention, the AFL set 1890 as the deadline for achieving the eight-hour day, and in 1898 the United Mine Workers union won an eight-hour day for its members. But going into 1900, there was still a gulf between national union contracts and local practice, and in every industry large numbers of unorganized workers were on the job for nine or ten hours. Duncan wanted eight hours to be the standard for every granite quarry and shop. Demand for memorials was still rising so he no doubt reasoned that manufacturers could afford to pay higher wages. He probably appreciated too that strike action built solidarity, made the local branches more dependent on the national union, and, providing the manufacturers caved in quickly, large numbers of independent cutters would come into the union fold.[18]

An article in the *Granite Cutters' Journal* listing thirteen answers to the question "Why eight hours?" suggested this was indeed Duncan's rationale. Eight hours—but really, the process of striking for eight hours—would "build up trade unions, and concentrated effort is the law of success in the militant world of industry." Aside from the claim that "the eight-hour day would increase the longevity of the workers," presumably in the case of granite cutters by reducing their exposure to dust, the other answers made spurious arguments. Three of the answers hinged on the assumption that shorter hours increased demand for labor, thereby raising the wages of those already

17. Synthesized primarily from GCNU-M, the *Granite Cutters' Journal*, and "GCNU Branch, Membership, and Strike Data," spreadsheet, compiled by author (and available on request), primarily from the *Granite Cutters' Journal*, GCNU records, and *Boston Globe* articles; in 1900, daily wages for bricklayers and masons in Hamburg were $1.43 and in Dresden $1.07, *Bricklayer and Mason*, 12:9 (September 1909), p. 209.

18. For a pro-union viewpoint, see Marion Cotter Cahill, *Shorter Hours: A Study of the Movement since the Civil War* (New York: Columbia University Press, 1932). Hourly-paid workers in developed countries generally work a standard eight-hour day, with overtime at 50 percent more and Sundays and holidays at double-time, and collective bargaining has even pushed the bar down to a seven-hour day in countries such as France. Still, many professionals in the United States, where efficiency per worker is the highest in the world, routinely work nine or ten hours for five days, while some, particularly lawyers and doctors who are building their careers, work sixty or even eighty hours for no additional remuneration, suggesting there is not necessarily any correlation between time spent at work and take-home pay or ill health, but rather that those with high job satisfaction and greater ambition may like to work longer hours.

working while at the same time putting more workers on the roles to make up for the shortfall in production, which would even "help the taxpayer by putting the tramp [to] work." A shorter day would "raise the standard of living, upon which business prosperity depends," thereby benefitting employers and employees alike. Other answers argued that a shorter workday created "greater opportunity for social and educational development." Workers, the logic went, would not use the extra time to lounge about at home or go to the bar earlier but would instead "have more time to understand [their] duties [as citizens]" and implement "desirable social reforms," while shorter hours would actually "promote temperance by removing the desire for stimulants which comes from long hours of labor."[19]

For their part, employers were prepared to accept the eight-hour day, which after all meant that they had the opportunity to work shorter hours too, but the GCNU's concomitant demand for higher wages was another matter. Speaking on behalf of the New England Granite Manufacturers' Association (NEGMA), James Milne of Quincy first took issue with an argument Duncan had made in a circular letter that employers could easily afford the new wage rate because the introduction of pneumatic surfacing machines had increased their profitability. In addition to the four-dollar daily cost of generating the compressed air, each machine required an operator as well as three to five cutters to rough off sufficient stone to justify running the machine, so the main advantage was in the improved quality of the stone rather than cost reduction. Milne's principal objection was Duncan's line that the new bill of prices included "'a slight advance'" of "a few cents per hour," when raising the daily minimum from $2.52 to $3.00 while reducing the hours from nine to eight actually represented a pay raise of one third, from 28 to 37½ cents an hour. As the deadline of 1 March approached, a handful of manufacturers signed the new bill but most refused, so Duncan brought his members out on strike.[20]

With angry undertakers demanding headstones, and companies in the more militant areas like Quincy still recovering from a protracted strike the previous year, there was soon a counter offer from the NEGMA to pay the old minimum rate for the new eight-hour day, or 31½ cents an hour. Duncan rejected this out of hand, as did the strike committee of the Milford, Massachusetts, branch when Norcross Bros. offered them 33 cents. Two weeks into the strike, cutters sensed victory when manufacturers in Barre went against the NEGMA by compromising with their local to pay an average—rather than a minimum—of three dollars for eight hours. Barre was home to some of the best quality and most profitable quarries in the country, as well as a large contingent of anarchist Italian cutters, so manufacturers there could afford to be prudent. Amid disaffection within the NEGMA at the Barre compromise, Quincy manufacturers retrenched and the GCNU local prepared for a long strike. Acting secretary Andrew Johnson reported in the *Granite Cutters' Journal*'s May edition that, "the boys

19. *Granite Cutters' Journal*, 23:276 (March 1900), p. 2.
20. Milne, *Boston Globe*, 18 February 1900, p. 6.

are determined not to accept anything less than 35 cents an hour, and the bosses on their side" were just as determined not to exceed their last offer, "that is 31½ cents minimum and 33 cents average." "Our membership," Johnson worried, "has thinned down considerably" as "many of the boys have left town and secured work in other places."[21]

Even as the strike in Quincy dragged on into a third month, and Quincy's skilled workers and memorial business drifted away, owners of quarries producing building stone, particularly at Redstone, New Hampshire, and North Jay, Maine, were conceding at the three-dollar rate. Duncan told a *New York Times* reporter that contracts for a million dollars ($24 million) to supply stone for former Senator William A. Clark were the deciding factor. Bored with a multimillion-dollar Tiffany-style mansion in his Butte, Montana, hometown, Clark, who had made fortunes in banking and copper mining, was now developing a home on Manhattan's Fifth Avenue for which the stone carving alone would cost $225,000. Anxious to finish his new mansion on schedule, Clark had presumably agreed to pay extra for the granite, which Duncan estimated would provide work for 1,200 cutters.[22]

Quincy manufacturers, who by this time had little business left to lose, held their ground until cutters voted to accept a slightly sweetened offer of 33 cents minimum and 35 cents average pay. Duncan declared "Victory!" in June's *Granite Cutters' Journal*, making the GCNU America's first union to achieve the eight-hour day across all its branches, and its members some of the highest paid craft workers in the country. A 1902 survey showed that when GCNU members in Portland, Maine, were earning a minimum of 35 cents an hour, longshoremen earned a minimum of 30 cents, carpenters, iron molders, and trainmen 25 cents, brick carriers 22 cents, and machinists 20 cents; only bricklayers' wages were comparable and then with the Portland granite cutters' average wage of 38 cents. But high wages for shorter hours were only part of the story. "Business is very dull here at present," Johnson reported from Quincy in June. Business picked up in July and August, probably from filling orders backlogged during the strike, because in November Johnson reported "a number of men laid off," and he anticipated a "dull winter." Figures showing the uninterrupted rise in Quincy's granite production, from some $2 million in 1899 to $3 million by 1910, were misleading too, because even before the strikes of 1899 and 1900, the profitability and the competitiveness of Quincy's shops had been declining, making it harder for owners to invest in machinery that would increase quality and save labor, which led to further uncompetitiveness in the face of rising labor costs. Real wage gains by GCNU members in 1899–1900, that is to say, benefitted a select group of unionized craft workers. They came at the cost of workers outside the union, and they undermined the long-term health and sustainability of the industry itself.[23]

21. Norcross, *Boston Globe*, 20 March 1900, p. 4; *Granite Cutters' Journal*, 23:278 (May 1900), p. 6; this edition is incorrectly numbered 277.

22. *NYT*, 17 May 1900, p. 1.

23. *Sixteenth Annual Report of the Bureau of Industrial and Labor Statistics for the State of Maine, 1902* (Augusta, ME:

Craft unions were narrowly selective, the GCNU being a case in point, for it did not enroll cutters of soft stones like sandstone or marble, nor quarry riggers who usually joined the Quarrymen's Union, and only begrudgingly did it enroll granite tool sharpeners, consigning them to a separate branch, like the Tool Sharpeners No. 1 at Quincy and the Tool Sharpeners No. 2 at Barre. Under Duncan's direction, moreover, the GCNU barred groups of skilled granite cutters that it deemed prone to strike breaking or ethnically unsuitable. Former convicts who had learned the trade while serving their sentence could not join and neither could Blacks. In 1896, a year after taking office, Duncan drew up an agreement with Venable Bros. of Atlanta, Georgia, to replace Blacks who were members of the Quarrymen's Union with GCNU cutters. That the workers' ethnicity was the issue behind their firing and not membership in a rival union was clear from Duncan's correspondence. When Gompers showed Duncan a letter from F.A. Davidson, the secretary of the Atlanta Federation of Trades, complaining that discriminating against Blacks played into the hands of employers, Duncan replied that Davidson's letter was "beautiful sentimentality bordering upon the ideal and covers a state of affairs which we all think ought to exist and hope may exist, but at the present time . . . is wholly unwarranted." Earlier, when he was acting president of the AFL in 1894, Duncan ordered the International Association of Machinists to remove the word *white* from its constitution, yet he hinted that many craft unions had "refused to admit a colored man without having any such provision in their constitutions, the matter being left absolutely with the local union as to whether or not they admit colored applicants."[24]

It is ironic—though understandable given the conceit inherent in his version of the American Dream—that Duncan strove to exclude immigrants from the GCNU. As part of an AFL delegation to the White House in 1906, Duncan and Gompers petitioned President Theodore Roosevelt on measures to protect the advantages that the AFL had won for its members. Roosevelt confirmed in his reply not merely a "deep conviction that we must keep out of the country every Chinese laborer, skilled or unskilled," but also "that all possible steps should be taken to prevent the importation of laborers under any form." While Roosevelt wanted the door left open to immigrants who could demonstrate they had "the right stuff in them to enter into life on terms of decent quality with our own citizens," he felt that only a "warped moral and mental attitude" would condone giving "succor [to immigrants] at the expense of pulling down our own people." Duncan's GCNU was reluctant to recognize Scottish union cards, and it was only on sufferance of the Italian members' growing numbers and influence that he agreed to print Italian language articles in the *Granite Cutters' Journal*. At the same time, Duncan used a combination of inducements and coercion to bring

Kennebec Journal Print, 1903), pp. 75–92; *Granite Cutters' Journal*, 23:279 (June 1900), p. 6, and 23:284 (November 1900), p. 6.

24. See Philip S. Foner, *History of the Labor Movement in the United States: From the Founding of the American Federation of Labor to the Emergence of American Imperialism* (New York: International Publishers, 1955), vol. 2, p. 357, and Duncan to Gompers, 16 June 1896, cited in ibid.; Philip Taft, *The A.F. of L. in the Time of Gompers* (New York: Harper & Brothers, 1957), pp. 309–10.

all non-unionized master granite workers into the GCNU. So aggressive had Duncan's tactics become by 1906 that a grand jury in Caledonia, Vermont, indicted him on conspiracy charges after ten cutters who withdrew from the GCNU to set up shops on their own account alleged that Duncan had tried to destroy their business. His methods worked. Membership swelled by almost a quarter during the year of the eight-hour strike, rose by another 1,100 to 7,000 in 1901, reached 11,300 in 1906, and plateaued at 13,500 during 1911–15, making the GCNU three times larger than when he took office.[25]

fig. 59: Duncan's home at 144 Glendale Road, a two-family in 2011

In as much as it represents a land where life is better and richer for everyone, with opportunities commensurate with ability and achievement, and even when it promises not merely high wages but a social order wherein newcomers can attain the fullest stature of which they are capable and receive recognition for what they are, Duncan lived the American Dream. He landed in New York in 1879 with nothing except a grade school education, a stonecutters' apprenticeship, and a bag of chisels. Within six years, he no longer hammered those chisels but donned a suit to earn a salary as the chief executive of first a local and then a national organization. At twenty-nine in January 1887, he married eighteen-year-old Lillian M. Holman, who bore him a son nine months later, to become what a reporter called a "home-loving man." Soon after relocating the *Granite Cutters' Journal*'s editorial office to Summer Street in Boston, Duncan bought a triple-decker on Glendale Road in Quincy that was every bit as

25. Roosevelt, *Boston Globe*, 22 March 1906, p. 1; indictment, *Boston Globe*, 24 January 1906, p. 3; membership, William Haber, *Industrial Relations in the Building Industry* (1930; repr., New York: Arno Press, 1971), p. 305.

imposing as the homes of all but the wealthiest of quarry owners (fig. 59). A hero to all the GCNU members he brought closer to the Dream, Duncan was "devoted to our form of Government and the governmental principles upon which it soundly rests," eulogized GCNU President William Green at his funeral in 1928. In the halls of the AFL, he "stood like a plumed knight battling against the hosts of error." Duncan, Green averred, was "an American in all that [the] word implies."[26]

Duncan left Aberdeen dreaming of higher wages and a better life, and he no doubt had the determination and work ethic to see that dream come true. When he landed in New York, he could have taken the path of fellow Aberdeen native Andrew Milne of the Milne & Chalmers Company, and the father of James Milne with whom Duncan sparred in February 1900. Milne worked as a journeyman polisher in Quincy for eleven years until going into partnership with two other polishers in 1880. In 1904 at the age of sixty-three, Milne bought out his partners to become the sole owner of a retail memorial polishing and engraving business that he built up to sixty employees by 1913, by which time he had also branched out into real estate. But Duncan immediately joined the cutters' union and became a professional activist for collective bargaining. Unlike Milne, he evidently brought with him from the cutting sheds of Aberdeen the socialist logic—though never Marxist, he was careful to say—that employees would always be poor workers oppressed by rapacious bosses with no hope of ever earning sufficient capital to become capitalists themselves. They must therefore organize collectively to defend their rights to a fair share in the profits. To the extent that Duncan strove for a trade unionism that would boost living standards for the common man, he did have a vision, yet one that was hardly enlightened. After dividing his world into capital versus labor, bosses versus workers, he divided it further into skilled granite cutters versus other laborers, and again, into GCNU members versus oppositionists and scabs outside the union. Yet competitive though these divisions might sound, Duncan's trade unionism stifled competition just as it took away an individual's free will. As the power and solidarity of Duncan's union grew, so the wages of granite workers moved closer to a uniform price throughout the industry, regardless of a given worker's ability to produce or a given shop's ability to pay. For hundreds of Scottish and Italian immigrant stonecutters, the American Dream of a better life came true in the 1890s–1900s. But theirs was a selfish, shortsighted reality, wrought by creating a society within a society, and it did not lead to a sustainable utopia.[27]

Granite Barons: Jonathan Swingle, Theophilus King

There is little in Quincy's history to indicate that the 1890s were America's "reckless decade," as one historian describes it. Indeed, the emphasis that local elites placed on temperance suggests that a prudence if not a downright prudishness ruled their lives. Where extravagance is evident today, it is in the grave art of Mount Wollaston

---

26. Eulogy, *Boston Globe*, 18 September 1928, p. 9.

27. Milne & Chalmers, in Arthur W. Brayley, *History of the Granite Industry of New England* (Boston: National Association of Granite Industries of the United States, 1913), vol. 1, pp. 97–98.

Cemetery and perhaps one downtown building, a bank. Two men who came closest to being the kind of industrial or commercial barons that historians like to contrast with disgruntled workers were Jonathan S. Swingle, owner of Quincy's largest quarrying business, and Theophilus King, an investment banker, although their social philosophy and public philanthropy were representative of the Progressive Era not the Gilded Age. Both Swingle and King, moreover, had only grade school education and started out poor, making them emblematic of the American Dream, but they also played their role in the social problem that the expectation of the Dream created.[28]

fig. 60: Jonathan S. Swingle, The Extra Dark Man, ca. 1924

Like Duncan, Swingle began as a granite cutter. Born in 1872 in Zanesville, Ohio, a farming, pottery-making, and quarrying community of ten thousand, Swingle moved to Quincy in the early-1890s, presumably after finishing his apprenticeship. He worked in a granite-cutting yard in South Quincy for a few years, building up his skills and saving what he could of his wages before going into partnership with a granite polisher, Angus D. Martin, to form the ambitiously named Empire Polishing Works. At that time, Martin was working for the Eagle Polishing Company, which meant he was moonlighting, as perhaps was Swingle. It is unclear how successful this venture was, but by 1897 when Swingle was twenty-five, he had a new partner, Alexander Falconer, another Aberdeen immigrant, with whom he operated a steam-powered shop employing thirty granite workers. Profits from this business by 1908 enabled him to buy a quarry in West Quincy, which turned out to contain an unusually deep seam of high quality granite. Within fifteen years, Swingle had

28. H.W. Brands, *The Reckless Decade: America in the 1890s* (New York: St. Martin's Press, 1995).

parlayed these ventures into the largest and most prestigious granite business in Quincy. Granite from Swingle's Quarry became almost black when polished and was the perfect stone for engraved memorials, and it, along with his debonair good looks and piercing eyes, lent him the moniker The Extra Dark Man. In a 1924 historical brochure by the Quincy Lodge of Elks, he promoted his business as "the most extensive and valuable group of quarries owned and operated by one man, in the world." In addition to a 1.6 million-cubic-yard hole in the West Quincy hills, Swingle left his mark on the city by presenting it in 1925 with a polished granite ball, cut from a twenty-four-ton block of Swingle's Extra Dark, which still shimmers outside Quincy City Hall.[29]

fig. 61: polished sphere of Swingle's Extra Dark outside Quincy City Hall

Theophilus King was born in 1844 in Rochester, southern Massachusetts, where his father owned the village mill. At fifteen, King had earned enough from odd jobs to buy a sixty-fourth share in a whaler, which he sold at the voyage's end, and with the proceeds moved to Boston. After eight years working up from a clerk to a factor in a leather firm, he went into partnership at age twenty-four to manufacture leather goods. Boston's Great Fire of 1872 sent the factory into bankruptcy, but King battled back to be sufficiently wealthy by the late 1880s to voluntarily pay off the creditors plus

29. Compiled primarily from obituary, *Boston Globe*, 12 March 1929, p. 9; *Historical Sketch of the City of Quincy: The Granite City* (Quincy, MA: Quincy Lodge of Elks, 1924), p. 11. For Martin, see Brayley, *Granite Industry*, vol. 1, p. 101; the Empire Polishing Company, founded by Martin and John A. Clark in 1905, was a successor. Swingle probably bought his quarry from Alphonse Reinhalter because at that time Thomas F. Mannex operated the adjacent Reinhalter Quarry, and, according to the *Globe* article, Swingle—at some stage—bought quarries from both of them. Listings of quarries, equipment, and owners are in T. Nelson Dale, *The Chief Commercial Granites of Massachusetts, New Hampshire, and Rhode Island* (Washington, DC: U.S. Geological Survey, 1908), pp. 98–120, and *The Mine, Quarry, and Metallurgical Record of the United States, Canada, and Mexico* (Chicago, IL: Mine and Quarry News Bureau, 1897), pp. 498–99.

6 percent interest and buy a house in Quincy with his wife and two children. It was an imposing property in Italianate style, on three floors with a setback wing, although like most houses in Quincy it was timber framed with clapboard siding. In 1909, he was a director of a dozen manufacturing companies as well as the president of the Quincy Quarries Company, which operated two large quarries, and of Quincy's main bank, the Granite Trust Company. In the late 1920s, King worked a deal with land owned by the Bethany Congregational Church so that the church could rebuild and he could have a new ten-story art deco bank building, which today dominates Hancock Street. During his last years, he built up and administered a million-dollar fund that contributed each year to over fifty charitable, philanthropic, and religious causes. He lies buried under a colossal polished granite sphere in Mount Wollaston Cemetery.[30]

fig. 62: Theophilus King's memorial, Mount Wollaston Cemetery

There is no record of whether Swingle liked to socialize over a relaxing drink at the end of a hard day, but many of his workers surely did, because King, who was determined to deprive them of the pleasure, counted forty-two licensed liquor vendors when he cofounded Quincy's No-License movement in 1882. Not that this was an unusually large number for a working-man's town of ten thousand, being one licensed establishment for 238 souls, compared with, say, English villages of a hundred or two residents that offered a choice between two or three pubs. Still, for King, who chaired the No-License committee, even one saloon was a moral blight on his town. Looking back in 1899 after seventeen alcohol-free years, he remembered how "young men were

---

30. Complied primarily from: "Theophilus King," in Samuel Atkins Eliot, ed., *Biographical History of Massachusetts: Biographies and Autobiographies of the Leading Men in the State* (Boston: Massachusetts Biographical Society, 1909), vol. 2, no numbering; "Theophilus King," in *Who's Who in America*, vol. 12, 1922–23 (Chicago: A.N. Marquis & Company, 1922), pp. 1789–90.

being led astray to an alarming extent, not only to drink, but to gambling and other associated evils." Since then, there had been a transformation, "a condition of peace and happiness in hundreds of homes," a safety on the streets, and a "proud distinction of a continuous temperance sentiment" that no statistics could measure. As a consequence of diverting what he estimated was $125,000 a year in liquor sales through "purer channels," the Quincy workman had grown more regular in his habits, and more able to pay honestly and provide comforts for his wife and children. Once the last saloon closed, the "quietness, temperateness and law-abiding character of the people have been notable." Quincy, he was convinced, had accordingly made "a decided advance in morals and public spirit."[31]

fig. 63: Theophilus King, ca. 1899

Perhaps King was right to close the saloons and banish alcohol from the lodges where Quincy's granite workers and bosses alike congregated after a tiring day. One drink could lead to another, drunkenness encouraged unruly behavior, and alcoholism did debilitate the body. Maybe Quincy had become a haven of peace and happiness since the No-License movement made it a dry town. But King, it seems, did not go out much, at least not after work, when he settled down in his library with a book. Officer P.H. Bradley, newspapers reported, had a "hard fight" on the night of 26 August 1900 while arresting a Finn for drunkenness. Other Finns had set on the officer in an effort to free their friend and a "battle royal" ensued. Passersby came to Bradley's assistance and he prevailed, marching his drunken prisoners into the station

31. Theophilus King, "The First Victory," in *No-License in Quincy*, ed. William Frederic Hoehn (Quincy, MA: Eastern Printing and Engraving, 1899), pp. 45–47.

with his uniform in tatters. Officers explained to the reporter that, "Finns who give the police most trouble drink a mixture of alcohol and oil of ether, which maddens them and seems to deaden their sense of pain." Unless the blow was "hard enough to fracture the skull," clubbing them was useless, so the officers' best tactic was to "engage them pugilistic fashion and try for a solar plexus blow." Most of Quincy's drinkers, though, were a quiet lot, maybe because they were in fear of pugilistic local police.[32]

During one crackdown in June 1903, Quincy police hauled eleven "ordinary" drunks into court, plus one man they had arrested at the train station after a Saturday night of drinking in Boston, and fined them from three to five dollars. Impetus for this particular cleanup campaign came not from Quincy, though, but from judge and newly appointed police commissioner William H.H. Emmons in Boston. As determined as King to stamp out what he called the "vice" of drinking, Emmons believed that throwing drinkers in jail would have "'considerable effect,'" because even if they were released the next morning, "'many won't get drunk after being arrested once.'" There was a backlash in Boston against Emmons's wholesale arrests, which on the Monday morning at the start of his moral crusade brought 231 men and 21 women into court, most after languishing in jail since Saturday night. One puzzled policeman thought that Emmons had "'not seen enough of the world.'" Would it not be better, another mused, to "'trust to the discretion of the police officer.'" "'I may know a man very well,'" the officer explained, "'and know that he would not disturb the public peace. He may attend a banquet or some other social function and be on his way home. It is a hard thing to enforce an order to arrest such a man when by letting him pass by he would be certain to go home of his own accord.'" Those arrested were a "respectable looking lot," according to defense lawyers. There was among them—the *Boston Globe* reported from South Station, the scene of several arrests—"a benevolent appearing elderly man, with glasses, who is said to be an eminently respectable and industrious mechanic." And a "young fellow of perhaps 21, fashionably dressed," who "if intoxicated at all, it must have been very slightly." Judging by at least five more arrests by Quincy police during the June crackdown, residents who could afford a train ticket and feared breaking the law in Quincy routinely enjoyed themselves in Boston. Closing the saloons and bars, therefore, did little to curb drinking, although it did criminalize the pleasure and may have encouraged excess, or at least snatching an extra one for the train, and it no doubt increased the cost, which is why poorer drinkers turned to dangerous moonshine or ether. In August 1903, Quincy District Court handled seventy-four cases of drunkenness and ten cases of selling intoxicating liquor.[33]

Swingle and King rose from humble beginnings to the heights of achievement through perspicacity and industriousness, personifying for Quincy's granite workers,

---

32. *Boston Globe*, 27 August 1900, p. 5.

33. Crackdown, *Boston Globe*, 16 June 1903, pp. 1, 3; elderly man and young fellow, *Boston Globe*, 14 June 1903, p. 10; other arrests, *Boston Globe*, 14 June 1903, p. 10 and 21 June 1903, p. 1; district court, *Boston Globe*, 1 September 1903, p. 2.

as well as would-be Scottish and Italian immigrants, the American Dream. But as they and their entrepreneurial cohort prospered, they distanced themselves from their wage-earning roots, if not by flaunting their newfound wealth then at least by the way they dressed, the company they kept, and the self-righteous morality they promulgated. Immaculate in starched shirt and dinner jacket, Swingle was a social fixture at the local chapters of business clubs and fraternal organizations like the Granite Manufacturers' Association, Elks, Masons, Knights Templars, and Bethany White Shrine, the last two being leading organizations in the temperance movement. These newly rich owner operators and businessmen supported good causes, contributed to charities, and made a lot of noise about progressive reforms and social uplift, yet because Swingle and King—and for that matter Duncan, too, who lived a short walk from both of them—no longer identified with those they employed nor appeared to care sufficiently about their workers' practical problems, the rift between so-called capital and labor grew wider and more acrimonious. But this culture of distancing was indicative of the paradox inherent to the American Dream. After all, if everyone succeeded then who would bother to push themselves to get ahead? Perhaps Quincy's wage earners wanted their bosses to appear wealthy and sophisticated. Perhaps, at some subliminal level, they wanted to feel hard-done-by, even to the extent of living dangerously, whether in the workplace or after hours. Moreover, through risk taking, illegal drinking, and fighting they could demonstrate their independence in the face of so much social pressure to change their habits and conform.

Living to Enjoy the Dream

Theophilus King died at the advanced age of ninety-one and James Duncan at seventy-one, although his less fortunate son who qualified as a doctor died at twenty-seven. Jonathan Swingle died at fifty-seven, which sounds premature, but even he bucked the trend because the national average life expectancy in 1900 for men was forty-eight, rising to only fifty by 1910. Granite workers lived on the wrong side of that statistic, for quarries were as dangerous as cutting sheds were dusty. Yet to the extent that they evaluated the risks as we might do today—smug in our hindsight, with the benefit of artificial fibers and the security of rigorous product testing and punitive litigation—they took them in stride. Granite working was their chosen profession, they were skilled at it, and they were proud of the memorials their art created. Being a granite cutter—being a brother member of the GCNU—was a defining identity. It was one's life, even as it may have shortened that life. When death came early for so many friends and relatives, fatalism made it possible to enjoy the day, while with bravado one could even have a bit of fun. When one worked on the edge then it was surely better, some no doubt felt, to live on the edge, to work hard and then play hard, down at Ostiria Astoria's, Joseph Sandora's, Mrs. Charles Ratti's place, or the other spots down on Water Street where beer, wine, and sometimes whiskey sold in defiance of Quincy's strict prohibition laws.[34]

---

34. Laura B. Shrestha, *Life Expectancy in the United States* (Washington, DC: Congressional Research Service,

fig. 64: Granite Rail Quarry, with derricks, ladders, and grout pile (top left). By this time (ca. 1928), there were lifting chains and oversized wire ropes yet none of the seven workers wore helmets

Granite quarries were full of edges (fig. 64), sharp edges to bash into and steep edges to fall over. Riggers could contain fractured blocks on the quarry walls with wires tensioned from eyebolts embedded in lead-filled holes they drilled into boulders on the surface. Blocks could still break loose, as could the grout pile of worthless stone that ringed the quarry walls. Descending into the quarry required negotiating a network of wooden ladders or riding what workers called a boat, a metal hopper suspended from steel wires lowered from a steam-powered derrick. Corroded nails or rotten rungs gave way, and the boat lurched if the derrick's engine malfunctioned. Subjective danger abounded in a quarry despite quarrymen's efforts to minimize it. William Larson, aged 35 and married with two children, died instantly one morning of a fractured skull, and three other men, including the Granite Rail Quarry's foreman, received serious powder burns and injuries from flying granite. A spark from the compressed air drill they were using had detonated gunpowder left over from a blast the day before that had seeped into a crack. When Bartholomew Gunning was guiding a stoneboat that removed grout from the quarry, the rope jerked unexpectedly, lassoed his ankles, and flung him into the quarry wall. He was lucky the doctors did not have to amputate his smashed leg. Pekka Kainkainen, twenty-two, died when a sixty-foot derrick at Oscar Djers's quarry fell on top of him. A rope supporting a boat in which John Cappacioli was riding snapped, tipping him out to the quarry floor where he escaped with a broken leg.[35]

These and other deaths and debilitating injuries, the details of which did not always reach the newspapers, added 3 percent to the payroll through injury compensation and insurance premiums, not to mention lost production, so owners as well as workers had an incentive to keep the quarries as safe as possible. And it was not only workers who died, as when a falling derrick killed Noak Anderson, married with two daughters, at the stonecutting plant of his firm Anderson & Carlson. Still, even with the limited technology at their disposal, quarry owners could have done more to implement safety procedures, just as workers could have done more to protect themselves. Metal hard hats did not appear until after World War I, and then workers complained that they were too heavy and uncomfortable, but by 1900 sensible bicyclists were wearing lightweight helmets made from strips of padded leather. One of these might have saved Larson. Similarly, reliable harnesses and carabiners did not begin to evolve into the workplace from mountaineering until the 1910s, but quarrymen could have tied their waists into short ropes permanently attached to the boat. Had Cappacioli done so he would not have been thrown out when one support wire snapped. But unless owners had enforced compliance by insisting that foremen fined violators, implementing such innovations would have been useless. As it was, old hands showed their experience by scaling precipices as if they were on a walk in the park, while junior quarrymen put on their best macho face.[36]

Granite cutters and engravers were less sanguine about dust, which irritated their eyes, gummed up their nose, and made them cough. In the days when they pounded drills by hand or surfaced granite with bush hammers, there had been dust too, but it had tended to settle between blows. Now the pneumatic drills and powered surfacing machines of the 1900s blew around the extra dust that spewed out continuously. For granite workers, as well as owner-managers who spent their days alongside them in the cutting and finishing sheds, the issue was not whether granite dust was an irritant but rather the extent to which a given level of it shortened their lives and, hence, how far they should to go to avoid inhaling it or to eliminate its presence.

Since before the Industrial Revolution, ceramists and coal miners had known about the dangers of potter's rot and miner's lung, which doctors began calling *silicosis* in the 1870s. As medical science and X-ray machines developed in the 1900s, researchers started to link occupational silicosis with phthisis—tuberculosis, or TB. By the mid-1920s, evidence was mounting that granite cutters were not only suffering from loss of breath from silicosis but were also dying at high rates from TB. In 1929,

35. Blast, *Boston Globe*, 13 September 1906, p. 6; hurled against granite, *Boston Globe*, 4 August 1909, p. 3; derrick, *Boston Globe*, 16 May 1916, p. 13; snapped rope, *Boston Globe*, 21 January 1923.

36. Anderson, *Boston Globe*, 7 April 1929, p. A25.

U.S. Public Health Service *Bulletin No. 187* gave a frightening picture of TB mortality among granite workers in Barre. For cutters, whose sheds contained 44 million particles per cubic foot (mp/cf), and carvers and letterers, whose sheds had 27 mp/cf, the TB mortality rate was 2,600 per 100,000 after twenty to twenty-four years of service, rising to 4,700 for workers with more than thirty-five years' service, or from 3 to 5 percent. *Bulletin No. 187* also reported that after four years, all workers with the highest exposure "were more or less affected" by shortness of breath or diminished chest expansion, and it concluded that, "a direct relation existed between dust exposure and damage to the lungs with particular tendency to succumb to tuberculosis."[37]

Union leaders and state officials were soon requiring owners who had not already done so to invest in mechanical extraction systems, as detailed in another public health service report of 1929, to rid the cutting sheds of dust. During the 1930s, it became common knowledge that the silicosis that had been killing granite cutters for decades was yet another instance of callous, greedy bosses harming their workers' health. Occupational Safety and Health Administration (OSHA) regulations since the 1980s have mandated zero-tolerance policies toward dusts in the workplace, particularly those that cause or might cause silicosis, and which OSHA and insurance company inspectors routinely enforce.[38]

Medical research has shown how regular inhalation of large quantities of dust particles—with sharp silica grains and pointy asbestos fibers being worse than, say, cotton or corn dust—defeats the body's inbuilt filtration system, eventually leading to pneumoconiosis, a shortness of breath caused by irreversible pulmonary cell damage, but which in only the most extreme cases is fatal. Chest x-rays may indicate advanced silicosis as patchy radiolucencies, but more commonly radiologists will spot tubercular lesions. Due to what researchers believe are immunogenic responses to silica particles in the respiratory passages, patients with even mild silicosis have a three-fold higher chance of contracting TB, an infectious bacterial disease that before modern treatments killed over half its victims. Epidemiologists have also concluded that workers exposed to high levels of silicate dusts, but who otherwise exhibit no symptoms of silicosis, are similarly three times more likely to contract TB. An indicator of the extent to which Quincy's granite workers—the focus of this chapter—suffered from silicosis, therefore, would be the rate at which they died from TB. A high TB death rate would not in itself prove that victims had silicosis because a small enough sample population could have had unusual exposure, say to the arrival of TB-infected immigrants who also had colds and were sneezing. But a low rate, particularly in the presence of a control population with a similarly low or average rate, would suggest that they

37. Leonard Greenburg, "Studies on the Industrial Dust Problem: 1. Dust Inhalation and Its Relation to Industrial Tuberculosis," *Public Health Reports*, 40:7 (13 February 1925), pp. 291–309; Albert E. Russell, et al., *The Health of Workers in Dusty Trades, II: Exposure to Siliceous Dust (Granite Industry)*, U.S. Public Health Service, *Bulletin No. 187* (Washington, DC: Government Printing Office, July 1929); see also, David Rosner and Gerald Markowitz, *Deadly Dust: Silicosis and the Politics of Occupational Disease in Twentieth-Century America* (Princeton, NJ: Princeton University Press, 1991), pp. 38–44.

38. J.J. Bloomfield, "A Study of the Efficiency of Dust-Removal Systems in Granite-Cutting Plants," *Public Health Reports*, 44:42 (18 October 1929), pp. 2505–22.

neither suffered from silicosis nor had dangerously high exposure to silicate dusts, because both these conditions, according to epidemiological research, would have elevated their TB incidence rate by a factor of three.[39]

In 1908, a typical year, the Quincy Public Health Department certified forty deaths from TB. Adjusting down from the 1910 census of 30,642 to 27,850 (population growth being about 5 percent per annum) gives a mortality rate of 144 per 100,000. This compares favorably with rates for Boston in 1908 of 171, Lawrence to the north at 158, Taunton to the south at 197, but not Brockton thirteen miles to the southwest at 96. Still, in none of those cities were there silicosis-prone quarrymen or stonecutters, although in Lawrence and Taunton there were thousands of workers in dusty textile mills. Twenty years later, in 1928, TB deaths in Quincy had fallen, as they had all over the state, to twenty, while the population had risen to 67,600, giving a rate of 30, whereas in Boston, where public health officials boasted of unusually low TB mortality, the rate was more than double, at 65 using 1931 figures. It is necessary to stress that tuberculosis mortality rates in the 1900s–30s varied widely, by country, demographics, nutrition, and occupation. A study by Rollo H. Britten showed that across ten U.S. states in 1930, mortality ranged from 26 for professional men, through 72 for skilled male workers, to 185 for unskilled male workers. Quincy's public health department, furthermore, did not provide breakdowns by occupation, its doctors and coroners may have misdiagnosed the cause of death, and Quincy's population was statistically small. Nevertheless, given the large percentage of craft workers, as well as the numbers of recent immigrants from Europe where TB rates were higher than America, a rate of 30 in 1928 is remarkably low, close to Britten's figure for a population of professional men and far removed from his average of 185 for regular workers. Even after adding in all deaths from respiratory diseases, the rate was only 80 (Quincy's total death rate in 1928 was 848).[40]

Based on these statistics for TB death rates, and allowing that silicosis increases the chances of contracting TB by three times, it is hard to argue that Quincy's army of granite workers suffered unduly from work-induced chronic or even mild silicosis, particularly when pneumatic cutting and polishing machines did not exacerbate the dust problem until the mid-1900s. If some 2,500[41] workers had spent two decades

39. See, for instance, R.L. Cowie, "The Epidemiology of Tuberculosis in Gold Miners with Silicosis," *American Journal of Respiratory and Critical Care Medicine*, 150:5 (November 1994), pp. 1460–62.

40. *Annual Reports of the Officers of the City of Quincy, Massachusetts, for the Year 1908* (Quincy, MA: George W. Prescott Publishing Co., 1908), p. 236; *City of Quincy, Massachusetts: City Government of 1929, Together with the Annual Reports of the Officials of the Year 1928* (Boston: Chapple Publishing Company, 1928), p. 162, and other respiratory deaths, p. 166; rates for cities in Philip P. Jacobs, "Misleading Mortality Statistics of Tuberculosis," *American Journal of Public Health*, 3:5 (May 1913), pp. 443–44, who stressed the importance of adjusting population across decade-wide census numbers; Britten cited in Milton Terris, "Relation of Economic Status to Tuberculosis Mortality by Age and Sex," *American Journal of Public Health*, 38:8 (August 1948), p. 1061; Boston rate for 1931, in *Boston Globe*, 1 January 1933, p. A13, and see also 17 October 1930, p. 17, for boasting about low TB death rates.

41. This figure may be conservative because according to a strike report in the *Boston Globe*, 1 March 1916, p. 8, "About 5,000 men employed in the granite industry in this city [Quincy] quit this morning," and that was before the peak years for memorial production; I am using here a commonly cited figure of 2,000 employed in, say, 1910, and adding 500 to allow for those granite workers who had retired or switched to other work and were still living in Quincy; see, for instance, Burke, *Quincy Industries*, p. 37.

inhaling dangerous quantities of granite dust then TB rates by 1928 should have been skyrocketing, not plunging as they were, from 143 in 1908 to 30. There was, moreover, a control group: of Quincy's twenty TB deaths in 1928, eight were women; similarly, of the fifty-four deaths from all other respiratory diseases, such as bronchitis and pleurisy, twenty-four were women. Women—who are slightly less prone to TB than men—also had dusty trades, like textile or leather working, but virtually none of them worked in the granite cutting and polishing sheds. Despite the received wisdom that the overwhelming burden of Quincy Hospital was to care for sick and dying granite workers, evidence, if anything, indicates that these men were a healthy lot, which should not be too surprising given their daily exercise, time outdoors, and ample wages for food. This is not to deny that some of them may well have coughed and wheezed, whether from granite dust, the tobacco they smoked, or the coal fumes they inhaled at home, nor that cleaner air at work would have prolonged their lives. Rather, it does not seem as if their work environment, per se, was unusually bad for their respiratory systems.[42]

fig. 65: a Quincy granite worker operating a pneumatic surfacing machine, ca. 1925; he is outdoors and wearing a dusk mask

What, then, explains the disparity between the high TB mortality rates, and hence the underlying silicosis, of granite workers in the Barre studies and the low rate in Quincy? Workers dying of TB might have left town, although this is unlikely because Quincy's public health department had operated a sanatorium since 1903. Perhaps this Contagious Hospital saved the lives of TB patients, but again this is improbable because effective antibiotics were not available until the 1940s, before which about half of all patients died, irrespective of treatments. Anecdote suggests one answer. Tony Bok, a Camden, Maine, farmer and cousin of Harvard president Derek Bok, would tell the story of Swedish granite cutters who insisted on working outdoors

---

42. *City of Quincy . . . 1928*, p. 166; even if all the twelve men who died of TB were exclusively granite workers, then their death rate among Quincy's 33,800 males would have been 35, and among their own group of 2,500, 480 per 100,000, or between a seventy-fourth and a fifth of the level for Barre, as reported in *Bulletin No. 187*; for hospital, see Stan R. Nikkel, *The City of Presidents: A Quincy Guidebook* (Quincy, MA: Sea Gull Publishing, 1992), p. 50.

throughout the coldest winters, to the amazement of newly arrived cutters from southern Italy who sought comfort in the heated sheds. There were Swedish cutters in Quincy, and they, along with the Aberdeen cutters whose homeland was also cold in winter, may well have instilled among their colleagues the importance of maintaining air circulation in the sheds and working outdoors whenever possible. Photographs from the time show granite sheds with doors folded back on one side and windows on the other (fig. 56), and workers operating pneumatic machinery in open yards (figs. 65–67). Those with the dustiest jobs—surfacing machine operators and monument engravers—could have tied scarves around their faces and even lined them with cotton wool, although extant photographs provide no evidence they did, but after the mid-1910s, some workers did wear full-face dust masks, which were adaptations of wartime rubber gas masks, with replaceable gauze filters (fig. 65).[43]

fig. 66: a Quincy granite carver bent over his pneumatic die grinder, ca. 1925; he is wearing one glove and is working outdoors but it is unclear if he is also wearing a dusk mask

Water suggests a more germane answer, as it is better not to make dust than try to remove it once it is already airborne. Gang saws relied on water streams to wash the iron-shot abrasive they used into the steel cutting wire or notched steel cutting disc, so they were inherently dust free (fig. 68). Workstations, at least in the larger sheds in which water pipes ran along the walls, had hoses that operators used to cool and lubricate their machines, and soak down stone as well as their work areas. As the gray carpet surrounding the operator working outside in fig. 67 suggests, pneumatic surfacing machines "were prodigious generators of airborne granite dusts," but industrial historian Paul Wood also points out that "they were later supplied with water to wet the stone and keep down airborne dust." Polishing machines generally produced little dust because, like the gang saws, they had a diaphragm or centrifugal pump that fed a slurry of fine metal shot or carborundum grit to the polishing head, which it drew

---

43. Cases of as opposed to deaths from TB reported by Quincy's public health department each year during 1919–25 averaged 87, which is consistent with a fatality rate of about 50 percent, *City of Quincy . . . 1928*, p. 15; Bok, conversation with Catherine Fonseca Chapman, August 1982.

from a sump under the machine (fig. 69). Tool grinders also used water in their sheds for lubrication and cooling.[44]

fig. 67: two Quincy workers operating pneumatic surfacing machines outdoors; in the foreground, the operator has protected his clothes with an apron but it is not possible to tell if he has also protected his lungs with a dust mask

fig. 68: Quincy granite workers operating a water-lubricated gang saw, ca. 1923

A further and more controversial explanation is that Progressive Era public health officials sought to expose what they presumed was the exploitation of industrial workers by heartless bosses, and hence they were insufficiently objective. A seminal study by Frederick L. Hoffman in 1922 relied on data provided by the GCNU, hardly an unbiased source, to correlate the rising TB mortality rates of New England's granite workers with the increased use of pneumatic equipment. It is revealing, for instance, that

---

44. Paul Wood, "Tools and Machinery of the Granite Industry, Part III," *Chronicle of the Early American Industries Association*, 59:4 (December 2006), pp. 131, 135, 140.

the GCNU reported TB deaths from the three Quincy branches during 1896–1903 at twenty-five, during 1904–11 at thirty-seven, and during 1912–18 at fifty, which may have been correct, yet Hoffman then used those numbers to arrive at mortality rates per 100,000 per year, the standard measure, giving figures of 518, 543, and 819 respectively. But the number of deaths provided by the GCNU were the total over each of the seven year periods, meaning that the true rates per year were seven times less, or 74, 77, and 117. Corrected on this basis, the figures for Quincy's granite workers were actually less than the numbers Hoffman provided for the general New England population, of 231, 188, and 137, indicating that Quincy's granite workers were, if anything, healthier not sicker than those in other jobs. While Hoffman's data did show the Quincy numbers going up when the general TB rate was going down, they were within random variations for such a statistically small number of deaths of between three and seven per year, and consequently meaningless. This is not to deny the hazard posed by granite dust in the workplace, nor to argue that this dust did not give granite workers silicosis or TB. Neither is it the intention here to denigrate the noble and well-meaning efforts by health workers and reformers like Hoffman to clean up hazardous conditions in America's workplaces. Rather, it is important to point out that Hoffman drew his influential conclusions from suspect data, Progressives and union officials found what they sought, and their well-documented sympathies have passed into received wisdom as fact.[45]

Once myths are enshrined in conventional wisdom, they are hard to dislodge. In 2004, the New England Press published *Men Against Granite*, an edited collection of fifty-two Works Progress Administration interviews from the late-1930s conducted by Mari Tomasi and Roaldus Richmond among the riggers, cutters, stone carvers, tool sharpeners, bartenders, prostitutes, and widows of the granite-working community of Barre. Lead editor of this project was Alfred Rosa, emeritus Professor of English at the University of Vermont and the founding president of the New England Press. It is a beautifully crafted book, redolent with stories of hardship and tragedy. Despite acknowledging that Tomasi and Richmond typed the accounts from memory after they had conducted the interviews, and that they later wrote novels inspired by their interviewing experiences, Rosa claims that "these interviews document history." Perhaps they do, but without a critical assessment, they may just as well document Depression-era fiction of the kind that Tomasi and Richmond subsequently produced. In the introduction, there is a photograph of a quarry worker using a pneumatic drill. Having dated the image to "circa 1900," Rosa's caption reads, "Note the lack of safety equipment such as goggles and a breathing mask." It is clear from the photograph that granite dust is falling onto the worker's pants and boots, and it may well be that he was

45. Frederick L. Hoffman, *The Problem of Dust Phthisis in the Granite-Stone Industry*, U.S. Department of Labor, Bureau of Labor Statistics, *Bulletin No. 293* (Washington, DC: Government Printing Office, May 1922), pp. 29, 28. My skepticism of Hoffman's data includes my derived critique of them, as suggested by the abnormally large figures in his "Numbers Exposed" column; do these represent his additions of union members for each of the seven years, his average of the GCNU's estimate of all granite workers per year, or might they include those whom the GCNU knew had moved out of the area? Hoffman's science did not run to such specificity.

inhaling dust that gave him silicosis, leading to a fatal pneumonia infection. And yet, it would be just as disingenuous to present a photograph of a 1965 Ford LTD convertible with the caption, "Note the lack of safety equipment such as seat-belts and airbags." For sure, granite working in 1900 without the benefit of plastic eye protectors was potentially dangerous, but it is debatable if the delicate glass goggles that aviators started to wear after 1903 would have been any safer. Lacking critical engagement with the material, *Men Against Granite* perpetuates the conclusion—at an advanced scholarly level—that immigrant granite workers were the hapless victims of exploitative, uncaring, capitalist manufacturers.[46]

fig. 69: a Quincy granite worker operating a polishing machine with a felt wheel and an abrasive slurry, ca. 1923

To the extent that Quincy workers were able to reduce their exposure to hazardous granite dust in the 1900s–20s through sensible measures, such as working outdoors, wearing a mask, or tamping down dust with water, further technological improvements alleviated though never eliminated the problem. Shop owners installed fan-powered extract ducts next to cutting heads, and those who could afford to do so replaced outmoded equipment with wet surfacing machines and die grinders, which anyway were more efficient and required less sharpening. Yet there were always quarrymen who drilled dry even when water was sitting in a pool next to them, just as there are plenty of workers today, often self-employed ones, from autobody refinishers to apartment refurbishers, who choose to work without a dust mask or respirator even when a pack of disposable filters is peeking at them from their tool bag. "America is a free country," they sometimes retort, when faced with compliance with a fresh crop of regulations.[47]

---

46. Mari Tomasi and Roaldus Richmond, *Men Against Granite*, Alfred Rosa and Mark Wanner, eds. (Shelburne, VT: New England Press, 2004), pp. 7–8, 2.

47. Wood, "Tools and Machinery . . . Part III," p. 141; Bloomfield, "Dust-Removal Systems." Many self-employed workers in the dusty building and metalworking trades travel to job sites in Boston from their homes in New Hampshire, where the state motto is "Live free or die."

fig. 70: Quincy City Hospital, ca. 1925

Fall of Quincy's Granite Industry

Other than 1922, when a calamitous, yearlong strike by the GCNU cost the manufacturers a million dollars ($24 million) in lost revenue alone, Quincy's granite industry generated sales of over $3.5 million a year throughout the 1920s, peaking in 1926 at $3.8 million. Quincy's Granite Manufacturers Association had a hundred members, there were over a dozen working quarries, two dozen large stone yards, several small businesses catering to the retail memorial trade, and about two thousand workers. When Quincy's Elks opened their expansive new three-story lodge in 1924, their souvenir book touted Quincy's "great Fore River shipyards, her iron works, the Great Tubular Rivet factories, her Pneumatic Scales factory, the Boston Gear Works, and a dozen other active industries," yet it stressed, nevertheless, that "Quincy's wealth lies in her quarries." Then, in 1929, business plummeted to little over a million and never recovered. By 1939, there were only six working quarries with thirty-one abandoned. In 1940, the New Haven Railroad shut down its Granite Branch to West Quincy, in operation for 114 years since Gridley Bryant built the Granite Railway, and two years later the Granite Rail Company went bankrupt. Swingle's, the last major working quarry, closed in 1963. How could an industry that had been central to Quincy's commercial and social life since Solomon Willard and Bryant developed the Bunker Hill Quarry in 1825 collapse so suddenly and then wither away?[48]

Looking at a graph of gross sales, an obvious answer would be to blame the Great Depression, macro-economic factors outside anyone's control. But sales were falling

48. *Historical Sketch*, p. 46; *Boston Globe*, 29 September 1940, p. D12.

steeply in 1928 months before the Wall Street Crash, and there was no recovery in the 1940s–50s when demand for expensive granite memorials and building stone rose. J. Nelson Clifford identified five reasons in his analysis of 1939, all of which blamed the manufacturers. First, had been "the lack of modernization of equipment and methods," whereas the competing centers of Barre and St. Cloud in Minnesota "adopted new inventions and processes as soon as they were developed." Second, dealers and producers had "deliberately contracted their market" by focusing on local retail sales rather than the interstate wholesale trade, and there had been a lack of cooperation between retailers, quarry owners, and manufacturers to the extent that the latter were now carving 60 percent of the monuments from imported granite. Third, "shortsighted" producers had "compromised the quality and reputation" of Quincy granite by doping monuments with a mixture of oil and lampblack to make inferior stone appear to be expensive dark grades. After a few years, the doping leached away leaving mottled memorials and angry relatives. Fourth, was the rise in injury compensation and insurance rates, from 2.4 percent of payroll in the 1920s to 12 percent in 1932 and 20 percent in 1939, although Clifford admitted this was as much a product of Massachusetts state regulations as employers running particularly dangerous workplaces. Fifth, because manufacturers had failed to build up sufficient capital reserves they operated on credit, skimped on advertising, and lost yet more business to competing centers, further weakening their confidence and making them more reluctant to invest.[49]

All of these charges had merit, particularly doping because isolated cheating by unscrupulous vendors is often enough to undermine an entire industry's reputation, and strict quality inspection by the Quincy Granite Manufacturer's Association, as practiced in Barre, could easily have policed such damaging abuses. Still, it was fashionable in the 1930s to point fingers at greedy manufacturers and sympathize with employees as hapless victims. It was as if, for any given industry, there were two antagonistic groups—bosses and workers—and sometimes a third, scab workers outside a union, whom employers also exploited as strike breakers. There was rarely any sense that an industry was about a group of professionals, albeit with different talents, abilities, experience levels, and monetary stakes, coming together to make a living for themselves by producing a particular good. Competition was not productive, between one business and the next, but destructive, between employers and employees within the business. Even when Clifford in his second reason mentioned that the local GCNU strike of 1922 "paralyzed the industry," leaving producers unable to fulfill orders and driving away "most of the interstate business," he did not attribute any blame to those who actually struck, the GCNU and its local members, let alone accuse *them* of shortsightedness despite admitting later in his paper that Quincy's workers already enjoyed the "higher wage levels characteristic of New England." Apportioning blame to the GCNU, and the climate of division it exacerbated if not created, suggests

49. Clifford, *Granite Industry*, pp. 149–50.

an interpretation that better fits the facts underlying Clifford's Depression-era reasoning.[50]

First, lack of modernization: strikes and wage increases, on one hand, drained away the profits necessary for investment in capital equipment. By April 1920, the three local Quincy GCNU branches were demanding $8 a day, or $46[51] for a 44-hour week, allowing for the four hours typical of a Saturday morning but with no other overtime. This was an increase of 270 percent since 1900, and came at a time when the average wage for skilled workers was $34 for a 49-hour week, for unskilled was $26, and for farm workers was $20. Consumer prices, admittedly, had risen during the Great War but, in April, they had been falling precipitously since January due to the postwar depression of 1920–21, which economist J.R. Vernon states was "the largest one-year percentage decline in the [GNP price deflator] series in the more than 120 years covered," being between 15 and 18 percent for the one-year period. Strikes kept pushing quarry and shop owners to the brink so that, far from being able to invest, all but the top few lost money or closed down. On the other hand, unionized workers at Quincy resisted the installation of new machinery because they believed it would put them out of work. Page after page of the *Granite Cutters' Journal* discussed at length the merits of socialism or the progress of strikes, just as meeting after meeting of the GCNU committee talked ad nauseam about fines for oppositionists or the payment of strike funds, but never about production machinery or methods. Only in *Stone* and *Monumental News*, the manufacturers' journals, were there articles about how new equipment or labor techniques could improve quality, boost production, and increase sales and profits, thereby strengthening the industry as a whole while protecting it from outside competitors.[52]

Second, contraction of the market: regular strikes for more pay by Quincy workers—in 1899, 1900, 1905, 1908, 1916, 1919, 1920, and 1922—disrupted production, eroded manufacturers' confidence and commitment, and drove away business. Not including minor or wildcat stoppages, these strikes totaled at least 472 days. Although, when averaged out and allowing for Sundays, there were only eighteen days of lost production a year, or 6 percent, the strikes of 1916 and 1919 lasted over a month, in 1908 lasted two months, and in 1922 dragged on from March to December. Third, doping: owners of finishing shops who had run out of quality stone because of quarry strikes, or who could not meet their escalating payroll bills, were more likely to risk unscrupulous activity if by doing so they might satisfy orders and defray bankruptcy. Fourth, compensation and insurance: repeated strikes left quarry and shop

50. Ibid., pp. 149, 150.

51. Today, this would be $1,058, or about $53,000 a year, allowing two weeks unpaid vacation, which does not sound excessive in comparison with, say, a skilled bricklayer or licensed electrician, but wages for such trades have risen disproportionately, in large part due to union activism; average wages for automotive mechanics, for instance, are $640 and $33,280, or about a third less.

52. *Boston Globe*, 4 April 1920, p. 16; figures from *Historical Statistics of the United States, Colonial Times to 1970* (Washington, DC: U.S. Bureau of the Census, 1976), series D843–44 and D840–41, p. 172, and farm workers without room or board at $3.30 per day, series K181; J.R. Vernon, "The 1920–21 Deflation: The Role of Aggregate Supply," *Economic Inquiry*, 29:3 (July 1991), p. 572.

owners undercapitalized and discouraged them from long-term planning, so they had little incentive to invest in anything unless it directly boosted short-term profits. Fifth, insufficient capital increased borrowing costs and curtailed advertising: yes, it had, but the reason for the insufficiency was that unremitting strikes and wage hikes had diminished profit; neither manufacturers nor banks usually show reluctance to invest capital into profitable businesses. Hubris may also have been a factor, with manufacturers and workers alike resting on the reputation of Quincy's quarries for providing the stone that built the Bunker Hill Monument. In Solomon Willard's time, there had been little competition, but now there were dozens of quarries—from Minnesota to South Carolina—producing granite that was superior to everything at Quincy, except perhaps Swingle's Extra Dark.[53]

Craft Working and American Trade Unionism

Duncan never understood how his interpretation of the Dream had stifled the life out of its promise, trapping his members in a closed, sociocultural box that inhibited their financial and intellectual development, as well as denying improvement and growth to the industry he chose to practice as a teenager. Instead of working with employers on how to make the workplace more efficient, nicer, or safer, he bickered incessantly with them over nuances of procedure. As the Quincy strike of 1908 dragged into its eighth week, he spent his time giving statements like: "I told the members of the executive committee that I would notify the Quincy union to prepare such an explanation and submit it when the bill was signed. I did not promise to make such an interpretation myself, as you can see by my letter to the secretary of the Quincy union, which was sent the morning after the executive committee met, and by the letter that was sent to the manufacturers' association here by the secretary of their national executive committee, which conferred with our committee." It was all, the *Globe* reporter lamented, "as complex as a Chinese puzzle." Four years earlier, Duncan had said that, "No contract should be more sacred than the trade agreement of organized labor." A union agreement was "a matter of honor between the contracting parties," one that could not be circumscribed like surety companies' bonds or compulsory edicts that "enslave the body or dwarf the mind." Yet Duncan never saw how the rigid, mind-numbing bureaucracy of unionization that he created had enslaved his members.[54]

Had Duncan left the compelling logic of socialist ideology and trade unionism behind in Aberdeen and instead parlayed his energy and talents into entrepreneurship in the United States, he may well have become the proprietor of one of the twenty-one leading granite firms in Quincy listed by Arthur W. Brayley in his 1913 history of the industry. Of those twenty-one, the owner-operators of seventeen were European immigrants, like Duncan, and all of them began as poor apprentices or laborers who made their dreams come true. One of these firms, Alexander Falconer, had employed workers who, in turn, founded two other firms on the list. John A. Clark, from

53. Strike data from Chapman, "GCNU Branch, Membership, and Strike Data."
54. *Boston Globe*, 27 May 1908, p. 9; *Boston Globe*, 20 November 1904, p. 27.

Edinburgh, Scotland, worked in a Canadian iron mine before learning the granite polishing trade in Quincy, with six years at Falconer's, when around 1900 he formed the
Empire Polishing Company, which Brayley judged to be the largest granite polishing
business in the world. Andrew Johnson, from Eslof, Sweden, had been a GCNU activist and an employee of Falconer's for eleven years before founding Hughes & Johnson
in 1903, since when the firm—a "model" business, according to Brayley, "with all the
latest tools and machinery"—had created employment for thirty granite cutters. But
all that was in 1913, when firms like Falconer's were still expanding and profitable.[55]

fig. 71: Alexander Falconer's version of the American Dream, 1905

For sure, the industry was changing from craft working to machine production.
But that did not have to mean there would be fewer jobs for skilled workers—those
who had trained as apprentices for seven years in return for their board and a bag of
tools—and that a union was therefore necessary to protect those jobs. Working with
granite, whether in 1900 or in 2000, required a range of skills learned primarily
through experience, such as judging the load bearing properties or color after polishing of a particular stone, and operating a surfacing machine was just as demanding as
hammering stone flat by hand. While it certainly takes fewer workers today to produce a curtain wall panel or a cemetery memorial, there are new job categories, from
granite kitchen top installers to architectural stone computer-aided designers. For
sure, quarries were dangerous and sheds were dusty. Yet the GCNU did little to enhance its members' safety and health. As with technological advances in production
equipment, articles about derrick loading or dust extraction systems appeared in the

---

55. Brayley, *Granite Industry*, vol. 1, pp. 95–107.

manufacturers' magazines not the *Granite Cutters' Journal*. In the long run, it was likely to be the smaller, nonunion quarries and shops that were the healthiest; big, profitable businesses presented attractive targets for strike action, so although they may initially have had the latest and most efficient equipment, lost sales and spiraling labor costs subsequently made it hard for them to outlay capital on nonproductive equipment like fans and ducting. For sure, employers will do all they can to minimize the cost of production, including wages, and wages in the 1900s–20s were far higher for unionized craft workers than, say, nonunionized farm workers. But aside from the fundamental problem that the escalating wages of Quincy's granite workers were unsustainable under prevailing market conditions, the nonunionized shops afforded a path to lucrative partnerships and sole proprietorships, at least for those who could stomach the extra risks and responsibilities of owning a business. Wages, moreover, find their own level based on market forces, as they had done for the efficient and well-paid granite workers of Willard's day, who even out-competed convicts at the Charlestown prison.

Ultimately, Duncan's efforts to increase wages, along with the free time to enjoy them, for a growing body of granite workers were counterproductive. National union membership peaked in 1911, hovered for four years, and then fell thereafter. In 1979, the GCNU, whose national headquarters had been permanently in Quincy since 1906, printed its last issue of the *Granite Cutters' Journal* and gave up its long fight for the working man. There was tragedy here. At about the same time, architects were specifying rich, polychrome granites for Boston's exciting new office towers, and affluent homeowners were spending thousands of dollars on the latest granite kitchen countertops. Yet much of this granite was from quarries in Mexico, Brazil, and Peru where staff were happy to work for wages that a relatively free global market could pay, rather than wages dictated by an introverted union bureaucracy. U.S. granite production survived, but by moving to a handful of specialist plants that truck or ship stone from quarries in South Carolina, Georgia, South America, or Europe, and cut and polish it into building veneer and countertops with huge semi-automated machines, like Georgia Stone Industries in Smithfield, Rhode Island. Quincy might have remained one of those specialized centers, but even its shipyards, gear works, and cymbal maker closed down or moved away, leaving it a forlorn commuter suburb of Boston. There are still plenty of recent immigrants, though, and many of them are living the American Dream, but now they work in the non-unionized service sector. Quincy's population stagnated in the 1960s and fell in the 1970s, but in the last fifteen years it has picked up. In large part due to the Portuguese-speaking Brazilians and Cantonese-, Vietnamese-, and Hindi-speaking Asians who are particularly likely to be staffing as well as owning the hundred or so licensed premises that are once again popular, this traditionally dry granite city is revitalizing.

David B. Williams, author of *Stories in Stone*, paints a vivid picture of "dangerous and debilitating" working conditions at the Quincy quarries. "Blocks of rock fell from derricks or exploded from the walls. Derricks collapsed and workers got crushed. Men froze in winter and baked in summer. They breathed toxic dust." In one memorably figurative passage, Williams likens the life of a Quincy quarryman to slavery: "Steel cables and iron chains whipped into men as they dug." He leaves his reader with no doubt that conditions in the quarries were "appalling." Everything Williams describes was, of course, true, but his are comfortable truths, the kind of selective shibboleths that buyers of popular histories like to read. An alternative story in stone might describe four or five Finns, part of the group of seventeen who crossed the Atlantic to Quincy in the late-1880s dreaming of a better life, and who had a fight with Officer Bradley in 1900 when they were still acculturating to Theophilus King's puritanical strictures. I see them walking up the hill to the top of Swingle's Quarry.[56]

Shadows of overnight mist swirled from a clump of trees or rose from the lake of a disused quarry. Fresh-fallen leaves strewed the frosted grass, sticking to their boots when they stepped off the path. As the foreman was late, they sat on a rock, rolled cigarettes, and savored a flask of coffee, strong and black as Finns prefer. They were soon chatting about the previous night's National Hockey League game and what to do on Sunday now that it was too cold for family picnics. Perhaps the bluefish were running in the Neponset. One of them noticed the morning sun rippling across the harbor from the east, then catching the taller buildings of downtown Boston. A hush fell over them. It had been a while since any of them were in the city, although they could picture the subways emptying workers into the busy streets, and the elegant offices, some built from granite they had quarried. "I'll have steam up soon," their foreman called, snapping them out of their reverie, and they walked over to the rim of the quarry. Even though they had been there a thousand times before, the sheer depth and scale of the hole they had made still filled them with awe. Adrenaline added its rush to the coffee and smokes as they made their way down the ladders and across the ledges, excited to begin another day in the knowledge that few other men not only had their skills but also the opportunity to practice them in such a unique and wondrous place. They were masters of their environment, those lithe Finns, and fiercely proud of it. On that crisp November morning, as the air hoses stiffened and started to hiss, and the sun beamed its orange light onto the quarry walls, there was no other place they would sooner have been.

---

56. David B. Williams, *Stories in Stone: Travels Through Urban Geology* (New York: Walker & Company, 2009), p. 27.

6. PAUL CELLUCCI: CONSPIRACY THEORY

It might seem odd that Americans, members of a free and open society who regard themselves as educated, rational thinkers, would be in thrall to so many popular conspiracy theories. Some theories have sought to blame outside conspirators for national misfortunes, such as Cuban nationalists for blowing up the USS *Maine* in Havana Harbor in 1898. More often, the presumed culprits are federal government officials, such as President Franklin D. Roosevelt for facilitating the 1941 Japanese attack on Pearl Harbor, or the Air National Guard for accidentally shooting down Trans World Airlines flight 800 off Long Island in 1996 and then denying culpability. Some conspiracies have a compelling logic, such as the assertion that the Pentagon instructed the pilot of Korean Airlines flight 007 to deliberately fly into Soviet airspace on 1 September 1983 to trigger early-warning systems while the space shuttle *Challenger* and a Ferret-D satellite were monitoring overhead, mistakenly presuming that the Soviets would not shoot down a passenger plane. Others, like the notion that the Federal Bureau of Investigation (FBI) ran a secret detention center for extraterrestrial aliens, as featured in the 1990s Fox television series *The X-Files* starring David Duchovny as Special Agent Fox Mulder, or that the George W. Bush administration orchestrated the 9/11 attacks, are harder to believe. Yet all these theories—and dozens more—have a dedicated following. Decades after official insistence that there was full governmental disclosure and no evidence of outside collusion, a Gallup Poll of 2003 showed that 75 percent of Americans did not believe that Lee Harvey Oswald acted alone in assassinating President John F. Kennedy on 22 November 1963. In 2004, A&E Television Networks' The History Channel ran a twelve-part documentary series, *Conspiracy?*, suggesting that conspiracy theories were suitable for serious, if not quite scholarly, analysis. For all their purported objectivity, scholars have added to the American fascination with conspiracies. In the 1970s, New Left political scientists and historians published titles like *The Paranoid Style in American Politics*, and *The Politics of Unreason*, portraying conservatives and right wingers as pathological crackpots, but these books themselves had a shrill tone that hinted at the conspiratorial. Scholars have given their imprimatur to the conspiracists by participating in the Annual Dallas JFK Assassination conferences organized by the Coalition on Political Assassinations, or by publishing detailed analyses of amateur video films of the assassination to argue that a second shooter fired from a manhole cover beneath a parked car.[1]

Yet given the moral exemplarism inherent in the enduring national core value symbolized by the shining city, and a founding ideology inherited from John Locke that cautioned against the wiles of corrupt, overbearing government, then Americans'

---

1. "Americans: Kennedy Assassination a Conspiracy," Gallup Poll 9751:19 of 10–12 November 2003, http://www.gallup.com/poll/9751/americans-kennedy-assassination-conspiracy.aspx (accessed 1 February 2012); this poll was consistent with the findings of six others conducted since the 1970s, ranging from 74 to 81 percent, but significantly higher than two polls conducted in 1963 and 1966, which indicated that only 50 percent of Americans believed there was a conspiracy. Richard Hofstadter, *The Paranoid Style in American Politics, and Other Essays* (1965; repr., Chicago: University of Chicago Press, 1979); Seymour Martin Lipset and Earl Raab, *The Politics of Unreason: Right-Wing Extremism in America, 1790–1977* (2nd ed.; Chicago: University of Chicago Press, 1978).

long fascination with conspiracy theories is not surprising. Americans have enjoyed a relatively free and open society, which makes a stage for Bible-thumping moralists, muckraking journalists, and spectacle-vending television news shows. Federal authorities and public officials, moreover, have provided the conspiracists with plenty of ammunition, sometimes literally. There really was a Watergate burglary, followed by a cover-up and denial at the presidential level. There really were CIA and National Security Council assassins, coup plotters, drug dealers, money launderers, and gunrunners, public knowledge of whose actions has invariably met with official denials and cover-ups.[2]

Popular, enduring conspiracy theories, such as the Kennedy assassination, share the same fundamental characteristics. There should be a real crime or malfeasance of national significance; a benign, official explanation in the face of suspicious circumstances and strange coincidences; alternative explanations of an outlandish nature that implicate government officials; and little chance of ever knowing what really happened. After voicing support for a conspiracy theory, particularly of a bizarre or unscientific nature, one's friends may express surprise, even ridicule, leading to pangs of cognitive dissonance, hence the necessity for convincing others of the theory's veracity, which in turn makes it a component of one's identity. At the same time, there is something appealingly human about discussing ridiculous conspiracies, albeit with a hint of sarcasm. Thousands of R.E.M. fans in the 1990s hummed along to this catchy lyric: "If you believed they put a man on the moon, man on the moon. / If you believe there's nothing up my sleeve, then nothing is cool." Because conspiracy theories typically implicate the government, their popularity blossomed in the climate of Vietnam War-era protests and distrust of information from federal sources. Fuelled by actual conspiracy convictions against government officials for authorizing the Fielding and Watergate burglaries, they became a weapon for members of the counterculture in their attacks on the establishment.[3] Like the Bunker Hill Monument's blank granite walls primed to receive the impress of orators Daniel Webster and Edward Everett, a good conspiracy is an open field for story tellers' flights of fancy.

Just as nationalism takes breath in the heady atmosphere of competing nation-states, so conspiracy theories, themselves of a nationalistic flavor, take root and grow in the muck of social discord and distrust. To whatever extent Americans are all Anglo-Protestants at heart, as historian Samuel Huntington would have it, ethnic, racial, and generational divides sundered Boston's society in the 1970s and on into the 1990s. This was the era of Irish Republican Army (IRA) gunrunning, forced school bussing, and antiwar protests, with Charlestown the locus for much of this countercultural angst. No wonder, then, that the Monument along with the Quincy quarries that supplied its granite blocks have been subjects for conspiracy theorists, beginning

---

2. Examples include the ouster of Iran's Mohammad Mosaddeq on 19 August 1953, assassinations run by Guatemala's CIA station chiefs during the 1950s–80s, and the cocaine trafficking, money laundering, and arms smuggling organized by the NSC's Col. Oliver L. North that constituted the Iran–Contra scandal of November 1986.

3. On 3 September 1971, President Richard M. Nixon's so-called plumbers burgled the office of psychiatrist Lewis Fielding in the hope of finding the medical file on Daniel Ellsberg who had leaked the Pentagon Papers.

in 1831 with the charge by Anti-Masons that the Monument, as an Egyptian obelisk resting on a silver plaque inscribed with necromantic hieroglyphs, was what amounted to a Masonic rocket ship or radio beacon for communing with nether-worldly spirits. Fierce controversies arose over possession of the Monument: did it belong to—did it stand for—the blue-collar Irish-American Townies who had lived in its shadow for generations, or to the invasion of BMW-driving Yuppies who, by snapping up expensive condominiums around Monument Square, were pricing Townies out of their rented apartments? At Quincy, did the quarries belong to the youths who had been colonizing them since the 1930s to bond, experiment, party, and escape their parents' control, or to city politicians seeking reelection and to their property-developing backers who were eager to build townhouses and golf courses? Fuelling this latter question was Boston's Central Artery / Tunnel Project, or Big Dig, which kicked fourteen billion dollars into the local economy, just as it created lucrative opportunities for political conflicts of interest if not necessarily kickbacks.[4]

Young people making their own fun at the quarries, a special place they adopted and which they turned into a unique, lived-history resource, became the unwitting actors and ultimate losers in what may have been a conspiracy by Massachusetts state and Quincy city government officials to fill the quarries with hazardous waste, thereby winning voter approval, solving a Big Dig problem, and benefitting contractors and property developers. To whatever extent this potential conspiracy might implicate Governor A. Paul Cellucci, it was under his watch that the quarries closed, for which a majority of voters were surely grateful. An Italian-American from Hudson, Massachusetts, a European immigrant shoe-making town twenty-three miles west of Boston, Cellucci was in many respects an exemplary governor, doing his best as a bipartisan, fiscal conservative to rein in the decades-old tax-and-spend policies of an entrenched and self-serving state legislature and boost flagging public education standards. Despite, or perhaps even because of, the runaway spending of the Big Dig project and the destruction of the Quincy quarries, Cellucci's governorship was that of an American hero fulfilling the American Dream.

Quarry Counterculture

Since at least thirty years before Swingle's ceased production in 1963, the quarries at West Quincy had been the wellspring of a unique, macho counterculture, centered on diving and partying. *Life* magazine's front cover of 8 August 1938 (fig. 72) featured four well-muscled youths "launching themselves outward and down," thirty-five feet, "in swift parabolas," while a dozen friends awaited their turn to show skill and bravery. "To young people of Norfolk County," the caption read, the quarries were "famed as the most thrilling and soul-satisfying swimming hole in New England." Cut out block by wedged block, then darkened by weather and overgrown, the quarries had an awesome naturalness, a chilling sense of the primordial that opencast bauxite or copper quarries, with their sculptured ramps and roads, seem to lack. Back then, when a

4. Samuel P. Huntington, *Who Are We? The Challenges to America's National Identity* (New York: Simon & Schuster, 2004).

few initials chiseled in the rock were the only graffiti, the quarries were soul-satisfyingly visceral. Unstable grout piles, submerged ledges, and snapping turtles made them tricky places for the unaware, and yet, in their extreme danger, they were surprisingly safe. A psychological parallel would be the treatment of roof-deck railings in the City of London, which must be over-engineered to protect against a crush of drunken revelers, and yet a clause of the same ordnance, albeit little used in these risk-averse times, permits builders to omit the railings altogether, on the assumption that a natural fear of heights will keep anyone from falling. Swimming is intrinsically risky, as some eight hundred Americans drowning in pools, rivers, and lakes annually attest. At roughly the same moment that *Life*'s photographer snapped the Quincy divers, experienced swimmer George B. Wright, fifteen, sank out of sight from an on-duty lifeguard at the Cowford swimming hole, Lumbar River, North Carolina. Nevertheless, deaths from recreational diving at Quincy during 1930–2010 averaged one a decade with the first occurrence in 1956, a remarkable statistic given the untold thousands of dives in a given season. Diving lore at Quincy passed down from experienced peers; neophytes and skilled divers alike honed their technique naturally, as they progressed through jumps of increasing height, learning the difficulties of staying in balance for the duration of the drop, and appreciating how much more solid water becomes with every foot added to the dive.[5]

Quarry-goers broadened in the 1960s to include nature lovers and rock climbers, although technical climbing was at that time a fringe sport. "A quarrying company owns the area, and tolerates climbers, swimmers, and skindivers in their abandoned quarries," Massachusetts Institute of Technology (MIT) Outing Club members William R. Crowther and Anthony W. Thompson assured readers of their *Climber's Guide to the Quincy Quarries* (1968). My well-thumbed copy came courtesy of a research chemist and MIT graduate Yuanshou Chen, an elderly but still lithe man when I met him in the early 1990s, whose eyes would always sparkle when talking of his trips to Quincy in the mid-sixties. Crowther and Thomas listed fifty-eight routes, ranging in difficulty from a simple 5.2 to an almost impossible 5.10, the maximum grade of difficulty originally specified for Class 5 rock climbs by the Sierra Club in the Yosemite Decimal System of the 1950s. One of the guide's four 5.10 routes, Yellow Knight, an "unrelenting series of small footholds far apart and terrible handholds," promised "practice in smooth deep knee bends." Although climbers typically learned hard routes by slipping from the holds, resulting falls at Quincy risked little more than dangling from the rope. Iron rings, anchored by quarrymen in lead-filled holes, and backed up by climbing bolts installed by club members, made for safe and convenient top-roping. As opposed to bouldering, soloing, or leading, all of which risk a fall either past an anchor or directly to the ground, in the top-roping system a nylon rope attached to the climber's harness passes through a locking carabineer slung from two

5. *Life*, 5:6 (8 August 1938), p. 9; Quincy quarries' statistics from "Deaths at the West Quincy Quarries, 1930–2012," spreadsheet, compiled by author (available on request), primarily from newspaper reports, but cross-checked with John A. Laukkanen, *Quincy Quarries: Gold and Gloom* (Victoria, Canada: Trafford Publishing, 2004), pp. 45–50; there were nine recreational drowning deaths in eight decades; *Robesonian*, 15 August 1938, p. 1.

or more ridge-line anchors, and is then pulled in through a friction lock or belay device by a partner on the ground. By the mid-1980s, sticky, rubber-soled shoes, chalked fingers, and physical techniques practiced in rock gyms enabled climbers to exceed 5.10; today, the hardest routes, climbed on sight, rate an astonishing 5.15. With the new equipment and techniques, along with greater leisure time and concerns for fitness, the popularity of rock climbing skyrocketed. In 1991, when Larry LaForge published *Boston Rocks*, an edition of *Climber's Guide* expanded to the Boston area, he listed 109 routes in the quarries.[6]

fig. 72: "Into a Quincy Quarry," *Life* front cover, August 1938

I first went to the Quincy quarries in the summer of 1986 with my climbing partner Richard Palmer, the opening manager of the Bostonian Hotel in Quincy Market.[7]

6. William R. Crowther and Anthony W. Thompson, *A Climber's Guide to the Quincy Quarries* (Cambridge, MA: MIT Outing Club, 1968), pp. 3, 16; Larry LaForge, ed., *Boston Rocks* (Cambridge, MA: MIT Outing Club, 1991).

7. Palmer managed this distinctive, independent hotel in the heart of downtown Boston for partners Arthur D. Winn, a developer of Section 8 affordable housing, and an Arab prince, from 7 September 1982 to 1996, when Hong

Palmer had been hiking on Mount Washington two winters prior when a wind gust swept two men from the ice-covered summit plateau. During the ensuing rescue, Palmer met Robbie Taylor, a local climber who was recovering from a fall on Mount Kilimanjaro; Taylor subsequently introduced him to a circle of Boston climbers, including Jeff Brewer and alpinist David Breashears, and it had not been long before they had given him the mountaineering bug. We had become friends shortly after I moved to Charlestown in 1985, in part because we were both expatriate Britons. Technical climbing was soon our shared hobby, our Sunday escape from the pressures of business. I will never forget the excitement of that first trip to Quincy. From the parking lot, we walked up Gridley Bryant's inclined plane (fig. 73), a few rusted iron strips still staked to the granite rails, and then along an overgrown trail that opened out onto the splendor of Granite Rail Quarry. Set in a pristine wetlands ecosystem, its serene lake glimmered in stark contrast to the raucous graffiti daubed anarchically over the surrounding rock walls and grout piles, the discarded granite blocks with their gaudy spray paint like the pieces of a giant's unfinished jigsaw puzzle. Before we started climbing, I wanted to see Swingle's, so we skirted Granite Rail, scrambled up some boulders, and came out on a hill with a commanding view of Boston, eleven miles away. I could sense the quarry's enormity before I saw it—some echoed sounds, a waft of cooler, fusty air. Then there it was, and a primal fear gripped me. Despite my relative comfort with heights, my heart was beating faster with every step nearer the rim, which I did not want to approach but could not resist. Tiptoeing the last few paces but still one pace shy, I stared down a 170-foot sheer drop to the water far below, further impressed to know that the quarry floor was another 260 feet beneath the surface.

fig. 73: Gridley Bryant's inclined plane, in 2011

Kong-based Regal Hotels purchased it; London-based Millennium Hotels bought out the failing Regal in 2000 and renamed it the Millennium Bostonian Hotel.

fig. 74: a climber top-roping Little Inch, rated an easy 5.4, in Little Railroad Quarry (his partner is belaying him from a stance off the picture to the bottom right)

Over the next fifteen years, I made dozens of trips to the quarries with my own expanding circle of climbing partners, and eventually with my son once he was sufficiently confident to handle a belay. In the Little Railroad Quarry, our preferred spot, we would set a rope from slings clipped to a couple of the quarrymen's old iron anchor hoops, and work out a route. Mingled Measure or Flake Direct to warm up, then perhaps Sticky Fingers or even Blood Streaks, so named for the can of slippery red paint someone had once tipped down the already-smooth granite face. One hot Sunday morning, feeling particularly inspired at the L face in Granite Rail, I managed to eke my way up the 5.8 Manic Depressive. With dragonflies skimming daintily over the mirror-like water, toads hopping off water lily leaves, excited sounds echoing around the rocks, and everywhere the towering, sheer mass of a million tons of raw granite, the atmosphere at the quarries on those summer days was always magical.

After a morning's exertions, we would frequently hike over to Swingle's for a view of Boston, the cool breeze, and to marvel at this wound wrought in nature by man's sheer grit and determination. One morning, a blood-curdling yell split the air, startling us out of our reverie. A half-naked bronzed youth had leapt into space from an intermediate ledge to our left, dubbed Heaven by jumpers. He had no doubt performed this death-defying tribal ritual before because he was confidently whooping and cycling his legs as he plummeted the seventy-two feet toward the lake. His three buddies were whooping too, and perhaps wondering if they would someday have the guts to follow him. Their girlfriends, standing well back from the brink, seemed suitably impressed with the daring performance. At the last minute, the diver straightened and crossed his legs, pointed his toes, buried his face in cupped hands pressed to the chest, and cut a clean, white hole in the dark water. After what seemed like an eternity, he bobbed back to the surface and free-styled across the lake to the far end, from where it was possible to clamber out and back up to the top. Of all the thousands of youths who dived from fifteen or even thirty feet into Granite Rail, only a few hardcore souls ever earned the accolade of having *jumped Swingle's*, to use local parlance.

fig. 75: climbers admiring Boston's skyline from West Quincy

Sporting action at the quarries was largely a male preserve, with girlfriends and hangers-on in the role of admirers. Even in the 1990s when rock climbing became popular among women, and Catherine Destivelle and Lynn Hill proved that they could compete with men at international climbing events and frequently win, it was a rare sight to see a female climber at Quincy, and I never once saw a woman perform a high dive. Still, while male youth culture predominated, all manner of folks frequented the quarries: tweed-jacketed naturalists and bird watchers; determined-looking members of the Massachusetts Audubon Society off for a hike into the Blue Hills

Reservation; emergency medical technicians (EMTs) practicing stretcher rescue techniques; macho U.S. Army Reservists kicking off from the rock in rapid rappels, their ropes writhing like angry snakes; young children splashing around and swimming in the shallows at the far side of Granite Rail; a toddler with a butterfly net; and, back down at the parking lot, senior citizens visiting the small, dusty, but nonetheless fascinating Quarry Museum located in the Granite Railway's old compressor house.

Quarry atmosphere was always as unique as it was liberating, a completely free and unstructured environment in which to hang out and do one's thing. "I've been climbing on these rocks for 20 years now," Alan Rubin enthused in the introduction to LaForge's *Boston Rocks*, "yet I still get enjoyment every time I go out." Repeating a climb for the hundredth time, Rubin found the same "thrill of effort and accomplishment" that he had enjoyed on the first ascent. Even more important was the comradeship. "Socializing with others who have a common interest but who have different backgrounds, either at the rocks, or in the bar afterwards, is a major component of the urban climbing scene." And yet, as the counterculture vs. the establishment conflicts of the 1970s gave way—or regressed, as some would see it—to the litigiousness, risk aversion, and ever-bigger, buttoned-down government of the 1990s, the quarries' freewheeling urban culture was precisely their undoing. For while aficionados valued them as a vital resource, a cabal of politicians and parents feared them as a challenge to their traditional ideals and as a world beyond their understanding and hence control. Simultaneously, with white flight from Boston's urban core fueling demand for luxury condominiums in the suburbs, developers were slavering over the golf-course potential, natural setting, and stunning views—of downtown, a safe distance away on Interstate-93—that the quarries offered. In a preemptive strategy, a group of climbers and outdoors activists campaigned for the Metropolitan District Commission (MDC), whose management at that time seemed to be on their side, to purchase the twenty acres still under commercial ownership. This brought Granite Rail under the MDC's jurisdiction, with adjacent Swingle's being the responsibility of the City of Quincy. In a hint of the fate awaiting the quarries, Rubin was skeptical that future administrations would honor the MDC's pledge to preserve their historic value and open-access format, particularly in light of the mixed motives it had demonstrated at other sites in its domain. "Over the years since climbing began here various outcrops have been closed or destroyed," he noted, and "this problem is even greater today as urban development tries to gobble up the remaining open terrain, and as landowners panic in the face of concerns over liability." On its website, the MDC recognized that the quarries were "eastern Massachusetts' best rock climbing" area, yet could not help mentioning how "the site possesses a rather eerie atmosphere."[8]

Leaving out the more esoteric pursuits of quarry diving and rock climbing, simply strolling around a quarry—just like boating, driving, or even crossing the street—is potentially fraught with subjective danger. There were never any handrails at Quincy.

8. LaForge, *Boston Rocks*, pp. 13, 12; Rubin wrote his piece in 1987, two years after the MDC purchased the twenty acres; http://www.state.ma.us/film/feefree/quincyquarries.htm (accessed 9 October 2000).

A few tattered signs indicated that a particular grout pile was unstable, or that the edge at a particular spot might crumble. Those who went there, nevertheless, understood the dangers and for the most part acted responsibly; there were almost no unforced accidents and, for that matter, remarkably few forced mishaps. On a typical weekend afternoon in the summer, when the quarries accommodated several hundred visitors, there might be forty or fifty jumps an hour into the cooling waters of Granite Rail. Although some youths brought beer with them to consume during the day, there was little in the way of daylight drinking, despite the absence of police patrols. After sunset, other groups, invariably with underage members given the legal drinking age of twenty-one, gathered to kick back and party, but even then, when cans were popping and marijuana joints were glowing in the moonlight, the quarries were a safe place for young people.

Closure: Bodies in the Quarries

In the eighty years since the first recorded non-work-related fatality in 1933, the West Quincy quarries claimed twenty-four bodies, two of which arrived from elsewhere, an average of 0.30 deaths per year.[9] Three were those of women, two were murder victims, eleven fell, nine drowned, and rock falls crushed two. Victims' average age was 20.4, which reduces to 17.4 on omitting the six victims over twenty, which is to say that 75 percent were teenagers. John A. Whalen, twenty-three of Dorchester, drowned while swimming solo in Cashman's Quarry in September 1933. In February 1942, John J. Grasselli, a twenty-two-year-old Quincy police officer, murdered Helen D. Cullen, an older married woman whom he had met in a bar in Boston's West End, and dumped her body into Carlson's Quarry. In September 1956, thirteen-year-old Ronald J. Fasulo drowned in Fuller's Quarry. Albert J. Moscatel, eighteen, died in 1960 in a rockslide in Swingle's; late one June evening two years later, Joel Ryan and Arthur O'Neil, both eighteen, similarly fell into Swingle's. Two Lowell men, Howard D. Trombly, forty-two, and Robert Francis Lavoie, twenty-three, fell into Swingle's in 1963 after triggering a rockslide. Lawrence Gray Foster, eighteen, of East Bridgewater, drowned in the Blue Hill's Quarry in August 1965. In 1970, Robert Callahan, seventeen, died while attempting a hundred-foot dive into Badger's Quarry, and the following year, Thomas Lee McAuley, seventeen, also drowned in Badger's. Another Swingle's rockslide crushed climbers Robert R. Hanson and his girlfriend Caroline Echardt, both seventeen, in December 1973. Thomas Fielding, sixteen, of Charlestown, dived into Granite Rail in August 1980 but hit a partially submerged wood block, one of several floated into the quarry by safety officials in an effort to deter jumpers. In June 1983, Paul S. Gooch, seventeen, successfully made his first fifty-three-foot jump into

9. Chapman, "Deaths at the West Quincy Quarries"; there were no deaths in the six years of 1974–79, the four years of 1966–69 and 1990–93, the three years of 1957–59 and 1986–88, or the two years of 1995–97; I have omitted Thomas James Scanlon Jr. who committed suicide in 1961 by driving his car into Granite Rail, and John Mezetti, an eight-year-old, who fell through ice in Gray Rock Quarry in February 1954; other than Mezetti's there were no deaths younger than thirteen. There were other deaths, all before 1963, in disused quarries and swimming holes in Quincy proper, east of I-93, which, once filled and developed, became part of Quincy's urban core; these were neither part of the West Quincy quarry counterculture nor relevant to the debate over bodies in the quarries under discussion here.

Swingle's only to drown after a second jump from seventy-two feet. Vincent M. Alcide, an eighteen-year-old Haitian-American from Mattapan, completed a dive into Fuller's but then drowned while swimming out. In May 1985, Gerald McHugh, twenty, was walking home with a friend after an evening's drinking when a blinking yellow highway construction sign suggested a game of target practice. A passing State Police trooper spotted their rock throwing and his cruiser's blue lights sent the pair running off. They separated in the dark and McHugh ran into nearby Old Colony Quarry, where police found his body next day. On New Year's Day 1989, Gerald Arroyo died after falling onto ice while climbing near the bottom of Swingle's. In 1997, Thomas L. Roberts, twenty-six, drowned during a seventy-five-foot dive into Granite Rail. In July 1998, Ryan N. Whitney, nineteen, a doctor's son who had recently left Milton High School without graduating, fell into Lyons Quarry at 1:30 AM after wandering away from his friends during a drinking party. And a month later, Christopher T. Griffiths, seventeen, while demonstrating bravado to his girlfriend, slipped off a ledge at Swingle's. Subjective danger was a factor in less than half of these twenty-one tragic deaths during 1942–99, while drinking, showing off to girlfriends, failure to follow standard climbing procedures, plain stupidity, and perhaps depression contributed to the rest.

Even as the cumulative death toll rose in consequence of the quarries' growing popularity, government officials, public safety officers, rescue personnel, newspaper editors, and heartbroken relatives could have continued to judge quarry deaths for what they were, the natural and inevitable result of young men coming of age: hanging out, having fun, horsing around, impressing girlfriends, daring each other, and testing their bodies. They could have studied motor vehicle crash statistics proving that adolescents at the quarries were safer than their friends who borrowed the family car—or, worse still, the five-liter Pontiac Trans Am that their well-meaning but naive parents had given them as a high school graduation present—for an eighty-mile-an-hour spin around South Shore towns with accommodating bartenders.[10] They could have appreciated that the two deaths in 1998, one of the worst years at the quarries, compared with a dozen South Shore boating fatalities that year, including two teenagers killed on jet skis.[11] They might have put aside their shock and grief over the isolated incidents to focus instead on the virtually free outdoors sport, relaxation, and friendship in a unique and unforgettable historic environment enjoyed by generations of young people at the quarries. But this was now the 1990s, and the criteria for sound judgment had shifted a notch toward paranoia. Three factors conspired to turn *bodies in the quarries* into a mass-media metanarrative whose result could only be the quarries' destruction.[12]

10. Of 42,000 motor vehicle traffic deaths in 1993 (a relatively safe year on America's roads, down from 49,078 in 1988), 3,165 drivers and 1,938 passengers (12 percent) were aged between sixteen and twenty; *AAMA Motor Vehicle Facts and Figures, '94* (Detroit, MI: American Automobile Manufacturers Association, 1994), p. 91.

11. "South Shore Boating Deaths, 1998," spreadsheet, compiled by author (available on request), primarily from newspaper reports.

12. For the mechanisms through which metanarratives and "megaspectacles" drive mainstream media culture, see

A media-generated preoccupation with *closure* was the first factor. Ever since early man went off to sea or to discover what might be on the other side of the mountain and then sadly never returned, his family and friends would live in desperate hope, until the day his body washed up on the beach or someone discovered it, frozen, on a high pass. They could then bury it, putting to rest what Asian societies call a wandering soul. This kind of closure was a balanced, personal response to coping with uncertainty and grief. But as a neologism for Americans of the 1990s, glued as many of them increasingly were to nightly television news shows, ambulance-chasing exposés, and crime-fighting soaps, *closure* in the media's hands became a sort of Pavlovian outpouring of communal angst. One family's private need for closure became the shared demand of a million voyeurs.

A keyword search of the WorldCat database of books brings up the first mentions of closure in Catherine Cameron's *Resolving Childhood Trauma* and William X. Kienzle's *Till Death*, both published in 2000. In what may be the first usage of the word in the context of shared grief over a missing body, George Marshall, a Minneapolis county judge ruling on a juvenile sex-ring case in December 1991, remarked that there was "an overriding state interest for closure," although he might just as well have been stating a wish to close the case. At any rate, by 1995, in the aftermath of the Oklahoma City Bombing, the national press had developed—and was exploiting—the closure phenomenon. "There is talk of closure," mooted the *Los Angeles Times* eight months after the bombing, "yet the staggering number of monuments and memorials and souvenir mementos has kept the emotions fresher than many survivors can stomach." Quoting George R. Sprague, the father of a rape-murder victim who had just heard that the suspected murderer had hanged himself, the *Boston Globe* first used the term in 1996, albeit in an altered sense: "[Dwayne] Vinson's death 'does, for the family, bring closure more quickly than it otherwise would have.'" It was on 29 November 1997 that the *Globe* first linked a death at Quincy quarries with the problem of closure.[13]

Following a night of drinking in local pubs, P.J. McDonagh, nineteen, a visiting business student from County Galway, Ireland, was at the Granite Rail Quarry in the early morning hours of 27 June 1994 for a few last beers, when, in circumstances unknown to his friend Mark Walsh who had fallen asleep at the scene, he disappeared. Police divers were unable to find his body, setting in train a media focus on closure and his relatives' grief, McDonagh having a large extended family on both sides of the Atlantic. When divers did recover the body three years later, the *Globe* was able to report that, "the sense of closure is palpable for the family." "'We are just not worrying or wondering anymore on where P.J. could be,'" said his aunt Noreen McDonagh of Dorchester. At the same time, the *Globe* mustered its arsenal of hyperbole to add

Henry A. Giroux, *Beyond the Spectacle of Terrorism: Global Uncertainty and the Challenge of the New Media* (Boulder, CO: Paradigm Publishers, 2006), esp. pp. 19–46.

13. *Minneapolis Star Tribune*, 21 December 1991; *Los Angeles Times*, 17 December 1995, p. A22; *Boston Globe*, 27 December 1996, p. B2.

ominously, "As one family neared closure after the recovery of P.J. McDonagh's body from the Granite Rail Quarry, another family yesterday continued to endure an excruciating wait beside its deep, murky waters." This was a reference to the parents of missing person Karen Hammond and, in turn, to murder victim Sonia F. Leal, two women whose disappearances created the most media-memorable of all the bodies-in-the-quarries stories of the 1990s.[14]

After murdering Leal, a Portuguese-American of seventeen who had been in foster care after repeatedly leaving her parents and had then supported herself by sex work, her three killers chose to dump the body into Granite Rail. That night, 10 November 1994, they wrapped it in a comforter weighted with three cinder blocks but, in their ignorance of the quarry's underwater topography, they had chosen a spot above a ledge fifteen feet down, where quarry-goers spotted it ten days later. Eight months after they recovered the body, police employed a new cryogenic technique to lift a fingerprint from duct tape that had bound the victim's hands, which led to the arrest of Shawn Kane. Awaiting trial for Leal's murder, Kane tried for a plea bargain by suggesting that another female homicide victim lay in the waters of Granite Rail. Police suspected this might be Hammond, a twenty-one-year-old mother of two from South Boston, whose boyfriend had last seen her at a convenience store at 4 PM on 3 January 1995. Other than Kane's claim, it is unclear why investigators, headed by Norfolk County District Attorney Jeffrey A. Locke, thought Hammond might be a murder victim, let alone why her body was in one of the Quincy quarries. Her father Charlie Hammond admitted that she was a prostitute who used drugs, so she probably frequented Boston's so-called Combat Zone to support an expensive habit, but there are prostitutes who do not become murder victims and drug users who lose themselves in different states or disappear in the process of taking their own lives.[15]

With Kane pointing into the waters of Granite Rail, State Police divers launched a high-profile search of the quarry on 14 November 1997, creating a daily diet of dramatic television footage and newspaper reportage. Aided by a robot-mounted video camera, at a depth of 178 feet and in conditions of poor visibility, divers in bulky pressure suits and domed helmets found and recovered a body, which medical examiners identified two days later as that of the missing Irish student McDonagh. At a spot roughly thirty feet away where they left a marker, the divers also claimed to have located a woman's body. When they returned to recover it, they found the marker but the body was no longer there. Because everyone, the divers included, were convinced that multiple bodies were in the quarry, the divers presumed it was the lightweight marker, rather than a heavier body, that had moved. "The woman's body was spotted before McDonagh's," the *Globe* reported, "but in the process of identifying and

---

14. *Boston Globe*, 29 June 1994, p. 27, and 1 July 1994, p. 24; *Boston Globe*, 29 November 1997, p. B1.

15. Leal, *Boston Globe*, 23 November 1994, pp. 1, 50, and 24 July 1995, pp. 1, 14; for Hammond as drug user, *Boston Globe*, 21 September 1997, p. B2, and "involved in prostitution," *Boston Globe*, 12 December 1997, p. B5; for Hammond as "a murdered prostitute," Deputy Chief of Staff Russell D. Aims to Cellucci, 2 February 1998, Governor's Papers, Weld/Cellucci/Swift, GO2/series 505, Governor's Office, Chief of Staff (hereafter cited as GPGO), b. 20, folder (f.) Quincy Quarry, Massachusetts Archives, Boston.

recovering the bodies, a location marker over the female body became dislodged." Even more categorically, the *Quincy Patriot Ledger* stated that Kane had implicated his codefendants Robert F. Larkin III and Kevin Lynch "in the murder of the woman found submerged 175 feet below the surface of the water Thursday." Given that this was a pending murder case, such sloppy reportage was as irresponsible as it was reprehensible. It left the public in no doubt that the police had found the body of a murdered woman in the quarry and all they had to do now was recover it and convict the suspects. No one was asking how the divers knew that the object they saw was the body of a woman, which were they correct would have suffered from thirty-four months of decomposition, albeit at a slow rate in the low temperature at such a depth. Locke promised that divers would return the following day, but stressed how the murky waters made it "'difficult for divers to see their hands in front of their faces.'" For another sixteen days, the frustrated divers searched, yet they never found a second body.[16]

There would be no closure for Charlie Hammond, who was keeping a daily vigil at the quarry. Standing mournfully in the cold, clutching a Styrofoam heart-shaped wreath embellished with a teddy bear and roses, which he so dearly wanted to throw into the water over the place where the divers would bring his daughter's body to the surface, he made a sight that viewers surely found pitiable. "'If there is someone down there, I'm hoping it's my daughter,'" said the distraught Hammond. "'It's been three years, and I know I can't take much more.'" Enthralled in the saga by television programmers and newspaper editors hungry for advertising revenue, the Massachusetts public could not take much more either.[17]

Cellucci's Reelection Campaign

A second factor behind the mass media preoccupation with bodies in the quarries, and which would soon conspire to bring closure to the suffering public, was the reelection campaigns of at least three career politicians, Norfolk District Attorney Jeffrey Locke, Quincy Mayor James A. Sheets, and Massachusetts's Acting Governor Paul Cellucci. In addition to the probe at the quarries, Locke, a Republican, in May 1997 had initiated a second high-profile investigation into allegations that Michael LeMoyne Kennedy—nephew of Senator Edward M. Kennedy (D-MA) and brother of Congressman Joseph P. Kennedy II (D-MA) who was planning a run for the governor's office—had sex with a babysitter when she was fourteen; that investigation ended in December when Kennedy skied into a tree while playing football on the slopes of Aspen, Colorado. Sheets, a "powerhouse politician" according to the local press, was looking to rally voter support for a sixth consecutive term, and, like his cohort of American politicians, was dependent on campaign contributions from wealthy commercial sponsors to fund advertising and entertainment costs. Cellucci, the son of an Italian-American politician, won election to the Massachusetts House of Representatives

---

16. *Boston Globe*, 29 November 1997, p. B1; identification of McDonagh, *Quincy Patriot Ledger* (hereafter cited as *QPL*), 27 November 1997, p. 1; bodies, *QPL*, 25 November 1997, p. 8; Locke ends search, *QPL*, 11 December 1997, p. 1.

17. *Boston Globe*, 29 November 1997, p. B1.

shortly after graduating from Boston College Law School in 1973. Running with the Republican Party's William F. Weld on a platform of fiscal conservatism, he became lieutenant governor in 1991, and then acting governor in July 1997 when Weld resigned after nomination by President William J. Clinton as ambassador to Mexico. By November 1997 when divers were searching Granite Rail, Cellucci was already campaigning for the September gubernatorial primary, in which he expected to face the well-connected State Treasurer Joseph D. Malone, prior to the 3 November 1998 election. Public fascination with bodies in the quarries, combined with a voyeuristic need for closure, provided these incumbent candidates with a perfect vote-winning opportunity, at no cost to the campaign budget and with little risk of backfire.[18]

fig. 76: Mayor James. A Sheets

Between them, Locke, Sheets, and Cellucci directed all the state and local agencies responsible for the criminal investigations and quarry searches, which made it easy for them to control the tempo, profile, and content of mass-media reportage. Identifying with and then acting to alleviate the distress of grieving relatives like Hammond showcased the candidates' compassion. Mounting ever more costly searches, made imperative by criminal proceedings and relatives' need for closure, provided them with an opportunity to demonstrate fiscal responsibility through the argument that closing the quarries, or better yet, filling them in once and for all, would curtail taxpayers' expense. And bringing criminals to book, particularly rapists and sex offenders, had long been the first act in a populist politician's playbook.

Going into 1997, Sheets for some years had fanned public fears of the constant danger the quarries posed. Even though he probably frequented them in his youth while attending Quincy's Eastern Nazarene College, a three-mile bicycle ride away, Sheets gave the quarries their enduring epithet of "death holes" and he cast quarry

---

18. "Powerhouse politician," *QPL*, 27 May 2010, p. 6.

jumpers as troublesome, immature "Tom Sawyers."[19] "'Despite the enormous expense and environmental concerns,'" Sheets insisted to reporters that he "'wanted every quarry drained and filled.'" Quincy's politicians closed ranks behind their mayor. "'We're always in a reactive position,'" regretted City Councilor Michael D'Amico. "'We need to secure these quarries once and for all.'" Playing on parents' heartstrings, D'Amico asked, "How many more kids do we want to lose up there?" Blame and guilt was the burden of responsibility he laid on Quincy's electorate: "'If we don't address this, we know what's going to happen.'" In response to an ongoing campaign by the Friends of the Blue Hills (FBH) to maintain and better manage the quarries as a recreational facility and nature reserve, Sheets retorted that, "'there's nothing natural about preserving a hole full of water, debris, cars, bodies and everything else.'" With each new body that police pulled out of the quarries, lobbying to save the quarries by the FBH's white-haired director David P. Hodgdon, even without the shrillness and desperation it assumed by 1999, had no answer to such devastating rhetoric from a powerhouse politician like Sheets. Hodgdon, anyway, had compromised the effectiveness of his campaign by advocating a managed solution for the quarries; any management by the MDC or the City of Quincy would have left these entities responsible and open to litigation. All that was workable at the quarries was the same treatment employed by the National Park Service at the Grand Canyon, where there have never been fences or handrails and anyone approaching the edge does so at their own risk.[20]

After Locke called off the divers in December 1997, Cellucci capitalized on the climate of fear and frustration to step up his own lobbying campaign, both in the mass media and state legislature. A sincere administrator rather than a self-aggrandizer, Cellucci needed encouragement in his drive to drain and fill the quarries, but that was coming in spades from his staff, politicians such as Representative Martin J. Walsh (D-Dorchester) as well as Locke and Sheets, and particularly Charlie Hammond who had become fixated on the hope that his daughter's body was in Granite Rail. Even though investigators had begun speculating that the body—the one divers claimed to have seen—was a different murder victim, Hammond left his job as a truck driver to spend all his time on promoting the search.[21]

Patrick McDonagh, P.J.'s father, had demonstrated throughout 1996–97 how to mobilize political support for and media interest in expensive, high-profile draining, searching, and recovery operations at the quarries. Then-governor Weld had won election in 1990 on a mandate to slash runaway public spending; he had trimmed 15,000 employees from the state's payroll but the escalating price of the Big Dig threatened his record, so he was reluctant to tap a $1 million appropriation for draining Granite Rail. At that time, moreover, Big Dig officials had not yet set their sights on the quarries as the perfect dump for their slurry and excavated fill. McDonagh recruited eager

19. James Sullivan, "Jumping from Heaven," *Yankee Magazine* (July 1996), p. 36; an ironic concurrence is the title of Mark Twain's unfinished novel, *Tom Sawyer's Conspiracy*.

20. *Boston Globe*, 1 August 1998, p. 1.

21. *Boston Globe*, 12 December 1997, p. B5; Walsh to Weld, 22 July 1997, GPGO, b. 20, f. Quincy Quarry.

Democrat opponents, such as James T. Brett who argued in a letter to Weld that the "[historic] restoration" of Granite Rail by draining and filling it would not merely bring peace of mind to the McDonagh family but also "ensure public safety and provide environmental protection," while further procrastination would only lead to "a higher human and financial cost to the taxpayers of the Commonwealth." Weld needed to keep in Brett's good graces for he was chairman of the Committee on Taxation, so Weld promised McDonagh that draining would begin, and, despite more foot-dragging, divers did bring closure by recovering the body. On assuming the governorship, Cellucci continued Weld's tactics, but by 1998 stalling was no longer an option.[22]

fig. 77: *Governor Argeo Paul Cellucci*, oil portrait by Ronald Sherr, 2002

Documenting Cellucci's involvement with filling the quarries is necessarily a matter of inference—state archivist John Hannigan was "surprised" by the lack of records in the governor's files relating to the Big Dig and Quincy quarries, probably "due to the ongoing legal struggles over the results of the project"—with extant memoranda stating only that aides were planning breakfasts, press conferences, visits, and meetings. For a meeting on 3 February 1998, Deputy Chief of Staff Russell D. Aims warned Cellucci that Hammond would ask, "'If it was [your] daughter in there, how long do you think it would take to drain the quarry?'" Aims joked that Hammond was "ready to start bailing out the quarry with buckets." Hammond's desperate pleading evidently worked because later that day Cellucci announced a two-phase plan, funded by the state, with "'Phase 1'" being "'a partial drain'" of Granite Rail, and "'Phase 2'" being "'What can we do for a permanent solution?'" Both phases, Cellucci intimated, would be expensive, but "'for there to be no more tragedies, it will take more than the $1 million'" that the legislature budgeted in 1996 after the disappear-

22. Brett to Weld, 24 May 1996, GPGO, b. 20, f. Quincy Quarry.

ance of McDonagh. A few days later, Cellucci's press secretary José M. Juves and Locke began organizing a breakfast ceremony in the Great Hall of the State House, ostensibly to honor the divers, police, MDC officials, and Quincy public safety personnel who had assisted in the McDonagh recovery but essentially as a publicity vehicle for Cellucci's and Locke's political campaigning while simultaneously raising the profile of the drive to drain and fill the quarries.[23]

On into 1999, MDC and Cellucci administration staff kept the draining and body-recovery efforts at Granite Rail Quarry in the newspapers and on television screens, nagging at the public's need for closure. Legal maneuvers by the Appalachian Mountain Club and the FBH to maintain the quarry in its historic form served only to fuel mass-media interest. When a group of rock climbers and FBH members visited the site on 3 August 1998, Cellucci's senior staff noted with evident satisfaction that, "the media was out in full force as were DA Locke and the family of Karen Hammond." Keeping the spotlight on Granite Rail was also distracting attention from work that was already underway to destroy Swingle's and other quarries at West Quincy.[24]

Hazardous Waste Conspiracy Theory

A Massachusetts state Department of Environmental Protection (DEP) ruling over slurry produced by Boston's Big Dig, along with a speculative property development deal signed by Sheets, was the third factor that determined efforts by Cellucci and Sheets to channel a public need for closure into the destruction of the Quincy quarries. Once Congress had overridden President Ronald Reagan's veto for federal funding for the Big Dig, peripheral work began in 1991 for what would be the biggest public works project in U.S. history. To transfer the Central Artery (I-93), a six-lane highway built in 1959 atop green iron girders, to tunnels under downtown Boston—the crux of the project—would necessitate the removal of fourteen million cubic yards of dirt, the pouring of 3.8 million cubic yards of concrete, and the threading of the tunnels through a maze of building foundations, subway lines, and utilities. It would take nine years longer than engineers initially projected, and cost $14.6 billion instead of $2.8 billion, giving new meaning to the phrase *state budget*.[25]

Invasive work downtown began in earnest after the state transferred the Big Dig's oversight to the newly created Massachusetts Turnpike Authority (MTA) in 1997, most noticeably in the construction of the Zakim Bridge and the digging of five miles of slurry walls. Because the road tunnels would pass through the landfill on which much of the city's harbor-line buildings sat, engineers opted for slurry-wall construction,

---

23. Hannigan to author, 17 July 2008; Aims to Weld, 2 February 1998, GPGO, b. 20, f. Quincy Quarry; *Boston Globe*, 4 February 1998, p. B3; Juves to Catherine McDonald, 10 February 1998, GPGO, b. 19, f. Quincy Quarry, EOPS.

24. Melanie Murray-Brown to Aims, including "suggested talking points" for Cellucci's press conferences, 4 August 1998, GPGO, b. 20, f. Quincy Quarry; "Quincy Quarries, 8/10/99, 6/8/00," VCR, GPGO, b. 164.

25. Adjusting for inflation improves the initial budget to $8.8 billion, but that is over the extra nine years. According to a detailed survey by the *Boston Globe*, 17 July 2008, p. A1, after adding interest payments the true cost was $22 billion; Massachusetts taxpayers and drivers shouldered 73 percent of the costs, incurring a debt that they will not pay off until 2038. Calculations for dirt, slurry, and other statistics based on "Big Dig Materials Handling and Disposal Data," spreadsheet, compiled by author (available on request), primarily from official and newspaper reports.

both to create tunnel walls and to buttress the elevated highway and other structures during excavation.

To form a slurry wall, a hydromill crane lowers a powered milling unit into the ground, cutting a trench about a meter wide. As cutting progresses, the hydromill extracts dirt and ground-up rock and replaces that excavated material with a dense slurry of bentonite clay and water, which ensures that the trench walls cannot collapse. Associated pumps and pipes pass the extracted material through a sophisticated mud treatment plant, consisting of scalper screens, hydrocyclones, and dewatering tanks, which separates rock and dirt from slurry, the former being trucked away and the latter returned to the system, although there is inevitably a degree of comingling, with bentonite trucked out with the dirt and clays and other impurities returned to the trench with the slurry. Modern hydromills can cut trenches to a depth of sixty meters. When the trench is finished, engineers lower in rebar reinforcement cages, then pump in concrete while pumping out the slurry; being twice as dense as the slurry, the concrete settles at the bottom of the trench, displacing the slurry above it. Once the concrete has cured through hydration, the new walls safeguard the integrity of tunneling work, which typically involves the simultaneous suspension from the walls of horizontal cast-concrete roofs, thereby constructing an underground box.[26]

Engineers and their state overseers must always have appreciated that there would be details of the highly complex and innovative Big Dig project that they would have to resolve as the work progressed, not least being what to do—exactly—with the fourteen million cubic yards of excavated material. Initial talk was of capping and beautifying Spectacle Island, a garbage dump in Boston's outer harbor, and this indeed occurred, but the logistics of transshipping the dirt by barge, the necessity for defense against storm erosion, and the island's small, eighty-acre size proved a costly undertaking to dispose of a million-odd cubic yards. Aside from Spectacle Island, some thirteen million cubic yards of dirt—primarily gray, sticky clay plus three centuries of accumulated fill debris such as oyster shells, rotting timber piles, and industrial wastes—sat in limbo. It is also unclear from accessible records where used slurry figured in the planning process. Because bentonite has value as a bagged, powdered material, the presumption was likely that the Big Dig's primary contractor, Modern Continental Construction, would recycle it, either for later use or for sale to other contractors nationwide. But once the project was underway and federal and state funds were flowing, a sort of feeding frenzy mentality set in, which left many details lost in the rush to bank profits, hire more workers, and complete icons to which politicians could attach their names. Whatever the plan for the slurry, recycling was no longer an option once DEP chemists had tested it and found that, in addition to traces of toxic heavy metal ions picked up by the absorbent bentonite from Boston's landfill, the slurry had an alkaline pH that exceeded 12.5, which alone was sufficient to classify

26. *Hydromill Method: Technology Information* (Cesena, Italy: Solimec Drilling and Foundation Equipment, 2010); calculations here, in pounds per cubic yard, assume concrete at 3,280, bentonite slurry at 1,726, and excavated dirt at 2,050.

it as a corrosive, hazardous waste. Not that this should have been a surprise to the planners and engineers because bentonite slurry, which itself has a pH of 9.1, is highly absorptive, and, as it cycled from trench to trench, was in frequent contact with liquid concrete, whose active ingredient, Portland cement, has a pH of 12.5–13.5.[27]

Once the legal designation of a commercial material shifts from being a lubricating oil, an antifreeze, a tire, or a bentonite slurry to a hazardous waste, a slew of regulations kick in, contravention of any of which, knowingly or from ignorance, and on a cradle-to-grave basis, results in draconian penalties. Handling, transportation, processing where necessary, and disposal of hazardous waste requires specialist contractors, purpose-built vehicles, expensive equipment, and lots of certification and regulatory filing. Whereas a trucking company might quote 23 cents per ton-mile to move loads of dirt across town, or about $180 to deliver a thirty-ton load from Boston to Quincy, a hazardous waste contractor would charge five or six times that amount. With the DEP ruling in place, not only had MTA planners and officials to find a home for all the excavated dirt but, with the slurry walls completed, they were now also saddled with disposing of 541,660 tons of sloppy, corrosive, hazardous waste. To a haulage contractor, that was eighteen thousand truckloads, worth some $16 million in transportation costs alone. Extra bills to dispose of hazardous slurry were just one slice of the Big Dig's mushrooming budget.[28]

It has proven beyond this study's means to document exactly when and under what circumstances the DEP made its ruling, or, for that matter, to document much of the hazardous waste and quarry filling story; crucial swathes of paperwork were off limits for many years due to pending litigation, at other times became lost in rooms full of unsorted boxes, and, in at least one case, a public official destroyed the documentary record. Yet that is perhaps as it should be, because the suggestion here is that there was a conspiracy, and proving otherwise would undermine Americans' ideological fascination with conspiracy theories. Still, circumstantial evidence, mostly from newspaper reports, can patch together an adequate picture. At 11:45 PM on 5 March 1998, when traffic was thankfully light, a ten-wheel dump truck operated by ODF Contracting of Dorchester was carrying slurry to Quincy when its tailgate gave way, spilling thirty tons of goo and closing three southbound lanes of the Southeast Expressway. There was no mention in the report that the slurry was a hazardous waste or that there was anything special about the truck. On 15 October 1999, another dump truck hauling slurry to Quincy on the Southeast Expressway swerved to avoid a disabled vehicle, slopping goo into the two fast lanes and causing a nine-car chain reaction that hospitalized three motorists and closed the highway for two hours during morning rush hour. Terry Brown, a Big Dig spokesman, said that the dump truck was one of fifteen, "specially modified" for the job, and that the slurry "cannot be recycled," meaning that the DEP had ruled it was hazardous. "'We thought it was OK," he

27. Chapman, "Big Dig Materials Handling and Disposal Data." In chemistry, pH is the indicator of a solution's acidity or alkalinity, with a value of 7.0 being neutral; a solution's maximum alkalinity, or concentration of hydroxyl ions, is 14.0.

28. Ibid.; total weight of slurry, from DEP Associate Commissioner Beth Nicholas, QPL, 7 June 2000, p. 1.

said offhand, making no mention of the slurry's legally hazardous nature. "'We will check it out again.'" Brown, who was apparently unaware of the major spill in 1998, mentioned that they had been trucking the slurry "'without problems for some months,'" so presumably the ruling came in the summer of 1999.[29]

At the receiving end, off Ricciuti Drive in West Quincy, other teams of contractors were pumping water out of Swingle's Quarry, enclosed, along with Granite Rail since early 1998, by barbed wire fences and security patrols, and pumping in the slurry. With announcements of cost overruns at the Big Dig coming faster than taxpayers' salary checks, with dump trucks slopping slurry onto highways, and with political rivals gearing up for a new round of elections, officials found themselves on the defensive. At a neighborhood meeting in Quincy in June 2000, Beth Nicholas, a DEP associate commissioner, likened the slurry to plain old cement used in driveways, which in its wet state was "[actually] 'highly corrosive.'" So, she implied, the DEP's ruling was more of a technicality than an environmental issue. Because the slurry had a pH in excess of 12.5 the DEP had to classify it as "'a corrosive hazardous waste,'" but "'once it sets, however, the fill is safe to the touch.'" Defending his city council's decision to fill Swingle's with Big Dig slurry, Quincy Public Works Commissioner David Colton dismissed recent newspaper allegations as "'exaggerations.'" Reports that "'we've created a hazardous waste dump in West Quincy couldn't be further from the truth,'" he insisted, and he passed around a lump of what he said was hardened slurry to prove its harmlessness.[30]

These official responses raise two questions that meeting participants did not ask. First, if the slurry was just like cement—and just as harmless, or at least no more harmful—then why did the DEP have to classify it as hazardous in the first place? Surely, if they had simply treated it as they did cement then they would not only have saved taxpayers millions of dollars in hazardous waste transportation, handling, and disposal fees, along with all the associated regulatory filings, but they would also have helped the environment by the energy saved through recycling half a million tons of bentonite. Calcium bentonite is intrinsically safe, with medicinal uses as a laxative and in skin creams. In granular form, it is commonplace in homes as cat litter and in workshops as oil dry. Had the DEP's officials been less doctrinaire, they could have made the distinction between a particular material being hazardous in one situation yet harmless in another. To the extent that highly alkaline cement—or lime, or bentonite—is hazardous to humans, it is when it makes prolonged contact with skin. Long before there is any painful skin perforation, someone working with cement typically notices a soapiness to the touch and washes it off, thereafter avoiding excessive contact or wearing gloves. Yet because of its very alkalinity, there are natural medicine practitioners who recommend drinking bentonite on a daily basis to ward off cancer, which they believe can only grow in acidic conditions.[31]

29. *QPL*, 6 March 1998, p. 9; *Boston Globe*, 16 October 1999, p. B7.
30. *QPL*, 7 June 2000, pp. 1–2.
31. See, for instance, Raymond Dextreit, *Earth Cures: A Handbook of Natural Medicine for Today* (New York:

Second, if the slurry hardened up, just like cement, then why did it not solidify when it was sitting for weeks in the bottom of slurry-wall trenches? Because of its unique hydraulic properties, once cement is wetted and mixed, it sets rock hard within a few hours, through a chemical reaction that occurs even under water. Conversely, bentonite's unique colloidal properties allow it to maintain state as a slurry, without sedimentation, for long periods; it only becomes solid when it dries out. Using Big Dig bentonite slurry to fill a quarry—a sump for groundwater, and half of which in the case of Swingle's was below sea level—suggested that when topped off with three hundred feet of dirt the underlying slurry might never dry, retaining its sloppy and alkaline state. Following the DEP's logic that it was the alkalinity that made the slurry hazardous, DEP officials surely appreciated the potential for environmental damage by dumping the slurry into Swingle's. NetRegs, the British government's Environmental Agency website, states that, "bentonite can be highly polluting to water," so contractors must "ensure that it is contained within your working area and does not enter any watercourses," adding that laboratory testing for hydrocarbons is essential before slurry disposal in a landfill. Like a giant syringe, tipping 250 feet of dirt onto 160 feet of wet slurry would generate a pressure at the bottom of Swingle's of 210 pounds per square inch (psi). With three-quarters of the dirt sitting above the water table, it was probable that watery alkaline slurry, bearing whatever heavy metals, hydrocarbons, and other toxins it had accumulated from Boston landfill, would push out through fissures in the quarry's granite walls and contaminate the surrounding groundwater, thereby damaging the local wetlands ecosystem and harming the environment that was the DEP's responsibility to protect.[32]

On the grounds of its mission to protect the environment from damage, let alone of saving energy or protecting the public from unnecessary expense, it is hard to fathom the DEP's rationale. Expedient, political, and commercial justifications, though, along with conflicts of interest and collusion with other state and city officials, are easier to find. In 1997, knowing that Big Dig officials were desperate for convenient locations at which to dump excavated dirt, Quarry Hills Associates (QHA) signed a fifty-year lease on public land with Sheets. QHA's ambitious plan was to cover a 450-acre site, which included the quarries and three municipal landfills, along with outlying land similarly leased from the City of Milton, and build a 27-hole golf course, clubhouse, 400-seat function hall, and parcels of at least three hundred luxury condominiums. Thanks to QHA and Sheets, Big Dig planners now had a home for 88 percent of the dirt at a convenient site eleven miles down the expressway. Although the City of Quincy would benefit from real estate taxes paid by condominium owners, from a share in profits from greens fees and functions at the golf course, and from the inclusion in the plan of a soccer field and four Little League baseball diamonds, QHA was exempt from real estate taxes on the leased land. QHA's partners were Quincy property magnate William O'Connell and his brother Peter, retired landfill operator

Citadel, 2000).

32. http://www.environment-agency.gov.uk/netregs/businesses/construction/62317.aspx (accessed 10 May 2012).

Charles Geilich, and former Quincy mayor Walter Hannon Jr. and his son Walter Hannon III, suggestive of a sweetheart deal for political insiders.[33]

For lead developer William O'Connel, fifty-seven and already a multimillionaire, the QHA deal was not simply another lucrative business opportunity. He evidently dreamed of making the Granite Links Golf Course his retirement realm, legitimating his career while providing an impressive entertainment facility for associates, friends, family members, and mayors like Hannon and Sheets. His longtime friend Brian Leonard would become the general manager of Granite Links. It was therefore essential to tame the wilderness site, which above all meant expunging the death holes featured so prominently in the media—Granite Rail and Swingle's Quarries—both physically and psychologically. There had to be closure.

There had to be closure, not just of quarries that could swallow up bodies, but of an ungovernable region where adventurous individuals had made their own society, beyond the reach of law enforcers, beyond the pale of American civilization. In a seminal paper of 1893, historian Frederick Jackson Turner advanced his frontier thesis, which argued that the American love of liberty depended on the existence of the frontier, far distant in space and character as that was from the dissolute wiles of the Old World. With the frontier finally tamed, Turner believed that Americans would lose their dynamism, competitiveness, and democratic ideals. Quincy quarries' countercultural frontier society represented simultaneously everything that was invigorating, productive, and transformative about republican America and everything that was defiant, dangerous, and immoral. Closing the quarries—closing the frontier—would weaken the national spirit, but, for all the folks who felt comfortable with their version of the American Dream, it would also reduce their angst.[34]

Filling in the Granite Rail Quarry, owned by the MDC but now encompassed by the QHA lease, promised to be a practical if costly undertaking. An MDC budget in May 2000 allowed $134,000 for draining the quarry's remaining thirty feet of water, a trifling sum in light of the $12,535,700 total estimate for rehabilitation. But the massive and far deeper Swingle's, owned by the City of Quincy and similarly part of the QHA lease, presented a slew of engineering challenges. Indeed, after consulting with engineers, FBH director Hodgdon had voiced the belief in August 1998 that it was a "logistical impossibility" to fill Swingle's.[35]

Swingle's contained some 203 million gallons of water, to a depth of 260 feet, with the bottom being 430 feet below the ground-level rim. Tipping the 51,000 truckloads of Big Dig dirt into Swingle's necessary to fill it to within twenty feet of the rim meant draining the water first, otherwise the resulting mud would make subsequent pumping impossible.[36] When Swingle's was operational, pumps to remove rain

33. *QPL*, 28 September 2001, p. 1; *QPL*, 19 December 2002, p. 2.

34. Frederick Jackson Turner, lecture to the American Historical Association in 1893, published as *The Significance of the Frontier in American History* (Madison: State Historical Society of Wisconsin, 1894).

35. "Granite Rail Material Disposal: Preliminary Cost Budget Estimate," posted on http://www.friendsofthebluehills.org/endpage/budget.htm (accessed 9 July 2008); *Boston Globe*, 1 August 1998, p. B1.

36. Before rehabilitation began, grout piles around the rim typically stood above the outlying grade, which shelved

and ground water sat on the quarry floor, pulling from a sump with a few yards of suction hose. Even then, with a relatively narrow four-inch discharge pipe, it was impractical to push a column of water weighing 2.3 tons at 206 pounds per square inch to the rim, so pumping was typically a multi-stage affair, initially into a storage tank on an intermediate ledge, and then by additional pumps and tanks to the top. With the quarry floor submerged, a sufficiently powerful centrifugal pump run by a diesel engine would have to sit on a barge, lowered to the water's surface by crane. At the outset of pumping, 170 feet down, a suitable 150-horsepower pump ought to achieve 800 gallons per minute without overload. With, say, six such pumps operating constantly, it would still take over thirty days to pump 203 million gallons. But with each foot the water level fell, the pumping rate would decrease, until the pumps were close to their maximum dynamic head of 450 feet, by which time the rate would be little better than 250 gallons per minute. Under ideal conditions, six pumps would take over three months to drain Swingle's, a calculation that presumes no more water would enter the quarry. In practice, it was likely to take twice that many pumps to keep pace, and a lot more time, which Big Dig planners did not have because as contractors completed the slurry walls there was an immediate requirement to dispose of the used slurry, the only storage space on site being dump trucks. There would be the problems of debris clogging the pumps' section heads, silt buildup nearer the bottom, and engineers predicted that with the water removed the sides of the quarry would become unstable and large sections might break away, taking workers on the top into the hole. Pumping so much water from such a depth, moreover, would be vastly expensive, costing upwards of $550,000 in diesel fuel alone.[37]

Hazardous waste slurry promised a win-win solution to the logistical impossibility of rehabilitating Swingle's Quarry. Pumping the 541,660 tons of Big Dig slurry into the bottom of the quarry would stem groundwater inflow, stabilize the quarry walls, and raise the water level by about 163 feet, thereby facilitating the pump-out operation. A treatment plant similar to those in use at the downtown worksites would clean the less dense water, returning any slurry that had mingled with it during the pumping process to the quarry. With the water gone, and after a few weeks of summer evaporation to harden the surface slurry, trucks could begin tipping dirt. There would be space for 955,000 cubic yards to bring the ground level to within twenty feet of the old quarry's perimeter, allowing for some attractive landscaping, a few safe outcrops for the climbers, and a wetlands pond in the middle for the nature lovers (figs. 78, 79). Instead of the hassle and cost of recycling far more used slurry than the U.S. construction market could absorb, Modern Continental could simply buy bags of fresh bentonite and sell them to the Big Dig. By burying the slurry hundreds of feet below ground—out of sight and out of mind—on land owned by the City of Quincy, and ruling it to be merely alkaline and therefore no more hazardous than concrete, the

off as a consequence; twenty feet allows for grout pushed into the quarry as well as for the maintenance of stable outcrops, such as around Granite Rail.

37. A typical pump, on which I have based these calculations, would be the HL5MS Dri-Prime centrifugal unit from Godwin Pumps, Bridgeport, NJ, as detailed in Godwin's specification sheet, GPASL.052.1005, 2005.

DEP absolved itself, the Big Dig, and contractor Modern Continental of liability over half a million tons of waste that may well have contained substantial quantities of hydrocarbons and other toxins. There would be lots of lucrative haulage and handling contracts to go around, portions of which might come back later as political campaign contributions. Sheets, Hannon, O'Connell, and friends would have their golf course. Affluent professionals could own condominiums with stunning city views, a tee shot away from a weekend's sport. Quincy parents would pay lower taxes due to income from the condominiums, and, on the new fields, their children would play baseball, a healthy, American game; no longer would parents live in fear of the adventures their children were having at the quarries. With the death hole filled, bringing closure at last, and the true costs lost in pages of line items and a spiraling overall budget, Massachusetts taxpayers would conclude that whatever the price of filling Swingle's it was money well spent.

There was an unfound body in Swingle's, that of Paul Gooch who had drowned after diving in 1983, but entombing it under the slurry did not impair any longing for closure on the part of his relatives. It had been Gooch's first time at the quarries and he was eager to test himself and prove his courage. After completing a jump from fifty feet into Swingle's, his friends spurred him into trying one from Rampa, a ledge adjacent to Heaven at seventy-two feet. In his inexperience, he entered the water leaning too far forward and never regained the surface. There had been serious—and expensive—efforts to recover the body, with underwater cameras and the pumping out of a hundred million gallons until the reduced water pressure triggered the fall of huge slabs into the quarry. After seventeen years, Gooch's father Paul L. seemed to have accommodated his grief, lavishing his love instead on daughter Kristen and her two grandchildren. But Gooch's mother, Patricia Bournival, could never forget him, never understand why he had jumped to his death, and perhaps blamed herself for the tragedy. With the approach of what would have been her son's thirtieth birthday, she visited his memorial plaque at the edge of Swingle's. His twentieth anniversary had been tough, she explained, "'the 25th not as bad, but the 30th really snapped me into something.'" She felt "'agitation. Discombobulation. Realizing Paul would have been 30, I kept wondering—would he have married his childhood sweetheart? Would he have had children? What would he have been like?'" According to James Sullivan, a former jumper himself who interviewed Bournival, she was at first angry with city policymakers for not closing the quarries, but then she had realized that "'my son was meant to die that day,'" and "'with that, you lose a lot of anger. You won't ever get over it, but you will learn to live with it.'" After watching the mostly Catholic jumpers bless themselves and then dive into Granite Rail, she said, "'I don't understand that. And the notion that someone who jumps can be a hero, I can't identify with that.'" Yet Bournival's was a personal grief. Her son died before *closure* hit newspaper and television reportage, when deaths at the quarries became the shared grief as well as the generational misunderstanding of a million parents.[38]

---

38. Sullivan, "Jumping From Heaven," pp. 36, 110.

fig. 78: top-roped climbers on the remnants of Granite Rail Quarry, 2011

In July 1999, contractors completed the draining of Granite Rail, which enabled Locke to solve the riddle of the woman's body that divers had failed to recover in 1997. There were no bodies in Granite Rail, but police did identify a clothing store mannequin. Waterlogged but still relatively light, it must have drifted away after the divers saw it, eerily white and death-like in the murky water, and marked its position. In addition to paying a testing fee of one dollar a ton on the 825,000 tons of dirt dumped into Granite Rail, another dollar a ton to the MDC, and $2,475,000 for trucking the dirt to West Quincy, Big Dig accountants paid QHA a tipping fee of $4,538,000. Exactly why Big Dig officials felt that the O'Connell, Hannon, and Geilich partners deserved the $4.5 million, or what they did with the money, does not appear to be a matter of public record, but it was presumably well worth it to be free of all that dirt and free of another death hole. QHA developers had little to do, it seems, to beautify the Granite Rail area of their lease, leaving them time to design the golf course, and build and market the condominiums. Big Dig officials spent an additional $134,000 to stabilize the remaining rocks so climbers would be safe, $20,000 on grading, loam, and grass seed, $80,000 on wetland restoration, $20,000 on historic resources preservation, and $300,000 on a hydrogeological study to make sure everything was just so. There were a few other line items in the $13.2 million budget, such as a $200,000 credit to QHA for "trucking delays." In exchange for taking the rest of the dirt, some eleven million tons, Big Dig officials paid $100 million to QHA in tipping fees, out of which QHA gave $2.8 million to the City of Quincy and $70.9 million to its general contractor McCourt Construction, owned by Richard McCourt of South Boston, leaving a balance of $26.3 million. This $100 million did not include the cost of 500,000 dump truck trips to Quincy. Presuming that McCourt included trees, shrubs, bags of grass seed, goal posts, and netting for the baseball diamonds in his $71 million dirt-spreading and landscaping contract, it is unclear how QHA's directors justified accepting—in good conscience—another twenty-six million dollars of public funds, especially as the deal provided them, free of charge, with 450 acres of prime real estate.[39]

Presumably, after budgeting a dollar a ton for laboratory testing, or some $13 million, the dirt spread to make recreation facilities, gardens, parks, and wetlands would not be hazardous to the environment, particularly when the overarching contractor was the state itself. And perhaps the dirt spread by McCourt for QHA was harmless stuff. Evidence from Melrose, where city officials similarly gave their enthusiastic imprimatur for the spreading of Big Dig dirt, suggests otherwise. On assurances by the DEP that it was safe, Melrose officials accepted 690,665 tons of dirt to improve the Mount Hood Memorial Park and Golf Course. *Accepted* is really the wrong word because the Melrose treasury expected to garner $490,000 in revenues. But as David Kassel, then at the Massachusetts Office of the Inspector General, noted online in 2008, "city officials failed to first do a project plan, design, or cost estimate," so, as truckloads of dirt kept coming, "wetlands in the park became flooded and sediment from the fill got into resource areas." This might not have been so bad, except that independent laboratory analysis showed that samples of the fill had detectable concentrations of Total Petroleum Hydrocarbons (TPH), one sample being as high as 189 milligrams per kilogram, or 189 ppm. Responding to the concerns of Nancy A. Naslas of the Melrose Conservation Commission in December 2000, Steven G. Lipman, Special Projects Coordinator at the DEP, made light of the TPH readings. Lipman pointed out that the other fourteen samples ranged from non-detects to 95 mg/kg, so the arithmetic average of all fifteen samples was 56 mg/kg, while under Section 310CMR 40.0900 of the stringent Massachusetts Contingency Plan, TPH levels would have to be over 200 mg/kg before the material was hazardous. He "did not believe," he assured Naslas, "that there are any health or environmental concerns from the intended use of the till material." Perhaps that was so, but, as Kassel reported, "trees and other vegetation in a number of areas [had] died or were stressed." In January 2002, John McElhenny of the Associated Press surveyed "the moonscape" where Big Dig dirt covered "what used to be a 5-acre woodland," to report that "instead of new playing fields, 15 months of dumping polluted two wetlands and two other low-lying areas, and made the 18-hole public course into a 17-hole affair." While the average TPH level of 56 mg/kg in the Melrose fill would seem insignificant at face value, the total tonnage tipped was 700,000, meaning that by Lipman's own admission the fill contained 39.2 tons of TPH hazardous waste, or more than would fit into an eighteen-wheel gasoline truck.[40]

39. Mannequin, *QPL*, 31 July 1999, p. 9; "Granite Rail Material Disposal"; given the cost overruns that plagued the Big Dig, I am presuming the finished work did not come in under budget.

40. Background information in *Review of the Mount Hood Public Works Project in Melrose* (Boston: Office of the Inspector General, October 2002), esp. pp. i, 79–81; Kassel, posted on the accountablestrategies.wordpress.com blog, 19 February 2008; Naslas to Lipman, 1 December 2000, and Lipman to Naslas, ca. 10 December 2000, courtesy Jason Turley (no longer on file at Melrose City Hall); McElhenny, cited in the online community newspaper *South Coast Today*, http://www.southcoasttoday.com/apps/pbcs.dll/article?AID=/20020105/NEWS/301059984 (accessed 13 July 2008).

Melrose Mayor Patrick Guerriero, who had resigned to become Acting Governor Jane M. Swift's deputy chief of staff and just announced that he would be her running mate in the gubernatorial election, explained how, "When you're mayor of a $40 million industry, you make good decisions some days, and you make conditionally bad ones." As a chief executive, there would always be things "you wish came out differently." Guerriero pleaded that he had not intentionally mismanaged the project. Still, its overseeing agent was Environmental Landscape Management (ELM), owned by his friend Steven Ziolkowski, and Guerriero had awarded work contracts to ELM, all without soliciting competing bids. Some Melrose residents, nonetheless, thought Guerriero did a fine job. In a September 2000 letter to the *Melrose Mirror* complimenting the city council, Len Dalton reckoned that the Big Dig had encouraged "righteous tree huggers to [come] out of the woodwork and [bark] about 'vernal pools' and clear cutting." Those pools "were little more than mosquito breeders and were well buried."[41]

fig. 79: Swingle's is now a nice place to walk the dog

A decade later, Boston's Central Artery tunnels had, as promised, shaved many minutes off suburbanites' morning commute. Climbers were once again enjoying top-roping at West Quincy on the safe, stabilized outcrops. Dogs were sniffing out new walks around the perimeter of Swingle's. Over at the impressively manicured Granite Links, where transplanted shrubs and trees along the fairways were in bud, Polo-shirted golfers were admiring each other's tee shots. Quarry Hills had a comfortable feel.

---

41. Guerriero, in ibid.; *Melrose Mirror*, 1 September 2000, http://melrosemirror.media.mit.edu/servlet/pluto?state=30303470616765303037576562506167653030326964303034343131032 (accessed 10 October 2008).

fig. 80: Granite Links club house, with a splendid view of downtown Boston

For the politicians, officials, developers, and contractors, life was not necessarily any better. Even after replacing MTA director and Big Dig project manager James J. Kerasiotes in 2000, Cellucci never lived down accusations that as chief executive the cost overruns, corruption, and quality control lapses were ultimately his responsibility. His subsequent ambassadorship at Ottawa was controversial, upsetting Canadians by trying to cajole them into increasing military spending. In a bruising campaign in 2001, Sheets lost the mayoralty of Quincy to his longtime Republican Party nemesis William J. Phelan, and Sheets, at the age of seventy-four, was still trying to make a comeback in 2010. An investigation conducted by the Massachusetts Office of the Inspector General concluded that before his term ended in January 2002, Sheets "removed and took possession of documents from the Mayor's Office," including files, particularly those on QHA, a chronicle of his meetings, and computer backup tapes, and he had instructed his staff to reformat computer drives. It is hard to see why Sheets would destroy the documentary record of his dealings with QHA and the filling of the quarries unless the importance of what he sought to hide was greater than the risk of prosecution for destroying public documents. In 2008, McCourt Construction and Richard McCourt's son Ryan pleaded guilty "to conspiracy to defraud the government," involving more than 1,500 cases of overbilling the Big Dig; sentencing in 2010 gave McCourt a $500,000 fine and Ryan McCourt two years' probation. Modern Continental filed for Chapter 11 bankruptcy on 23 June 2008, four years after its owner, Italian immigrant Les Marino, died amid multiple law suits and charges that his company's shoddy workmanship had caused slurry wall leaks and the detachment of a concrete ceiling panel that crushed a car and its driver. In September 2011, prosecutors arraigned William O'Connell, by then seventy-two, on charges of cocaine trafficking and four counts of statutory rape of a minor that began when she was fourteen. At least one of O'Connell's friendships seemed nonetheless to have endured. In February 2012, Norfolk County Superior Court Judge Kenneth J. Fishman allowed the paroled O'Connell to fly to Rome for a month's holiday, on the pretext that it would enable him "'to have a religious experience by having many private guided tours of the Vatican.'"[42]

Neither did the massive public-works project at West Quincy put an end to bodies in the quarries nor, for that matter, bodies anywhere else, because youths will always find a way to practice their skills, learn their limits, prove their mettle, kick back with some cold beers, and generally come of age, and if not at a relatively deserted quarry then on a public road behind the wheel of a car, where they are far more likely to add other bodies to their own. "Marine falls, dies in Quincy quarry," headlined the *Boston Globe*'s Metro section on 20 June 2009, as its editors remembered their readership's voyeuristic fascination with the quarry dramas of the 1990s. Patrick J. Coughlin, twenty-one and recently returned from a tour of duty in Iraq, was at home when three friends called from a bar to ask if he would join them for a 2 AM swim at Fuller's, an outlying quarry they had frequented as teenagers; it was a chilly, rainy night, making it an odd request. According to the *Globe* report, Coughlin and another friend were about to jump when Coughlin slipped, hitting his head on a rock before landing in fifteen feet of water, but the details, along with any attempt to understand young men's love of the quarries, were lost in a celebration of Coughlin's heroic service for his country in battle. Coughlin had earned an "Iraq Campaign Medal," reporter John R. Element noted, "the Global War on Terrorism Medal, the Sea Service Deployment Ribbon, the Armed Forces Reserve Medal, and the National Defense Service Medal." Leo Coppens said tearfully at the site that his nephew was "'one of the finest Americans,'" a Marine who "'loved his country.'" Fuller's lay inside the boundary of the Granite Links Golf Club, a "semipublic" course, as the *Globe* put it. Perhaps McCourt's bulldozers had run out of Big Dig dirt by the time they made it as far as Fuller's, or perhaps it had simply been out of sight and out of mind. At bottom, as safety officials and parents surely recognize, youths enjoy jumping into cool water on summer days. Happily, there will always be swimming holes and yet sadly this means there will inevitably be tragedies, ones that no amount of diligence can prevent. On Sunday morning, 1 July 2012, Lamar Thompson, fun-loving and eighteen, drowned while swimming to shore after a dive off a public pier near Quincy Yacht Club.[43]

Whether any of the politicians and public officials mentioned here failed to address conflicts of interest with contractors and developers, engaged in collusion,

42. *The City of Quincy: Investigation into the Removal of Records and Erasure of Computer Files from the Former Mayor's Office* (Boston: Massachusetts Office of the Inspector General, June 2003), p. i; McCourt, *Boston Globe*, 1 March 2008, p. B4; *QPL*, 16 February 2012, p. 1.

43. Background from Annemarie Stanton, Coughlin's former teacher; *Boston Globe*, 20 June 2009, p. B1; *Globe*, 2 July 2012, B3.

feathered their own nests, or wasted public funds is not the issue. It may well be that they did all they could under difficult circumstances, and that the end result was the best outcome for taxpayers and constituents. For their beneficiaries and patrons, for those who now enjoy Boston's waterfront unencumbered by what four-term mayor Thomas M. Menino once dubbed the "other Green Monster," and for those among them who accept as truisms that power inevitably corrupts and human nature is what it is, they are American heroes. That heroism stems, in part, from the delicious notion that somewhere in the bowels of the Big Dig there might have been the odd conspiracy, and that is the issue here. Since 2001 when I began mentioning elements of the hazardous waste conspiracy story—on a plane, at a historians' conference, in a barber's chair, over a barroom beer—the excited responses have amazed me. Random strangers have struck up two-hour conversations, stayed in email contact, and forwarded packets of city council documents. A good conspiracy, they imply, is marvelously American. Instead of consternation, they exhibit pride, as if the process of theorizing about a conspiracy confirms the health of the Founding Fathers' republican system, whereby it is still sufficiently open to keep public officials on their toes but secret enough to stop everyone from going to jail.[44]

Townies, Provos, and the Code of Silence

To the extent that class or job description was a denominator, quarry counterculture, like Quincy itself, was traditionally blue collar. Since the 1960s, particularly during the oil shocks and stagflation of the 1970s, and through into the 1990s, Quincy was a troubled city in decline. Its population fell by 3.7 percent in the 1970s and was virtually the same in 1990 as it had been in 1960, while its poverty and unemployment rates were high for a city in eastern Massachusetts. *Quincy Tomorrow*, a presentation of the Planning Board's best hopes for 1966 and beyond, put a brave face on the painful shift from heavy industry and manufacturing to the service sector, hinting merely in the preface that "if there is something 'wrong,' with a city physically or otherwise, [then . . .]," and "where a community problem exists, a response is called for." Health care, financial services, and insurance companies breathed new life, as did the spending power of commuters to Boston, eleven miles up the expressway. Aside from the connection between the Bunker Hill Monument and the quarries that supplied its granite, Charlestown in its transition from blue collar to young professional culture— that of the Yuppie in 1980s' parlance—had much in common with Quincy, although the stresses there at times verged on pitched battle. Both communities were predominantly Catholic and second- or third-generation immigrant, in the case of Charlestown from Ireland. Both had War of Independence-era history and National Park Service sites popular with tourists, the Adams National Historic Park in the case of Quincy, which preserves the homes of John Adams and John Quincy Adams. Both had newspapers with *Patriot* in their titles. Despite but no doubt because of their immigrant roots, citizens of both communities had a strong sense of national as well as local

44. *Boston Globe*, 14 November 2002, p. 5, and "second green monster," 21 December 2003, p. B7.

identity. And both were insular, in part from their geography, but in Charlestown's case from a distrust of outsiders that bordered on loathing.[45]

Charlestown in the mid-1980s was a rough and tumble neighborhood of tired clapboard rowhouses, smoky saloons, and public housing projects. Along the broad southeast flank of Charlestown's triangular configuration and cutting it off from the Navy Yard waterfront and the USS *Constitution* tourist area, a rusting elevated highway rumbled over what was formerly the elegant City Square on its way to the Maurice J. Tobin Memorial Bridge, towering 250-feet over the Mystic River. Starting underneath the bridge, sandwiched between Medford Street and Bunker Hill Street and extending along a third of the triangle's northeast flank, moldered forty blocks of low-income and special needs housing, the Bunker Hill Street housing project. Completing the northwest flank, a forlorn tract of derelict warehouses lined the Mystic River, up to the narrow neck with Somerville, itself isolated from Charlestown proper by the Sullivan Square bus and subway stations. Down the southwest flank, ran a mess of elevated highways, train tracks, parking lots, the Bunker Hill Community College, and the mounds, chutes, and mixers of Boston Sand & Gravel Company. Running south from Main Street to City Square, the nearest, and maybe safest, accessible point to downtown Boston over the Charlestown Bridge, there were growing pockets of gentrification, as there were too around Monument Square. Fifteen years had passed since the war between Somerville's Winter Hill Gang and George Patrick McLaughlin's Charlestown gang claimed sixty lives, but there was still plenty of color, sometimes red and on the streets.

On 22 February 1984, ten months after police shot dead her brother who was robbing a subway station collector's booth, a man killed Judith Ann Lawrence, twenty-five and a mother of two, in her apartment at the Bunker Hill projects. "'There's too much guns and drugs,'" said Lawrence's sixteen-year-old stepbrother, a Charlestown High School sophomore, who blamed the neighborhood for the deaths. "'You see drugs everywhere.'" In October 1984, police arrested Arthur L. "Butchie" Doe Jr., twenty-six, outside the Cobblestone Restaurant on Medford Street, where he and another man were intending to murder Jeffrey Crowley, the survivor of a previous murder attempt in 1983, with the gun that Doe was carrying. At the projects in March 1985, Michael J. Burns, nineteen, his face covered with a ski mask, confronted Joel Durham, twenty-five, firing five bullets into his chest. After a vicious brawl with two men at the Celtic Tavern on Friday, 18 October 1985, Robert "Booboo" Barrett, a twenty-five-year-old beer deliveryman, left with a piece of someone's earlobe in his mouth. A woman in the bar had apparently blamed Barrett for shooting her brother the year before, which started the fight. When Barrett called his mother, she told him, "'Bobby, be careful, they're going to kill you.'" Responding to a call at 2:20 AM on Monday morning, police found Barrett on the sidewalk outside the Celtic with two gunshots to the abdomen and one to the head. Cars were speeding off, one of which the police stopped and arrested an occupant for possession of cocaine. Police believed

---

45. James E. Lee, *Quincy Tomorrow* (Quincy: Planning Board of Quincy, Massachusetts, 1965), p. 1.

that Barrett's killer shot him in the bar then dragged the body outside. Barrett's family maintained that there were thirty people in the bar at the time of the shooting, or at least "'several,'" according to the police. None of these witnesses would say anything. "'Maybe they won't sleep for the rest of their lives. Maybe it will happen to one of theirs, because it will,'" said Barrett's sister Lori. "'The killing won't stop in Charlestown because no one ever sees anything.'" On November 1986 at 2:30 AM in what police suspected was a drug deal gone awry, Dennis J. Quirk, seventeen, and Joseph A. DeAngelo, eighteen, shot into the car of Arthur Godfrey, twenty-nine, and his eighteen-year-old girlfriend Jennifer Peckham. They both survived this assault, but Quirk and DeAngelo chased the fleeing Godfrey, felling him on Main Street. In three of these five murders and attempted murders over thirty-three months within Charlestown's 1.3 square miles, police charged a suspect. In the other two, and in a dozen other shooting incidents in which no one died, they made no arrests, in large measure because of Charlestown's fabled code of silence.[46]

Charlestown's bars were colorful places in the mid-1980s, with their green plastic shamrocks, red Leatherette stools, and customers sporting yellow and black Bruins hockey jerseys, if not through skin tone, which was uniformly white. From October 1985, when I moved to Charlestown's Navy Yard, to December, I checked out all of them, from the pretentious Warren Tavern to the anonymous Sully's overlooking the Rutherford Ave. highway, where the sign had fallen down years before but no one had bothered to hang it back up. In a few, I would assume an Irish accent and play drunk, so I got by and even traded rounds of drinks. One morning, police "do not cross" tape adorned Macovoy's bar across the street from the Big Potato where I had been drinking the night before, but with the lapse of almost thirty years and the bar demolished during the Big Dig, I have not been able to reconstruct the shooting there, although no one died. Still, having seen fights in London's pubs, Charlestown's seemed civilized enough to me. Petty crime, though, was rampant, particularly directed against the property of Yuppie newcomers. Yuppies would come home to a busted door lock; they would go to their car in the morning to find it sitting on bricks instead of wheels, or, worse, not there. Broken glass from vehicles' side windows glistened in the gutters like freshly fallen snow. I only made the mistake once of parking my VW Golf in Charlestown; when I returned an hour later, its passenger window was more snow and a hole in the dash replaced the Blaupunkt stereo. Townies who would never harm a vehicle they dreamed of one day owning, like a shiny red Ferrari or Corvette, scratched their keys down the sides of many a 3-Series BMW.

Toward the Sullivan Square end of Medford Street, near the deserted Schrafft's candy factory, the Cobblestone Restaurant fronted as a fundraising and support center for Provisional IRA activists, or Provos. British security forces, along with the U.S. federal government, called the Provos terrorists. Boston's Irish saw them as heroic freedom fighters. By 1984, Patrick Nee, a Gaelic-speaking immigrant and an associate of

46. Lawrence, 23 February 1984, p. 1; Doe, 8 October 1985, p. 28; Durham, 9 March 1985, p. 23; Barrett, 22 October 1985, p. 20; Godfrey, 23 November 1986, p. 34, all *Boston Globe*.

James J. "Whitey" Bulger and his Somerville-based Winter Hill gang, had raised sufficient funds to load seven tons of AK-47 assault rifles (about 1,500 plus ammunition) onto a Gloucester, Massachusetts, fishing trawler, the *Valhalla*, in Boston Harbor. But an informant in the IRA tipped off British police who intercepted the cargo; at the Boston end, Bulger tortured and killed a second informant. In 1990, police arrested Nee during an armored truck robbery in Abington, Massachusetts, after which he served ten years of a thirty-seven year sentence, and he wrote a memoir that in part inspired a series of films about Charlestown's version of the counterculture.[47]

fig. 81: "IRA Provos" across the Monument's southeast face, in 2008 before further sandblasting

Plumb in the center of all this unlawful activity, all this unfolding history, was the Bunker Hill Monument, not so much casting its shadow as defining the identity and legitimating the mores of the gang members and drug dealers, car thieves and bank robbers, plasterers and plumbers, barbers and bartenders, Townies and Provos who lived, worked, and operated around Monument Square. Heroes to themselves but villains to outsiders, victimized by a culture that celebrated poverty, drugs, heavy drinking, and crime, trying to escape but trapped by that powerful thing called home, and resentful of the successful professionals who moved into renovated condominiums with designer kitchens and whirlpool baths, the Irish-Americans of Charlestown took the Monument as their own. In the right light, despite repeated efforts by crews with sandblasters, the slogans "Brits Out" and "IRA Provos" in four-foot spray paint are still visible across the northwest and southeast faces of the Monument's lower two courses, marking perhaps the only occasion that a group has physically possessed the Monument since Boston's elite Freemasons laid their silver plaque under its cornerstone. Surely, the graffiti artist seemed to be saying, the Monument marked the spot where the

47. Patrick Nee, *A Criminal and an Irishman: The Inside Story of the Boston Mob–IRA Connection* (Hanover, NH: Steerforth Press, 2006), pp. 152–53, 157–58, 161, 169–70.

heroes of 1775 fell and where the heroic Irish-American counterparts of those fighting in the 1968–98 Troubles in Northern Ireland stood. Like them, it stood for gritty determination, for resistance, for mortal struggle against tyranny, particularly against the hated British. Claiming it for the Provos was a reaffirmation of that long, historic struggle. Now it would celebrate the spot at the Long Kesh prison outside Belfast where in 1981 Bobby Sands, IRA freedom fighter and Member of Parliament for Fermanagh and South Tyrone, died on hunger strike.

By the late-1990s, something of a ceasefire prevailed in Charlestown. Higher rents had squeezed out poorer Townies, while others who owned property had sold out. Newcomers had learned from experience to swap their German sedans for used American trucks with *C-Town Hockey* or *Teamsters Local 25* bumper stickers. In the condo-ed brownstones around Monument Square and the new brick townhouses at the Boston end of Main Street, upcoming Irish-American professionals were enjoying barbecues with the upcoming Yankee-American professionals from next door. Over in the projects and finding themselves in the minority, Townies were coming to workable arrangements with their neighbors from Haiti and the Dominican Republic. Living standards were rising and gang members were dead or in jail. Police detectives, moreover, began to hear voices in Charlestown's code of silence.

In 1998, Jill Medvedow, director of Boston's Institute of Contemporary Art (ICA), with encouragement from National Park Service historian Marty Blatt, commissioned a nineteen-minute video by Krzysztof Wodiczko for projection onto the Monument. As an artist born into suffering during the Warsaw ghetto uprising of 1943, Wodiczko had no hesitation in selecting the code of silence for his theme and the victims' mothers for his actors. For three September evenings from 8:00–10:00 PM, mothers tens of feet high clutching candles or photographs of their dead sons animated the blank granite while loudspeakers narrated their grief. Wodiczko's *Let Freedom Ring*, the *Boston Globe*'s Judy Rakowsky reported, put the mothers' faces "on one of the most aggressively masculine pieces of sculpture in Boston," Charlestown's "phallic obelisk." A young man who had lost three brothers to gunshots admitted in the narration that, "we know a lot more in the streets than we tell the outside world—or the police." One of the mothers of a son whose murderer the police had never apprehended stressed that, "if you want something, you have to work for it, and that includes justice."[48]

Coming in a recession year that threatened to set back Charlestown's recent gains, *Let Freedom Ring* opened up old wounds, and it also smacked of a conspiracy. It upset many Townies—male Townies—who took it to be an assault on their character as well as an attack on the Monument. Part way through the first showing, James Conway, owner of the *Patriot-Bridge* newspaper and Charlestown's unofficial mayor, berated a shocked Medvedow for unfairly sullying Charlestown's image. Conway's angry outburst may have highlighted for the equally shocked visitors to the projection the gendered sore still festering behind the code of silence debate. Real estate broker William

48. Krzysztof Wadiczko, *Let Freedom Ring*, video projection, 19 min., Institute of Contemporary Arts, Boston, 24–26 September 1998; *Boston Globe*, 25 September 1998, p. D1.

Gavin—a man—dismissed Charlestown's criminal image, telling Rakowsky, "'I was born on Monument Ave. and I never saw any crime committed,'" as if his inability to witness a murder proved that there had been none. Cofounder of Charlestown After Murder, Sandy King—a woman—disagreed with the complaints by Conway and Gavin that the projection presented an overly negative view of Charlestown. "'Too bad,'" she said. "'Murder is negative.'" Rakowsky asked a youth, Anthony Sorrentino, sixteen, why he was shaking his head and walking away. "'I've had so many people in my life die,'" he replied, "'I don't want to watch it.'" In part, Townies like Conway were incensed because the projection took on the form of a conspiracy between the National Park Service, a foreign artist, and a Brahmin–Yuppie cabal at the ICA to wrest the Monument from their control, to possess it, even to emasculate it with wailing mothers. Unlike the "Brits out, IRA Provos" graffiti, Wodiczko's projection left no physical mark, yet so vivid were the images and so poignant the memories that the attack may have seemed more invasive. It was as if there had been a second Battle of Bunker Hill. Working-class Townie rebels were defending the Monument in the name of American liberty against a police action by the wealthy Brahmins who patronized the ICA. It was an action by aristocratic descendants of the Yankee elites like Joseph Warren and John Hancock who, in June 1775, so brilliantly deflected a pending revolution by discontented, underemployed journeyman and apprentices against their growing power into a counterrevolution to throw out the British officials, usurp their authority, and assume full power and control.[49]

Unbeknownst to Medvedow or Blatt when they picked a weekend for *Let Freedom Ring*, a feature film about Charlestown's killings, directed by Ted Demme and starring Denis Leary, premiered at the Boston Film Festival on 25 September, the second evening of the projections. At $11 million to make but with a box office take of $334,000, *Monument Ave.* was hardly a popular film, though it deserved better, if only for two memorable sequences. In one, Leary's character Bobby O'Grady, car thief Mouse, and Seamus, a cousin off the plane from Dublin, partied on cocaine until a gibberish debate about the merits of scoring another eight ball ended with them crashing on the sofas. In the other—an old story but brilliantly told—Mouse burgled a Yuppie condo only to fall asleep on the waterbed after making a ham 'n three-cheese sandwich and becoming engrossed in an album of rare baseball cards. When the condo owner, played by local hockey star Cam Neely, returned home, he startled the napping Mouse who bolted. Neely duly reported the burglary and the police asked what the thief had taken, to which Neely replied, "a nap." In the film's climax, O'Grady gunned down crime boss Jackie and his sidekick Shay who, between them, had ordered and carried out the execution of a presumed informant in a crowded bar and, later, the naive Seamus who happened to witness the execution.[50]

49. Interview by author with National Park Service historian Marty Blatt, 30 September 2011, and *Boston Globe*, 26 September 1998, p. B1.

50. *Monument Ave.*, dir. Ted Demme, 93 min., Miramax Films, 1998.

Yet just as *Monument Ave.* confronted the social implications of Charlestown's code of silence, it also celebrated its Townie culture as all-American. O'Grady and his friends stole cars, used drugs, treated women as sex objects, and assaulted a Black newcomer to Charlestown. Despite adding the double murder of Jackie and Shay to his film-long string of criminal and antisocial activity, O'Grady emerged as a rugged American hero set in the vigilante tradition of the Western frontier. After the double murder, Detective Hanlon (Martin Sheen) intercepted O'Grady on the street. Hanlon frisked him to find not a gun but a fat packet of cash. Knowing it was O'Grady who had finally rid Charlestown of the evil mob boss Jackie, Hanlon entered into a conspiracy with him, whereby he pocketed the cash in return for keeping his own silence about the murders. This ironic twist turned the code of silence on its head, portraying senior police officials as corrupt villains, and murderers as unbadged marshals meeting out summary justice when law enforcement proved incapable. *Monument Ave.*'s conspiratorial message was that O'Grady's crimes were understandable, pardonable, even, given his deprived upbringing; they were victimless, stealing cars from Yuppies who flaunted their easily won wealth and claimed the loss on their insurance. Charlestown's crimes were not the moral responsibility of the gangsters who committed them and then killed their friends for snitching to the police but rather the product of official corruption. In the closing barroom sequence, viewers could join with the film's relieved survivors to buy a round of shots and toast, "Here's to Bobby O'Grady."[51]

Imagining the Monument

By the first years of the new millennium, Charlestown—and its young men—had come of age. Charlestown High's Asian- Latino- Black- and Irish-American students were winning scholarships to prestigious universities. Harvard-Kent, a model elementary school with some of the most dedicated teachers in the Boston Public School system, was placing growing number of students at Boston Latin. There was still some drug dealing over in the projects, but residents there were taking care of their neighborhood and working to police it themselves. Single women were choosing Charlestown as a safe home from which to walk to downtown offices. A German sedan parked overnight was no more at risk than anywhere else in Boston. Todd English's Figs and Olives restaurants were the talk of gourmands across the city; the Big Potato had become the Ironside Grill, a sophisticated sports bar with a choice of Angus beef or veggie burgers; and while Sully's changed little, its customers now had a spectacular view of the Zakim Bridge and downtown Boston.[52] With the Big Dig complete, landscapers turned City Square into one of the prettiest little parks in the city. There was newfound prosperity. Johnnie's Foodmaster stocked a cabinet of French cheeses, McCarthy's Liquors not only sold Heitz cabernet but Rich McCarthy could also offer customers his opinion on a particular vintage, and Pat Owens at the Bunker Hill Barber Shop was charging more for a trim than city-center salons. There was newfound confidence, newfound pride.

51. *Monument Ave.*
52. Before its upscale refit, the Big Potato had changed its name to the Sweet Potato.

Townie pride had always been at its best for the Bunker Hill Day parade, on the nearest Sunday to 17 June. Side streets held their own block parties, grills smoked in the back yards, on-street tipplers hid their beers in Styrofoam cups, grandparents as well as children wore silly hats and threw cracklepops, and everyone had a ball. In 2011, when the Bunker Hill Pipe Band stopped at Elm and Bunker Hill Streets to perform a Celtic reel (fig. 82), the corner had tony gas lamps, mature trees, and prim condos with vinyl siding and shuttered windows. Six sets of beaming parents and grandparents had babies on their shoulders, laps, or in strollers. There were politicians squeezing hands, girls dancing in the street, men with bushy beards and others with monogrammed golf shirts or touting SLR cameras, a boy blowing bubbles, and everywhere the kind of engaged yet relaxed contentment that comes when one's world is mellowing if not quite yet in harmony. When the redcoat reenactors marched past the Carr Funeral Home at School Street (fig. 83), there, watching their pride with a twinkle of irony on its blank granite slabs, was the Bunker Hill Monument, a constant reminder of Charlestown's history and a totem for both its conflicts and its concord.

fig. 82: Bunker Hill Pipe Band, performing on Bunker Hill Street, Bunker Hill Day parade, 2011

Through the silent presence of its historic power, the Monument has continued to spread its watchful influence far beyond Charlestown's residents and even its tourists, entering the imagination of a nation of Americans, no more so than in recent years via the seductive medium of film. Despite making the briefest of appearances, it was the pivot around which *Monument Ave.* hinged, starting with the opening shot of the Monument silhouetted against a mysterious sunset, the only other discernible features being car headlights, two smoking factory chimneys, and the bactrian humps of the Mystic Bridge. Six minutes into the film, when O'Grady, Mouse, and Seamus left a bar and sauntered up Monument Ave. kicking cars to set off their alarms, there was the Monument looming over them, ethereal in blue light, all-seeing all-knowing, part alien rocket ship, part Egyptian sphinx.

fig. 83: redcoat reenactors, with the Monument watching

Reaching millions more viewers than *Monument Ave.*, Ben Affleck's box office blockbuster *The Town* (2010) similarly pivoted its gripping action around the Monument, but Affleck went further, giving it a starring role. An opening caption explained that, "one blue-collar Boston neighborhood has produced more bank robbers and armored car thieves than anywhere in the world," namely Charlestown, followed by an anonymous quotation: "I'm proud to be from Charlestown. It ruined my life, literally, but I'm proud." Then, taking a cue from *Monument Ave.*, *The Town*'s first shots were of the Monument, silhouetted against a fast-frame sunrise, followed by a panoramic aerial sequence in which the camera revolved around the Monument before centering it between the Custom House Tower and the twin obelisks of the Zakim Bridge, in stunning granite fengshui alignment on the two-dimensional screen (fig. 84). Cognizant, no doubt, of the Zakim's sibling-like symbolism, Affleck gave it a supporting or perhaps amplifying role, with the Zakim and the Monument making the same number of appearances—ten apiece—throughout the film. Those appearances came at crucial junctures, as when a panoramic shot of the Monument preceded Townie bank robber Douglas "Doug" MacRay (Affleck) giving Yuppie bank manager

Claire Keesey (Rebecca Hall) a diamond necklace and suggesting that they leave Charlestown to start a new life. At face value, *The Town* was standard Hollywood melodrama of multiple murders, car chases, steamy sex, and sufficient firepower to turn Boston's streets into a war zone. And yet, on a deeper, subliminal level, Affleck's achievement was to underlay the gratuitous violence and implausible plot lines with a morality play of American core values. Conveying the salience of those values, as well as legitimating them, was their juxtaposition with the Monument's power and history. For sure, *The Town* was about grossing three times its outlay by engrossing viewers in a fantasy world of violence and romance. But it was really about explaining what it meant to be an American, with the Monument in the dual roles of silent narrator and heroic exemplar.[53]

fig. 84: silent star of *The Town*—the Monument, with Custom House Tower and Zakim Bridge, in granite fengshui alignment

Through the Monument's legitimacy, *The Town* conveyed five core American precepts, each of which related to and underpinned the others: First, above all else, morality lies at the very heart of existence—Americans exist in a moral world—and yet morality is relative. In the spirit of *Bonnie and Clyde* and a hundred Hollywood Westerns and Dirty Harrys, *The Town*'s message was that murder was a terrible sin but bank robbery was a borderline offense, even a pardonable one depending on the social circumstances. Stealing money from a bank was another victimless crime, and those who robbed banks and armored cars were latter day Robin Hoods, stealing from the rich—or, in the American case, the federal government—to pay the poor. Near the film's climax, Doug told crime boss Fergie (Pete Postlethwaite) that he would commit to a robbery at the Fenway Park baseball stadium. A silhouette of the twin obelisks of the Zakim Bridge against a fast-frame sunrise played into an aerial shot of Charlestown and the Monument, followed by Doug visiting Claire, who was gardening at her public vegetable patch near the projects. By that point in the plot, Special Agent Adam

53. *The Town*, dir. Ben Affleck, 125 min., Warner Brothers, 2010; budget $37 million, box office sales $154 million. Affleck took liberties here because the *Boston Globe* article that the caption references (19 March 1995, p. 28) states that Charlestown was "a community to which more armored car robbers are traced than any other in the country [America], according to FBI statistics," and the quotation is more of a paraphrase as the anonymous convicted drug dealer told reporter Judy Rakowsky, "I'm mighty proud of where I come from. It's ruined my life, literally, but I'm proud."

Frawley (Jon Hamm) had turned Claire against Doug, with whom she had fallen in love, by telling her that it was Doug's gang that had robbed her bank (at the start of the film) and taken her hostage.   Doug knew that he had lost Claire, but he at least wanted her to believe that he was a decent guy.   "I will never lie to you again," he told her.   "Really?"   "Yes, I promise you.   Ask me anything you want."   Angry and confused, Claire asked, "How many banks have you robbed?"   "Six trucks, two banks," Doug replied.   Claire glanced aside before her eyes again probed his: "Have you ever killed anyone?"   "No."   Claire was almost in tears as Doug turned to leave, registering his parting words: "I will never lie to you, I will never hurt you, and if I lose you I will regret that for the rest of my life."   Reassured that Doug was a mere thief and not a murderer, Claire could again find a place in her heart for him.

Second, redemption is possible for all Americans.   A rising hockey star in his youth, Doug had blown his chance of signing with the Boston Bruins because he had fallen into an OxyContin drug habit.   After time served for a failed robbery, he broke his addiction and became a regular at Alcoholics Anonymous meetings.   Although Doug continued to rob armored cars and banks, unlike his fellow gang members and in the face of their chiding, he resolutely refused drugs and alcohol.   Robbing banks was simply Doug's career, one that he adopted reluctantly and then because Charlestown's coercive, blue-collar social climate had deprived him of other choices for personal advancement.   Yet for a true Townie like Doug, the American system worked, redeeming drug users, alcoholics, and even murderous bank robbers.   By the film's end, Doug had a new, legal career catching crawfish.

Third, vigilantism and frontier justice are one with the rule of law and necessary when the legal system cannot or has failed to function.   Soon after the start of their relationship, Claire told Doug that she had sold her Toyota Prius because someone had vandalized it, and that during her walks to work through the projects men there had verbally abused her and then thrown bottles at her, since when she walked "the long way" around.   From her description, Doug identified them as Hispanic-American drug dealers.   Rounding up his psychotic friend and partner James "Jem" Coughlin (Jeremy Renner), the two busted their way into the dealers' apartment in the projects, beat them senseless, and told them to leave town or face death.   In a climax that mirrored *Monument Ave.*'s, Doug shot Fergie and his sidekick Rusty.   This brazen double murder in Fergie's florist's shop came in spite of Doug's proud statement to Claire that he had never killed anyone.   But Affleck cast Fergie as the epitome of evil, chemically castrating Doug's father Stephen as punishment for trying to leave the crime ring, and addicting his mother Doris to drugs, which led to her suicide.   Once the law had proved incapable of protecting single women walking to work, or of prosecuting drug-dealing crime bosses who drove mothers to kill themselves, it was then morally justifiable, even praiseworthy, for hero Doug to mete out punishment that fit the crimes.   Hints of the frontier throughout *The Town* reinforced its promulgation of the five core values.   Claire's vegetable patch sat on the frontier with the lawless projects.   When

Jem met Doug in Sully's barroom to advocate killing Claire, the view from the window behind them was of fences separating a no-man's land of highways and train tracks from the office towers of civilized Boston lying beyond, suggesting that Charlestown itself lay outside the frontier. Most poignantly, the closing shot showed Doug, in what would pass for homespun pants and with a full beard, living in a log cabin on a deserted frontier-like lagoon in Florida.

Fourth, rugged individualism, itself a product of the frontier spirit, is as much the essence of American liberty as it is the fount of the American Dream. With his rough-shaven looks and brooding physique, Doug exuded a quiet pugnacity, moving with a calculated determination but rarely with unplanned haste; not even in a hailstorm of swat-team bullets did he lose his self-control, and only once did he break stride and then into a slow lope. At the outset, after the first bank robbery when his gang drove off with the cash and hostage Claire, Doug was a subservient antihero, taking orders from Fergie as to which bank to rob next, at best an equal partner in the gang's decision-making and sometimes in a subordinate role to Jem. To change his life and to change what had gone so blatantly wrong with Charlestown, and by inference Thomas Jefferson's republican experiment, Doug increasingly exerted his willpower. He argued with Jem against doing another job for Fergie to the point where the two friends fought, and only when Fergie threatened to kill Claire did Doug grudgingly agree. As the only member of the gang left standing after the Fenway Park heist miscarried, Doug demonstrated his ability to stand up to Fergie—literally—in a magazine-emptying duel he survived because he was wearing a bullet-proof vest.

Fifth, Americans must act on their core values of moral relativism, vigilantism, and rugged individualism if they are to face down and prevail against an overbearing, corrupt federal government. Affleck did not go as far as *Monument Ave.* in showing a police officer taking a bribe from a killer in return for silence and he buried no explicit conspiracy within *The Town*'s plot, and yet Frawley's consistent contempt for and corruption of the legal process was arguably worse than Hanlon's deal with O'Grady. "This isn't a very libertarian thing to say," Frawley told Claire, giving his standard answer to suspects and witnesses alike who asked for a lawyer, "but anyone who lawyers up is guilty." Frawley's modus operandi was to intimidate or coerce potential informants by catching them doing something wrong and then threaten them with retribution from other prisoners once they were in jail. In Frawley's mind, everyone was guilty until proven innocent, and anyone guilty had put themselves beyond the law, so arranging for one prisoner to torture or kill another while in federal custody was just an extension of their punishment. Frawley tried to intimidate petty drug dealer Krista "Kris" Coughlin (Blake Lively)—Jem's sister and Doug's former girlfriend—into becoming an informant by threatening arrest and the loss of her baby daughter to foster care. When Kris requested a lawyer, Frawley instead told her about Doug's relationship with Claire, which led to Kris loading up on OxyContin and crashing her car. At the hospital, Frawley renewed his threat to have Social Services take her baby away, and, in her drugged depression, she relented. Perhaps in the public interest of arresting a gang of dangerous bank robbers, Frawley's illegal tactics warranted moral sanction, but in his zeal to jail Doug, whose street craft made him look stupid, Frawley repeatedly rode roughshod over the law that was his duty to uphold. Following the robbery of an armored car in Boston's North End and a chase that left smashed police cruisers littering the streets like a video game, Frawley determined to arrest Doug's gang for questioning on trumped up warrants based on crime-scene fingerprints he did not have. "Get me something that looks like a print so I can shake their tree," Frawley ordered detective Dino Ciampa. "'Cause the not fucking around thing is about to go both ways." In the interrogation room, Frawley said to Doug, "You're here today so I could tell you personally that you're going to die in federal prison. And so are all your friends. No deal. No compromise." Nevertheless, after the gang's final shootout against FBI swat teams massed outside Fenway Park like regiments of soldiers, Doug was still able to cock a snoot at the power of government forces by calmly driving away in a police cruiser. With Doug dressed in a police officer's uniform and Frawley unshaven in scruffy clothes, toting a shotgun, their roles reversed, and it was while dressed as an officer that Doug killed Fergie.

fig. 85: Charlestown Youth Hockey Association's Monument-centric flag, from *The Town*

Like *Monument Ave.*, *The Town* turned morality on its head, challenging viewers to accept FBI agents as corrupt villains, and murdering bank robbers as heroic law enforcers. After outwitting Frawley and the combined talent of the FBI, Doug left Claire with much of his share of the gang's proceeds and escaped Charlestown's depravity for the rugged yet clean living of the virtual frontier. Instead of handing over the cash—some of it stolen from the bank of which she was the former manager—to the police,

Claire used it to a endow a charity to renovate the Charlestown hockey rink, which for some years had no ice due to lack of funds. In *The Town*'s closing scene, four pee-wee hockey players passed a puck on the new ice, underneath four flags prominently strung from the rafters, those of the United States, the Commonwealth of Massachusetts, Charlestown, and the Charlestown Youth Hockey Association, which depicts the Monument erect, in Irish green, thrusting through the letter C, against a pair of crossed hockey sticks (fig. 85). Claire, with Doug's aid, had achieved what the MDC could not afford or did not care to do: she had reopened the rink, providing sport for youths who would otherwise have drifted aimlessly into drugs and crime. Viewers who associated the MDC with state corruption and waste would likely have appreciated the goodness that can accrue from the efforts of individual citizens to challenge and defeat the system, and hence the salience of Doug's all-American heroism.

While Affleck's *The Town* did not advance a conspiracy theory per se, his critically acclaimed *Gone Baby Gone* (2007) did. Set not in Charlestown but Dorchester, another traditionally Irish-American Boston neighborhood, *Gone Baby Gone* opened with the abduction of Amanda, a young girl, presumably by a child molester. Believing that the police would mishandle the search, a family member hired private investigator Patrick Kenzie (Casey Affleck), who soon uncovered a different explanation: a drug trafficker had taken Amanda as ransom for money stolen from him by Amanda's mother and her boyfriend. But all seemed lost when a botched nighttime exchange at the Quincy quarries ended with the loud splash of Amanda's tragic death, or at least with Amanda's doll floating on the water. There was puzzling evidence, nevertheless, and Kenzie was not the type to lose heart. He subsequently figured out that the abductor was not a low-life criminal but rather the corrupt police chief Jack Doyle, who intended to make Amanda the child he and his wife had always wanted. To throw Kenzie off the trail and close the case, Doyle had set up the botched exchange. It was a play, in other words, by director Affleck on the bodies-in-the-quarries metanarrative familiar to him from his long association with Boston. Despite its brilliance, Affleck may not have realized the irony inherent to his plot in light of that irony's relevance to conspiracy theory.[54]

Claire's philanthropy, Doug's execution of an evil crime boss, and Kenzie's unmasking of a conspiracy at the Boston Police Department might seem insignificant acts in the face of a government so massive, remote, unresponsive, and inefficient, but that is precisely the paradox that the movies—and the Bunker Hill Monument itself—address: the paradox of powerlessness in the face of overbearing power; the paradox of the single citizen's worth in a society of millions; the paradox of an American's freedom in the land of a national security state whose founding purpose was to uphold—not curtail—that freedom. Swat teams swarming a ballpark clad in fatigues with full body armor and high-powered automatic weapons illustrate the Whiggish fear of standing armies becoming the tools of tyrants and the justification for the Second Amendment right to keep and bear arms. Yet all those paramilitaries, police,

---

54. *Gone Baby Gone*, Ben Affleck, director, 114 min., Miramax Films, 2007.

and FBI officers could not solve the cases, stop the crimes, nor arrest the felons. Private citizens O'Grady and Doug executed the bosses who orchestrated the crimes. Private investigator Kenzie unmasked the corrupt cop. And anonymous citizen Claire donated the money to rehabilitate a public ice rink when MDC officials had their minds on filling quarries at Quincy and facilitating developers' golf-coursed condominiums. If more individual citizens acted independently and responsibly for the public good, these films argue, then there would be less need for big government and standing armies.

When George Washington Warren looked at Solomon Willard's finished Monument he realized that whereas from a distance it was a single monolith, close up it comprised many blocks of close-fitting granite. *E pluribus unum*, he said, *out of many, one.* Yet however big the monolith and however many the blocks, removing just one would bring the edifice down, in the same way that every block was supporting the cumulative load. As Americans have learned from the experience of constant bickering, to the extent of fighting a civil war, therein lay the problem of independence and the paradox of freedom. Real freedom—the dizzying lightness of infinite choice, mobility, and temptation that Kierkegaard identified as the source of angst—is as unsettling for individuals as it is dangerous for society. It is easy to talk about freedom but a disquieting matter to live it. Few successful bank robbers—or business tycoons—with a million in cash seize the opportunity to start a new life in a different country, and, when they do, they seclude themselves in an imprisoning facsimile of their former home. For nineteenth-century Americans, taming the frontier meant the weakening of rugged individualism just as it meant curtailing the lawlessness of hoboes and freebooters. Greater freedom for twenty-first-century Americans has equated to greater personal responsibility and the rising national cost of safeguarding that freedom. Still, it is easy to mistake the Monument's genius, not for cementing liberty-loving individuals into the consensus-seeking members of a powerful nation-state but rather for encouraging and then legitimating ideological and cultural difference. As all things to all comers, the Monument's genius has been to solve the paradox.

Willard caused nothing to interfere with the Monument's smooth, unblemished granite; he brooked no embellishments nor inscriptions that would mar its blank slate. Edward Everett knew that it marked the spot. Daniel Webster understood that it spoke through him. Freemasons and Provos sought to possess the Monument because it endowed their eccentric clannishness with universal Americanism. Film directors gave it starring roles because it made real their far-fetched stories and lent truth to their actors' upturned morality. Proud tourists climb its 294 stairs to soak up its republican history, look out over Boston, and know that theirs is still the shining city on a hill. Boston's Bunker Hill Monument, as well as the granite cities it spawned, has been writing that history since a French marquis laid its cornerstone in the name of liberty. It will continue to write history as long as there are Yankee heroes and American dreamers who believe that theirs is an exceptional land guided by a Providential hand.

BIBLIOGRAPHY

Archival Sources and Unpublished Documents

Adams, John Quincy. Papers. Massachusetts Historical Society, Boston. Microfilm edition. Ed. Frederick S. Allis Jr. 1972.

The Adams Papers. Massachusetts Historical Society, Boston. Microfilm edition.

Everett, Edward. Papers. Massachusetts Historical Society, Boston. Microfilm edition. Ed. Frederick S. Allis Jr.

Governor's Papers, Weld/Cellucci/Swift. Massachusetts Archives, Morrissey Boulevard, Boston.

Granite Cutters' International Association of America Records, 1877–1978. Archives of the University of Massachusetts, Amherst.

Perkins, Thomas Handasyd. Papers. Massachusetts Historical Society.

Warren, George Washington. "Bunker Hill Monument Scrapbook, 1829–1892." Leather bound notebook of press clippings, manuscript N-324. Massachusetts Historical Society, Boston.

Published Documents and Reports

AAMA Motor Vehicle Facts and Figures, '94. Detroit, MI: American Automobile Manufacturers Association, 1994.

American State Papers, Class 1, Foreign Relations. Vol. 5. Washington, DC: Gales & Seaton, 1858.

Annals of the Congress of the United States. 18th Cong., 1st Sess. Washington, DC: Gales & Seaton, 1856.

Annals of the Massachusetts Charitable Mechanic Association, 1795–1892. Boston: MCMA, 1892.

Annual Reports of the Officers of the City of Quincy, Massachusetts, for the Year 1908. Quincy, MA: George W. Prescott Publishing Co., 1908.

Bloomfield, J.J. "A Study of the Efficiency of Dust-Removal Systems in Granite-Cutting Plants." *Public Health Reports*, 44:42 (18 October 1929), pp. 2505–22.

British Parliamentary Papers: Select Committee Reports on the East India Company and Trade with China, 1821–31. China, vol. 36. Shannon: Irish University Press, 1971.

Burke, Helen F. *Quincy Industries, 1625–1943.* Quincy: City of Quincy, Massachusetts, 1943.

Celebration of the Centennial Anniversary of the Battle of Bunker Hill. Boston: Rockwell and Churchill, 1875.

Celebration of the Two Hundred and Fiftieth Anniversary of the Settlement of Boston, September 17, 1880. Boston: City Council, 1880.

The City of Quincy: Investigation into the Removal of Records and Erasure of Computer Files from the Former Mayor's Office. Report, 45 pp. Boston: Massachusetts Office of the Inspector General, June 2003.

City of Quincy, Massachusetts: City Government of 1929, Together with the Annual Reports of the Officials of the Year 1928. Boston: Chapple Publishing Company, 1928.

"Commercial Statistics." *Merchants' Magazine and Commercial Review*, 6:2 (1 February 1842), pp. 177–91.

Dale, T. Nelson. *The Chief Commercial Granites of Massachusetts, New Hampshire, and Rhode Island. Bulletin No. 354*. Washington, DC: U.S. Geological Survey, 1908.

Forty-Sixth Report of the Select Committee, Session 1840. London: Houses of Parliament, 1840.

Founding Families: Digital Editions of the Papers of the Winthrops and Adamses. Ed. C. James Taylor. Boston: Massachusetts Historical Society, 2007.

Greenburg, Leonard. "Studies on the Industrial Dust Problem: 1. Dust Inhalation and Its Relation to Industrial Tuberculosis." *Public Health Reports*, 40:7 (13 February 1925), pp. 291–309.

Historical Statistics of the United States. Cambridge: Cambridge University Press, 2009, online.

Historical Statistics of the United States, Colonial Times to 1970. Washington, DC: U.S. Bureau of the Census, 1976.

Hoffman, Frederick L. *The Problem of Dust Phthisis in the Granite-Stone Industry*. U.S. Department of Labor, Bureau of Labor Statistics. *Bulletin No. 293*. Washington, DC: Government Printing Office, May 1922.

Jacobs, Philip P. "Misleading Mortality Statistics of Tuberculosis." *American Journal of Public Health*, 3:5 (May 1913), pp. 431–47.

The Mine, Quarry, and Metallurgical Record of the United States, Canada, and Mexico. Chicago, IL: Mine and Quarry News Bureau, 1897.

Proceedings of the Bunker Hill Monument Association, at the Fifty-Fifth Annual Meeting, June 17, 1878. Boston: Bunker Hill Monument Association, 1878.

"Progressive Wealth and Commerce of Boston." *Merchants' Magazine and Commercial Review*, 15:1 (1 July 1846), pp. 34–50.

Register of Debates in Congress, Comprising the Leading Debates and Incidents of the Second Session of the Nineteenth Congress. Washington, DC: Gales & Seaton, 1829.

Report (brought from The Lords, 7 May 1821) Relative to the Trade with the East Indies and China, in British Parliamentary Papers: Select Committee Reports on the East India Company and Trade with China, 1821–31. China, vol. 36. Shannon: Irish University Press, 1971.

Report of Record Commissioners. Charlestown Land Records, 1638–1802. 2nd edition. Boston: N.p., 1883.

Review of the Mount Hood Public Works Project in Melrose. Boston: Office of the Inspector General, October 2002.

Russell, Albert E., et al. *The Health of Workers in Dusty Trades, II: Exposure to Siliceous Dust (Granite Industry)*. U.S. Public Health Service. *Bulletin No. 187*. Washington, DC: Government Printing Office, July 1929.

Sixteenth Annual Report of the Bureau of Industrial and Labor Statistics for the State of Maine, 1902. Augusta: Kennebec Journal Print, 1903.

Terris, Milton. "Relation of Economic Status to Tuberculosis Mortality by Age and Sex." *American Journal of Public Health*, 38:8 (August 1948), pp. 1061–70.

Vital Records of Petersham, Massachusetts, To the End of the Year 1849. Worcester, MA: Franklin P. Rice, 1904.

[Webster, Daniel.] *The Papers of Daniel Webster*. Ed. Charles M. Wiltse. Hanover, NH: University Press of New England, 1974.

Published Addresses, Letters, Memoirs, Novels, and Contemporary Works

Adams, James Truslow. *The Epic of America*. 1931; repr., Boston: Little, Brown, and Company, 1939.

[Adams, John Quincy.] *An Address Delivered at the Request of a Committee of Washington; on the Occasion of Reading the Declaration of Independence, on the Fourth of July, 1821.* Washington, DC: Davis and Force, 1821.

Adams, John Quincy. "Lecture on the War with China, Delivered Before the Massachusetts Historical Society, Dec. 1841." *Chinese Repository*, 11:5 (May 1842), pp. 276–88.

———. *Memoirs of John Quincy Adams.* Ed. Charles Francis Adams. Philadelphia: J.B. Lippincott, 1875.

———. *The Writings of John Quincy Adams, 1816–1819.* Vol. 6. Ed. Worthington Chauncey Ford. New York: Macmillan Company, 1916.

———. *The Diary of John Quincy Adams, 1794–1845.* Ed. Allan Nevins. New York: Longmans, Green and Co., 1928.

Brackenridge, Hugh Henry. *The Battle of Bunkers-Hill: A Dramatic Piece, of Five Acts in Heroic Measure, by a Gentleman of Maryland.* Philadelphia: Robert Bell, Printers, 1776.

Bunyan, John. *The Holy Citie: Or, The New-Jerufalem.* London: Francis Smith, 1665.

Cary, Thomas G. "Thomas Handasyd Perkins." In *Lives of American Merchants*, pp. 33–101. Ed. Freeman Hunt. New York: Office of Hunt's Merchants' Magazine, 1856.

Crowther, William R., and Anthony W. Thompson. *A Climber's Guide to the Quincy Quarries.* Cambridge, MA: MIT Outing Club, 1968.

Cummings, Charles A. "Architecture in Boston." In *The Memorial History of Boston, including Suffolk, Massachusetts, 1630–1880*, vol. 4, pp. 465–88. Ed. Justin Winsor. Boston: James R. Osgood and Company, 1881.

Dana, Richard Henry, Jr. *Two Years Before the Mast: A Personal Narrative.* 1840; repr., Boston: Houghton Mifflin Company, 1912.

Davis, Emerson. *The Half Century.* Boston: Tappan and Whittemore, 1851.

Dearborn, Henry. *An Account of the Battle of Bunker's-Hill, printed with Daniel Putnam, A Letter to Maj. Gen. Dearborn, Repelling His Unprovoked Attack on the Character of the Late Maj. Gen. Israel Putnam.* Boston: Munroe & Francis, 1818.

Description de L'Égypte, ou recueil des observations et des recherché qui ont été faites en Égypte pendant l'expedition de l'armée Française. Paris: De L'Imprimerie Impériale, 1809.

Drake, Samuel Adams. *Bunker Hill: The Story Told in Letters From the Battle Field by British Officers Engaged.* Boston: Nichols and Hall, 1875.

———. *Old Boston Taverns and Tavern Clubs.* Boston: W.A. Butterfield, 1917.

Eliot, Samuel Atkins, ed. *Biographical History of Massachusetts: Biographies and Autobiographies of the Leading Men in the State.* Vol. 2. Boston: Massachusetts Biographical Society, 1909.

[Emerson, Ralph Waldo.] *Journals of Ralph Waldo Emerson, 1820–1872.* Vol. 6. Eds. Edward Waldo Emerson and Waldo Emerson Forbes. Boston: Houghton Mifflin Company, 1911.

Everett, Edward. "Coray's Aristotle [Affairs of Greece]." *North American Review*, 17:2 (October 1823), pp. 389–424.

[Everett, Edward.] *Orations and Speeches on Various Occasions by Edward Everett.* Boston: American Stationers' Company, 1836.

The First Railroad in America: A History of the Origin and Development of the Granite Railroad at Quincy, Massachusetts. Boston: Granite Railway Company, 1926.

Fu Lo-shu, ed. and trans. *A Documentary Chronicle of Sino–Western Relations, 1644–1820.* Vol. 1. Tucson: University of Arizona Press, 1966.

Gilman, Arthur Delavan. "Architecture in the United States." *North American Review*, 58:2 (April 1844), pp. 436–80.

Gompers, Samuel. *Seventy Years of Life and Labor: An Autobiography*. 2 vols. 1925; reissued in one volume, New York: E.P. Dutton & Company, 1943.

[Greenough, Horatio.] *A Memorial of Horatio Greenough*. Ed. Henry T. Tuckerman. New York: Benjamin Bloom, 1853.

———. *Letters of Horatio Greenough, American Sculptor*. Ed. Nathalia Wright. Madison: University of Wisconsin Press, 1972.

Grissell, Thomas. "Account of the Scaffolding Used in Erecting the 'Nelson Column,' Trafalgar Square." Discussion 667. *Institution of Civil Engineers*, 3 (1844), pp. 203–23.

Hale, Sarah Josepha. *Northwood, a Tale of New England*. Boston: Bowles & Dearborn, 1827.

———. *Northwood, or Life North and South: Showing the True Character of Both*. New York: H. Long & Brother, 1852.

Historical Sketch of the City of Quincy. Quincy, MA: Quincy Lodge of Elks, 1924.

Hoar, George Frisbie. *Autobiography of Seventy Years*. Vol. 1. New York: Charles Scribner's Sons, 1903.

Hunt, Freeman, ed. *Lives of American Merchants*. New York: Office of Hunt's Merchants' Magazine, 1856.

Johnson, Edward. *Wonder-Working Providence of Sions Saviour in New-England*. London, 1654. In William Frederick Poole, ed. Andover, MA: Warren F. Draper, 1867.

[King, Martin Luther, Jr.] *A Testament of Hope: The Essential Writings and Speeches of Martin Luther King Jr*. Ed. James Melvin Washington. New York: HarperSanFrancisco, 1986.

King, Theophilus. "The First Victory." In *No-License in Quincy*, pp. 45–48. Ed. William Frederic Hoehn. Quincy, MA: Eastern Printing and Engraving, 1899.

[Lafayette, Marquis de.] *Mémoires, correspondance et manuscrits de Général Lafayette, publiés par sa famille*. Brussels: Société Belge de Librairie, 1839.

LaForge, Larry, ed. *Boston Rocks*. Cambridge, MA: MIT Outing Club, 1991.

Laukkanen, John A. *Quincy Quarries: Gold and Gloom*. Victoria, Canada: Trafford Publishing, 2004.

[Lawrence, Amos.] *Extracts from the Diary and Correspondence of the Late Amos Lawrence, with a Brief Account of Some Incidents in his Life*. Ed. William R. Lawrence. Boston: Gould and Lincoln, 1855.

Lee, James E. *Quincy Tomorrow*. Quincy: Planning Board of Quincy, Massachusetts, 1965.

Ljungstedt, Andrew. *Historical Sketch of the Portuguese Settlements in China; and of the Roman Catholic Church and Mission in China*. Boston: James Munroe & Co., 1836.

Lodge, Henry Cabot. *Daniel Webster*. Boston: Houghton Mifflin Company, 1883.

Mills, Robert. "Essay on Architectural Monuments." *Analectic Magazine*, 1 (1820), pp. 278–88.

Nee, Patrick. *A Criminal and an Irishman: The Inside Story of the Boston Mob–IRA Connection*. Hanover, NH: Steerforth Press, 2006.

Perkins, Samuel G. "Insurrection in St. Domingo." *Proceedings of the Massachusetts Historical Society* (April 1886), pp. 305–74.

Preble, George Henry. "The Navy, and the Charlestown Navy Yard." In *The Memorial History of Boston, including Suffolk, Massachusetts, 1630–1880*, vol. 3, pp. 331–68. Ed. Justin Winsor. Boston: James R. Osgood and Company, 1881.

Quincy Granite: Lasting Until Everlasting. Quincy, MA: Granite Manufacturers' Association, 1932.

Quincy, Josiah. *Figures of the Past: From the Leaves of Old Journals.* Boston: Roberts Brothers, 1883.

Stuart, C.B. *A Brief Memoir of Gridley Bryant, Civil Engineer.* Boston: Henry W. Dutton & Son, 1871.

Sullivan, James. "Jumping From Heaven." *Yankee Magazine* (July 1996), pp. 34–37, 110–12.

Swett, Samuel. *History of Bunker Hill Battle, with a Plan.* Boston: Munroe and Francis, 1827.

———. *Original Planning and Construction of Bunker Hill Monument.* Pamphlet, 12 pp. Albany, NY: J. Munsell, 1863.

Tomasi, Mari, and Roaldus Richmond. *Men Against Granite.* Eds. Alfred Rosa and Mark Wanner. Shelburne, VT: New England Press, 2004.

Walker, Alexander. "Judah Touro." In *Lives of American Merchants*, pp. 441–67. Ed. Freeman Hunt. New York: Office of Hunt's Merchants' Magazine, 1856.

Warren, George Washington. *The History of the Bunker Hill Monument Association During the First Century of the United States of America.* Boston: James R. Osgood and Company, 1877.

Webster, Daniel. *A Discourse, Delivered at Plymouth, December 22, 1820, In Commemoration of the First Settlement of New-England.* Boston: Wells and Lilly, 1821.

———. *An Address Delivered at the Completion of the Bunker Hill Monument, June 17, 1843.* Boston: Tappan and Dennet, 1843.

———. *Two Orations by Daniel Webster: The Bunker Hill Monument; Adams and Jefferson.* Boston: Houghton Mifflin Company, 1893.

———. *Webster's First Oration Bunker Hill Oration.* Ed. A.J. George. Boston: D.C. Heath & Co., 1894.

———. *The Writings and Speeches of Daniel Webster.* Boston: Little, Brown, & Company, 1903.

Wheildon, William W. *The New Custom House: Strictures on an Article in the North American Review, for April, 1844, entitled, "Architecture in the United States."* Boston: W.D. Ticknor, 1844.

———. *Memoir of Solomon Willard, Architect and Superintendent of the Bunker Hill Monument.* Charlestown, MA: Bunker Hill Monument Association, 1865.

———. *New History of the Battle of Bunker Hill, June 17, 1775, Its Purpose, Conduct, and Result.* Boston: Lee and Shepard, 1875.

Willard, Margaret Wheeler, ed. *Letters on the American Revolution, 1774–1776.* Boston: Houghton Mifflin Company, 1925.

Willard, Sidney. *Memories of Youth and Manhood.* Vol. 1. Cambridge, MA: John Bartlett, 1855.

Willard, Solomon. *Plans and Sections of the Obelisk on Bunker's Hill, with the Details of Experiments Made in Quarrying the Granite.* Boston: Chas. Cook's Lithograph, 1843.

Winsor, Justin, ed. *The Memorial History of Boston, including Suffolk County, Massachusetts, 1630–1880.* Vols. 3, 4. Boston: James R. Osgood and Company, 1881.

Winthrop, John. "A Modell of Christian Charity." In *Collections of the Massachusetts Historical Society*, 3rd series, vol. 7, pp. 31–48. Boston: Charles C. Little and James Brown, 1838.

Winthrop, Robert C. *Address at the Unveiling of the Statue of Colonel William Prescott, on Bunker Hill, June 17, 1881.* Boston: J. Wilson and Son, 1881.

Films and Visual Media

Gone Baby Gone. Dir. Ben Affleck. Starring Casey Affleck and Michelle Monaghan. 114 min. Miramax Films, 2007.

Monument Ave. Dir. Ted Demme. Starring Dennis Leary. 93 min. Miramax Films, 1998.

The Town. Dir. Ben Affleck. Starring Ben Affleck and Rebecca Hall. 125 min. Warner Brothers, 2010.

Wadiczko, Krzysztof. *Let Freedom Ring: Bunker Hill Monument Projection.* Video projection, 19 min. Institute of Contemporary Arts, Boston, 24–26 September 1998. And DVD, 22 min. ICA/Vita, 1998.

Secondary Sources: Books, Journal Articles, Dissertations

Allison, Robert J. *The Crescent Obscured: The United States and the Muslim World, 1776–1815.* Chicago: University of Chicago Press, 1995.

Bartlett, Irving H. "Daniel Webster as a Symbolic Hero." *New England Quarterly*, 45:4 (December 1972), pp. 484–507.

Blight, David W. *Race and Reunion: The Civil War in American Memory.* Cambridge, MA: Belknap Press of Harvard University Press, 2001.

Bowditch, Nathaniel. *New American Practical Navigator.* New York: Edmund M. Blunt, 1826.

Brands, H.W. *The Reckless Decade: America in the 1890s.* New York: St. Martin's Press, 1995.

Brayley, Arthur Wellington. *History of the Granite Industry of New England.* 2 vols. Boston: National Association of Granite Industries of the United States, 1913.

Briggs, L. Vernon. *History of Shipbuilding on North River, Plymouth County, Massachusetts.* Boston: Coburn Brothers, 1889.

Brooks, Victor. *The Boston Campaign: April 1775–March 1776.* Conshohocken, PA: Combined Publishing, 1999.

Bruun, Ole. *Fengshui in China: Geomantic Divination Between State Orthodoxy and Popular Religion.* Honolulu: University of Hawaii Press, 2003.

Burstein, Andrew. *Jefferson's Secrets: Death and Desire at Monticello.* New York: Basic Books, 2005.

Cahill, Marion Cotter. *Shorter Hours: A Study of the Movement since the Civil War.* New York: Columbia University Press, 1932.

Cameron, E.H. "Of Yankee Granite: An Account of the Building of the Bunker Hill Monument." *Technology Review*, (May 1952), pp. 359–64, 368, and (June 1952), pp. 419–22, 438, 440, 442, 444, 446.

Campbell, David. *Writing Security: United States Foreign Policy and the Politics of Identity.* Minneapolis: University of Minneapolis Press, 1998.

Chapman, Michael E. "Taking Business to the Tiger's Gate: Thomas Handasyd Perkins and the Boston–Smyrna–Canton Opium Trade of the Early Republic." *Journal of the Royal Asiatic Society Hong Kong Branch*, 52 (2012).

Clifford, J. Nelson. "Granite Industry of Quincy, Massachusetts." *Economic Geography*, 15:2 (April 1939), pp. 146–52.

Cline, Myrtle A. *American Attitude Toward the Greek War of Independence, 1821–1828.* Atlanta, GA: Higgins-McArthur Company, 1930.

Coolidge, Mabel Cook. *The History of Petersham, Massachusetts.* Petersham, MA: Petersham Historical Society, 1948.

Cowie, Robert L. "The Epidemiology of Tuberculosis in Gold Miners with Silicosis." *American Journal of Respiratory and Critical Care Medicine*, 150:5 (November 1994), pp. 1460–62.

Crosby, Irving B. *Boston Through the Ages: The Geological Story of Greater Boston.* Boston: Marshall Jones Company, 1928.

Dickerson, O.M. "John Hancock: Notorious Smuggler or Near Victim of British Revenue Racketeers?" *Mississippi Valley Historical Review*, 32:4 (March 1946), pp. 517–40.

Edwards, William Churchill. *Historic Quincy, Massachusetts.* Quincy, MA: City of Quincy, 1957.

Ellis, George E. *History of the Battle of Bunker's (Breed's) Hill, on June 17, 1775.* Boston: Lockwood, Brooks, & Company, 1875.

Erkkila, Barbara H. *Hammers on Stone: A History of Cape Ann Granite.* Gloucester, MA: Peter Smith, 1987.

Ferling, John. *A Leap in the Dark: The Struggle to Create the American Republic.* Oxford: Oxford University Press, 2003.

Festinger, Leon. *A Theory of Cognitive Dissonance.* Stanford: Stanford University Press, 1957.

Field, James A., Jr. *America and the Mediterranean World, 1776–1882.* Princeton, NJ: Princeton University Press, 1969.

Finley, Ruth E. *The Lady of Godey's: Sarah Josepha Hale.* Philadelphia: J.B. Lippincott Company, 1931.

Foner, Philip S. *History of the Labor Movement in the United States.* Vol. 2, *From the Founding of the American Federation of Labor to the Emergence of American Imperialism.* New York: International Publishers, 1955.

Franchot, Jenny. *Roads to Rome: The Antebellum Protestant Encounter with Catholicism.* Berkeley: University of California Press, 1994.

French, Allen. *The First Year of the American Revolution.* Boston: Houghton Mifflin Company, 1934.

Frothingham, Paul Revere. *Edward Everett: Orator and Statesman.* Boston: Houghton Mifflin Company, 1925.

Frothingham, Richard. *The Battle-Field of Bunker Hill: With a Relation of the Action by William Prescott and Illustrative Documents.* Boston: By author, 1876.

———. *History of the Siege of Boston and of the Battles of Lexington, Concord, and Bunker Hill.* Boston: Little, Brown, and Company, 1903.

Fuess, Claude Moore. *Daniel Webster.* Vol. 2. Boston: Little, Brown, and Company, 1935.

Gallagher, H.M. Pierce. *Robert Mills: Architect of the Washington Monument, 1781–1855.* New York: Columbia University Press, 1935.

Giroux, Henry A. *Beyond the Spectacle of Terrorism: Global Uncertainty and the Challenge of the New Media.* Boulder, CO: Paradigm Publishers, 2006.

Gleason, Hall. "Old Ships and Shipbuilding Days of Medford." *Medford Historical Register*, 32:1 (March 1929), pp. 10–16.

Goldsmith, Larry. "'To Profit By His Skill and to Traffic on His Crime,' Prison Labor in Early 19th-Century Massachusetts." *Labor History*, 40:4 (1999), pp. 439–57.

Goldwater, Leonard J. *Mercury: A History of Quicksilver.* Baltimore, MD: York Press, 1972.

Gutstein, Morris A. *Aaron Lopez and Judah Touro: A Refugee and a Son of a Refugee.* New York: Behrman's Jewish Book House, 1939.

Haber, William Haber. *Industrial Relations in the Building Industry.* 1930; repr., New York: Arno Press, 1971.

Huntington, Samuel P. *Who Are We? The Challenges to America's National Identity.* New York: Simon & Schuster, 2004.

Hydromill Method: Technology Information. Pamphlet. Cesena, Italy: Solimec Drilling and Foundation Equipment, 2010.

Inguanti, Joseph J. "Domesticating the Grave: Italian-American Memorial Practices at New York's Calvary Cemetery." *Markers*, 17 (2000), pp. 8–31.

Jennings, Francis. *The Creation of America: Through Revolution to Empire.* Cambridge: Cambridge University Press, 2000.

Johnson, Paul E. *The Early American Republic, 1789–1829.* New York: Oxford University Press, 2007.

Kaempffert, Waldemar, ed. *A Popular History of American Invention.* New York: Charles Scribner's Sons, 1924.

Kaplan, Lawrence S. "The Monroe Doctrine and the Truman Doctrine: The Case of Greece." *Journal of the Early Republic*, 13:1 (Spring 1993), pp. 1–21.

Kasson, John F. *Civilizing the Machine: Technology and Republican Values in America, 1776–1900.* New York: Hill and Wang, 1999.

Kay, Jane Holtz. *Lost Boston.* Boston: Houghton Mifflin Company, 1980.

Ketchum, Richard M. *Decisive Day: The Battle for Bunker Hill.* 1962; repr., New York: Henry Holt and Co., 1999.

Kierkegaard, Søren. *The Concept of Anxiety: A Simple Psychologically Orienting Deliberation on the Dogmatic Issue of Hereditary Sin.* Ed. and trans. Reidar Thomte. 1844; repr., Princeton, NJ: Princeton University Press, 1980.

Kilham, Walter H. *Boston After Bulfinch: An Account of its Architecture, 1800–1900.* Cambridge: Harvard University Press, 1946.

Klooster, Wim. "Inter-Imperial Smuggling in the Americas, 1600–1800." In *Soundings in Atlantic History: Latent Structures and Intellectual Currents, 1500-1825*, pp. 141–80. Eds. Bernard Bailyn and Patricia L. Denault. Cambridge, MA: Harvard University Press, 2009.

Lancaster, Lynne. "Building Trajan's Column." *American Journal of Archaeology*, 103:3 (July 1999), pp. 419–39.

Larrabee, Stephen A. *Hellas Observed: The American Experience of Greece, 1775–1865.* New York: New York University Press, 1957.

Mandel, Bernard. *Samuel Gompers: A Biography.* Yellow Springs, OH: Antioch Press, 1963.

Martin, Lawrence. "Women Fought at Bunker Hill." *New England Quarterly*, 8:4 (December 1835), pp. 467–79.

Matthewson, Timothy M. "George Washington's Policy Toward the Haitian Revolution." *Diplomatic History*, 3:3 (Summer 1979), pp. 321–36.

McKee, Harley J. *Introduction to Early American Masonry: Stone, Brick, Mortar, and Plaster.* Washington, DC: National Trust for Historic Preservation, 1973.

Miller, Naomi, and Keith Morgan. *Boston Architecture, 1975–1990.* Munich: Prestel-Verlag, 1990.

Mondale, Clarence. "Daniel Webster and Technology." *American Quarterly*, 14:1 (Spring 1962), pp. 37–47.

Morrissey, Brendan. *Boston 1775: The Shot Heard Around the World.* London: Osprey Military, 1993.

Mullin, Robert Bruce. *The Puritan as Yankee: A Life of Horace Bushnell.* Grand Rapids, MI: William B. Eerdmans Publishing Company, 2002.

Murdock, Harold. *Bunker Hill: Notes and Queries on a Famous Battle.* Boston: Houghton Mifflin Company, 1927.

Mytum, Harold. "Popular Attitudes to Memory, the Body, and Social Identity: The Rise of External Commemoration in Britain, Ireland, and New England." *Post-Medieval Archeology*, 40:1 (2006), pp. 96–110.

Nikkel, Stan R. *The City of Presidents: A Quincy Guidebook.* Quincy, MA: Sea Gull Publishing Co., 1992.

O'Connor, Thomas H. *Bibles, Brahmins, and Bosses: A Short History of Boston.* Boston: Boston Public Library, 1991.

Oren, Michael B. *Power, Faith, and Fantasy: America in the Middle East, 1776 to the Present.* New York: W.W. Norton & Company, 2007.

Popkin, Richard H. *Disputing Christianity: The 400-Year-Old Debate over Rabbi Isaac Ben Abraham of Troki's Classic Arguments.* Amherst, NY: Humanity Books, 2007.

Puffer, Evelyn H. "A Great Business Lawyer." *Bulletin of the Business Historical Society*, 16:3 (June 1942), p. 61.

Purcell, Sarah J. "Sealed With Blood: National Identity and Public Memory of the Revolutionary War, 1775–1825." PhD diss., Brown University, 1997.

Quintal, George, Jr. *Patriots of Color, "A Peculiar Beauty and Merit": African Americans and Native Americans at Battle Road and Bunker Hill.* Boston: Boston National Historical Park, 2004.

Ramsay, David. *The History of the American Revolution.* Dublin: William Jones, 1795.

Remini, Robert Vincent. *Daniel Webster: The Man and His Time.* New York: W.W. Norton, 1997.

Resch, John P. "Politics and Public Culture: The Revolutionary War Pension Act of 1818." *Journal of the Early Republic*, 8 (Summer 1988), pp. 139–58.

Roeser, Patricia. "Bunker Hill Monument in Memory and Rhetoric." PhD diss., Arizona State University, 2010.

Rogers, Sherbrooke. *Sarah Josepha Hale: A New England Pioneer.* Grantham, NH: Tompson & Rutter, 1985.

Rose, Alexander. "Marksmanship in 1775: Myth or Reality?" *American Rifleman*, 158:7 (July 2010), pp. 45–47, 70.

Rosner, David, and Gerald Markowitz. *Deadly Dust: Silicosis and the Politics of Occupational Disease in Twentieth-Century America.* Princeton, NJ: Princeton University Press, 1991.

Scotland: The Rough Guide. 4th edition. London: Rough Guides, 2000.

Seaburg, Carl, and Stanley Patterson. *Merchant Prince of Boston: Colonel T.H. Perkins, 1764–1854.* Cambridge, MA: Harvard University Press, 1971.

Shammas, Carole. "How Self-Sufficient was Early America?" *Journal of Interdisciplinary History*, 13 (1982), pp. 247–72.

Shrestha, Laura B. *Life Expectancy in the United States.* Washington, DC: Congressional Research Service, Library of Congress, 2006.

Skehan, James W. *Roadside Geology of Massachusetts.* Missoula, MT: Mountain Press Publishing Company, 2001.

Smith, Chard Powers. *Yankees and God.* New York: Hermitage House, 1954.

Stelle, Charles C. "American Trade in Opium to China, Prior to 1820." *Pacific Historical Review*, 9:4 (December 1940), pp. 425–44.

———. "American Trade in Opium to China, 1821–1839." *Pacific Historical Review*, 10:1 (March 1941), pp. 57–74.

Stephenson, Michael. *Patriot Battles: How the War of Independence Was Fought.* New York: HarperCollins Publishers, 2007.

Story, Ronald. "Class and Culture in Boston: The Athenaeum, 1807–1860." *American Quarterly*, 27:2 (May 1975), pp. 178–99.

Taft, Philip. *The A.F. of L. in the Time of Gompers.* New York: Harper & Brothers, 1957.

Teed, Paul E. *John Quincy Adams: Yankee Nationalist.* New York: Nova Science Publishers, 2006.

Townshend, Charles Hervey. *The British Invasion of New Haven, Connecticut, Together with Some Account of Their Landing and Burning the Towns of Fairfield and Norwalk, July 1779.* New Haven, CT: Tuttle, Morehouse and Taylor, 1879.

Turner, Frederick Jackson. *The Significance of the Frontier in American History.* Madison: State Historical Society of Wisconsin, 1894.

Van Dyke, Paul A. *The Canton Trade: Life and Enterprise on the China Coast, 1700–1845.* Hong Kong: Hong Kong University Press, 2005.

Varg, Paul A. *Edward Everett: The Intellectual in the Turmoil of Politics.* Selinsgrove, PA: Susquehanna University Press, 1992.

Vernon, J.R. "The 1920–21 Deflation: The Role of Aggregate Supply." *Economic Inquiry*, 29:3 (July 1991), pp. 572–80.

Wermiel, Sara E. "California Concrete, 1876–1906: Jackson, Percy, and the Beginnings of Reinforced Concrete Construction in the United States." *Proceedings of the Third International Congress on Construction History* (May 2009), pp. 1509–16.

Whitehill, Walter Muir, and Lawrence W. Kennedy. *Boston: A Topographical History.* Cambridge, MA: Harvard University Press, 2000.

Whitlock, Brand. *La Fayette.* Vol. 2. New York: D. Appleton and Company, 1929.

Who's Who in America. Vol. 12, 1922–23. Chicago: A.N. Marquis & Company, 1922.

Williams, David B. *Stories in Stone: Travels Through Urban Geology.* New York: Walker & Company, 2009.

Wilson, Daniel Munro, and Timothy J. Collins. *Three Hundred Years of Quincy, 1624–1925.* Quincy, MA: City Government of Quincy, 1926.

Wilson, Susan. *Boston Sights and Insights.* Boston: Beacon Press, 1994.

Wood, Paul. "Tools and Machinery of the Granite Industry, Part I." *Chronicle of the Early American Industries Association*, 59:2 (June 2006), pp. 37–52.

———. "Tools and Machinery of the Granite Industry, Part II." *Chronicle of the Early American Industries Association*, 59:3 (September 2006), pp. 81–96.

———. "Tools and Machinery of the Granite Industry, Part III." *Chronicle of the Early American Industries Association*, 59:4 (December 2006), pp. 130–51.

———. "Tools and Machinery of the Granite Industry, Part IV." *Chronicle of the Early American Industries Association*, 60:1 (March 2007), pp. 10–32.

Wood, W.J. *Battles of the Revolutionary War, 1775–1781.* Chapel Hill, NC: Algonquin Books of Chapel Hill, 1990.

Young, Alfred F. *The Shoemaker and the Tea Party: Memory and the American Revolution.* Boston: Beacon Press, 1999.

Zheng Yangwen. *The Social Life of Opium in China.* Cambridge: Cambridge University Press, 2005.

Zimmer, Edward Francis. "The Architectural Career of Alexander Parris (1780–1852)." PhD diss., Boston University, 1984.

LIST OF ILLUSTRATIONS

*   *   *

ACKNOWLEDGEMENTS

My sincerest thanks to those who read chapters and through whose criticisms the manuscript improved, particularly Joe McCarthy, Robert Niebuhr, Stephen Watson, and four anonymous reviewers. Joe: I appreciate that even in your busy retirement, with chickens clucking for meal and crops to hoe, you still found time to send six pages of line items; I regret I never had the chance to repay my gratitude in kind. Colleagues, friends, librarians, and archivists have shared information, sourced materials, and generally supported this eleven-year-long endeavor, including Rich McCarthy in Charlestown, Marty Blatt at the National Park Service, John Hannigan and Jennifer Fauxsmith at the Mass. State Archives, Linda Beeler at the Thomas Crane Public Library, Jim O'Toole and the late Tom O'Connor at Boston College, along with Anne Kenny at the O'Neill Library, and especially David Quigley to whom I am indebted not only for his continuing encouragement but also for the award of a visiting scholarship. Two BC students enjoyed helping with background research on the Custom House Tower and Quincy quarries, Chris Collins and Justyna Szulc. I learned about conspiracy theory from Scott Gurman, quarry counterculture from jumper John Barron and teacher Annmarie Stanton, Melrose's golf club from Jason Turley, and Charlestown's colorful history from Ironside's bartender Mike. My special appreciation must go to Boston itself for providing me with what—for almost thirty years—I have had the privilege to call *home*.

MICHAEL E. CHAPMAN, PEKING UNIVERSITY & BOSTON COLLEGE, 2012

Trebarwyth Press welcomes inquiries, comments, and criticisms: mail@trebarwyth.com

INDEX

Federal Bureau of Investigation, 209; portrayed in *The Town*, 251
Federalism, 79
fengshui: of Monument, 49, 49n9; of Boston's granite, 163–69; in China, 164; in *The Town*, 247, 248i84
Festinger, Leon, 150n71. *See also* cognitive dissonance
Fielding (Lewis) burglary, 210, 210n3
Fielding, Thomas, 218
Finn, Henry J., 83
Finnish Americans, 190–91, 208
First Church, of Charlestown, 108, 108n49
Fishman, Kenneth J., 238
flèches, 4, 7
Foley, James J., 160–61
Forbes, Thomas T., 134
Foster, Lawrence Gray, 218
founding myth, 1, 9–17, 19, 20, 107; Monument primed for, 35; upheld by Webster, 54–55; woven by Webster, 40, 42
France: failure of republicanism in, 25, 41
Franklin, Benjamin, 115: as Freemason, 87
Franklin, Dexter: as BHMA director and JP, 60
freedom: America as exemplar of, 41, 120; American Dream of, 171; as core value, 54, 120, 171; the Enlightenment's promise of unlimited, 150, 253; IRA fighters for, 241; Greeks' fight for, 140; Monument as birthplace of, 38; Monument as spirit of, 83–84; paradox of, 252–53; vs. slavery for the new republic, 14
Freedom Trail, v
Freemasonry, 85, 86–88, 90, 172; and BHMA members, 17, 22, 79; business connections of, 14; and cornerstone laying, 36, 37, 242; despite Mills's, 30; and Monument as space ship, 211; in Quincy, 192; as republican 87
French Revolution: contrasted, 22, 25; Perkins's aid during, 127
Friends of the Blue Hills, 224, 226, 231
Frothingham, Richard, 14
Fuller, Timothy, 144, 146
Fulton, Robert, 115

Gage, Thomas, 2–4, 12
Gallatin, Albert, 145
Garrison, William Lloyd, 81, 125
Gavin, William, 243–44
Geilich, Charles, 231, 234
Gellner, Ernest, 21n40
geomancy. *See* fengshui
George III, 114, 150
George VI, 150
George, A.J., 39

Georgia Stone Industries, 207
Germantown, Quincy, 58
Gibbons, Lewis Grassic, 178
Gilman, Arthur D., 123–24
globalization, 126
global village, vi
Glover, Jose, 108n49
God, 79, 84, 91, 107–9; gave Americans ordered liberty, 170; favored Protestants, 93; fitted the English for self-governance, 114; liberty spread by, 40; plan of, 39, 147; had role for women, 92; made American exemplars, 41–42, 120; and gave ordered liberty, 170; rebuked Cain, 97; smile of, 37; implanted sense of the spot, 96; tabernacle of, 94; and trade, 147. *See also* Providence
Goddard, James, 133
Godey, Louis Antoine, 100
Godey's Lady's Book. See Ladies' Magazine
Godfrey, Arthur, 241
Goldberger, Paul, 163
Gompers, Samuel, 179, 184
Gone Baby Gone, 252
Gooch, Paul L., 233
Gooch, Paul S., 218–19, 233
Gorham, Benjamin, 140, 142–43; as BHMA director and JP, 60
Gorham, Steven: as BHMA director and JP, 60
Granary Burying-Ground, 122
granite: ashlar construction, 57–58; Cape Ann, 158; Chelmsford, 23, 27, 56, 58; colors of, 156–57; and convicts, 59–61; doping, 203, 204; early production of, 55–56; as exceptional, 121; facing of Boston skyscrapers, 161–62; fengshui, 163–69; fire resistance of, 156; geology of, 63–64; imported, 207; industry, 121–22, 207; and Lewis clamps, 75; polychrome, 158i42, 207; rootedness, of Boston, 163; shipping, 72–73; for sidewalks, 165–66; surfacing, bush hammer, 71–72; surfacing, pneumatic 182, 194, 197–99; for tombstones and memorials, 173–75; West Quincy granite, 56–59, 63–64, 202–5; working, hazards of, 59, 193–94
Granite Cutters' Journal, 178, 184, 185, 204; closes, 207
Granite Cutters' National Union, 178; burial benefit, 180; disbands, 207; dues, 180; and eight-hour day, 181–83; membership, 180; and TB data, 199–200; wages, 180, 204
Granite Links Golf Club, 231, 238
Granite Manufacturers' Association, 174, 192. *See also* New England Granite Manufacturers' Association
Granite Railway, 64–70, 64n40, 72; shuts down, 202
Granite Trust Company, 189

Custom House, 123; on Ladies' Fair, 103; on Mills, 32
Whig Party, 102, 102n40
Whiskey Rebellion, 21
whites of their eyes, 10
Whitney, Ryan N., 219
Whittlesey (Buell), Martha, 89
Wilcox, Benjamin C., 136
Willard, Joseph, 45, 53
Willard, Katherine, nee Wilder, 45
Willard, Samuel, 53
Willard, Solomon, 28, 43, 44; appointment as superintendent, 53; as architect, 48; and building the Monument, 70–77, 99, 109, 117–18; death of, 156; discharged, 78; moral character of, 52, 53; as draughtsman of Monument, 49–51; develops Bunker Hill Quarry, 64–66, 70–71; early years of, 45–47; granite industry of, 121–22; and Monument budget, 78; and need for quarry, 61–62; plans building lots, 88; and prison labor, 70; and Yankee mystique, 53–54, 62; Yankeeness of 44–45, 52, 75–76
Willard, William, 45
Williams, David B., 207–8
Williams, John D., 86
Wilson, Henry, 154
Wilson, Susan, 64
Wilson, Woodrow, 179
Winter Hill Gang, 240
Winthrop, John, v, 108, 114, 118, 119
Winthrop, Robert Charles, 151
Winthrop, Thomas L., 140
Winsor, Justin: *Memorial History* of, 47, 60, 156

Wodiczko, Krzysztof, 243, 244
Wolfe, Edward, 150
women: against code of silence, 243–44; at bake sale, 102–5; as conservators of morality, 79; left out by BHMA, 44; rock climbers, 216
Wood, Paul, 198
Woodmass, Edward, 129
Woodmass & Offley, 129, 132, 146
Woods, Tiger, 54
Works Progress Administration, 200
Wright, George B., 212

The X-Files, 209

Yankee: asceticism, 82; birthright of Everett, 95; business connections, 51; contemporary elites, 243, 244; hegemony over Union, 156; heroes, 253; industriousness, 69, 70–76; inventiveness, 68–70; origin of the term, 16–17; morals, 115; pride, 78, 161; qi, 165; restlessness, 150; tinkering, 45, 50, 150; virtue, 98–99, 101–2; women, 100
Yankee mystique, 44, 53–55, 62, 75, 107
Yankeeness, vi, 44–45, 52; of American Dream, 172; and harmony, 75; immigrant emulation of, 172; of Monument, 75–76; Old Testament principles of, 107. *See also* Willard, Yankee mystique
Yankees, 105, 107, 121; tinkering, 150
Yongle (Zhu Di), 168
Young, Ammi B., 122, 158, 166
Yuppies, 211

Ziolkowski, Steven, 236